Normal Rationality

Normal Rationality

Decisions and Social Order

Edna Ullmann-Margalit

EDITED BY
Avishai Margalit
and Cass R. Sunstein

OXFORD

UNIVERSITY PRESS

Great Clarendon Street, Oxford, OX2 6DP,
United Kingdom

Oxford University Press is a department of the University of Oxford.
It furthers the University's objective of excellence in research, scholarship,
and education by publishing worldwide. Oxford is a registered trade mark of
Oxford University Press in the UK and in certain other countries

Published in the United States of America by Oxford University Press
198 Madison Avenue, New York, NY 10016, United States of America

British Library Cataloguing in Publication Data
Data available

Library of Congress Control Number: 2017932561

ISBN 978-0-19-880243-3

Contents

Acknowledgments

The essays in this book were originally published as follows. Permission to reprint them is gratefully acknowledged:

Picking and Choosing (with Sidney Morgenbesser): *Social Research*, 44 (4) (Winter 1977):757–85.

On Presumption: *Journal of Philosophy*, 80:3 (1983): 143–63.

Second-Order Decisions (with Cass R. Sunstein): *Ethics*, Vol. 110, No. 1 (October 1999): 5–31.

Big Decisions: Opting, Converting, Drifting: *Political Philosophy*, ed. Anthony O'Hear (Cambridge University Press, 2006): 157–72.

On Not Wanting to Know: *Reasoning Practically*, ed. Edna-Ullmann Margalit (Oxford University Press (1999): 72–84.

Holding True and Holding as True (with Avishai Margalit): *Synthese* 92:2 (1992): 167–87.

Revision of Norms: *Ethics* 100 (1990): 756–67.

Invisible Hand Explanations: *Synthese* 39(2) (1978): 263–91.

The Invisible Hand and the Cunning of Reason: *Social Research*, Vol. 64, No. 2 (Summer 1997): 181–98.

Solidarity in Consumption (with Cass R. Sunstein): *Journal of Political Philosophy*, 9(2): 129–79.

Trust, Distrust, and in Between: *Distrust*, ed. Russell Hardin (Sage 2004): 60–82.

The Case of the Camera in the Kitchen: Surveillance, Privacy, Sanctions and Governance: *Regulation and Governance*, Vol. 2, Issue 4 (2008): 425–44.

Considerateness: *Iyyun* 60 (2011): 205–44.

Final Ends and Meaningful Lives: *Iyyun* 41 (1992): 73–82.

The author expressed her deep gratitude (in print) for comments and suggestions received from the following people: for chapter 1, Avishai Margalit and Robert Nozick; for chapter 2, Sidney Morgenbesser, members of the philosophy department at Princeton University, L. Jonathan Cohen, Derek Parfit, Isaac Levi, J. R. Lucas, Avishai Margalit, Joseph Raz, P. F. Strawson, and J. L. Mackie; for chapter 3, Saul Levmore and Richard Posner; for chapter 4, Avishai Margalit, Pasquale Pasquino, Cass Sunstein, and Eric Dickson; for chapter 5, Harry Frankfurt, Avishai Margalit, and Cass R. Sunstein; for chapter 6, Jonathan Malino and reviewers for *Synthese*; for chapter 7, Thomas Christiano, Alan Hamlin, David Heyd, Avishai Margalit, and Cass Sunstein; for chapter 8, Avishai Margalit, Robert Nozick, and Sidney Morgenbesser; for chapter 9, Avishai Margalit, Cass Sunstein, and Harry G. Frankfurt; for chapter 10, Avishai Margalit, Jill Hasday, Eric Posner, Richard Posner, Randy Picker, and Gil Kalai; for chapter 11, Russell Hardin, Cass Sunstein, and Avishai Margalit; and for chapter 12, Gil Kalai, Maya Bar-Hillel, Michael Biggs, Avishai Margalit, and Cass Sunstein.

Editors' Introduction

Edna Ullmann-Margalit was an unorthodox and deeply original philosopher whose work illuminated the largest mysteries of human life. Much of her writing focuses on two fundamental questions. (1) How do people proceed when they cannot act on the basis of reasons, or project likely consequences? (2) How is social order possible? Ullmann-Margalit's answers, emphasizing what might be called *biased rationality*, are important not only for philosophy, but also for political science, psychology, sociology, cognitive science, economics (including behavioral economics), law, and even public policy.

Ullmann-Margalit demonstrates that people have identifiable strategies for making difficult decisions, whether the question is small (what to buy at a supermarket) or big (whether to transform one's life in some large-scale way). She also shows that social dilemmas are solved by norms; that invisible-hand explanations take two identifiable (and dramatically different) forms; that trust can emerge in seemingly unpromising situations; and that *considerateness* is the foundation on which our relationships are organized in both the thin context of the public space and the intimate context of the family.

One of the distinguishing features of Ullmann-Margalit's work is its close attention to the details of human experience, and its use of those details to offer fresh understandings of social phenomena. Within economics, it is often suggested that people calculate the costs and benefits of alternative courses of action, but Ullmann-Margalit shows that if we look at how choices are actually made, we will find multiple domains in which no such calculations should or can be made. Within sociology, it is often suggested that consumption behavior involves the atomistic satisfaction of individual preferences, but Ullmann-Margalit draws attention to the widespread phenomenon of "solidarity in consumption." Within political philosophy, it is sometimes suggested that families must be just, and that a veil of ignorance is a good way to understand justice within the family; but Ullmann-Margalit draws attention to the "family deal," the need to proceed with "eyes wide open," and the centrality of considerateness.

We hope that this book will bring some of her most influential work to the attention of a larger audience. We also believe that her papers (including some of the less well-known) cast new light on a diverse assortment of problems in philosophy, social science, and individual lives.

I. Difficult Decisions

Some of Ullmann-Margalit's most illuminating essays explore how people proceed when acting on the basis of reasons is especially difficult. For example: What happens when two options we face are equally attractive (or equally unattractive), such that we have no evident reason to prefer one option over the other? And what happens when our decisions are so large that one or another choice will end up changing our own preferences and values?

In such cases, she argues, ordinary rationality fails us. Ullmann-Margalit agrees that as human agents, we have reasons to act—we are hardly indifferent to the world around us. We value some things more than others. But sometimes we face "symmetrical situations," in which there are equal considerations on both sides—and sometimes our very identity is at stake, as in the case of decisions that are personal and transformative.

The idea of symmetrical situations in philosophy is not new: the eleventh century philosopher, Al-Ghazali, discussed the case of a famished man being unable to choose between two identical dates. But Ullmann-Margalit and Sidney Morgenbesser, in their seminal *Picking and Choosing,* observe that the dilemma of the dates, which may seem contrived, is in fact a familiar one, not least in our modern, highly commercialized life. Facing a row of Campbell's Soup cans in the supermarket poses a similar dilemma: We have no reason to choose one can over the other, but we do have a reason to end up with one can. In such a case, Ullmann-Margalit and Morgenbesser argued, we do not *choose* a can of soup. We *pick*.

Any bias when we pick—picking the can on the far-left, say, because we are left-handed—can be rational, even though the far-left was not better. Ullmann-Margalit and Morgenbesser demonstrate that picking is a pervasive feature of human life, which would be much harder to navigate without it. In some cases, companies are undoubtedly in a position of picking rather than choosing—in deciding, say, to launch a product in January rather than March. The same is true for governments, not only when they select the timing of an announcement, but also when they are making personnel decisions, even high-level ones, among candidates who seem equally matched.

Some of the most difficult decisions in law and ordinary life are simplified by the use of some kind of presumption. Accused criminals are presumed to be innocent, and most of the time, legislative acts are presumed to be constitutional. And when people do not know what to do, they often adopt a presumption of some kind—for example, sticking with the status quo, or perhaps in favor of making a specific change. In *On Presumption,* her extensive engagement with the central idea, Ullmann-Margalit shows the immense importance of presumptions in helping people to extricate themselves from difficult situations. With close reference to the use of presumptions in law, she also shows that presumptions can serve as a way of breaking an initial symmetrical situation by using "supposition not fully justified, yet not quite rash either"—favoring one action over the other.

Some of her ideas about picking and presumptions are generalized in *Second-Order Decisions* (with Cass Sunstein). Ullmann-Margalit and Sunstein argue that when the consequences of various courses of action are difficult or impossible to calculate, people often make a *second-order decision,* or a decision about decisions, which makes the calculation unnecessary. They adopt rules or presumptions; they create standards; they delegate authority to others; they take small steps; they pick rather than choose.

Ullmann-Margalit and Sunstein offer grounds for choosing among the various strategies in both legal and nonlegal contexts, by exploring the extent to which they minimize the overall costs of decision and costs of error.

If choice without preference usually amounts to picking in small decisions about soup cans, Ullmann-Margalit moves to the other end of the spectrum in her essay *Big Decisions*. She defines "big" decisions as those that are both *transformative* and *irrevocable*. Such decisions, like that a CEO of a high-tech company who decides to become a Buddhist monk, have transformative effects on people's values and preferences. *After* the decision is made, and the CEO becomes a monk, reasons that existed before his transformation change in retrospect; they did not motivate that decision in the first instance. To explain decisions of this kind, Ullmann-Margalit introduces the idea of "opting"—a kind of analogue to picking—which she contrasts to converting and drifting.

Some people believe that it is generally or always rational to "want to know." In an argument that recalls her claims about minimizing the burdens of decisions, Ullmann-Margalit contends that people sometimes do not want to know, and that this is perfectly rational. To avoid boredom or pain, to retain impartiality, to retain surprise, and to avoid undesirable entanglements, people might not want to have access to relevant information. Building on concrete cases in which not wanting to know is perfectly reasonable, Ullmann-Margalit explores, and ultimately rejects, the idea that people should adopt a rebuttable presumption in favor of wanting to know. She urges instead that people should undertake a kind of cost-benefit analysis, balancing the advantages and disadvantages of receiving more information.

Much of Ullmann-Margalit's work deals with decisions, not beliefs. But some of her arguments bear on the latter as well. In *Holding True and Holding as True* (with Avishai Margalit), she argues that there is "nothing absurd about holding a sentence true without believing the proposition it expresses." Indeed, she and Margalit contend that this possibility captures a wide range of important phenomena. For example, people often hold Holy Scriptures to be true without necessarily understanding them. "What we have here are cases of division of epistemic labor, as it were." People hold many propositions as true because they trust others, such as scientists or priests, who are taken to understand them. There are close links here, drawn explicitly, with Ullmann-Margalit's work on presumptions.

II. Social Order

Much of Ullmann-Margalit's work investigates the foundations of social order, and what makes it possible. With reference to social norms, invisible hands, and the idea of considerateness, she explores how individually rational people, often concerned about their own self-interest, end up solving collective action problems and producing social stability. Under the influence of Thomas Hobbes and Thomas Schelling, she often enlists game theory to investigate these questions. But her insights turn out to be startlingly original.

Ullmann-Margalit's classic 1976 book, *The Emergence of Norms*, contends that social norms can be seen as solutions to serious problems posed by certain types of social interaction. Her claim is one of "rational reconstruction," involving not historical evidence, or indeed anything at all empirical, but instead a plausible claim about how a practice or a phenomenon might have emerged. Ullmann-Margalit treats three such situations as paradigmatic or "core," involving prisoner's dilemmas, coordination, and inequality. In all three situations, familiar social norms turn out to resolve the specified problems. In her view, norms typically have that effect insofar as they impose "a significant social pressure for conformity and against deviation," alongside a "belief by the people concerned in their indispensability for the proper functioning of society," and an expectation of clashes between the dictates of norms "on the one hand and personal interests and desires on the other."

In prisoner's dilemma situations, for example, people cannot easily produce a mutually beneficial state of affairs without some kind of norm, backed by appropriate sanctions. Suppose, for example, that the question is whether to pay one's income tax, to vote in a general election, to keep a promise, or to cut through a neighbor's well-tended lawn. In each case, a norm might turn out to be especially important, all the more so "the larger and the more indeterminate the class of participants, and the more frequent the occurrence of the dilemma among them." In short, norms operate as stabilizing devices.

Her essay in this volume, *Revision of Norms*, focuses on how norms break down. As she explains, they often shift from conclusive to presumptive—as when, for example, there is an across-the-board taboo against abortion, which is revised to a taboo that can be overcome in specified cases (as, for example, when the mother's health is at stake). Sometimes the presumption actually reverses, as in the case of smoking in public places. Ullmann-Margalit draws a distinction between "norm change (evolutionary, spontaneous) and norm revision (initiated)," but suggests that the distinction is not dichotomous. Sometimes "a gradual and 'evolutionary' process of change in societal attitudes and values eventually gets the official cachet on the level, mostly, of institutional policy revision." Norms with respect to sex equality and same-sex relations are examples.

With respect to norms, many of Ullmann-Margalit's arguments draw on invisible-hand explanations, which suggest that social practices are often a result of human action but not human design. To those who are interested in such explanations, Ullmann-Margalit insists, in *Invisible-Hand Explanations*, on the great importance of distinguishing between explanations of the *emergence* of practices and explanations of the *persistence* of practices. As she puts it: "One way to account for something's existence is as an answer to the question of origin: How did it come into being, how did it begin to exist? The other is as an answer to the question of endurance: Why does it persist (regardless of how it came about in the first place), why does it continue to exist?"

The kind of invisible-hand explanation that accounts for the emergence of practices might turn out to be altogether different from the kind that accounts for their persistence. In her view, the emergence of practices is often best explained by *aggregating* explanations: Diverse and dispersed action by numerous people might produce some kind of pattern, even if they did not foresee it or intend to bring it about. (Consider the wisdom of crowds.) By contrast, practices often persist because of *evolutionary* explanations. They survive some sort of competition. Survival value may have nothing to do with the emergence of a practice in the first place.

In *The Invisible Hand and the Cunning of Reason*, she enlists these points to demonstrate that invisible-hand explanations have a curious ideological career, and that those who invoke such explanations to defend longstanding practices often err. During the Scottish Enlightenment, such explanations were used to promote ideals of secular progress, while most recently they have been used inversely, to promote conservative reverence toward traditions—and in a sense to oppose the very idea of enlightenment. She contends that the ideological use of the idea of the invisible hand, by conservatives arguing against social planners, has been made plausible as a result of a failure to distinguish between the two kinds of invisible-hand explanations.

She notes, for example, that Friedrich Hayek seems to have thought that "all the institutions constituting our social fabric can—and should—be explained invisible-handedly, that invisible-hand explanations are evolutionary explanations, and that evolutionary explanations presuppose a functionalist outlook." Ullmann-Margalit responds that Hayek failed to see that the explanations he was offering for social institutions "were not explanations of emergence at all." She adds that evolutionary explanations of persistence cannot really be counted as *justifications*—and that it is necessary "to subject each existing social institution to a critical examination, free of presuppositions, in order to ascertain whether it was indeed of such positive social function and of such pedigree as to make it worthy of respect and preservation."

Drawing on her work on norms, Ullmann-Margalit argues that people often enjoy "solidarity in consumption." She urges (with Cass Sunstein) that contrary to a common picture of relationships in a market economy, people often express communal and membership-seeking impulses via consumption choices, purchasing goods and services because other people are doing so as well. Consider, for example, the decision to read a popular book (such as Harry Potter) or to see a popular movie (such as Star Wars). In such cases, an expression of some kind of solidarity might be involved. In a set of claims that bear on contemporary uses of social media, she argues that shared identities are maintained and created in this way. Sports events, such as the World Cup, are evident examples; people enjoy watching in a full stadium not in an empty one (in contrast to basking on an empty beach rather than a crowded one). These claims help explain why some products turn out to be far more successful than their creators ever dreamed, and why market success is essentially unpredictable; it also shows why people often comply with laws even if they are rarely enforced.

Ullmann-Margalit's arguments about norms and presumptions have clear implications for questions about trust and distrust. In *Trust, Distrust, and In Between,* she points to the existence of a gap between trust and distrust, and to the possibility of being suspended between the two. Since both trust and distrust require reasons, the question is what to do if there are no reasons, or at any rate no sufficient reasons, either way. This kind of situation—of being suspended between two poles without a sufficient reason to opt for either one of them—calls for a presumption. In some of the literature on trust, it seems to be taken almost for granted that generalized distrust is justifiable in a way that generalized trust is not, supporting a presumption of distrust. But Ullmann-Margalit raises serious doubts about that idea. She does so by introducing the idea of "soft distrust," a version of the stag-hunt game, in which the players "may coordinate in such a way as to enter into a relationship of cooperation and neither will be tempted to deviate to distrust in the future."

In much of Ullmann-Margalit's work, social norms solve problems. But they can also create them, by interfering with people's purely private judgments or by compromising their privacy. In *The Case of the Camera in the Kitchen: Surveillance, Privacy, Sanctions, and Governance,* she draws a series of intriguing lessons from the installation of a closed-circuit TV camera in the kitchen of the Center for the Study of Rationality at the Hebrew University of Jerusalem. (At the time, she was the Director of the Center and faced the problem; she decided to remove the camera.) Ullmann-Margalit suggests that this seemingly small incident turns out to be full of implications for large questions about surveillance and privacy in modern society. She discusses the many arguments brought forward in the resulting debate, such as that those who have "nothing to hide" should not fear the camera; that it is legitimate for people to object to being watched, even if they are doing nothing wrong; that communal spaces create a reasonable expectation of privacy; and that camera surveillance is acceptable only for grave risks (such as terrorism). Part of the fascination of this essay is Ullmann-Margalit's demonstration that on such issues, similar people have sharply opposed and sometimes apparently intractable intuitions.

Toward the end of her life, Ullmann-Margalit turned to a subject that has received essentially no academic attention: considerateness. She defines a considerate act as one "designed to decrease someone else's discomfort at near-zero cost to oneself." She urges, quite boldly, that "considerateness is the foundation upon which our relationships are to be organized in both the thin, anonymous context of the public space and the thick, intimate context of the family." Focused not on the emergence of norms but on their consequences, she notes that while a lover might send "a bouquet of a hundred roses," families typically have smaller, more routinized gestures and "deals," which reflect "their preferences and aversions, their different competencies and skills, their relative strengths, weaknesses, and vulnerabilities, as well as their fantasies, whims, and special needs." Ullmann-Margalit argues that in that context, it may be too much to aspire to justice. But a good family can certainly be fair.

With respect to the family, Ullmann-Margalit was focused both on mutual advantage and on partiality. She insisted that we cannot proceed " 'with eyes wide shut'—namely, in an imagined original position, behind a veil of ignorance." On the contrary, "the fair family deal is adopted considerately and partially, 'with eyes wide open'—namely, with the family members sympathetically taking into account the full particularity of each, and in light of fine-grained comparisons of preferences between them." Note that in this sentence, the word "partially" is paired with "considerately"; she sees a form of partiality as connected or at least compatible with fairness.

The concluding chapter in this book, *Final Ends and Meaningful Lives*, is a kind of epilogue. In a brisk but ambitious set of comments on an essay by Harry Frankfurt, she contends that for "the meaningfulness of life a mere additive function of locally mean-ingful moments will not do." She emphasizes the importance, in making meaning, of the "active and creative task of constructing one's past, of interpreting it, of using the 'raw material' of the succession of events to put it in the form of a narrative." She adds that it "is the narrative as a whole which is capable of endowing the constituent events with meaning or depriving them of it. I think that this notion of perspective in which one sees one's life, past as well as future, is indispensable for the notion of the meaning-fulness of life." That is a large claim, and it might help point the way toward a solution to the most fundamental mystery of all.

List of Tables

PART I
Decisions

1

Picking and Choosing

The notion of reasoned choice is central to most discussions of decision and action. It is usually anchored, in the more formal of these discussions, in a binary relation of preference over alternatives. The preference relation being but a partial ordering, however, it is quite standardly augmented by the equivalence relation of indifference to render it complete. This, then, is where the notion of indifference enters the picture—and this is usually where it is left: as merely subservient to the notion of preference, as a mere device in virtue of which the latter is made amenable to satisfactory systematization. But does it deserve to be left there?

This paper raises some philosophical questions that may be asked about the notion of indifference and attempts to answer some of them. It is a plea not to be indifferent to indifference.

Choosing, Picking, Selecting

We speak of *choosing* among alternatives when the act of taking (doing) one of them is determined by the differences in one's preferences over them. When preferences are completely symmetrical, where one is strictly indifferent with regard to the alternatives, we shall refer to the act of taking (doing) one of them as an act of *picking*. We adopt the term *selection* as the generic term, neutral with respect to choosing and picking.

More precisely, a simple picking situation will be a selection situation with the alternatives A and B such that: (i) the agent cannot select both A and B ("cannot" being construed as deontic prohibition, practical impossibility, or whatever); (ii) the agent is indifferent between A and B; (iii) the agent prefers the selection of either A or B, whichever it may be, to the selection of neither: one—or the other—is better for him than none.

Given this characterization, statements like Leibniz's "In things which are absolutely indifferent there can be no choice . . . since choice must have some reason or principle,"[1] or Collingwood's "Choice is choice between alternatives, and one must in some way

[1] Gottfried Wilhelm Leibniz, *Theodicy*, translated by E. M. Huggard (London: Routledge & K. Paul, 1951), pp. 148–9. See also G. H. R. Parkinson, *Logic and Reality in Leibniz's Metaphysics* (Oxford: Clarendon Press, 1965), p. 100.

present itself as more attractive than the other, or it cannot be chosen,"[2] become analytically true. Choosing is choosing for a reason, and this presupposes preference. However, to the extent that, through equating "choice" with (our generic) "selection," these statements purport to deny the existence of selection situations without preference—or indeed to deny the possibility of picking—this paper aims to render them doubtful, if not downright wrong.

As an example, consider the story attributed to Algazel (al-Ghazali) about the hungry man in front of whom are put two dates that are equally distant from him, equally accessible to him, and are completely alike in size, shape, and color, in beauty and in freshness. If the man is allowed only one of the dates, he cannot possibly choose since by assumption there is nothing in respect of which one of them is preferable. This is an earlier version of the much more famous story about Buridan's ass who, according to some,[3] is destined to starve to death owing to there being no ground on which to prefer one bale of hay over the other, and thus to there being no possibility of choice between them.

In view of the perplexities of this situation a recurrent line of reasoning throughout the historical discussions relating to the problem of Buridan's ass maintained that no situation of completely symmetrical preferences is feasible. Furthermore, if in a situation which *appears* to be one of strictly indifferent preferences a selection of one of the alternatives is as a matter of fact made, this only proves, on this view, that the given situation was after all *not* one of completely symmetrical preferences. Thus Montaigne says:

...nothing is presented unto us, wherein there is not some difference, how light so ever it bee: And that either to the sight, or to the feeling, there is ever some choise, which tempteth and drawes us to it, though imperceptible and not to bee distinguished.[4]

---

[2] R. G. Collingwood, *The Idea of Nature* (Oxford: Clarendon Press, 1945), p. 41.

[3] As some of the more striking examples, consider the following passages: "Between two foods, distant and moving in like measure, a man being free would die of hunger, before he should bring one to his teeth" (Dante Alighieri, *The Paradise*, edited with translation and notes by Arthur John Butler [London: Macmillan, 1885], p. 38); "And who should place us betweene a Bottle of wine, and a Gammon of Bacon, with an equall appetite to eat and drinke, doubtlesse there were noe remedy, but to die of thirst and of hunger" (Michel Equem de Montaigne, *Essays*, translated by John Florio, 3 vols. [London: J. M. Dent & Sons, 1965], 2: 333); "I say that I entirely grant that if a man were placed in such a state of equilibrium [like the ass of Buridanus] he would perish of hunger and thirst, supposing he perceived nothing but hunger and thirst, and the food and drink which were equidistant from him. If you ask me whether such a man would not be thought an ass rather than a man, I reply that I do not know" (Benedict de Spinoza, *Ethics*, translated by W. Hale White, revised by Amelia Hutchinson Stirling, 4th ed. [London: Oxford University Press, 1937], p. 102). Buridan's own position on this matter, incidentally, is not known. In fact, the story about the ass is not to be found in his writings. Thomas Reid's editor, Sir William Hamilton, offers this comment as a note to a passage by Reid mentioning the problem of Buridan's ass (the passage itself is quoted in n. 14, below): "The supposition of the ass, etc. is not, however, as I have ascertained to be found in his writings. Perhaps it was orally advanced in disputation, or in lecturing, as an example in illustration of his Determinism; perhaps it was employed by his opponents as an instance to reduce that doctrine to absurdity" (Thomas Reid, *The Works of Thomas Reid, D. D.*, preface, notes and supplementary dissertations by Sir William Hamilton, Bart., 4th ed. [Edinburgh: MacLachlan & Steward, 1854], p. 238).

[4] Montaigne, *Essays*, 2: 333.

And according to Leibniz:

There is never any indifference of equipoise.... There will therefore always be many things in the ass and outside the ass, although they may not be apparent to us, which will determine him to go to one side rather than the other.[5]

A somewhat weaker version of this position maintains that while selection situations with completely symmetrical preferences are possible, and thus present a genuine theoretical problem, they are not of any practical interest: "We are," says Rescher, "rarely in real-life situations confronted with strictly indifferent choices."[6] Even those who acknowledge the feasibility of such situations are hard put to produce convincing examples. The only good example, as well as the most popular one, seems to have been that of a selection situation involving a number of coins (or new dollar bills) any one of which will answer both the buyer's and the seller's purposes equally well.[7]

Are There Genuine Picking Situations?

Questions crowd in: Are there picking situations—and if so are they rare and inconsequential or rather pervasive and possibly revealing of our social or human situation? Are picking situations always transformable into choosing ones? If not, how do we pick and can we do so reasonably? Is the evidence for picking incompatible with well-entrenched lawful sentences or with apparent conceptual truths? There are many more, and we begin by asking: Are there genuine picking situations?

Our answer to this question is a firm yes; moreover, we maintain that they are numerous rather than rare. Supermarket shelves supply us with paradigmatic examples of social picking situations proper.[8]

---

[5] Leibniz, *Theodicy*, sees. 46–9.

[6] Nicholas Rescher, "Choice without Preference," *Kant Studien* 51 (1959–60): 143. We want to acknowledge our debt to Rescher's paper, from which we drew most of the references to the traditional writings on the problem of Buridan's ass.

[7] Compare: "...whence the election of two indifferent things commeth into our soule (and which causeth, that from out a great number of Crownes or Angells we rather take one than another, when there is no reason to induce us to preferre any one before others)" (Montaigne, *Essays*, 2: 333); "...for surely a man who has occasion to lay out a shilling, or a guinea, may have two hundred that are of equal value, both to the giver and to the receiver, any one of which will answer his purpose equally well" (Reid, *Works*, p. 609); "Such situations [of strictly indifferent choice] do however appear to exist. For example, if a person were offered a choice between two fresh dollar bills, the only perceptible difference between which is a difference in serial numbers, we would be greatly astonished if this selector could offer us a 'reason' for choosing one of them rather than the other, which could reasonably be regarded as valid. While a difference between the bills does indeed exist, it simply does not constitute a valid difference as regards their preferability as objects of choice" (Rescher, "Choice without Preference," p. 143).

[8] A picking situation is social if A arranges it for B. Often when a person arranges a selection situation he may not know whether he is arranging a picking or a choosing one. Thus the more food and drink our generous hosts offer us, the more choices they may believe they are making possible for us—but then the more confusion or indifference they may in fact be introducing. (See the remarks below on the taxonomy of selection situations according to types of personality.) We are assuming here that the guests are constrained to select some food or other; this indeed is how we propose to construe component (iii) in the description of

To be sure, given the variety of products on display and given your preferences, you may *choose* to get a can of soup. You may, further, choose to get tomato rather than mushroom soup, and you may, if you are particular about such matters, choose to get Campbell's tomato soup rather than Heinz's. But we hold that usually you cannot, and as a matter of fact do not, *choose* the can you end up throwing into the carriage: you *pick* it. That is, if it is the case—as it usually is—that, having eliminated from among the rows upon rows of Campbell tomato soup cans the less conveniently accessible ones as well as the conspicuously damaged ones, you are still facing at least two cans neither of which is discernibly superior to the other(s), then you are in a picking situation, willy-nilly.

This is not to deny, of course, that there may be differences among the cans, even differences which could make a difference. Thus a scientific weighing of the contents of the cans may yield that one of them was slightly fuller, or a careful examination of the inside of the cans may reveal that one of them was rustier than the others, etc. The point, however, is that as far as the ordinary consumer in the ordinary shopping situation is concerned one cannot seize upon these possible differences and claim that owing to them the situation is one of *choosing*. For all that the ordinary consumer in the ordinary shopping situation can determine for himself in a rough-and-ready way the alternatives up for selection are essentially identical and so his situation vis-à-vis them is one of *picking*. The fact that a thorough laboratory examination of the cans and their contents may provide some bits of information that could help differentiate between the cans is of no consequence here. For one thing, the cost of obtaining this additional information far exceeds the marginal utility the ordinary shopper stands to gain from it:[9] after all, how much are you willing to invest in order to find out which of the many soup cans you face is *really* "the best"? Besides, sending the cans off for this examination presumably requires the prior purchase of all of them from the shop, thus frustrating your initial aim of buying just one; and if you mark for examination not all but only some of them, this already involves picking anyway.

There is a further point, though, that is made in the Montaigne and Leibniz passages quoted above and that merits consideration here. It is neatly compressed in Leibniz's concept of the *petites perceptions*[10] and its gist is that once it is conceded that the alternatives up for selection are not absolutely identical and that it is likely that there are

---

picking situations given above. When this constraint is lifted, the description of the situation is no longer apparent. A man goes into a supermarket, sees two or more types of soup, pauses a while, then leaves. Did he pick to leave? Or did his initial preference for soup over no-soup give way to a more "fundamental" kind of preference—to evade the selection situation altogether rather than face a picking situation?

[9] This applies to the ordinary consumer in the ordinary shopping situation. Matters are different, of course, when we consider a survey conducted by a consumers protection organization. Here the possible differences among the ostensibly identical cans are of significance and may well be worth exposing. Note that a possible conclusion of such a survey is that the cans of firm A are of a more uniform quantity and quality than are the cans of firm B, and thus constitute a more genuine picking situation for the consumers.

[10] Gottfried Wilhelm Leibniz, *New Essays Concerning Human Understanding*, translated by Alfred Gideon Langley (New York: Macmillan, 1896).

some discoverable differences among them, it must thereby be conceded as well that the situation is one of choosing, not picking: it is, on this view, these subliminal differences which, "though imperceptible and not to bee distinguished," determine one's choice. All that we shall say at present in order to dispose of this argument is that, whether or not these (potential) subliminal differences are indeed capable of "tempting" and "drawing" you toward just one of the alternatives before you, they cannot be your *reasons* for selecting that particular alternative. As far as your perception of the situation is concerned, you are facing essentially identical alternatives. And to the extent that you are also aware that there may be some minuscule differences among them you at the same time surely realize that access to this potentially differentiating information is either not worth your while or else peculiarly defeating of your aim. And so, for all that you know and care, you are in a picking situation. (We shall have an occasion later to revert to the issue of reasons for choosing vs. causes that might determine picking.)

Generalizing somewhat, we contend that in this era of mass production and automatized assembly lines there is an abundance of essentially identical products and consumer goods that repeatedly place every one of us in picking situations. We may choose the *type* but we often can do no better than pick the *token*, whether it be a toothpaste tube or a copy of a book, a king-size bed or a motorcar. It may not be all that surprising, we feel, that thinkers of past ages did not grapple with the notion of selection situations with strictly symmetrical preferences: given that the inventory of items available for their consideration consisted basically of products of nature on the one hand and of handmade artifacts on the other, it is quite understandable that the notion of essentially identical picking items would seem to them merely hypothetical, if not altogether untenable.

Let us agree to refer to the picking situations of the Campbell-soup-cans variety discussed so far, those that involve essentially identical alternatives, as *picking situations proper*. We want now to mention a different type of picking situation. As illustrations of it, consider the following cases, (a) You are to draw a card from a well shuffled deck of cards; if the color is right (or the number, or the suit), you win. (b) Two identical boxes are placed before you: one of them contains $1000, the other is empty. You do not know which is the prize box, and you are allowed to select just one. (c) F. R. Stockton's story, "The Lady, or the Tiger?"[11] tells of a ruler whose method of administering justice was to throw the accused into an arena with two identical doors at the back. Behind one there was a fierce and hungry tiger; behind the other, a young and handsome lady. The fate of the accused—and it goes without saying that the question of his guilt or innocence as well—was to be settled by his opening one of the doors, not knowing which was which.

What these cases have in common is obvious. Each of them involves a selection situation in which the selecting agent has a clear preference for one outcome (or perhaps one type of outcome) over the other(s). Due to the structure, or design, of the situation,

---

[11] Frank R. Stockton, *The Lady, or the Tiger? and Other Stories* (New York: Scribner's, 1884).

however, the information as to which of the alternatives up for selection will yield the preferred outcome is inaccessible to him. In other words, even though the selection alternatives here are not identical, it is inherent to cases of this sort that they are presented to the agent in an identical guise so that he is unable to determine the identity of the preferred one. Thus (reverting to example (b)) the agent clearly prefers—and hence would want to choose—the prize box, but in the circumstances he can do no better than pick one or the other. Or again, he may have very good reasons for preferring the prize box over the empty one, but he has no reason for preferring box A over box B. Furthermore, given that he has as a matter of fact selected box A, the appropriate description would *not* be "He chose the empty box A"; rather, it would be "He picked box A which turned out to have been the empty one." These situations, in distinction from the picking situations proper presented earlier, will constitute what may be labeled picking situations *by default*.[12]

Having thus made out the case that there are selection situations that deserve to be classified as picking situations, we shall now proceed to ask: How is picking possible?

How is Picking Possible?

We are all familiar with the standard story about choice: Given your beliefs and utilities, whenever in a selection situation choose so as to maximize (expected) utility. But how are we to act in a picking situation proper, in face of essentially identical alternatives? Need we pick? Can we? That is, is picking conceptually absurd?

A survey of the traditional discussions of the problem of choice without preference reveals, as we saw earlier, that some deny the very existence of such situations. Among those who acknowledge that picking situations may exist, or who are anyway willing to entertain the notion of a picking situation as at least a hypothetical one, some tenaciously maintain that such situations are bound to end up in an impasse, that picking is impossible.[13] There is little doubt that these writers are in the grip of a mechanistic picture. Just as a physical object, suspended between identical forces, remains in equilibrium, or again just as a piece of metal, interposed between two identical and equidistant magnets, is at rest, so also a man who is equally drawn by the various

---

[12] We may perhaps describe the situation as one in which we pick to believe. But it is not clear what is gained thereby, and the issues involved in this suggestion are too complex to be dealt with here. Notice, as a sample, that writers often give the impression that (a) we are free to believe, but at the same time (b) we ought to choose (pick?) to believe in a reasonable way. And, furthermore, when we are confronted with two equally well-confirmed scientific theories, then (c) we are to choose (pick?) to believe the simplest.

[13] In addition to the passages quoted in n. 3, we ought perhaps to refer the reader to the passage in Aristotle where the earliest mention (though not a discussion) of the problem in hand is to be found and to which all later writers on the subject revert: "If...the place where the earth rests is not its natural place, but the cause of its remaining there is the constraint of its 'indifference' (on the analogy of...the man who is violently but equally hungry and thirsty, and stands at an equal distance from food and drink, and who therefore must remain where he is), then..." (Aristotle, *De Caelo* 2. 13. 295b24 [translated by W. K. C. Guthrie]; see also Plato, *Phaedo* 108e–109a).

alternatives he faces will, on this view, be destined to inaction.[14] And in response to the opponents of this position, who reasonably point out that nobody who is placed in the Ultimate Picking Situation will be ass enough to die for want of food and that in general people eventually settle for one or another of the alternatives, the categorical rejoinder to them is that to the extent that selection *has* been effected this in itself is a proof that the situation was not truly a picking but rather a choosing one. The upshot of this view, then, is that the act of selection presupposes preference: no selection without gradation.

It is quite possible, it seems to us, that at the root of this no-picking-is-possible position lies a biased and misleading mode of expression. The adherents of this view, as well as others, invariably couch the description of an agent's act of selection of one alternative out of two available ones in the formula: "The agent selected (grabbed, did) A rather than B." Now this "rather than" terminology is construed in such a way that it is taken to entail, or presuppose, the formula: "The agent preferred A to B." And this, in turn, amounts to interpreting the agent's selection of A as his having *chosen* A.[15] In other words, the very description under which the act of selection is taken to fall prejudges the issue in that it seems to analytically yield the fact that the situation was one of choosing to begin with.

---

[14] See Pierre Bayle, *Dictionnaire*, art. "Buridan." In his "Essays on the Intellectual Powers of Man," Thomas Reid has a section called "Of Analogy" where he strongly attacks the tendency to carelessly and uncritically use (or abuse) the mind-body analogy that is so often suggested by common, though misleading, modes of expression in our language. As a paradigmatic example of how misleading this analogy can get, he takes the favorite parallel drawn between the act of deliberation on the one hand and the physical act of scales-weighing on the other. The passage merits quotation in full: "When a man is urged by contrary motives—those on one hand inciting him to do some action, those on the other to forbear it—he deliberates about it, and at last resolves to do it, or not to do it. The contrary motives are here compared to the weights in the opposite scales of a balance; and there is not, perhaps, any instance that can be named of a more striking analogy between body and mind. Hence the phrases of weighing motives, of deliberating upon actions.

"From this analogy, some philosophers draw very important conclusions. They say, that, as the balance cannot incline to one side more than the other when the opposite weights are equal, so a man cannot possibly determine himself if the motives on both hands are equal.…And on this foundation some of the Schoolmen maintained that, if a hungry ass were placed between two bundles of hay equally inviting, the beast must stand still and starve to death, being unable to turn to either, because there are equal motives to both. This is an instance of that analogical reasoning which I conceive ought never to be trusted; for the analogy between a balance and a man deliberating, though one of the strongest that can be found between matter and mind, is too weak to support any argument. A piece of dead inactive matter, and an active intelligent being, are things very unlike; and, because the one would remain at rest in a certain case, it does not follow that the other would be inactive in a case somewhat similar.…

"The conclusion I would draw from all that has been said on analogy, is, that, in our inquiries concerning the mind and its operations, we ought never to trust to reasoning drawn from some supposed similitude of body to mind; and that we ought to be very much upon our guard that we be not imposed upon by those analogical terms and phrases, by which the operations of the mind are expressed in all languages" (Reid, *Works*, pp. 237–8).

[15] It seems that something like this procedure underlies the behavioral economists' notion of "revealed preference," according to which it is the consumer's act of purchasing a (certain quantity of a) certain commodity, rather than his declarations in response to an interviewer's questionnaire, that reveal his preferences (or his preference ordering over a given range of alternatives). Shouldn't this notion undergo some revision in view of the possibility of picking?

As a step toward thwarting this analytical connection we propose to describe an agent's act of selecting alternative A in a picking situation thus: "The agent selected (grabbed, did) A *to the exclusion of* B." This lingo is intended not to prejudge the issue in that it is supposed to be free of any presupposition, or entailment, of preference: it is simply supposed to amount to saying that the agent picked A where B was an alternative.

A word about formulating all this in terms of *reasons* for action. In the case of a choosing situation, where the agent selects A rather than B, we are generally held to be licensed to say that the agent (must have) had reasons for selecting A rather than B; and this is further unpacked into saying that the agent's overall reasons—in terms of his beliefs and utilities—for the selection of A outweighed his overall reasons for the selection of B: hence the preference for and choice of A. In the case of a picking situation, on the other hand, where the agent selects A to the exclusion of B, we may still say that the agent (must have) had reasons for selecting A to the exclusion of B. But, far from being further unpacked into saying that the agent's reasons for A outweighed those he had for B, this formulation is—and is intended to be—compatible with saying that the agent also had reasons for selecting B to the exclusion of A, so that any inference of preference and choice is undercut. Indeed, it is constitutive of picking situations that there will be reasons for the selection of A to the exclusion of B as well as reasons for the selection of B to the exclusion of A, and, furthermore, that these reasons be as good and as weighty.

Note that while in a picking situation proper, where by assumption each of the selection alternatives will satisfy him equally, the agent has no reason to *prefer* one alternative to the other(s), the other side of the same token is that if he has—somehow—effected a selection in such a situation, he will have no reason to *regret* it. Also, even though the agent has no outweighing *reason* for the selection of A, once he has—somehow—effected the selection of A he is nevertheless immune to any charges of having acted *unreasonably*. While it may not be a law that when we act we do so rationally (i.e., that we select the alternative that maximizes expected utility), it may be a law that when we act we do so reasonably (i.e., that we do not select a dominated alternative). Still this may not be the end of the matter. It may turn out that picking situations are always replaceable by choosing ones, and if so we can perhaps always act rationally.

This suggests that it may be possible for us to extricate ourselves from a picking situation by appropriately replacing it with a nonpicking one. But is it? If it *is*, will accounts of extrication by replacement avoid all reference to the ability to pick, and hence exempt us from having to remove the difficulties involved in the notion of this ability? And if it is *not*, how do we extricate ourselves directly?

Extrication from a Picking Situation

A rather natural suggestion as to how to go about picking is to select randomly by casting lots or, more generally, by resorting to the use of a random device. This suggestion amounts in effect to the following declaration: Since in a picking situation I find myself at an impasse, I call upon chance to extricate me by supplying me with an extrinsic sufficient reason for selecting one alternative to the exclusion of all the others. In other words, I delegate the power to effect a selection to chance, so that the mere singling out of one alternative by the random device will play, for me, the role of *force majeure*.

Let us examine this suggestion. It is quite clear, first, that with regard to trivial picking situations of the Campbell-soup variety, having recourse to a chance device may be just too costly in terms of time, attention, etc. Thus the outlay involved in securing a state of affairs in which each of the alternatives up for selection has equal probability of being singled out by the chance device often already outweighs the marginal utility to be gained from securing such a state of affairs: after all, each alternative, regardless of *how* it is picked, is by hypothesis supposed to be equally satisfactory. Second, resorting to a random device in itself involves a decision, namely, the decision *to* resort to chance, and this decision most likely involves the selection of the appropriate device—a selection that may quite plausibly be imagined to be of the picking variety. But the most serious objection to this method is that, far from providing a solution, it merely pushes the problem one step back. For suppose the picking situation comprises just two alternatives, A and B, and suppose that you have decided to toss a coin to settle the matter (and, indeed, that you have already somehow picked the coin that will be assigned the task). You will now have to match alternative A to heads (or tails) and B to tails (or heads). But this, of course, is inherently a matter of picking—so much so that it may deserve to be regarded as the picking situation par excellence. In other words, the very use of a random device is premised on the possibility of picking, that is, on our capacity to extricate ourselves from a picking situation: the matching of each of the alternatives up for selection with some one of the possible outcomes of the device is, inherently, a matter of picking.

Another suggestion that appears to merit consideration is the one espoused by Nicholas Rescher as a solution to the problem of choice without preference. Recognizing that recourse to a physical chance device may often be costly or cumbersome, he recommends the adoption of a random selection *policy*, such as "When confronted with a choice in the face of symmetric knowledge, or preference, always to select the first-mentioned (etc.) alternative."[16] By way of criticizing this idea let us note, first, that talk of a policy implies systematicalness and consistency (this is surely implicit in Rescher's use of "always"). Now while being systematic and consistent may doubtless be of help in extricating oneself from some picking situations one encounters, there is just no justification whatsoever for *requiring* it. Besides, such a policy needs to be *adopted*, and the adoption of a picking policy is of course itself a matter of picking: why the first-mentioned rather than the penultimate-mentioned alternative? Thus Rescher's own use of "etc." is question begging. Also, such a policy will in fact have to consist of numerous contingency plans: pick the first mentioned (or whatever) when the alternatives are orally presented to you, the right-most (or whatever) when they are serially ordered in space, the first (or whatever) alphabetically when names are

---

[16] Rescher, "Choice without Preference," p. 170.

involved and they are scattered or in a circle, the uppermost (or whatever) when there is a heap, and so on and so forth—not to mention the necessary higher-level disambiguating rules for cases where two or more of these contingency plans apply and conflict. When all of this is spelled out, with all the meta-picking that is involved, there is some room for doubt as to whether it can seriously be maintained that this method is practically less cumbersome and theoretically more satisfying than resorting to the use of an external, physical, randomizer.

Finally, it is of some interest to note that in recommending the use of a random selection policy in place of a physical random device Rescher says that it is indeed possible to use the human mind so as to arrive at such a policy since "men are capable of making arbitrary selections, with respect to which they can be adequately certain in their own mind that the choice was made haphazardly, and without any 'reasons' whatsoever."[17] Given such a categorical statement of our capacity to arbitrarily select a picking policy, one wonders about the point of the detour: why should it not be possible for us to do without the mediation of the policy, and simply put this capacity for making arbitrary selections to use directly in any picking situations we may face? (Note that it may be misleading to suggest that when we pick we do so arbitrarily: we have already said that we may in fact be acting reasonably. As for the converse: at a race A may bet on x to win because x's name is "Jerusalem" and A loves the city. Did A pick, albeit with a reason, or did he choose, though arbitrarily?)

There are some other prospective means of extrication that are worth commenting on. *Convenience* may be mentioned only to be quickly disposed of. If considerations of convenience happen to converge on one particular alternative in a given picking situation and single it out as the most conveniently pickable, then surely the problem of picking is avoided. To wit: we began with a situation in which we perceived the alternatives as, say, soup can A vs. soup can B. Between these we were indifferent. We then realize that the situation can be redescribed as follows: can A by selection s_1 vs. can B by selection s_2. Between *these* alternatives, owing to the consideration of convenience, we realize that we are not indifferent and so we can choose. But of course it may be simpler and better to say that just these considerations will have affected the utilities involved in such a way as to render the most readily accessible alternative preferred to the other(s) to begin with, so that the problem of picking in truth *dis*solves into one of simple choice. If, however, the picking situation is such that two or more of the alternatives turn out to be equally convenient to pick, then the factor of convenience is a superfluous one and we are back to where we started.

The case of *habit* is both similar to and different from that of convenience. A habit—like reaching for the left—may on some occasions resolve a picking situation. Where it does *not*, either because it does not apply to the picking situation in hand (e.g., because it is novel) or because it still squares with the picking of two or more of the alternatives, it is of no consequence. The interesting case is when, due to some habit, a resolution of

---

[17]   Rescher, "Choice without Preference," p. 169.

the picking situation *is* achieved: some one of the alternatives, that is, is in some sense habitually picked to the exclusion of all the others. Unlike the convenience consideration, the habit cannot be said to have supplied the agent with a *reason* for his selection (even though there may be reasons for a person to act in accordance with his habits); nor can it be incorporated, therefore, into the agent's utility assessments regarding the available alternatives. At the same time the habit can in a case of this sort be considered to have played a causal role in extricating the agent from the picking situation, and as such it may contribute to an *explanation* of his picking act.

Having surveyed some of the difficulties encountered by the various solutions—actually proposed or naturally proposable—to the problem of extrication, the problem itself is still with us. For although it may sometimes be possible to replace a picking situation by a choosing one, there is no reason to believe that it is always possible to do so. So we shall at this point state our basic contention that there is no evidence, either conceptual or empirical, to challenge the thesis that people have the ability to pick. This amounts, on one level, to the conjecture that where a genuine picking situation is involved the sentence "A picked x" and the sentence "A picked y" may each be compatible with any acceptable scientific corpus. And, on another level, it has to do with the observation that picking situations do not, normally, paralyze us, nor do they lead us to an impasse. Also, it would seem that we do not in principle depend for our extrication from these situations on any artificial or extrinsic device, on second-order decisions, or, for that matter, on the operation of the "will" as traditionally envisaged:[18] we simply have the capacity to extricate ourselves directly from such situations; we have the ability to pick. One may indeed go further and say that when we are in a genuine picking situation we are in a sense transformed into a chance device that functions at random and effects arbitrary selections (our misgivings about "arbitrary" notwithstanding; still others can be added about "random").

To be sure, the assertion that we have the capacity to pick at random need not be taken as a metaphysical one: an epistemic construal would suffice. That is, it does not pertain to the level of determining causes of the act of picking, and it is not in principle incompatible with there being explanations (as well as predictions) of this act from the vantage point of an all-knowing Laplacean machine. What is being claimed, rather, is that on the level of reasons for action, for all that we know we can, and often do, randomly pick. This is much like saying that while the course of a tossed die may

---

[18] From some of the traditional writings on the problem of choice without preference, one may often get the impression that for these writers a picking situation is one in which, as soon as the agent realizes that his preferences and motives are "ever so evenly balanced" and that a threat of an impasse is lurking, he summons from the arsenal that dependable, powerful, secret weapon, the will, which is held in reserve for just such cases and which enables him to accomplish the feat of "homing in" on some one of the alternatives. But for the will, they suggest, we would be asses.

Let us add that the rejection of this highly unsatisfactory "picking-will" view seems to have been the main motivation for the adoption of what was historically considered its only tenable rival, namely, the mechanistic view mentioned earlier.

be completely physically determined, for us it nevertheless functions as a chance device due perhaps to irremediable human ignorance of initial conditions.[19]

Is this the end of the story? In many ways it is only the beginning, even when we consider the simplest picking situations with which we began, namely, the ones in which the alternatives are mere replicas of one another. It seems that even here we can add to the mechanism that may actually be at work. Often enough, or perhaps typically, what occurs in a selection situation you identify as a picking one is that you haphazardly focus your *attention* on some one of the available alternatives. Once you do that, however, then—by hypothesis—none of the other alternatives attracts you more, and there is no room for qualms or second thoughts. So, given the absence of either detracting or distracting factors, there is nothing to prevent you from going ahead and grabbing (or doing) that focused-on alternative.[20]

Picking or Choosing

When the alternatives up for selection are essentially identical, that is, when they can in some objective sense be classified as "picking items," they determine what we termed a picking situation proper. One selects, however, on the basis of one's beliefs and utilities. It is reasonable to suggest, therefore, that it may not be necessary that the alternatives be (objectively) essentially identical, nor that the agent believe them to be such, for him to judge these alternatives as being of equal utility to him. Put differently, since choice presupposes preference, and preference relevant differences, and given that the relevance or irrelevance of the differences among alternatives varies with one's interests, what presents itself as a choosing situation to one person may be conceived of as a picking situation by another. Thus you may pick your tie in the morning while others

---

[19] Would an omniscient being, however, be capable of extricating himself from a picking situation? If this capacity is attributed to such a being, it would have to be metaphysical and not merely epistemic. But then the traditional arguments based on the principle of sufficient reason would seem not to go through: for one thing, God *could* in such a case pick a time to create the world. If, on the other hand, this capacity is denied this being, would he be omnipotent?

[20] In his comment on Aristotle's passage quoted earlier (n. 13), Simplicius seems to give vent to this idea of the unproblematic arrest of attention that leads to the resolution of a picking problem: "And if neither this nor that [i.e., neither hunger nor thirst] presses more, he will choose whatever he *first happens on*, as when two pleasant sights lie equally in our view" (quoted in Rescher, "Choice without Preference," p. 145, n. 8; emphasis added). See also Reid (*Works*, p. 609) in the passage immediately preceding the coin-picking example quoted in n. 7: "Cases frequently occur, in which an end that is of some importance, may be answered equally well by any one of several different means. In such cases, a man who intends the end finds not the least difficulty in taking one of these means, though he be firmly persuaded that it has no title to be preferred to any of the others. To say that this is a case that cannot happen, is to contradict the experience of mankind."

This sketchy attempt to reduce the notion of picking to that of attention (or arrest of attention) cannot get off the ground, however, unless an account of attention can be given in such a way that it is not described as an act. Otherwise it would be a dubious; replacement that is submitted rather than a helpful reduction. We feel that such an account can indeed be given, but we have none to offer yet.

choose theirs. It seems, then, that relative to your beliefs and utilities perhaps *any* selection situation that you face may be taken by you as a picking situation.

Often this takes the form of a second-order decision: with regard to any given selection situation you may choose—indeed you are free to choose—to allow it to be a picking situation. Selecting a rain hat in a department store, having been caught in a sudden pour, I may well be aware that there exists an optimal choice of a hat that suits me best. And yet, my overall priority being to get out of there fast—before the train leaves or before my toddler wrecks the place—I may choose to forgo all weighing and balancing and simply pick. Or again, you may know all there is to know about the differences between the two holiday resorts you are considering for your upcoming vacation and, what's more, these differences may well be relevant to you. And yet, being at a loss as to how to weigh all the different considerations and "calculate," or "see," what it is that you prefer most, you may choose to end the tormenting process by treating the situation as one of picking.[21]

Let us mention in this connection the story told about S. Y. Agnon, who apparently conceded that he often resorted to tossing a coin in cases of indecision. When asked by his puzzled interviewer how he could account for placing such reliance on chance, his answer is reported to have been that of course he did *not* let chance decide for him. Rather, gauging his reaction to the outcome of the toss, he would ascertain whether he was in fact pleased with or disappointed by it, and would accordingly know where his preferences really lay. This seems to indicate that the (second-order) decision to treat a given selection situation as one of picking could at times be self-correcting in that it may expose the situation as having been one of choosing all along.

Be that as it may, note that the decision to pick rather than choose in a given selection situation is by no means incompatible with the received model of the rational decision maker who is supposed to be maximizing (expected) utility. Once it is granted that the complete information about the alternatives is not "there," given free, gratis,

---

[21] It may well be asked, for the sake of symmetry if nothing else, whether it makes sense to talk not just about *choosing to pick* but also about *picking to choose*. Consider the case depicted in Figure 1.1. You may opt for *a*, in which case you get a sure prize, or for *b*, in which case you will have a choice between *c* and *d*. If you are indifferent between *a* and *b*, you may pick one to the exclusion of the other. If you pick *b* to the exclusion of *a*, you may be said to have picked to choose. It may be possible to *pick a choice*. In Figure 1.2, both *a* and *b* are supposed to lead to a choosing situation. If you are indifferent between them, you may pick one to the exclusion of the other, in which case you will have picked your choice.

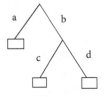

Figure 1.1

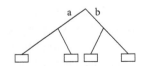

Figure 1.2

and for nothing, but rather has to be obtained at a cost, and once constraints of cost apply to the process of weighing and balancing as well, the appropriate meta-utility considerations may point in favor of picking some one of the alternatives instead of laboring to secure the choice of the "best."

So let us ask: Is it indeed the case that *any* selection situation could be taken by some agent as a picking situation? That is, aren't there actually selection situations that merit to be "objectively" classified as choosing situations proper? And once the question is put this way one may go on to question the departure point of this paper and wonder whether what were introduced as picking situations proper cannot perhaps present themselves—to certain agents and under certain circumstances—as cases of choosing. In addition it is instructive to inquire into the possibility that there may be methods designed to convince, influence, or perhaps manipulate us to exchange our perception of a given selection situation so that we shall come to take it as one of choosing, having previously treated it (or having been inclined to treat it) as a picking situation, or the other way round. We shall take up these questions in turn.

Are There Choosing Situations Proper?

It is in fact quite easy to list examples of selection situations that can hardly be thought of as presenting a picking problem for anyone. Thus one normally chooses rather than picks a spouse, a child's name, a dwelling house, a piece of jewelry, an employee, etc.: the importance, as well as a certain degree of irreversibility of the selection, and the individuality of the alternatives seem to suggest that these are as close as one can get to paradigm cases of choosing.

And yet even here it is not impossible or outrageous to imagine that one's choice is finally narrowed down to just two alternatives such that one is either practically indifferent between them or else downright incapable of weighing the relevant differences between them against each other. When this happens one may at the end resort to, or perhaps be reduced to, picking. Besides, note that whether a given selection situation is perceived by you as a picking or as a choosing situation depends not only on your purposes but also on the description. Thus the rather natural assumption that a book is usually chosen, not picked, presupposes the (standard) aim of reading as well as the description of the situation as that of selecting a book-for-reading. However, given such nonstandard aims as wanting to stop the door from slamming or to kill a mosquito or to look absorbed when someone enters your office door, and given that you have already made the (higher-level) decision that the job is to be assigned to a book, then your selection from the shelf of *that* particular book rather than—or to the exclusion of—the others may well be a matter of picking. In these cases the selection alternatives fall under such descriptions as "door-stopping books," "mosquito-killing books," etc.

Are there, then, no choosing situations proper? Are we to conclude that there is no selection situation such that the alternatives it presents may appropriately be described as relevantly different in some absolute or objective sense?

There is an argument of Goodman's concerning the aesthetic domain which, at least under one interpretation, amounts to a qualified denial of this conclusion.[22] We propose to reconstruct it as follows: Every two paintings differ in some physical aspects. A physical difference between two paintings is in principle always perceptible ("since a single quantum of light may excite a retinal receptor"[23]), even if it is not, at any given time, actually perceived. As such, any physical difference between two paintings potentially constitutes an aesthetic difference between them; moreover, "minute perceptual differences can bear enormous weight...indeed, the slightest perceptual differences sometimes matter the most aesthetically."[24] Therefore, when facing two paintings that seem identical to you—in particular, when facing two paintings one of which is an original work of art and the other a perfect forgery of it—the fact that you are unable to see any difference between them does not entitle you to take the situation of selecting one of them (on aesthetic grounds alone, that is) as a picking situation.

Thus reconstructed, Goodman's argument in fact falls short even of claiming that there exists a certain well-delineated class of choosing situations proper. All that it apparently amounts to is that "the fact that we cannot tell our two paintings apart merely by looking at them does not imply that they are aesthetically the same"[25] and hence does not imply that the selection situation they constitute is a picking one, not even of the "by default" variety.

It is quite doubtful whether this conclusion may be generalized and strengthened so as to yield the claim that the aesthetic domain does not admit of picking situations altogether. And in any case the shift in the discussion to the aesthetic realm should not be welcomed since it means dealing with selection alternatives (i.e., works of art) that may be approached in terms of *absolute values* while our picking/choosing distinction was primarily intended to pertain to the realm of selection alternatives that are in principle always substitutable and to which the consideration of *alternative cost* is inherently applicable.

Pickers and Choosers

Given the tentative conclusion that it is by and large the attitude of the agent to the selection situation that determines whether he will pick or choose, is it possible that what we termed picking situations proper will be treated as choosing ones? The answer is yes: children do it all the time. A plate full of "identical" candies presents us, hopeless grown-ups, with a clear case of picking, but for our children it often poses a serious and elaborate problem of choosing. While any piece of candy would be substitutable *salva valetudine* for our picked one, often none is for their chosen one. Children, we say, see differences where we do not see any, or take trifling differences to be relevant—that is,

[22] Nelson Goodman, *Language of Art* (London: Oxford University Press, 1969), pp. 99–109.
[23] Goodman, *Language of Art*, p. 107 n.   [24] Prior, "Can Religion Be Discussed?" p. 108.
[25] Goodman, *Language of Art*, p. 109.

to be sufficient reasons (usually patently ad hoc) for preference. Indeed we generally regard it as a sign of growing up when a child stops "behaving childishly" and is able to take a picking situation proper as just that (rather than fight with his or her little brother over who gets which).

Being able to take a picking situation proper for what it is is not just an indication of maturity, however, but in a way of sanity, or normalcy, too: neurotics, especially of the obsessive-compulsive type, often find picking situations intolerable. Their personality being characterized, among other things, by "a tendency toward massive attention to unimportant detail,"[26] the process of weighing the available alternatives for preference is for them at times practically interminable, and the (second-order) decision to pick all but impossible.

It is of some interest to note a certain shift that has taken place in the course of the discussion. While at the outset the picking/choosing distinction was relativized to types of selection situations, we have at this point come to relativize it to types of personality. There are, it seems, choosers and there are pickers; people may have a disposition to belong to one camp or to the other. The pedantic, meticulous, self-conscious type will presumably tend to be a chooser—as will the gourmet, the refined, and the person of sophisticated tastes—whereas the indifferent, nonchalant, or care-free one, a picker. It will in general be the person's beliefs and utilities, however, that will be affected by, and will reflect, these dispositions. And so it still holds good, of course, that given a particular selection situation this person will assess the relevance for himself of the discerned differences among the alternatives on the basis of his over-all beliefs and utilities, and will accordingly come to ultimately treat it as a picking or as a choosing situation. As for the proposal of an "objective" classification of selection situations into choosing vs. picking ones, the balance of the foregoing discussion indicates that it would not do. Instead it would be helpful to think of there being *core cases* of picking situations—those determined by what we termed "picking items" and referred to as picking situations proper—at one pole of some vague range and of some paradigmatic cases of choosing at the other. These clear cases at the two extremes may then help form the basis for standard expectations concerning the behavior patterns of people in certain selection situations, with deviations from these presumptive patterns (i.e., choosing in a clear case of picking or vice versa) calling for an explanation.

The Effect of Additional Information

An agent's beliefs about the alternatives up for selection, and in particular about the differences among them, play as we know a causal role in determining whether he will ultimately come to treat the selection situation as one of choosing or as one of picking. It follows that additional information about the alternatives may effect a change in his attitude toward the selection situation he faces. This is the light in which we may now

---

[26] *Encyclopedia Britannica*, art. "Neuroses."

view the role of the *expert*. Consulting an expert, you may find out that the selection of a film for your camera is not, as you tended to believe, a matter of picking but that there are in fact differences among the various products of different manufacturers, and moreover that these differences are indeed relevant to your photographic needs and wishes. So, enlightened now, you will choose. Thus the expert, who possesses more information and hence is able to "see" more differences, may turn a situation which you took to be one of picking (a television set, a rug, a watermelon, or what have you) into one of informed choosing. But his expertise may work in the opposite direction too. Not only does he see more differences: he may also see through superficial and artificial differences to an underlying sameness. Disconcerted, for example, by the huge variety of cosmetics of conflicting claims on display, you may seek the advice of an expert only to learn that as far as the chemical constitution that actually affects the facial skin is concerned they are all identical. So that, if you are indifferent to such additional aspects of the product as its perfume or package, you might as well pick.

Having said this we may now restate one of the major aims of commercial advertising as that of preventing people from mere haphazard picking. It is designed to influence, or manipulate, the consumer to choose the advertised product rather than pick among the various available alternatives. Given that the competing brands of, say, antacids (or bleachers, or toothpastes, etc.) are essentially identical, or at any rate that they are liable to be taken as such, the advertisement will play up some aspect (either "central" or "marginal," genuine or contrived) of the product in such a way as to lure the consumer into believing that *it* is a sufficient reason to prefer the advertised brand over its competitors. Thus commercial advertising is often presented under the guise of an expert's advice, informing the consumer of relevant differences.

But of course the advertising agencies do not rest content with tampering with our beliefs alone: they assault our utilities as well. That is, the ad often not only points out to us some differences among various products which we might otherwise have taken to be essentially identical picking-goods, but it also is designed to enlighten us to the fact that these differences indeed make a difference, that we just cannot be indifferent to them, that they are relevant to our own desires.

Note, incidentally, that all of this pertains *both* to honest advertising, where the advertised product does indeed give you more value for your money (whether because of the cartoons on the package that delight your children or simply because it performs better the job it is supposed to perform) *and* to deceitful advertising devised to mislead you into false beliefs.

Deeper-Level Picking

Is the notion of picking doomed to remain on the Campbell-soup-cans level? We want, finally, to hint at some other, deeper levels where this notion may belong. Indeed, some philosophical literature may be interpreted as suggesting that at the very deepest level of selection, involving the ultimate and most significant alternatives confronted by man, there can only be picking, there being no possibility of a reasoned choice. Somewhat less loftily put, it might be said that, *given* our beliefs and utilities, we pick or we choose as the case may be; but as to our utilities or values themselves, to the extent that they can be thought to be selected at all, they can only be picked.[27]

The Existentialist notion of the *absurd*, bound up as it is with the notion of the free moral *project* that man "launches out of his own nothingness,"[28] is underlain by the fundamental fact that

the goal itself and any general moral principles that may have dictated its selection must be thought of as choices that are subject to no causal influences and no rational controls at all. Such choices are, in the last analysis, "unjustifiable," because the reasoning that is commonly thought of as providing independent guidance for choice is itself an expression of that choice.[29]

But not only are our ultimate moral principles and goals in the last analysis unchoosable. So also, for some, is faith. In his brilliant dialogue "Can Religion be Discussed?" A. N. Prior lets his protagonists discuss two hypotheses for the explanation of religious faith: the hypothesis that it is an illusion (along the lines suggested by Psychoanalyst) and the hypothesis that it is not, that is, "that God is real, and faith is his gift."[30] Barthian Protestant says of the first that "it is probably just as good as the other—that there is nothing to choose between the two." He refers to the act of picking between these two options as an act of "jumping" this way or that. Logician does not find "this idea of taking 'leaps of faith' when confronted with two standpoints between which there seems to be nothing to choose" at all objectionable, since "we are always doing it, and there is nothing in such 'leaps of faith' that contravenes the 'Laws of Thought.'" (What he does object to, of course, is the idea that these two hypotheses constitute a picking situation: "There is everything to choose between *these* two hypotheses; for one of them makes sense and the other doesn't.") To be sure, for Barthian Protestant (in contrast to Sartre), even though the "leap" toward faith or away from it is a genuine act of picking in the sense that one can have no reasons to prefer one option to the other, once taken it is an

---

[27] To be sure, this is different from the paradigmatic cases of picking discussed so far in that it is not because of *symmetry* of preferences that one picks but because of the *absence* in principle of preferences that one picks. It may in fact never be the case empirically that one is in a completely preferenceless state. It is not implausible to suggest that we are "born into" preferences, or conditioned in various ways to having them. If that is the case, then there is room for talk of a conscious process of evaluating ("from within," so to speak) the preferences one finds oneself equipped with so that one eventually opts either to continue having them and acting on them or else to exchange them for different ones. But *this* process would seem to involve only acts of choosing, not picking. However, once the context is not the empirical one of actually *acquiring* our preferences but rather that of *justifying* them, it would seem that at the deepest level there can only be picking.

[28] William Barrett, *Irrational Man* (New York: Doubleday Anchor, 1962), p. 247.

[29] F. A. Olafson, "J.-P. Sartre," *Encyclopedia of Philosophy*, edited by Paul Edwards, 8 vols. (New York: Macmillan, 1967), 7: 292.

[30] A. N. Prior, "Can Religion Be Discussed?" (1942), in A. G. N. Flew and Alasdair MacIntyre, eds., *New Essays in Philosophical Theology* (London: SCM Press, 1955). All quotes are from pp. 7–9.

act which does admit of explanation since one jumps, as he puts it, "the way one has to." The leap toward faith is explained by divine intervention; it is "an inward miracle of God's mercy."

And so not only in our most common and trivial experiences as consumers in a plentiful society do we pick, but we may in fact pick—or sometimes we had better pick—in a variety of other selection situations. And it just may be that, whether to our delight or to our dismay, it is picking rather than choosing that underlies the very core of our being what we are.

2

On Presumption

Presumptions have to do with assumptions made ahead of time, in advance. The concept is suggestive, I think, of a supposition not fully justified, yet not quite rash either. There is in presumption a sense of an unquestioned taking for granted, but at the same time of some tentativeness, overturnability. Given this fertile soil of gently contrasting connotations, it is hardly surprising that philosophers have not altogether shunned the use of this notion.[1] But their employment of it is neither systematic nor critical, and the notion itself has not so far been the focus of proper philosophical attention. I shall in this paper give it the attention I think it deserves.

The clarification of the epistemic claims that presumptions have on us—or rather on our set of beliefs—is undoubtedly part of any adequate account of the notion of presumption. But this will not be the orientation of the explication I shall offer. I shall look, rather, to the role that the notion of presumption can be made to play within the theory of action. That is to say: rather than treat a presumption as an assumption made in advance of some theoretical venture, I shall treat it as an assumption made in advance of practical deliberation. Furthermore, rather than view presumption as a logical prerequisite for the launching of a theoretical inquiry, I shall view it as a rational prerequisite for arrival at a variety of decisions about action.[2]

I. Presumptions in the Law

Explication is usually guided by the pre-systematic, everyday usages of the notion under consideration. In the present instance, however, it seems to me that the ordinary-language analysis of the notion of presumption (or such cognates as 'presumably', 'a presumptive such-and-such') will not get us very far. Guidance in the present case is to be sought rather in the realm of the law. Within the framework of the law and, more specifically, within the law of evidence presumptions are both extensively used and

---

[1] Among the articles using 'presumption' in their *titles*: James W. Lamb, "Knowledge and Justified Presumption," this journal, LXIX, 5 (Mar. 9, 1972): 123–7; Louis I. Katzner, "Presumptions of Reason and Presumptions of Justice," also this journal LXX, (Feb. 22, 1973): 89–100; J. E. Llewelyn, "Presuppositions, Assumptions and Presumptions," *Theoria*, XXVIII (1962): 158–72.

[2] This might be contrasted with Nicholas Rescher's treatment of presumptions in his *Methodological Pragmatism* (New York: NYU Press, 1977). His framework is not practical deliberation, but what he refers to as the "cognitive venture," where presumptions are conceived of, roughly, as working hypotheses.

made the center of much theorizing.[3] It will be rewarding, therefore, to devote some space to unraveling the nature of legal presumptions, in spite of the fact that theoretical discussions about their status are not free from controversy and that there is no unanimity of opinion among lawyers even about their mode of functioning. It is not my intention to try to arrive at an exhaustive summary of the issue of presumptions in the law, nor to scrutinize all the uses of this notion in the legal literature. My intention is different: to locate the hard core of the use of presumptions within the law, in order that this may serve as a starting point for the task of philosophical explication. Accordingly, at various stages along the way, the explication will be halted momentarily and a point will be checked in the legal realm so as to clarify the direction in which the explication is to proceed. It should be stressed, then, that the reference to the law is for purposes of guidance and illustration only. My aim is to import the notion of presumption from the law into philosophy, not to export philosophical advice for the use of lawyers.

Here, first, is a sample list of legal presumptions: that a child born during lawful wedlock is legitimate; that a person who, without reasonable explanation, has not been heard from for at least seven years is dead; that a marriage regularly solemnized is valid; that a child under fourteen years of age has no criminal intention; that if A buys property from B and directs it to C, C was intended to be a trustee for A; that when in a common disaster the death occurs of two or more persons related as to inheritance, the younger (or healthier) person survived longer. Also: that a person accused of crime is innocent; that every person is sane; that a person intends the natural consequences of his or her actions.

Consider the first presumption cited above. "There is a presumption that a child born in wedlock is legitimate (i.e., that its father is the mother's husband)." In stating this, what is the law actually saying? Let us consider what consequences follow, if any, from these two premises:

(1) There is a presumption that a child born in wedlock is legitimate.
(2) Adam (a particular child) was born in wedlock.

More specifically, are there conditions under which the conclusion:

(3) Adam is legitimate (i.e., Adam's father is his mother's husband).

can be validly drawn from (1) and (2)? Or perhaps the conclusion should be

(4) There is a presumption that Adam is legitimate.

---

[3] Every text on the Law of Evidence contains a chapter on presumptions. Among the eminent authors of such texts are Phipson (1892, 8th edition 1942), Jones (1896, 5th edition 1958), Wigmore (1904, 3rd edition 1940) and Stephen (1925).

The *locus classicus* of theorizing on presumptions is the chapter devoted to them in James Bradley Thayer's *A Preliminary Treatise on Evidence at Common Law*, Boston, 1898. Also of special significance are two articles by Edmund M. Morgan: "Some Observations concerning Presumptions," *Harvard Law Review*, LXIV (1931): 906–34, and "Instructing the Jury upon Presumptions and Burden of Proof," *Harvard Law Review*, XLVII (1933): 59–83.

But then we shall want to know what it is that (4) is saying, and how it is related to (3). Does it actually say anything about Adam? It may perhaps be felt that (4) is not *asserting* anything at all, or at any rate not primarily, but that its import lies elsewhere.

The law itself has some things to say about what it is saying, or perhaps doing, by means of its presumption statements. Here are just two authoritative passages from the law of evidence:

A presumption means a rule of law that courts and judges shall draw a particular inference from a particular fact, or from particular evidence, unless and until the truth of such inference is disproved (Stephen).

A presumption may be defined to be an inference *required* by a rule of law drawn as to the existence of one fact from the existence of some other established basic facts. It is a true presumption of fact in the sense that another fact is assumed from established basic facts. It is a presumption of law in the sense that a rule of law requires the assumption to be made (Jones).[4]

The way a specific presumption, that of death upon the expiration of seven years of unexplained absence, is put to work is illustrated thus:

…*if* they [the jury] find the fact of absence for seven years unheard from, and find no explanatory facts to account for it, then *by a rule of law they are to take for true the fact of death*, and are to reckon upon it accordingly in making up their verdict upon the whole issue (Wigmore, §2490).

Above all, it is the notions of *taking something for true* and of "reckoning upon it" which interest me in this explicative venture.

The picture that begins to emerge is this. Suppose the descent of a certain man's estate is at stake. The fact in issue before the triers of fact (judge or jury) may be whether or not Adam is this man's legitimate heir (or, *mutatis mutandis*, whether or not this man, long absent, is still alive, or whether or not this man died before his wife in the airplane crash that killed them both). In the absence of evidence on this issue, or in case of conflicting evidence, how are the fact triers to proceed? Considerations of statistical, or of "prior" probability, even where they can be appealed to, will clearly not do as substitutes for particular evidence in each particular case. However, the law sometimes intervenes by laying down rules, in the form of presumptions, which effect the inference (or "inference") from certain basic facts already established to the existence of the fact in issue, as long as no evidence (or no sufficient evidence; see below) to the contrary is produced. These rules supply, where they apply and pending rebuttal, a ready-made answer, prescribed rather than ascertained, to the factual question involved. "When an inference derives from the law some arbitrary or artificial effect and is obligatory upon judges and juries, that inference is a true presumption" (Jones §11).

---

[4] There are also several further distinctions in the law concerning presumptions, notably (a) between presumptions of law and presumptions of fact; (b) between rebuttable presumptions and irrebuttable, or conclusive, presumptions. The first is commonly taken to be rather confused and confusing, a presumption of fact being perhaps an altogether redundant notion (see Thayer's attack on this distinction, Thayer's *Preliminary Treatise*, pp. 339–42). The second is interesting, but will not occupy us here.

I would go one step further and claim that there is not only an element of arbitrariness or artificiality in presumptions, but also an element of bias. Given that there are two possible answers to the factual question under consideration, either "yes" or "no," the presumption rule is partial toward one of them and favors it in advance over the other. What we have here is not the proverbial situation of gauging, preferably blindfold, which side of an evenly balanced scale turns out to tip the balance. Rather, we are deliberately putting the thumb on one side of the scale to begin with.[5]

Before we are ready to move on from the law, then, a rough preliminary answer to our question concerning the import of sentence (4) suggests itself: for purposes of coming to a verdict and provided that no (sufficiently strong) evidence to the contrary is in, the trier of fact is (instructed by the law) to take Adam's legitimacy for true.

II. The Explication

Sentences like (1) will be referred to as *presumption formulas*. The presumption formula will be represented by the string 'pres (P,Q)'. 'P' stands for the *presumption-raising fact* (the lawyers call it the *basic fact*)—in our example, being born in wedlock. 'Q' stands for the *presumed fact*—in our example, being fathered by the mother's husband. Capital letters indicate that generic descriptions of states of affairs are involved; lower-case letters will stand for particular descriptions.

The presumption formula is read, then, as 'P raises the presumption that Q',[6] or, alternatively, as 'There is a presumption from P that Q'. When it is said that it *applies* in a certain concrete instance, this should be taken to mean that the presumption-raising (generic) fact is instantiated in that concrete instance.

I proceed now to interpret the presumption formula in terms of a *presumption rule*. The presumption rule expressed by the formula 'pres (P,Q)' is directed to any person who is engaged in a process of practical deliberation whose resolution materially depends, among other things, on an answer to the factual question of whether q is or is not the case. Such persons may be referred to as the *rule subjects*. The rule is this:

Given that p is the case, you (= the rule subject) shall proceed as if q were true, unless or until you have (sufficient) reason to believe that q is not the case.

(a) "Proceed...": the nature of the rule

What sort of a rule is a presumption rule? What does it actually instruct its subjects to do?

Note first that the presumption formula is propositional in nature ("P raises the presumption *that* Q"); it is ostensibly about facts. However, I submit that it is concerned

---

[5] See Barbara D. Underwood's paper under the suggestive title "The Thumb on the Scales of Justice: Burdens of Persuasion in Criminal Cases," *Yale Law Journal*, LXXXVI, 7 (1977): 1299–348.
[6] Note: 'raises' not in the sense of "increases" but of "creates," "brings about."

not so much with *ascertaining* the facts as with *proceeding* on them, as its rule interpretation brings out. Presumption rules belong in the realm of praxis, not theory. Their point is to enable us to get on smoothly with business of all sorts, to cut through impasses, to facilitate and expedite action. But there is no specific action that a presumption rule charges its subjects with. It instructs its subjects to hold a certain proposition as true so as to have a foothold (as it were) for action. Put somewhat differently, the instruction is this: given *p*, make *q* a premise in the rest of the pertinent piece of your practical reasoning.

What are we to make of the quasi-jussive mode ("you shall proceed as if...") in which the presumption rule is cast: is it, or is it not, a mandatory rule?

In the law it is: the triers of fact are *required* to draw the inference from the *P*-fact to the *Q*-fact. Outside the law, with respect to the rather looser and more amorphous framework of practical deliberation in general, the answer is less clear-cut. I tend to think of presumption rules as offering *a way out* and, therefore, tend to regard the question of their status—i.e., whether they prescribe or permit, license, or enjoin—as slightly beside the point. What matters, in my view, is that they *entitle* the deliberators to make—and to ground their subsequent course of action in—an assumption they are otherwise not justified in making.

At the same time, as with many rights and norms, waiving such entitlements or failing to exercise them may be censurable. The very offer of a way out creates the expectation that it will be resorted to in the appropriate circumstances. Thwarting such expectations may well count as violation of a norm and be subject to disapprobation.

(b) "... as if q": an inference?

Are presumption rules concerned with inference? Is it their point that the presumed fact is inferred, in some sense or under certain conditions, from the presumption-raising fact?

To avoid confusion, let me draw attention to a distinction. Quite apart from whether or not presumption rules are *about* inference, there is associated with them a rule *of* inference. It is the formal rule governing the operation of the 'pres' operator: from (i) pres (*P,Q*) and (ii) *p*, it follows that (iii) pres *q* [compare sentences (1), (2), and (4) above].

This underscores the following feature of the operator: that it functions either as a two-place operator, its two variables standing for generic descriptions of states of affairs (the presumption formula), or as a one-place operator, its single variable standing for a particular description of a state of affairs (the presumed fact). The connection between these two functions is at the same time understood as well. Note, too, that a 'pres *q*' formula in effect presupposes a 'pres (*P,Q*)' formula. That is, if it is the case that, for some *q*, pres *q*, then there is a state of affairs represented by '*p*' such that both *p* and the appropriate presumption rule expressed by the formula 'pres (*P,Q*)' obtain.

So, the conclusion of the rule of inference associated with presumption rules is to the effect *that a certain fact is presumed*. But this is not to be confused with an inference *to the presumed fact.* And the question with which we started was whether or not what presumption rules are about is inference to the presumed fact(s). In answer to this question I submit that the presumption rule involves no commitment to, nor guarantee of, the truth value of the presumed fact q. It makes no claims upon its subjects' cognitive or epistemic systems. The rule entitles one to hold q as true for the purpose of concluding one's practical deliberation on the impending issue; it neither requires nor entitles one to believe that q.

In light of these considerations I shall avoid talking of presumption rules as being about, or prescribing, inference. Rather, I shall say of the presumption rule expressed by 'pres (P,Q)' that, with a view to its subjects' pertinent practical purposes, it sanctions for them the passage from p to q. Somewhat more succinctly, the phrase to be adopted is that a presumption rule *sanctions the practical passage* from p to q.

(c) "Unless or until...": the rebuttal clause

The ordinary-language word 'presumption' is suggestive of something tentative, contestible, reversible. There are various terms used, or usable, in this connection: a presumption may be said to be rebutted, overcome, overridden, reversed, defeated, displaced, nullified, and more. I shall single out the first of these and speak of the "unless or until" clause of the presumption rule as *the rebuttal clause*.

The question before us now is, What is it for a presumption to be rebutted? More specifically, we shall want to know what the rebuttal consists in and what it takes to bring it about.

Recall the rule: given that p, you shall proceed as if q unless or until you have (sufficient) reason to believe that q is not the case. This rule sanctions the practical passage from p to q while at the same time acknowledging the possible falsity of q. The rule should be understood as setting some sort of mechanism in motion. It sets its subjects on a certain course of action, namely, that of proceeding to act on the assumption that q. This course can be blocked only *if* (this is the perfective sense conveyed by the 'unless') or *once* (this is the continuate sense conveyed by the 'until') the rule subject has (sufficient) reason to believe that q is not the case. When this happens, the presumption is rebutted; so long as it doesn't, the presumption stands and is operative.

Note: it is the presumption-that-q which is rebutted, not the presumption rule itself. Given a presumption rule expressed by the formula 'pres (P,Q)' and a certain rule subject A, the presumption that q is rebutted for A if the circumstances are such that p is the case and A has (sufficient) reason to believe that not-q: the "unless" clause having been fulfilled, the proceed-as-if-q injunction lapses. (The presumption rule, though strictly speaking not rebuttable, is nevertheless revisable.[7])

---

[7] Any presumption rule is revisable, even those relating to so-called "conclusive," or irrebuttable presumptions. In "Analyticity by Way of Presumption" (Edna Ullmann-Margalit and Avishai Margalit, *Canadian Journal of Philosophy*, XII, 3 (1982): 435–52) the distinction between revisability and rebuttability, as well as the notion of conclusive presumption, are used to shed some new light on the notion of analyticity.

The question of what it takes to bring about the rebuttal of a presumption concerns the allocation of duties, and corresponding benefits, by the presumption rule. It has to do with the twin notions of the *burden of proof* and the *benefit of the doubt*. Let us once again take our cue from the law. In litigation, where a presumption rule applies, if and as long as no (sufficient) evidence-that-not-q is in, the triers of fact are to proceed as if q were established to be the case. With legal presumptions, then, it is *evidence* that rebuts them, and it takes the production of evidence to bring the rebuttal about. Now since in an adversary system evidence can be produced only by one or the other of the litigants, the law has to be clear about who is charged with the task of producing such rebutting evidence. The answer is indeed straightforward. To the extent that the unrebutted presumption serves to further the case of one of the parties, referred to as the "presumption proponent," it is up to the other party, referred to as the "presumption opponent," to attempt to rebut it. This is so regardless of who it was who established the presumption-raising fact to begin with, or, for that matter, regardless of where the over-all burden of persuasion lies. (The law distinguishes further between the so-called "persuasive burden" and the evidential burden, but this need not detain us here.)

So, in addition to the substantive aspect of the presumption rules, viz. the sanctioning of the practical passage from p to q, these rules also have a procedural aspect, that of casting a burden of producing counterevidence upon the presumption opponent. The presumption proponent becomes entitled to something: to the fact-triers' proceeding on q; the presumption opponent is charged with something: with the burden of showing that not-q. And the entitlement holds as long as the burden has not been discharged.

How can this be related to the wider and looser framework of practical deliberation, where no procedures for "going forward with evidence", and no pair of disputing parties, are part of the picture?

In the foregoing discussion it was already suggested that rebuttal in this framework consists in the deliberator's having (sufficient) reason to believe that q is not the case. That is, it is reasons for belief which rebut a presumption, and it takes the deliberator's coming to have them to bring the rebuttal about. It may not be idle to note at this point that it is not the *existence* of reasons for believing that not-q, but rather the deliberator's *having* them, which counts so far as rebuttal is concerned. Otherwise, the plain and "objective" fact that q is not the case would by itself rebut the presumption.

It follows that here, in contrast with the legal context, the presumption rule's procedural aspect of casting a certain duty on some specified person or party is rather diffuse. Anyone or anything that provides the deliberating agent with the appropriate reason for belief rebuts the presumption for him (or for her). It may, but it needn't be, another person who convinces the deliberator that q is not the case. It is in general just up to the deliberator to check that no available counterindication has been overlooked before he or she is both entitled and enjoined to proceed as if q; and any such (sufficiently weighty) counterindication that turns up may rebut the presumption, thereby halting the mechanism that was set in motion by the presumption rule. There is, then, some mild version of the principle of total evidence at work here. But there is still the question of the length to which one is to go in active search of such counterindication, how far away from the region of the immediately at hand and into the regions of the reasonably accessible or potentially obtainable. This question, however, cannot be given a general answer. It can be answered only relative to the pressures and constraints, notably time constraints, that the deliberator is under. (Another factor here is the strength of the presumption, to be taken up presently.) Indeed, it may turn out that the very point of some presumption rules (e.g., the conversational) is not that of coming to the aid of a person whose process of deliberation gets stuck, but rather to anticipate and preclude the deliberation process altogether, by providing the agent with a baseline for action which is to be abandoned just in case some counterindication is more or less thrust upon him.

Be that as it may, it is important to note the asymmetry that goes to the heart of the matter: whereas the presumption (that q) and the injunction corresponding to it (to proceed as if q) are triggered *in the absence of* certain reasons for belief, it is only *the possession of* certain reasons for belief which rebuts the presumption and annuls the injunction. Where one has reasons for belief sufficient for the grounding of action, there is no deliberation problem; it is to pave the way to action in default of such reasons that presumption rules come about.

(d) The strength of the presumption[8]

The presumption that q is rebutted for A when A has *sufficient* reasons to believe that not-q. How much is sufficient?

The "sufficient" qualifier is, I contend, a place holder. It should be replaced by an indication of the weight of the reasons for belief required for the rebuttal. Correlated with this measure will be an index of the strength of the presumption. Thus, a presumption rule relating to a strong presumption will be expressed by the formula 'pres$_s$ (P,Q)', read as "P raises a *strong* presumption that Q." Spelled out, it will say, "Given that p, you shall proceed as if q unless or until you have a *conclusive* reason to believe that not-q." Similarly, the presumption rule relating to a presumption of an intermediate strength will be worded in terms of *good* or *prima facie* reasons for belief, and the rule relating to a weak presumption in terms of *some* reason for belief.[9]

The situation underlying the working of a presumption rule relating to a weak presumption is this. Take a rule subject who is constrained to act and whose choice of course of action depends on whether or not he believes q to be the case. Suppose now that he has no reason for belief either way, i.e., he is in a state of ignorance regarding the

---

[8] I am indebted to Ronald Dworkin for illumination on the topic of this section.

[9] This is an extension of the grading of legal presumptions according to their strength. The presumptions of legitimacy and of innocence are strong presumptions in Anglo-American jurisdictions, requiring conclusive counterevidence for their rebuttal. The presumption of sanity is sometimes considered weak in the sense that it lapses as soon as *some* counterevidence is in [see Durham *v.* United States, 214 f. 2d 862 (D.C. Cir. 1954), 741–9]. Most legal presumptions, however, are intermediate in degree of strength.

answer to the factual question q or not q. Such persons cannot act on the balance of reasons since the proverbial scales are for them empty and in equipoise. But, given that a (weak) presumption rule applies to their deliberation situation, they are to proceed on q. One may think, for example, of the variety of interpretative presumptions that come to our aid in resolving practical deliberations which turn on the ascription of intentions and motivations in the case of a piece of human behavior, either verbal or nonverbal. Prominent among them is the Interpretative Presumption of Cooperation, which enjoins the hearer to interpret his converser's utterance as if it is an appropriate contribution to the accepted purpose or direction of the talk exchange between them, unless or until he has some reason to believe it is an *in*appropriate contribution thereto.[10]

No such lack of reasons for belief underlies the working of presumption rules relating to the stronger presumptions. The situation in which the rule subjects find themselves may broadly be characterized as one of doubt regarding the factual question of whether q is or is not the case. They may well have some reasons to believe q not to be the case, and these reasons may even be weightier than the reasons they have, if any, to believe the opposite. So there *is* in principle a possibility of acting on the balance of reasons here. Yet if these reasons are perceived as not sufficiently weighty for the person concerned to proceed to act on them, if there isn't sufficient conviction, there remains a deliberation problem. Now insofar as a presumption rule applies to this situation, it may operate so as to sway the deliberator toward acting on q. The situation here may be pictured not as one of evenly balanced scales, the presumption rule operating so as to tip the balance, but rather as one where the presumption rule operates so as to tilt the *un*evenly balanced scales toward the other side.

As a case in point, consider the situation where the future academic employment of a junior faculty member is to be decided upon at the end of a certain probationary period. If the person either excels or obviously fails there is no deliberation problem. But if the person succeeds somewhat, there may well remain a deliberation problem. It can be resolved, however, if the institution adopts a clear presumptive tenure policy, e.g., a policy that treats the academic job as belonging to the person hired as qualified for it, unless he or she proves *in*capable of meeting the professional standards of the university within the specified probationary period.[11]

But this is not quite accurate enough. If a presumption rule applies in a certain instance, it is there prior to the deliberation process and may at times preempt it altogether. The situation is more correctly to be pictured, then, as involving scales which, because of the presumption rule and the bias inherent in it, are tilted (toward

---

[10] Implicit in this is the proposal, which I develop elsewhere (see note 23 below), to recast Grice's well-known Cooperative Principle (in H. P. Grice, William James Lectures, Harvard 1968, 2nd lecture) as a principle governing the *interpretation* of utterances rather than as a principle governing the *production* of utterances; as such it becomes a Presumption of Cooperation.

[11] See Margaret Atherton, Sidney Morgenbesser and Robert Schwartz, "On Tenure," *Philosophical Forum*, x, 2–4 (Winter-Summer 1978–79): 341–52.

the q side) *to begin with*, and where the balance can be reversed only when a certain weight is put on the other side: when one has some reason to believe not-q in the case of a weak presumption, good (prima facie) reasons to believe not-q in the case of a presumption of intermediate strength, or downright conclusive reason to believe not-q in the case of strong presumptions.

It is this image of some fancied scales being atilt prior to any weighing which is conveyed by the 'pre-' of 'presumption'. And it is the strength of the presumption which determines the weight required for reversing the balance. As for the question of the factors that determine the differential strength of presumptions, these have to do with the relative strength of the considerations in which the justification of each presumption is grounded, as well as with the "work" it is expected to do. There are no generalizations that can be made here, except perhaps for the tentative observation that strong presumptions can hardly be expected to be encountered outside of the framework of the law. We turn now to the issue of justification.

III. The Justification of Presumptions

The central question up to now was, What are presumptions (or presumption rules)? The question to be taken up now is, *Why* presumptions?

There are in point of fact two justificatory tasks involved. The first concerns the justification for there being a presumption rule, some presumption rule, rather than none: Why are there, or why should there be, presumption rules? The second concerns the justification of the specific presumption espoused by a presumption rule: Why this presumption rather than some alternative?

These two tasks are obviously connected. Only if the first can be met satisfactorily is there any point in embarking upon the second. And also this: the fact that the second can, in certain cases, be answered constitutes part of the answer to the first.

(a) Why presumption rules?

A presumption rule, we recall, comes to the aid of a deliberating agent when he or she is called upon to act, when the choice of the course of action to be taken hinges in a material way on whether a certain state of affairs obtains, and when the agent is in a state of ignorance or doubt concerning the answer to the question. The significant factor in the description of the situation is that the person concerned is constrained to take action, *some* action, before his or her deliberation can be terminated: the time to act precedes the rational resolution of the deliberation process.[12] (Note that this may

---

[12] In his "Reasons for Action, Decisions and Norms," in Joseph Raz, ed., *Practical Reasoning* (New York: Oxford, 1978), pp. 128–43, Raz says: "It should be remembered that a decision is reached only when the agent (1) reaches a conclusion as to what he ought to do and (2) forms the belief that it is time to terminate his deliberations" (134). He is there concerned to emphasize that the first condition is not enough. What I wish to point out is that often the second condition is met but the first is not; it is in this context that various means of extrication have a role to play.

comprise cases where one is constrained to act, or perhaps to react, not just before concluding one's deliberations but even without having started to deliberate.) In particular, the wait-and-see option allowing for suspended judgment is supposed to be ruled out in this type of situation on either logical or practical grounds.

This is a description of a deliberation process which, whether because inconclusive, aborted, or altogether preempted, is unresolved. Unresolved deliberations, to be sure, need not be unresolvable. But from the standpoint of the deliberating agents, constrained as we imagine them to be by time pressure as well as by such "extraneous" factors as emotional stress, distraction, and languor, resolvability-in-principle is all but beside the point. The agents may be in need of some means of extrication. Now a variety of rules, or strategies, or second-order reasons for action, have been suggested and explored by writers on the subject. I cannot here, however, delve into that.[13] The pertinent point I wish to make as a starter on the justification issue is that presumption rules should be regarded as coming to satisfy just such a need: they function as a method of extrication, one among several, from unresolved deliberation processes. What they do is supply a procedure for decision by default.

In order to grasp the rationale of presumption rules qua means of extrication, I suggest that we revert once again to the law and look at the working of the presumption of innocence, which in more ways than one forms a class of its own.

A criminal trial is a process at the end of which the triers of fact must reach an unambiguous verdict for or against the defendant, however inconclusive the evidence before them may be. There is a point beyond which no more evidence is, or can be, introduced, and there is a time at which the fact triers' deliberations must terminate. If the evidence is conclusive and leaves no doubt in their minds as to the defendant's guilt or innocence, there is no problem. But where doubt persists, should they decide by mere preponderance of evidence, however slight? And what if the scales are evenly balanced?

This situation paradigmatically calls for a generic means of extrication. It is not to function as a surrogate for the deliberation process in each particular case. It is, rather, to provide a general direction for solution for the unresolved deliberation processes. The defendant—any defendant—is either to be acquitted for lack of proof of guilt or else is to be found guilty for lack of proof of innocence. Structurally speaking, either of these two counterpresumptions will do; both supply a procedure for decision by default. (Indeed, the old modes of trial—by ordeal, by wager of law, or by battle—were controlled by a presumption of guilt: a man charged with a criminal offense would be punished unless he managed to clear, or rather to "clear" himself.) The question whether to adopt one of these two counterpresumptions—and, if so, which—already slides us into the second justificatory task.

---

[13] I would just like to mention in this connection the treatment of the notion of *picking* as a means of extrication from unresolved deliberation problems of a rather special and restricted nature, in Edna Ullmann-Margalit and Sidney Morgenbesser, "Picking and Choosing," which is chapter 1 of this book.

Taking stock: presumption rules function as, and are thus justified qua, means of extrication from unresolved deliberation processes. They are called for in situations which, when described generically, present a recurrent pattern inherent to which is a decision problem such that those required to act can be anticipated to be stuck with an inconclusive or an aborted déliberation process. They are thus called for where arbitrary or haphazard decisions are otherwise likely to be made.

But the mere need for extrication does not in itself suffice to justify the institution of a presumption rule. What such a rule in effect offers is a policy of extrication based on a systematic bias favoring one of the available alternative-types over the other(s). And it is the independent justifiability of such a biased solution which is crucial for the institution of a rule espousing it to be justified.

A presumption rule may be seen, then, as replacing arbitrariness with something like rational prejudgment; although plainly prejudging an issue, it may nevertheless be defended as rational[14] in the following twofold sense: (i) in any particular instance the presumption it relates to is open to rebuttal; (ii) the bias it promotes is independently justifiable.

There remain to be discussed the grounds on which a specific presumption, i.e., the biased solution promoted by a presumption rule, may be justified, once the need for some presumption rule in the pertinent type of situation has been established.

(b) Why the specific presumption?

The justification of a specific, though generic, presumption-that-Q is, I suggest, a blend of two major types of consideration, sometimes supplemented by a third ancillary one.[15] They are these:

(i)   inductive-probabilistic considerations
(ii) value-related considerations
(iii) procedural considerations

Considerations of inductive logic and probability, in a broad sense, have to do with the likelihood of Q, given P. Broadly speaking, they underlie most presumptions. Most people unexplainably absent for upward of seven years are in fact dead; most people living together as man and wife are in fact man and wife; most people mean what they say (most of the time); the evidence of our senses is trustworthy in most cases; a descriptive word is mostly correctly applied to an object displaying certain antecedently specified features;[16] and so on. When the presumed fact-type Q is routinely a concomitant

---

[14] An altogether different approach to the question of the rationality of presumptions is offered by Louis I. Katzner "Presumptions of Reason," who addresses himself to the question whether the presumptivist principle of formal justice is rational in the specific sense of whether or not it is necessarily true.

[15] On the interplay of these considerations with regard to legal presumptions see Thayer, *A Preliminary Treatise on Evidence at Common Law* (1898) and Morgan "Some Observations," (1931).

[16] For more on the issue of presumptions of reference see Ullmann-Margalit and Margalit "Analyticity" (1977).

of the presumption-raising fact-type P, it would seem to be a waste of time and energy—sometimes even to the point where the very purpose of the action to be taken is defeated—to begin an investigation as to whether q is indeed the case in any instance of the occurrence of p. It would seem to make good practical sense to proceed on the assumption that q so long as no indications to the contrary crop up.

So with presumption rules relating to presumptions that accord with the normal balance of probability the chance of an error (i.e., proceeding on q while in fact q is not the case) is reduced. The nature and function of the inductive-probabilistic considerations in justifying a specific presumption vis-à-vis its counterpresumption is thus straightforward enough. The point to be emphasized about these considerations, however, is this: they cannot by themselves provide the ground on which a presumption is justified and, hence, on which the institution of a presumption rule is justified. If the sole rationale of the proceed-as-if-q injunction of a presumption rule expressed by the formula 'pres (P,Q)' were the fact that P probabilizes Q, then we would have on our hands just a piece of practical advice in accordance with some canons of inductive reasoning, not a presumption rule properly so called. Indeed, to the extent that pre-systematic or nontechnical uses of the term 'presumption' merely convey the notion of some probability connection, I consider the term to be devoid of its special significance. For a presumption rule to count as such, its justifying considerations from the realm of inductive logic and probability, to the extent that they exist, have to combine with *other* justifying considerations.

Moreover, considerations of the second, normative type may even outweigh those of the first and lead to the espousal of a presumption-that-q in spite of the fact that the odds may possibly favor not-q. Thus, consider the presumption of innocence: it is not even clear in that case whether the relevant probabilistic consideration relates to the entire class of human beings or to the much narrower class of persons charged with criminal offenses. This is a tricky question. But the point is that, even if the relevant class is taken to be that of persons charged and even if it turns out that most of the people in this class are actually guilty of the crimes attributed to them, the presumption in favor of proceeding as if the person charged is innocent may nevertheless be retained and defended; it may fly in the face of the probabilistic consideration. Or take the case of the presumptive principle of equality, in situations falling under the broad heading of the administration of distributive justice.[17] The proponent of this presumption will hold on to its injunction, i.e, to proceed as if the people to be treated were similar in all relevant respects unless or until relevant differences among them are shown, regardless of whether people are in fact likely or unlikely to be thus similar.

---

[17] For discussions of the presumptivist principle of equality (or of justice) see, e.g., S. I. Benn and R. S. Peters, *Social Principles and the Democratic State* (London: Allen & Unwin, 1959), p. 111, and *The Principles of Political Thought* (Glencoe, Ill.: The Free Press, 1965), pp. 127/8; Joel Feinberg, *Social Philosophy* (Englewood Cliffs, N.J.: Prentice-Hall, 1965), pp. 100–2; Katzner, "Presumptions of Reason."

So the justification of presumptions may, and perhaps commonly is, couched in inductive-probabilistic terms; but such considerations are neither necessary nor sufficient to justify the presumption rules relating to them.[18]

It is the justification of presumptions in normative terms which touches what I take to be the core of the concept of presumption. If the first type of consideration had to do with the *chance* of error, this normative type of consideration has to do with the *acceptability* of error. Presumption rules operate in situations where actions have to be decided upon in the light of insufficient information and often under external pressures and constraints. Errors (i.e., proceeding on q when not-q is in fact the case and vice versa) are bound to occur. There is no question of avoiding errors; at best there is the question of reducing their number. But a different sort of question is whether one type of error is to be preferred, on grounds of moral values or social goals, over the other(s). Evaluative considerations may exist which justify a systematic and generic bias in favor of erroneously proceeding on Q rather than erroneously proceeding on not-Q, given that P and given lack of sufficient reasons in the circumstances to believe either q or not-q to be the case.

Thus, in his *Treatise on Judicial Evidence* Jeremy Bentham[19] says that "in doubtful cases [the judge should] consider the error which acquits as more justifiable, or less injurious to the good of society, than the error which condemns." Hence the presumption of innocence. It is, then, as a corrective device that this presumption, as well as others, may be thought of: as regulating in advance the direction of errors, where errors are believed to be inevitable.

Similarly, take Louis Katzner's view with regard to the two rival presumptions, against treating people differently/similarly in any respect until grounds for distinction/similarity have been shown:

The only possible basis for opting for one of them rather than the other is which state of affairs one would rather see—that in which some of those who are similar are treated differently or that in which some of those who are different are treated similarly.—*[I]t comes down to a question of goals or values* (*cf*, note 1; emphasis added).[20]

Consider now the case of the various so-called "conversational" presumptions, like the presumption of truthfulness, or sincerity, or Grice's Cooperative Principle (see fn 10 above). It is easily realized that spending time and effort, in each and every instance in

---

[18] Consider this statement by David Lyons [*Forms and Limits of Utilitarianism* (New York: Oxford, 1965), p. 124], who joins issue with Marcus Singer and claims: "A presumption against lying, for example, is fully compatible with most instances of lying, or lying in most kinds of cases, not being wrong. We might say that presumptions as such have no qualitative implications."

[19] Extracted from the manuscript by M. Dumont (London: J. W. Paget, 1825), pp. 197/8.

[20] Joel Feinberg argues that to presume equal treatment "would be to make a presumption every bit as arbitrary as the presumption in favor of *unequal* treatment in the absence of knowledge of the relevant similarities and differences of the persons involved" (*Social Philosophy*, p. 102). He concludes that neither of the two opposing presumptions is independently justifiable, on moral grounds (he ignores all other considerations altogether).

which one's interlocutor has uttered something, to find out to one's satisfaction whether or not it is indeed true or sincere or whether or not it indeed contributes appropriately to the purpose of the talk exchange in which one is engaged, before one proceeds to respond to that utterance is quite likely tantamount to undermining the particular piece of conversation under consideration, if not interpersonal communication in general. It is along such lines, then, of the general interest in the smoothness of talk exchanges, that the justifying considerations for there being conversational presumption rules (*some* presumption rules, rather than none) are to be couched. But which presumptions shall they be? Can a specific presumption in this area be independently justified?

It may or may not be true that most utterances of indicative sentences by most human speakers in situations of communication are true, or are uttered in sincerity. Again, it may or may not be true that most utterances of most speakers constitute appropriate contributions to the (accepted, mutually recognized) goal or direction of the talk exchange in which they are engaged. To the extent that these things *are* true, there will be inductive-probabilistic considerations in favor of the presumptions in question. But regardless of the question whether or not a given utterance is likely to be true (etc.), there is the further question of which—if any—of the following alternatives is morally or socially "better": to proceed (respond, react) erroneously on the assumption of truth (sincerity, appropriateness of contribution), or to proceed erroneously on the assumption of falsity (insincerity, inappropriateness of contribution). Now it is my contention that if there is no commitment to some value according to which one type (or "zone") of errors is judged as preferable to the other, then talk of presumption in this area is inappropriate.[21] And it is further my contention that such a value judgment is indeed congenial to anyone who accords primacy to such notions as the dignity of persons in one's thinking about the fundamentals of ethics. This evaluative consideration comes, of course, on top of the factor of social desirability, if not necessity, of maintaining and sustaining interpersonal communication, which is furthered by the conversational presumptions of truth, sincerity, and appropriateness of contribution and not by any of their contrary presumptions. The normative consideration we are dealing with, in sum, can be viewed as two-tiered: it has to do (i) with the question of which sort of error is morally or socially more acceptable, and (ii) with the moral or social evaluation of the regulative effect on people's behavior of the presumption rule's being instituted and operative.

---

[21] Quine's Principle of Charity, the way he formulates it, is in this sense not a presumptive principle: "Assertions startlingly false on the face of them are *likely* to turn on hidden differences of language" [*Word and Object* (Cambridge, Mass.: The MIT Press, 1960), p. 59, my emphasis]; "One's interlocutor's silliness, beyond a certain point, is *less likely* than bad translation" (ibid.). It seems to me, however, that this principle can be viewed as a presumptive principle to the extent that the charitable interpretations it calls for are perceived not just as more likely to be true but also as conforming better with one's moral conception of one's fellow men and women; to the extent, that is, that giving credit where credit is not due is judged more pardonable, and of a higher moral order, than denying credit where it is in fact due.

There is yet another consideration intermingled here, which ought nevertheless to be kept analytically separate. It may perhaps be labeled the *determinateness consideration*.[22] Sometimes it is the case that, once the need for *some* presumption rule has been recognized, there is little real choice in the matter of *which* presumption it should espouse. For example, the presumption in favor of equal treatment even where there is ignorance as to the characteristics of the persons to be treated is determinate, whereas the counterpresumption, in favor of *un*equal treatment in the absence of knowledge of the relevant similarities and differences among the persons involved is so indeterminate (or, as one might say, merely determinable) as to be quite useless. The same might seem to apply to the presumption of sincerity (or that fluent speakers mean what they say): any contrary presumption would be determinable rather than determinate, and as such could hardly be of use as a guide for action.

In such cases, where it is primarily the determinateness consideration that decides which specific presumption shall be espoused by the presumption rule, regardless of whether or not it is supported by inductive-probabilistic considerations, the following stipulation needs to be made: where no separate normative argument is available according to which erroneously proceeding on q is judged morally or socially superior to erroneously proceeding on not-q, it ought at least to be the case that no such normative argument is available to justify any *contrary* presumption.

A consideration distinct from those dealt with thus far, and often appealed to in the law, is that of procedural convenience. In the case of a railway passenger who is injured by wreck or derailment, the presumption is that the railway company was negligent. Morgan (1931, p. 931, cf. note 3) conjectures that this presumption is grounded in a combination of all three types of justifying considerations: in the normal balance of probability, in a normative judicial policy directed toward protecting the public, *and* in the procedural consideration of the comparative convenience with which the parties can be expected to produce pertinent evidence. In general, the procedural consideration has to do with the question of what presumption will be the most useful to adopt as an initial step in the process of deliberation, what will "help the game along best"—quite apart from the question whether the conclusion to which the adoption of this rule points is likely to be true, as well as from the question whether there exists a standard by which one sort of error is judged as more acceptable than the other.

Obviously, if the answer given to the procedural question conflicts with the answer given to the other two questions, the procedural consideration will be outweighed. But in those cases where there is no conflict, where it is in line with the answers to the other questions, or indeed where it is the only clear and solid answer available, it counts.

I would like, finally, to return to the discussion raised above (section IIb) about the nature of the inference involved in presumption rules and to offer the following observation. Underlying the notion of presumption rules there lies a conception of reasoning peculiar to the practical sphere and different both from deductive and from

---

[22] I am indebted to the late John Mackie for this point.

inductive reasoning. In deductive reasoning, once the premises are specified, arrival at the conclusion is a matter of *derivation*, in accordance with some rules. In inductive reasoning, once the premises are specified, the arrival at the conclusion is, roughly speaking, a matter of *calculation*, in accordance with some canons. With presumption rules, once the premises (presumption-raising facts) are specified and provided the context is practical rather than theoretical, arrival at the conclusion (the presumed fact) is in principle a matter of a prior, generic *decision*. It is the decision to sanction the practical passage from *P* to *Q*. This decision may be motivated, to a lesser or to a greater degree, by the canons governing inductive reasoning, but not exclusively by them. As we have seen, it must be motivated also by certain evaluative considerations which are primarily concerned with the differential acceptability of the relevant sorts of expected errors: the fact that one sort of error is judged to be, in the long run and all things considered, preferred on grounds of moral values or social goals to the alternative sort(s) constitutes an overriding reason for the decision underlying the presumption rule. The presumption rule itself, which such a (generic) decision underlies, then enables the deliberating agents to arrive, when necessary, at a (specific) decision by default in each concrete instance to which it applies.

This concludes my systematic presentation. Clearly, this is but a bare skeleton. The question whether these dry bones can live will be answered only when some flesh and sinews—in the form of detailed illustrations and case studies—are brought upon them. This, however, is a task for another time.[23]

---

[23] This task is partially carried out in my "Some Presumptions," in Leigh S. Cauman et al., eds, *How Many Questions: Essays in Honor of Sidney Morgenbesser* (Indianapolis: Hackett, 1983).

3

Second-Order Decisions

I. Introduction

In making decisions, people sometimes calculate the costs and benefits of alternative courses of action, and choose the option that maximizes net benefits, however these may be described and understood. Certainly this is a conventional picture of practical reason in both private and public life.[1] When deciding what to buy, where to travel, whether to support legislation, or how to vote in a dispute over constitutional rights, people might seem to proceed in this way. A common idea about decision-making is that agents are typically in the business of maximizing or optimizing. At the time of choice, this is their basic method and their basic goal.

A moment's introspection shows that this picture is inaccurate or at least too simple. The cost of deliberation is often high. When and because the stakes are extremely low, people may use simplifying strategies; when and because the stakes are extremely high, people may seek approaches that relieve them of the burden of or the responsibility for choice. Sometimes calculation of costs and benefits of alternative courses of action is exceedingly difficult, or in any case tedious and not worthwhile. Every bureaucrat knows that cost-benefit analysis may fail cost-benefit analysis, and almost everyone, bureaucrat or not, is sometimes willing to do a great deal in order to reduce or to eliminate the burdens of decision. Often agents very much want *not* to make (particular) decisions. Often they know that they will want not to make decisions even before they undertake the particular calculations involved in those particular decisions. Part of what it means to optimize is to try to reduce the burdens of judgment, a fact that can lead people not to calculate at all, or to do so in a sharply truncated fashion. Noncalculative or truncated decisions can in turn have substantial individual and social consequences.

This is true for decisions both large and small, and for decisions both by individuals and by institutions, political and otherwise. When people are deciding what cereal to buy at the grocery store, whether to buckle their seatbelts or lock their car doors, what route to take to the movie theatre, or what to say in response to the question, "how are you," they may want, almost more than anything else, a simple way of proceed. Reduction of the burdens of decision and choice is valued in less routine settings

[1] See, e.g., Gary Becker, *Accounting for Tastes* (Cambridge, MA: Harvard University Press, 1996).

as well. Consider the decision whether to purchase a house, to get married, to move to another city, to have a child, or, in the political realm, to create a new right, to reduce spending on welfare programs, or to make war or peace; here people often find themselves in a poor position to calculate ultimate consequences, and they seek to produce simpler strategies for choice.

The point very much bears on ethics, politics, law, and institutional design. To be sure, people often believe that it is important to face the responsibility for decision, even though another strategy would produce a better outcome. Sometimes elected officials—simply because of the democratic legitimacy that comes from their election—refuse to relinquish responsibility to those with superior knowledge; democratic considerations may force them to make decisions on their own. But when officials decide whether to sign a civil rights law, or to support affirmative action, they may not be in a position to calculate net benefits, and hence they may choose some other decision-making strategy for political or strictly cognitive reasons. Public institutions generally operate on the basis of this understanding; some institutions, like the Environmental Protection Agency and the Food and Drug Administration, owe their existence partly to the legislature's desire to reduce the burdens of judgment. Or consider adjudication. When deciding cases, judges are constantly in a position to decide how much (and to some extent whether) to decide, and different judges, with different assessment of how to weigh the cognitive burdens, often split on just this question.

Our particular interest here is in *second-order decisions*. The term requires some clarification. In the case of second-order desires, one deals with desires-about-desires; in the case of second-order beliefs, one deals with beliefs-about-beliefs. In the case of second-order decisions, however, one does not exactly deal with decisions-about-decisions. Rather, one deals with the decision about appropriate strategies for avoiding decisions or for reducing their costs. More particularly, our concern is with *strategies that people use in order to avoid getting into an ordinary decision-making situation in the first instance*. Thus people (and institutions) might be said to make a second-order decision when they choose one from among several possible second-order strategies for minimizing the burdens of, and risk of error in, first-order decisions. Second-order decisions about second-order strategies are thus our basic topic.

The procedure of choice might, for example, be a delegation to some other person or institution ("I'll ask what my wise friend John thinks; he'll know how to handle that question" or "the Environmental Protection Agency will decide how to solve the problem of groundwater pollution"). Or the chosen procedure may involve a judgment, before ultimate decision-making situations arise, in favor of proceeding via some rule settled in advance ("I always buckle up my kids in the back seat, even on short rides," or "whenever the bill to be paid is less than $50, I shall pay cash," or "if the opposing party proposes a tax increase, do not support it"). As we understand it here, the term "second-order decisions" refers to strategies chosen before situations of first-order decision in order to eliminate the need for ordinary choice or to reduce the calculative demands of choice.

Second-order decisions are a pervasive part of ordinary life and a major aspect of ethics, politics, and both private and public law. But they have not been studied systematically. In this essay, we attempt to make some progress on the topic. One of our strategies is to see what might be learned by exploring analogies and disanalogies between the cases of individuals and institutions. Each of us lives according to a wide range of second-order decisions, many of them so reflexive and so thoroughly internalized that they do not seem to be decisions at all. Political and legal institutions often confront or embody second-order decisions. Indeed, one of the most important tasks for a Constitution itself is to make a series of second-order decisions. Even after a Constitution is in place, political actors face a range of further second-order decisions, and well-organized private groups tend to know this, at least where the stakes are especially high.

Part of our purpose is simply to organize this topic by providing a taxonomy of strategies—the first step toward understanding the adoption, at the individual and social levels, of one or another second-order decision. We also try to provide some guidance on positive and normative issues. Both individual people and collective bodies may face an interesting meta-decision: Which of the possibilities on the menu is the suitable one with regard to a given kind of cases? Should an agent or an institution adopt a rule or a presumption? When is it best to take small steps, or instead to delegate to another party?

Second-order strategies differ in the extent to which they produce mistakes and in the extent to which they impose informational and other burdens on the agent and on others either *before* the process of ultimate decision or *during* the process of ultimate decision. Thus a second-order decision might well be based on a judgment about how best to (1) reduce the overall costs of decision and (2) regulate the number, magnitude, and quality of mistakes. There are three interesting kinds of cases. *First,* some second-order strategies impose little in the way of decisional burdens either before or during the ultimate decision. This is a great advantage, and a major question is whether the strategy in question (consider a decision to flip a coin) produces too much unfairness or too many mistakes. *Second,* some second-order strategies greatly reduce decisional burdens at the time of ultimate choice, but they require considerable thinking in advance (consider, for example, the creation of rules to govern emissions from coal-fired power plants, or to govern misconduct by one's children). Decisions of this kind may be burdensome to make in advance; but the burdens may be worth incurring if they remain far less than the aggregate burdens of on-the-spot decisions. Here too there is a question of how to regulate the number, magnitude, and quality of mistakes. *Third,* some second-order strategies impose little in the way of decisional burden in advance, but may impose high burdens on others who must make the first-order decision; a delegation of power to some trusted associate, or to an authority, is the most obvious case.

We attempt to understand these different kinds of cases by drawing on actual practices, individual and institutional. The result is to provide some guidelines for seeing when one or another strategy will be chosen, and also when one or another makes best sense. In the process we introduce some ethical, political, and legal issues that are raised by various second-order decisions.

II. A Taxonomy

People determined to ease the burdens of decision have a number of available strategies. The following catalogue captures the major alternatives. The taxonomy is intended to be exhaustive of the possibilities, but the various items should not be seen as exclusive of one another; there is some overlap between them, a point to which we shall return.

1. Rules

People anticipating hard or repetitive decisions may adopt a rule, in the form of an irrebuttable presumption. A key feature of a rule is that it amounts to a full, or nearly full, ex ante specification of results in individual cases. All, or nearly all, of the work of decision is done in advance.

In order to ease the burdens of decisions, people might say, for example, that they will never cheat on their taxes or fail to meet a deadline, or that they will never borrow money, or that in their capacity as friend, they will always keep secret anything told in confidence. While dieting, you might adopt a rule against eating dessert; a former smoker might adopt a flat ban against having a cigarette, even a single one late at night. There are many institutional analogues. A legislature might provide that no one may smoke on airplanes; or that judges can never make exceptions to the speed-limit law or the law banning dogs from restaurants; or that everyone who has been convicted of three felonies must be sentenced to life imprisonment. Irrebuttable presumptions are widespread in law, partly because they greatly reduce the burdens of judgment in the course of individual cases.

Importantly, rules produce many mistakes (in the sense of bad results) simply because rebuttal is not allowed. Rules are typically overinclusive and underinclusive by reference to the reasons that justify them.[2] If taken very seriously, a rule-bound speed limit law will produce some extremely bad outcomes (imagine an unusually safe driver rushing his friend to the hospital); so too for mandatory imprisonment for three-time felons; so too with a ban on any dogs in restaurants (suppose a police officer needs help from his bomb-sniffing German Shepherd). Good friends and good doctors tend to have a flexible attitude toward rules.[3]

It is because of their generality that rules are often criticized as a pathology of unnecessarily rigid people and (still worse) of modern bureaucratic government[4];

---

[2] See Frederick Schauer, *Playing By The Rules* (New York: Oxford University Press, 1993).

[3] On doctors and rules, see Kathryn Hunter, *Doctor's Stories* (Princeton: Princeton University Press, 1993).

[4] See Eugene Bardach and Robert Kagan, *Going by the Book: The Problem of Regulatory Unreasonableness* (Philadelphia, Temple University Press, 1982); see also the popular treatment in Philip Howard, *The Death of Common Sense* (New York: Random House, 1994).

but they might be defended as a way of minimizing the burdens of decision while producing good results overall. The rigidity of rules can also produce serious interpretive difficulties, as when a rule confronts an unanticipated case and produces, in that case, a transparently absurd outcome; here the question is whether the rule should operate as something like a presumption. A good deal of interpretive dispute in law is focussed on such problems, which is why rules often are nearly full, rather than full, ex ante specifications of outcomes.[5]

2. Presumptions

Often ordinary people and public institutions rely not on a rule but instead on a presumption, which can be rebutted. A presumption is typically rebuttable only on the basis of a showing of a certain kind and weight.[6] People might say, for example, that they will presume against disclosing a confidence; or they might say that they will violate the speed-limit only in compelling, unusual circumstances (like saving a life); or that the government may discriminate on the basis of race only if there is an especially strong reason for doing so. In order to obtain greater accuracy, rules may be "softened" in the direction of presumptions. The result, it is hoped, is to make fewer mistakes while at the same time limiting decisional burdens.

It is important here to distinguish between a presumption and a rule-with-exceptions, though the distinction is subtle. A rule with exceptions tends to have the following structure: "Do X—except in circumstances A, in which case do non-X (or, in which case you may be exempt from doing X)." Thus, for example, "observe the speed limit— except when you're driving a police car or an ambulance in an emergency, in which cases you may exceed it." By contrast, a typical presumption says something like: "Act on the assumption that P—unless and until circumstances A (are shown to) obtain, in which case, stop (or reconsider or do something else)." The two amount to the same thing when the agent knows whether or not circumstances A obtain. The two are quite different when the agent lacks that information. With a presumption, you can proceed without the information; with a rule-with-exceptions, you cannot proceed, that is, you are justified neither in doing X nor in not doing X. Thus presumptions function as default rules; they free up the agent, who has a set course of action without knowing whether there are rebutting circumstances.

In law, the distinction between rules-with-exceptions and presumptions is sometimes conceived as a distinction between ex ante specification and ex post specification of rebutting circumstances. Thus a speed limit law may have specified exceptions (police officers and ambulance drivers may violate it); a prohibition on killing does not apply in cases of self-defense. With a presumption, the rebutting circumstances are not identified in advance; it is understood that life may turn up problems that could not have been anticipated. Here the idea of a presumption overlaps with the idea of a "standard," to be taken up presently.

---

[5] See H. L. A. Hart, *The Concept of Law* 127–30 (2d ed. Oxford: Clarendon Press, 1996).
[6] See Edna Ullmann-Margalit, "On Presumptions", 80 *J. Phil.* 143 (1983).

Many important presumptions result from the suggestion that in the case of uncertainty or lack of information, an individual, or a government, should "err" on one side rather than another. Consider, for example, the presumption of innocence and the notion of "prevention" as the strategy of choice in environmental law. Folk wisdom is captured in the notion, "better safe than sorry," an idea that often has an ethical dimension and that has analogues in many areas of law and politics. There are also presumptions in favor of liberty and equality. Daily decisions are permeated and much simplified by presumptions—in favor of particular grocery stores, routes to the downtown area, lunch plans. Often there is also an implicit but widely shared understanding of the kinds of reasons that will rebut the relevant presumptions. Thus Ronald Dworkin's influential claim that rights are "trumps" can be understood as a description of rights as strong presumptions, rebutted only by a demonstration of a particular kind.[7]

Presumptions play an important role in the law of contract and statutory interpretation.[8] Described as "default rules," much of contract law is founded on an understanding of what most parties would do most of the time; the parties can rebut the presumption by speaking clearly. These "market-mimicking" default rules produce continuing debates about the extent to which courts should attempt to ask, not what most parties would do, but what these particular parties would have done if they had made provision on the point; the more specific inquiry increases the burdens of decision but promises to increase accuracy. Sometimes contract rule presumptions are "information-eliciting," that is, they attempt to impose on the party in the better position to clarify contractual terms the obligation to do precisely that, on pain of losing the case. In the law of statutory interpretation, there is a similar set of presumptions, designed to discern what Congress would have done or instead to impose the duty to obtain a clear statement from Congress on the party in the best position to do so. It is possible to see disputes over liberty and equality as rooted in presumptions, more or less crude, about appropriate social states, presumptions that can be rebutted by special circumstances.

3. Standards

Rules are often contrasted with standards.[9] A ban on "excessive" speeds on the highway is a standard; so is a requirement that pilots of airplanes be "competent," or that student behavior in the classroom be "reasonable." These might be compared with rules specifying a 55 m.p.h. speed limit, or a ban on pilots who are over the age of 70, or a requirement that students sit in assigned seats. In daily life, you might adopt a standard

---

[7] See Ronald Dworkin, *Taking Rights Seriously* (1975); this is an effort to read Dworkin through the lens provided by the discussion of exclusionary reasons in Joseph Raz, *Practical Reason and Norms* 37–45 (2d ed. (Princeton: Princeton University Press, 1990).

[8] See Ian Ayres and Robert Gertner, "Filling Gaps in Incomplete Contracts," 99 *Yale L.J.* 87 (1989).

[9] See, e.g., Kaplow, "Rules and Standards: An Economic Analysis," 42 *Duke L.J.* 189 (1992); Sullivan, "Foreword: The Justices of Rules and Standards," 105 *Harv. L. Rev.* 22 (1993).

in favor of driving slowly on a snowy day, or of being especially generous to friends in distress. The degree of vagueness is of course highly variable among standards.

The central difference between a rule and a standard is that a rule settles far more in advance and allows on-the-spot judgments to be quite mechanical. Standards can structure first-order decisions, more or less depending on their content, but without eliminating the need to continue to deliberate. In law, the contrast between rules and standards identifies the fact that with some legal provisions, interpreters have to do a great deal of work in order to give law real content. The meaning of a standard depends on what happens when it is applied. Of course the nature of the provision cannot be read off its text, and everything will depend on interpretive practices. Once we define the term "excessive," we may well end up with a rule. Perhaps officials will decide that a speed is excessive whenever it is over 60 miles per hour.

An important illustration here comes from standards of proof and in particular from the notions of "clear and convincing evidence" and "beyond a reasonable doubt." Judges have refused to assign numbers to these ideas. Thus the legal system has standards rather than rules. Why should the "reasonable doubt" standard not be said to call for, say, 97 percent certainty of guilt? Part of the answer lies in the fact that this standard must be applied to many different contexts—different crimes, different police behavior, different defendants, and so forth—and across those contexts, a uniform formula may well be senseless. The "reasonable doubt" standard allows a degree of adaptation to individual circumstances, and this is part of its advantage over any single number. This is also its disadvantage, for it imposes substantial burdens on those who must make the ultimate decision.

4. Routines

Sometimes a reasonable way to deal with a large decisional burden is to adopt or to continue a routine. By this term we mean something similar to habits, but more voluntary, more self-conscious, and without the pejorative connotations of some habits (consider the habit of chewing one's fingernails). Thus a forgetful person might adopt a routine of locking his door every time he leaves his office, even though sometimes he will return in a few minutes; thus a commuter might adopt a particular route and follow it every day, even though on some days another route would be better. The advantage of a routine is that it reduces the burdens of decision even if it produces occasional error. The adoption of routines is of course a common phenomenon in daily life, as people act "without thinking." These are the "standard operating procedures" by which people negotiate their daily affairs.

We have said that routines are related to habits; they are also related to rules. Often they are the concrete specifications of how precisely a rule is to be followed. If, say, the rule is that in a snowstorm, when driving conditions are hazardous, schools are to be called off, then the routines, taken as standard operating procedures, will specify exactly how the responsibilities for carrying this out are to be allocated: what key features in the weather report should trigger the cancellation, who should notify whom (local radio stations, local TV stations, possibly some particular parents), in what order the school buses are to go out, and so forth. Something similar happens when visiting dignitaries come to a nation; the rules of protocol say who will receive special treatment (the "red carpet") and the routines specify what steps will be taken, who does what and when. In this way routines work like manuals; their point is to minimize the discretion allowed to the accidental people who happen to be there when the event occurs—all the thinking is done in advance.

Institutional practices entrench routines as well. Any parliament is run in large part by routines, many of them unwritten. To the extent that a legal system relies on precedent, it follows a practice of this general kind. In fact respect for precedent can be seen an especially important kind of routine. Judges follow precedents not because they believe that past decisions are correct—they usually do not even ask whether they are— but because doing so is a routine. If an account is to be offered, it is (roughly) that a legal system will be better if judges follow precedent, because adherence to precedent promotes planning, decreases the burdens of decisions, and accomplishes both of these goals without, on balance, creating more mistakes than would be created without reliance on precedent. Thus following precedent is a kind of "enabling constraint"—a constraint on the power of choice that helps to simplify and to facilitate choice.[10]

5. Small steps

A possible way of simplifying a difficult situation at the time of choice is to attempt to make a small, incremental decision, and to leave other, larger questions for another day. When a personal decision involves imponderable and apparently incommensurable elements, people often take small, reversible steps first.[11]

For example, Jane may decide to live with Robert before she decides whether she wants to marry him; Marilyn may go to night school to see if she is really interested in law; the government might experiment with certain subsidies to independent movie producers before committing itself to a full-scale program. A similar "small steps" approach is the hallmark of Anglo-American common law.[12] (If it appears at this point that the common law can run afoul of the rule of law ideal, the appearance captures reality, or at least so many people now urge.[13]) Judges typically make narrow decisions, resolving little beyond the individual case; at least this is their preferred method of operation when they are not quite confident about the larger issues. It is sometimes suggested that because of the likelihood of unintended bad consequences, government do best, in certain domains, if their steps are small and incremental.[14] The notion of

---

[10]   See Stephen Holmes, *Passions and Constraint* (Chicago: University of Chicago Press, 1995).

[11]   See Edna Ullmann-Margalit, "Opting: The Case of 'Big' Decisions," in *The 1984/5 Yearbook of the Wissenschaftkeleg Zu Berlin*, available at: https://www.wiko-berlin.de/fileadmin/Dateien_Redakteure/pdf/Jahrbuecher/Wiko-JB-1984-85.pdf.

[12]   See Edward Levi, *An Introduction to Legal Reasoning* (Chicago: University of Chicago Press, 1948).

[13]   The tension between the rule of law and the common law method is the basic theme of Antonin Scalia, *A Matter of Interpretation* (Princeton: Princeton University Press, 1997).

[14]   See James Scott, *Seeing Like a State* (New Haven: Yale University Press, 1998).

"pilot programs" is based on this idea. In the psychological literature, the "small steps" approach has been identified with both steady, reliable success ("small wins"[15]) and recurrent error.[16]

6. Picking

Sometimes the difficulty of decision pushes people to decide on a random basis. They might, for example, flip a coin, or make some apparently irrelevant factor decisive ("it's a sunny day, so I'll take that job in Florida"). Or they might "pick" rather than "choose" (taking the latter term to mean basing a decision on reasons).[17] Sometimes this happens when the stakes are very low. In the supermarket, busy shoppers often pick; if they were to choose (among, say, toothpastes or pain relievers or cereals) they might find themselves shopping for an intolerably long time. There are many public analogues. A legal system might, for example, use a lottery, and indeed lotteries are used in many domains where the burdens of individualized choice are high, and when there is some particular problem with deliberation about the grounds of choice, usually because of underlying asymmetries among the alternatives.

While people sometimes pick because the stakes are low, they may pick in the extreme opposite case too: When the differences between the alternatives are enormous, too big and confusing to contemplate, or in some respect incommensurable. They may pick because they do not know where to begin (so to speak). Or the consequences for decision may be so large that people do not want to take responsibility for making the decision; hence they pick (consider Sophie's Choice). Here delegation might be an alternative to picking as the second-order strategy.

7. Delegation

A familiar way of handling decisional burdens is to delegate the decision to someone else. People might, for example, rely on a spouse or a friend, or choose an institutional arrangement by which certain decisions are made by other authorities established at the time or well in advance. In actual practice, such arrangements can be more or less formal; they involve diverse mechanisms of control, or entirely relinquished control, by the person or people for whose benefit they have been created.

Sometimes the principal grants full authority to the agent to whom power has been delegated; "trustees" often have authority of this sort. Sometimes the principal retains ultimate power of decision. Thus, for example, in a system of separated and divided powers, war-making decisions are typically delegated to specified officials, subject to

[15] See Karl Weick, "Small Wins," 39 *Am. Psych.* 40 (1984). Keick urges, "[I]t seems useful to consider the possibility that social problems seldom get solved, because people define these problems in ways that overwhelm their ability to do anything about them. . . . Calling a situation a mere problem that necessities a small win . . . improves diagnosis, preserves gains, and encourages innovation. Calling a situation a serious problem that necessities a larger win may be when the problem starts." (at 48).

[16] See Daniel Kahneman and Don Lovallo, "Timid Choices and Bold Forecasts: A Cognitive Perspective on Risk Taking," 39 *Mgmt. Sci.* 17 (1993).

[17] See Edna Ullmann-Margalit and Sidney Morgenbesser, Picking and Choosing, chapter 1 in this book.

various safeguards. In the private sphere, people may rely on the wisdom of those in whom they have great confidence, and here there is a continuum from mere consultation to a delegation of full authority over the outcome.

8. Heuristics

People often use heuristic devices, or mental short-cuts, as a way of bypassing the need for individualized choice. For example, it can be overwhelming to figure out for whom to vote in local elections; people may therefore use the heuristic of party affiliation. When meeting someone new, your behavior may be a result of heuristic devices specifying how to behave with a person falling in the general category in which the new person seems to fall. The relevant category may be age, gender, education, race, religion, demeanor, or something else. What is important is that decisions are a product of heuristic devices that simplify a complex situation and that can also lead to error.

A great deal of attention has been given to heuristic devices said to produce departures from "rationality," understood as a result of decisions based on full information.[18] And sometimes heuristic devices do lead to errors, even systematic ones. But often heuristic devices are fully rational, if understood as a way of produce pretty good outcomes while at the same time reducing cognitive overload or other decisional burdens.

III. Decisions and Mistakes

A. Costs of Decisions and Costs of Errors

Under what circumstances will, or should, an agent or institution choose one or another second-order strategy? Begin with a somewhat crude generalization: Rational people attempt to minimize the sum of the costs of making decisions and the costs of error, where the costs of making decisions are the costs of coming to closure on some action or set of actions, and where the costs of error are assessed by examining the number, the magnitude, and the kinds of errors. We understand "errors" as suboptimal outcomes, whatever the criteria for deciding optimality; thus both rules and delegations can produce errors. If the costs of producing optimal decisions were zero, it would be best to make individual calculations in each case, for this approach would produce correct judgments without compromising accuracy or any other important value. This would be true for individual agents and also for institutions.

Two qualifications are necessary. The first is that people may want to relieve themselves of responsibility for certain decisions, even if those people would make those decisions correctly. This is an important reason for delegation (and hence for institutional arrangements of various kinds, including the separation of powers). A second

---

[18] See, e.g., John Conlisk, "Why Bounded Rationality?" 34 *J. Econ. Lit.* 669 (1996).

qualification comes from the fact that special problems are created by multi-party situations: public institutions seek to promote planning by setting down rules and presumptions in advance, and the need for planning can argue strongly against on-the-spot decisions even if they would be both correct and costless to achieve. We will take up these qualifications below.

The chief motivation for second-order decisions is that most people know two important facts: their own (first-order) decisions may be wrong, and arriving at the right decision can be very difficult, or have high costs. For any agent these costs are of qualitatively diverse kinds: time, money, unpopularity, anxiety, boredom, agitation, anticipated ex post regret or remorse, feelings of responsibility for harm done to self or others, injury to self-conception, guilt, or shame. Things become differently complicated for multimember institutions, where interest-group pressures may be important, and where there is the special problem of reaching a degree of consensus. A legislature, for example, might find it especially difficult to specify the appropriate approach to affirmative action, given the problems posed by disagreement, varying intensity of preference, and aggregation problems; for similar reasons a multimember court may have a hard time agreeing on how to handle an asserted right to physician-assisted suicide. The result may be strategies for delegation or for deferring decision, often via small steps.

The costs of decision and the costs of error move people to make and to stick to second-order decisions. There are a number of general reasons why one or another second-order strategy might be best. Consider the pervasive tendency to delegate decisions to others. People tend to delegate the power of choice when the cognitive or emotional burdens of decision are especially high and when the costs of error are likely to be much reduced by giving the power of decision to some other person or institution. Thus those who feel unusual stress at certain decisions are likely to find someone who can make those decisions for them. More formally, certain actors are said to have "authority" if giving them the power of decision can promote accuracy while reducing decisional burdens.[19] In industrialized nations, the grant of power to administrative agencies stems largely from a judgment to just this effect; the political or informational costs of specific decisions about (for example) the regulation of coal-fired power plants or sex discrimination press legislators in the direction of broad and somewhat open-ended standards, to be given particular content by administrative delegates. Thus the Federal Communications Commission and the Environmental Protection Agency are effectively Congress' delegates. We will return to this point below.

An institution facing political pressures may have a distinctive reason to adopt a particular kind of second-order decision, one that will *deflect responsibility for choice*. Jean Bodin defended the creation of an independent judiciary, and thus provided an initial insight into a system of separated and divided powers, on just this ground; a monarch is relieved of responsibility for unpopular but indispensable decisions if he

---

[19] Cf. Joseph Raz, *The Morality of Freedom* 23–31 (discussing authority).

can point to a separate institution that has been charged with the relevant duty. This is an important kind of enabling constraint.[20] In modern states, the existence of an independent central bank is often justified on this ground. Consider the Federal Reserve Board in the United States. The President has no authority over the money supply and indeed no authority over the Chairman of the Federal Reserve Board, partly on the theory that this will prevent the President from being criticized for necessary but unpopular decisions (such as refusing to increase the supply of money when unemployment seems too high); the fact that the Federal Reserve Board is unelected is an advantage here. There are analogues in business, in workplaces, and even in families, where a mother or father may be given the responsibility for making certain choices, partly in order to relieve the other of responsibility. Of course this approach can cause predictable problems.

B. Restricting Options and Reducing Knowledge

These various points are closely related to two important phenomena: wanting not to have *options* and wanting not to have *knowledge*. Through restricting options and reducing knowledge, people can simplify decisions, and hence they often adopt a second-order strategy to accomplish these goals.

It is sometimes suggested that people would always prefer to have more choices rather than fewer, and on conventional assumptions about how people "maximize," the suggestion makes a great deal of sense. There is a familiar exception: options consisting of threats disguised as offers. But the exception does not come close to exhausting the field. Even if we put threats to one side, we can readily see that often people would like fewer rather than more options, and they would much like to be in a position to take certain possibilities off the agenda.[21] Indeed, they may be willing to do or to pay a lot to reduce the option set. Sometimes this is because the addition of options increases the burdens of decision without increasing, much or at all, the likelihood of a good decision. Thus 1000 television channels, or 500 selections on the menu of your favorite restaurant, might well increase decision costs without improving outcomes, in such a way as to produce a net loss. As a second-order decision, people familiarly truncate the universe of options: I want shoes, I want to shop around for an optimal buy, but I decide in advance to limit my hunting to all the shoe stores in one particular mall. Or I want to go to graduate school, but I might be overloaded with too many choices, so I apply to only five schools (knowing that some of those to which I have not applied may be better than the best of the five to which I am admitted). There are other examples of enabling constraints; consider legislative procedures, or rules of order and relevance, designed to reduce the number of issues that can be considered at any one

---

[20] See Stephen Holmes, supra n.10.

[21] A good discussion, highly relevant to second-order decisions, is Gerald Dworkin, "Is More Choice Better Than Less," in Gerald Dworkin, *The Theory and Practice of Autonomy* (New York: Cambridge University Press, 1991).

time. When something is considered "out of order," by informal or formal rule, it is because this limitation, embodying a second-order decision, simplifies judgment by reducing options.

Sometimes both people and institutions want not to have options for a quite different reason: they suffer from weakness of will and fear temptation. They know that if cigarettes or chocolates are available, they may "succumb," and they therefore attempt to close off the universe of possibilities. Legal systems are frequently responsive to this problem. Consider mandatory "cooling off" periods for certain purchases, or mandatory payments to a social security system. In circumstances of temptation, second-order decisions usually take the form of rules embodying precommitment strategies.

It is reasonable to think that more knowledge is usually better than less, but both individuals and institutions often seek to be or remain ignorant.[22] Whether or not ignorance is bliss, no one searches for all available information. Sometimes this is because of the sheer difficulty of obtaining all relevant facts. But people take positive steps—are willing to incur substantial costs—to prevent themselves from finding things out. This may be because knowledge creates strategic problems or biases decisions in the wrong direction. The goddess Justice is blindfolded; the blindfold symbolizes a kind of impartiality. The law of evidence is based largely on a judgment that certain information will prejudice the jury and should not be heard, even if it is material to that decision.

Similarly, people may have a second-order reason for denying themselves knowledge that will make them choose wrongly, impose on them unwanted feelings of responsibility (as when an acquaintance confides a deep secret), or otherwise produce harm to self or others. The notion of "plausible deniability," made famous in the Watergate era, can be taken as a metaphor for decisions not to obtain information that may compromise the person who has become informed. Presidents and Supreme Court justices prevent themselves from knowing many relevant facts. Thus many second-order decisions consist of a failure to secure more information, especially but not only if it is costless to do so. People fail to seek options or information, or take affirmative steps not to get either of these, in order to minimize the burdens of decision and the number and magnitude of errors, or to reduce actual or perceived responsibility.

C. Burdens Ex Ante and Burdens Ex Post

Thus far we have offered a taxonomy of second-order strategies and suggested some general grounds on which someone might pursue one or another approach. It will be useful to organize the discussion by observing that several of them require substantial thought before the fact of choice, but little thought during the process of ultimate choice, whereas others require little thought both before and during the process of choice. Thus there is a temporal difference in the imposition of decision costs, which

---

[22] See Edna Ullmann-Margalit, "Not Wanting to Know," in Edna Ullmann-Margalit ed., *Reasoning Practically* (Oxford: Oxford University Press, 1998).

we describe with the terms "High-Low" and "Low-Low." To fill out the possibilities, we add "Low-High" and "High-High" as well. Note that by the terms decision costs we refer to the overall costs, which may be borne by different people or agencies: the work done before the fact of choice may not be carried out by the same actors who will have to do the thinking during the process of ultimate choice. Consider Table 3.1:

Table 3.1. Burdens Ex Ante and Burdens Ex Post

	little ex ante thinking	substantial ex ante thinking
little ex post thinking	Low-Low: picking; small steps; various heuristics; some standards (1)	High-Low: rules; presumptions; some standards; routines (2)
substantial ex post thinking	Low-High: Delegation (3)	High-High: Hamlet; characters in Henry James novels; dysfunctional governments (4)

Cell 1 captures strategies that seem to minimize the overall burdens of decision (whether or not they promote good overall decisions). These are cases in which agents do not invest a great deal of thought either before or at the time of decision. Picking is the most obvious case; consider the analogous possibility of flipping a coin. Small steps are somewhat more demanding, since the agent does have to make some decisions, but because the steps are small, there need be comparatively little thought before or during the decision. As we have noted, cell 1 is the typical procedure of Anglo-American common law; we shall soon investigate this method in more detail. The most sharply contrasting set of cases is High-High, Cell (4). As this cell captures strategies that maximize overall decision costs, it ought for our purposes to remain empty. Fortunately it seems to be represented only by a small minority of people in actual life (consider Hamlet or certain characters in Henry James novels and their real-world analogues, and also incompetent bureaucracies).

Cell (2) captures a common aspiration for national legislatures and for ordinary agents who prefer their lives to be rule-bound. Some institutions and agents spend a great deal of time deciding on the appropriate rules; but once the rules are in place, decisions become extremely simple, rigid, even mechanical. Everyone knows people of this sort; they can seem both noble and frustrating precisely because they follow rules to the letter. Legal formalism—the commitment to setting out clear rules in advance and mechanical decision afterwards—is associated with cell (2); indeed, the ideal of the rule of law itself seems to entail an aspiration to cell (2).[23]

When a large number of decisions must be made, cell (2) is often the best approach, as the twentieth-century movement toward bureaucracy and simple rules helps to confirm. Individual cases of unfairness may be tolerable if the overall result is to prevent the system from being overwhelmed by decisional demands. Cell (2) is also likely to be the best approach when a large number of people is involved and it is known in

---

[23] See Antonin Scalia, *A Matter of Interpretation* (1997).

advance that the people who will have to carry out on-the-spot decisions constantly change. Consider institutions with many employees and a large turnover of employees (the army, entry levels of large corporations, and so forth). The head of an organization may not want newly recruited, less-than-well-trained people to make decisions for the firm: rules should be in place so as to insure continuity and uniform level of performance. On the other hand, the fact that life will confound the rules often produces arguments for institutional reform in the form of granting power to administrators or employees to exercise "common sense" in the face of rules.[24]

An intermediate case can be found with most standards. The creation of the standard may itself require substantial thinking, but even when the standard is in place, agents may have to do some deliberating in order to reach closure. Decisions are not mechanical. Of course there are many different kinds of standards, and it is possible to imagine standards that require a great deal of thought ex ante and standards that require very little, just as it is possible to imagine standards that greatly simplify or standards that give relatively little guidance.

Cell (3) suggests that institutions and individuals sometimes do little thinking in advance but may or may not minimize the aggregate costs of decision. As we have seen, delegations may require little thinking in advance, at least on the substance of the issues to be decided, and the burdens of decision will be felt by the object of the delegation. Of course some people think long and hard about whether and to whom to delegate, and of course some people who have been delegated power will proceed by rules, presumptions, standards, small steps, picking, or even subdelegations. Note that small steps might be seen as an effort to "export" the costs of decision to one's future self.

It is an important social fact that many people are relieved of the burdens of decision through something other than their own explicit wishes. Consider prisoners, the mentally handicapped, young children, or (at some times and places) women; there is a range of intriguing cases in which society or law makes a second-order decision on someone else's behalf, often without any indication of that person's own desires. The usurpation of another's decisions, or second-order decisions, is often based on a belief that the relevant other will systematically err. This of course relates to the notion of paternalism, which can be seen as arising whenever there is delegation without consent.

In some cases, second-order decisions produce something best described as Medium-Medium, with imaginable extensions toward Moderately High-Moderately Low, and Moderately Low-Moderately High. As examples consider some standards, which, it will be recalled, structure first-order decisions but require a degree of work on the spot, with the degree depending on the nature of the particular standard. But after understanding the polar cases, analysis of these intermediate cases is straightforward, and hence we will not undertake that analysis here.

We now turn to the contexts in which agents and institutions follow one or another of the basic second-order strategies.

---

[24] See Phillip Howard, *The Death of Common Sense* (1996).

IV. Low-High (with Special Reference to Delegation)

A. Informal and Formal Delegations

As a first approximation, a delegation is a second-order strategy that reduces the delegator's costs both before and at the time of making the ultimate decision, through exporting those costs to the delegate. Informal delegations occur all the time. Thus, for example, one spouse may delegate to another the decision about what the family will eat for dinner, what investments to choose, or what car to buy; a dieting teenager may delegate to his older sibling or best friend the decision whether and when dessert may be eaten; an author may delegate to his coauthor the decision how to handle issues within the latter's expertise. These delegations often occur because the burdens of decision are high for the delegator but low for the delegate, who may have specialized information, who may lack relevant biases or motivational problems, or who may not mind (and who may even enjoy) taking responsibility for the decision in question. (These cases may then be more accurately captured as special cases of Low-Low.) The intrinsic costs of having to make the decision are often counterbalanced by the benefits of having been asked to assume responsibility for it (though these may be costs rather than benefits in some cases). Thus some delegates are glad to assume their role; this is important to, though it is not decisive for, the ethical issue whether to delegate (consider the question of justice within the family). And there is an uneasy line, raising knotty conceptual and empirical questions, between a delegation (with a delegator and a delegate) and division of labor (consider the allocation of household duties).

Public institutions, most prominently legislatures, often delegate authority to some other entity. There are many possible factors here. A legislature may believe that it lacks information about, for example, environmental problems or changes in the telecommunications market; the result is an Environmental Protection Agency or a Federal Communications Commission. Alternatively, the legislature may have the information but find itself unable to forge a consensus on underlying values about, for example, the right approach to affirmative action or to age discrimination. The legislature may be aware that its vulnerability to interest-group pressures will lead it in bad directions, and it may hope and believe that the object of the delegation will be relatively immune. Interest-group pressures may themselves produce a delegation, as where powerful groups are unable to achieve a clear victory in a legislature but are able to obtain a grant of authority to an administrative agency over which they will have power. Or the legislature may not want to assume responsibility for some hard choice, fearing that decisions will produce electoral reprisal. Self-interested representatives may well find it in their electoral self-interest to enact a vague or vacant standard ("the public interest," "reasonable accommodation" of the disabled, "reasonable regulation" of pesticides), and to delegate the task of specification to someone else, secure in the knowledge that the delegate will be blamed for problems in implementation.

B. When to Delegate

Obviously a delegation is sometimes a mistake—an abdication of responsibility, an act of unfairness, a recipe for more rather than fewer errors. But when is delegation the right option? Delegation deserves to be considered whenever an appropriate delegate is available and there is a sense in which it is inappropriate for the agent to be making the decision by himself. Before delegating, comparison with other possible approaches may well be in order. As compared with making all first-order decisions on an all-things-considered basis, a delegation promises to lower decision costs, certainly for the delegator and on certain assumptions on balance; this depends on the capacities of the delegate (can he or she make decent decisions quickly?). If the delegate is trustworthy, the delegation may well produce fewer mistakes.

Compared to a High-Low approach, a delegation will be desirable if the legislature, or the delegator, is unable to generate a workable rule or presumption (and if anything it could come up with would be costly to produce) and if a delegate would therefore do better on the merits. This may be the case on a multimember body that is unable to reach agreement, or when an agent or institution faces a cognitive or motivational problem, such as weakness of will or susceptibility to outside influences. A delegation will also be favored over High-Low if the delegator seeks to avoid responsibility for the decision for political, social, or other reasons, though the effort to avoid responsibility may also create problems of legitimacy, as when a legislator relies on "experts" to make value judgments about environmental protection or disability discrimination.

As compared with small steps or picking, a delegation may or may not produce higher total decision costs (perhaps the delegate is slow or a procrastinator). Even if the delegation does produce higher total decision costs, it may also lead to a higher level of confidence in the eventual decisions, which, if the delegate is good, will be sound. It follows, unsurprisingly, that the case for delegation will turn in large part on the availability of reliable delegates. In the United States, the Federal Reserve Board has a high degree of public respect and hence there is little pressure to eliminate or reduce the delegation. But a delegate—a friend, a spouse, an Environmental Protection Agency—may prove likely to err, and a rule, a presumption, or small steps may emerge instead.

There is also the independent concern for fairness. In some circumstances, it is unfair to delegate to, for example, a friend or a spouse the power of decision, especially but not only because the delegate is not a specialist. Issues of gender equality arise when a husband delegates to his wife all decisions involving the household and the children, even if both husband and wife agree on the delegation. Entirely apart from this issue, a delegation by one spouse to another may well seem unfair if (say) it involves a child's problems with alcohol, because it is an abdication of responsibility, a way of transferring the burdens of decision to someone else who should not be forced to bear them alone.

In institutional settings, there is an analogous problem if the delegate (usually an administrative agency) lacks political accountability even if it has relevant expertise.

The result is the continuing debate over the legitimacy of delegations to administrative agencies.[25] Such delegations can be troublesome if they shift the burden of judgment from a democratically elected body to one that is insulated from political control. So too, there is a possibly illegitimate abdication of authority when a judge delegates certain powers to law clerks (as is occasionally alleged about Supreme Court justices) or to special masters who are expert in complex questions of fact and law (as is alleged in connection with a proposed delegation in the Microsoft litigation). Avoidance of responsibility may be a serious problem here.

C. Complications

Three important complications deserve comment. First, any delegate may itself resort to making second-order decisions, and it is familiar to find delegates undertaking each of the strategies that we have described. Sometimes delegates prefer High-Low and hence generate rules; almost everyone knows that this is the typical strategy of the Internal Revenue Service, a delegate of Congress that likes to proceed via rule. Many spouses, delegated the power of decision by their husbands or wives, operate in similar fashion. Presumptions may be favored over rules for the now-familiar reason that they can reduce ex ante costs and promote greater "flow." Alternatively, delegates may use standards or proceed by small steps. This is the general approach of the National Labor Relations Board, which (strikingly) avoids rules whenever it can, and much prefers to proceed case-by-case. Or a delegate may undertake a subdelegation. Confronted with a delegation from her husband, a wife may consult a sibling or a parent. Asked by Congress to make hard choices, the President may and frequently does subdelegate to some kind of commission, for some of the same reasons that spurred Congress to delegate in the first instance. Of course a delegate may just pick. She may, for example, choose to flip a coin, or she may decide without doing much thinking about what decision is best.

The second complication is that the control of a delegate presents a potentially serious principal-agent problem. How can the person who has made the delegation ensure that the delegate will not make serious and numerous mistakes, or instead fritter away its time trying to decide how to decide? There are multiple possible mechanisms of control. Instead of giving final and irreversible powers of choice to the delegate, a person or institution might turn the delegate into a mere consultant or advice-giver. A wide range of intermediate relationships is possible. In the governmental setting, a legislature can influence the ultimate decision by voicing its concerns publicly if an administrative agency is heading in the wrong direction, and the legislature usually has the power to overturn an administrative agency if it can muster the will to do so. Ultimately the delegator may retain the power to eliminate the delegation, and to

---

[25] Compare David Schoenbrod, *Power Without Responsibility* (New Haven: Yale University Press, 1993) with Jerry Mashaw, *Chaos, Greed, and Governance* (New Haven: Yale University Press, 1997).

ensure against (what the delegator would consider to be) mistakes, it may be sufficient for the delegate to know this fact. In informal relations, involving friends, colleagues, and family members, there are various mechanisms for controlling any delegate. Some "delegates" know that they are only consultants; others know that they have the effective power of decision. All this happens through a range of cues, which may be subtle.

The third complication stems from the fact that at the outset, the costs of a second-order decision of this kind may not be so low after all, since the person or institution must take the time to decide whether to delegate at all and if so, to whom to delegate. Complex issues may arise about the composition of any institution receiving the delegation; these burdens may be quite high and perhaps decisive against delegation altogether. A multimember institution often divides sharply on whether to delegate and even after that decision is made, it may have trouble deciding on the recipient of the delegated authority.

D. Intrapersonal Delegations and Delegation to Chance

Thus far we have been discussing cases in which the delegator exports costs to some other party. What about the intrapersonal case? On the one hand, there is no precise analogy between that problem and the cases under discussion. On the other hand, people confronted with hard choices can often be understood to have chosen to delegate the power of choice to their future selves. Consider, for example, such decisions as whether to buy a house, to have another child, to get married or divorced, to move to a new city; in such cases agents who procrastinate may understand themselves to have delegated the decision to their future selves.

There are two possible reasons for this kind of intrapersonal delegation, involving timing and content respectively. You may believe you know what the right decision is, but also believe it is not the right time to be making that decision, or at least not the right time to announce it publicly. Alternatively, you may not know what the right decision is and believe that your future self will be in a better position to decide. You may think that your future self will have more information, suffer less or not at all from cognitive difficulties, bias, or motivational problems, or be in a better position to assume the relevant responsibility. Perhaps you are feeling under pressure, suffering from illness, or not sure of your judgment just yet. In such cases, the question of intra-personal, intertemporal choice is not so far from the problem of delegation to others. It is even possible to see some overlapping principal-agent problems with similar mechanisms of control, as people impose certain constraints on their future selves.

From the standpoint of the agent, then, the strategy of small steps, like delay, can be seen as a form of delegation. Also, the strategy of delegation itself may turn into that of picking when the delegate is a chance device. When I make my future decision depend on which card I draw from my deck of cards, I've delegated my decision to the random card-drawing mechanism, thereby effectively turning my decision from choosing to picking.

V. High-Low (with Special Reference to Rules and Presumptions)

We have seen that people often make second-order decisions that are themselves costly, simply in order to reduce the burdens of later decisions in particular cases. When this process is working well, there is much to do before the fact of decision, but once the decision is in place, things are greatly simplified.

A. *Diverse Rules, Diverse Presumptions*

We have suggested that rules and presumptions belong in this category, and frequently this is true. But the point must be qualified; some rules and presumptions do not involve high burdens of decision before the fact. For example, a rule might be picked rather than chosen—drive on the right-hand side of the road, or spoons to the right, forks to the left. Especially when what it is important is to allow all actors to coordinate on a single course of conduct, there need be little investment in decisions about the content of the relevant rule. A rule might even be framed narrowly, so as to work as a kind of small step. A court might decide, for example, that a law excluding homosexuals from the armed services is unconstitutional, and this decision might be framed as a rule; but the court's opinion could be issued in such a way as to leave undecided most other issues involving the constitutional status of homosexuals. Rules often embody small steps. Of course the same points can be made about presumptions, which are sometimes picked rather than chosen and which might be quite narrow.

For present purposes we focus on situations in which an institution or an agent is willing to deliberate a good deal to generate a rule or a presumption that, once in place, turns out greatly to simplify (without impairing and perhaps even improving) future decisions. This is a familiar aspiration in law and politics. A legislature might, for example, decide in favor of a speed limit law, partly in order to ensure coordination among drivers, and partly as a result of a process of balancing various considerations about risks and benefits. People are especially willing to expend a great deal of effort to generate rules in two circumstances: (1) when planning and fair notice are important and (2) when a large number of decisions will be made.[26]

In most well-functioning legal systems, for example, it is clear what is and what is not a crime. People need to know when they may be subject to criminal punishment for what they do. The American Constitution is taken to require a degree of clarity in the criminal law, and every would-be tyrant knows that rules may be irritating constraints on his authority. So too, the law of contract and property is mostly defined by clear rules, simply because people could not otherwise plan, and in order for economic development to be possible they need to be in a position to do so.

When large numbers of decisions have to be made, there is a similar tendency to spend a great deal of time to clarify outcomes in advance. In the United States, the need

---

[26] See Louis Kaplow, "Rules and Standards: An Economic Analysis," 42 *Duke L.J.* 557 (1992).

to make a large number of decisions has pushed the legal system into the development of rules governing social security disability, workers' compensation, and criminal sentencing. The fact that these rules produce a significant degree of error is not decisive; the sheer cost of administering the relevant systems, with so massive a number of decisions, makes a certain number of errors tolerable.

Compared to rules, standards and "soft" presumptions serve to reduce the burdens of decision ex ante while increasing those burdens at the time of decision. This is both their virtue and their vice. Consider, for example, the familiar strategy of enacting rigid, rule-like environmental regulations while at the same time allowing a "waiver" for special circumstances. The virtue of this approach is that the rigid rules will likely produce serious mistakes—high costs, low environmental benefits—in some cases; the waiver provision allows correction in the form of an individualized assessment of whether the statutory presumption should be rebutted. The potential vice of this approach is that it requires a fair degree of complexity in a number of individual cases. Whether the complexity is worthwhile turns on a comparative inquiry with genuine rules. How much error would be produced by the likely candidates? How expensive is it to correct those errors by turning the rules into presumptions?

B. Of Planning and Trust

Often institutions are faced with the decision whether to adopt a High-Low strategy or whether instead to delegate. We have seen contexts in which a delegation is better. But in three kinds of circumstances the High-Low approach is to be preferred. First, when planning is important, it is important to set out rules (or presumptions) in advance. The law of property is an example. Second, there is little reason to delegate when the agent or institution has a high degree of confidence that a rule (or presumption) can be generated at reasonable cost, that the rule (or presumption) will be accurate, and that it will actually be followed. Third, and most obviously, High-Low is better when no trustworthy delegate is available, or when it seems unfair to ask another person or institution to make the relevant decision. Hence legislatures tend in the direction of rule-like judgment when they have little confidence in the executive; in America, parts of the Clean Air Act are a prime example of a self-conscious choice of High-Low over delegation. Liberal democracies take these considerations as special reasons to justify rules in the context of criminal law: The law defining crimes is reasonably rule-like, partly because of the importance of citizen knowledge about what counts as a crime, partly because of a judgment that police officers and courts cannot be trusted to define the content of the law.

When would High-Low be favored over Low-Low (picking, small steps)? The interest in planning is highly relevant here and often pushes in the direction of substantial thinking in advance. If the agent or institution has faith in its ability to generate a good rule or presumption, it does not make much sense to proceed by random choice or incrementally. Hence legislatures have often displaced the common law approach of case-by-case judgment with clear rules set out in advance; in England and America, this has been a great movement of the twentieth century, largely because of the interest in planning and decreased faith in the courts' ability to generate good outcomes through small steps.

Of course mixed strategies are possible. An institution may produce a rule to cover certain cases but delegate decision in other cases; or a delegate may be disciplined by presumptions and standards; or an area of law, or practical reason, may be covered by some combination of rule-bound judgment and small steps.

C. Private Decisions: Ordinary People, Intrapersonal Collective Action Problems, and Recovering Addicts

Thus far we have been stressing public decisions. In their individual capacity, people frequently adopt rules, presumptions, or self-conscious routines in order to guide decisions that they know might, in individual cases, be too costly to make or be made incorrectly because of their own motivational problems. Sarah might decide, for example, that she will turn down all invitations for out-of-town travel in the month of September, or John might adopt a presumption against going to any weddings or funerals unless they involve close family members, or Fred might make up his mind that at dinner parties, he will drink whatever the host is drinking. Rules, presumptions, and routines of this kind are an omnipresent feature of practical reason; sometimes they are chosen self-consciously and as an exercise of will, but often they are, or become, so familiar and simple that they appear to the agent not to be choices at all. Problems may arise when a person finds that he cannot stick to his resolution, and thus High-Low may turn into High-High, and things may be as if the second-order decision had not been made at all.

Some especially important cases involve efforts to solve the kinds of intertemporal, intrapersonal problems that arise when isolated, small-step first-order decisions are individually rational but produce harm to the individual when taken in the aggregate. These cases might be described as involving "intrapersonal collective action problems."[27] Consider, for example, the decision to smoke a cigarette (right now), or to have chocolate cake for dessert, or to have an alcoholic drink after dinner, or to gamble on weekends. Small steps, which are rational choices when taken individually and which produce net benefits when taken on their own, can lead to harm or even disaster when they accumulate. There is much room here for second-order decisions. As a self-control strategy, a person might adopt a rule: cigarettes only after dinner; no gambling, ever; chocolate cake only on holidays; alcohol only at parties when everyone else is drinking. A presumption might sometimes work better: a presumption against chocolate cake, with the possibility of rebuttal on special occasions, when celebration is in the air and the cake looks particularly good.

---

[27] Cf. Thomas Schelling, "Self-Command in Practice, in Policy, and in a Theory of Rational Choice," 74 *Am. Econ. Rev.* 1 (1984).

Well-known private agencies designed to help people with self-control problems (Alcoholics' Anonymous, Gamblers' Anonymous) have as their business the development of second-order strategies of this general kind. The most striking cases involve recovering addicts, but people who are not addicts, and who are not recovering from anything, often make similar second-order decisions. When self-control is particularly difficult to achieve, an agent may seek to delegate instead. Whether a delegation (Low-High) is preferable to a rule or presumption (High-Low) will depend in turn on the various considerations discussed above.

VI. Low-Low (with Special Reference to Picking and Small Steps)

A. Equipoise, Responsibility, and Commitment

Why might an institution or agent pick rather than choose? When would small steps be best? At the individual level, it can be obvious that when you are in equipoise, you might as well pick; it simply is not worthwhile to go through the process of choosing with its high cognitive or emotional costs. As we have seen, the result can be picking in both low-stakes (cereal choices) and high-stakes (employment opportunities) settings. Picking can even be said to operate as a kind of delegation, where the object of the delegation is "fate," and the agent loses the sense of responsibility that might accompany an all-things-considered judgment. Thus some people sort out hard questions by resorting to a chance device (like flipping a coin).

Small steps, unlike a random process, are a form of choosing. High school students tend to date in this spirit, at least most of the time; often adults do too. Newspapers and magazines offer trial subscriptions; the same is true for book clubs. Often advertisers (or for that matter prospective romantic partners) know that people prefer small steps and they take advantage of that preference ("no commitments"). In the first years of university, students need not commit themselves to any particular course of study; they can take small steps in various directions, sampling as they choose.

On the institutional side, consider lotteries for both jury and military service. The appeal of a lottery for jury service stems from the relatively low costs of operating the system and the belief that any alternative device for allocation would produce more mistakes, because it would depend on a socially contentious judgment about who should be serving on juries, with possibly destructive results for the jury system itself. The key point is that the jury is supposed to be a cross-section of the community, and a random process seems to be the best way of serving that goal (as well as the fairest way of apportioning what many people regard as a social burden). In light of the purposes of the jury system, alternative allocation methods would be worse; consider stated willingness to serve, an individualized inquiry into grounds for excuse, or financial payments (either to serve or not to serve). For military service, related judgments are involved, in the form of a belief that any stated criteria for service might be morally suspect, and hence a belief that random outcomes produce less in the way of error.[28]

B. Change, Unintended Consequences, and Reversibility

Lotteries involve random processes; small steps do not. We have said that Anglo-American judges often proceed case-by-case, as a way of minimizing the burdens of decision and the consequences of error. In fact many legal cultures embed a kind of norm in favor of incremental movement. They do this partly because of the distinctive structure of adjudication and the limited information available to the judge: in any particular case, a judge will hear from the parties immediately affected, but little from others whose interests might be at stake. Hence there is a second-order decision in favor of small steps.

If, for example, a court in a case involving a particular patient seeking a "right to die" is likely to have far too little information, and if it attempted to generate a rule that would cover all imaginable situations in which that right might be exercised, the case would take a very long time to decide. Perhaps the burdens of decision would be prohibitive. This might be so because of a sheer lack of information, or it might be because of the pressures imposed on a multimember court consisting of people who are unsure or in disagreement about a range of subjects. Such a court may have a great deal of difficulty in reaching closure on broad rules. Small steps are a natural result.

Judges also proceed by small steps precisely because they know that their rulings create precedents; they want to narrow the scope of future applications of their rulings given the various problems described above, most importantly the lack of sufficient information about future problems. A distinctive problem involves the possibility of too *much* information. A particular case may have a surplus of apparently relevant details, and perhaps future cases will lack one or more of the relevant features, and this will be the source of the concern with creating wide precedents. The existence of (inter alia) features X or Y in case A, missing in case B, makes it hazardous to generate a rule in case A that would govern case B. The narrow writing and reception of the Supreme Court's decision in the celebrated Amish case, allowing an exemption of Amish children from mandatory public schooling, is an example.

Quite apart from the pressures of inadequate information, too much information, and disagreement, small steps might make special sense in view of the pervasive possibility of changed circumstances. Perhaps things will be quite different in the near future; perhaps relevant facts and values will change, and thus a rule that is well suited to present conditions may become anachronistic. Thus it is possible that any

---

[28] On ethical and political issues associated with lotteries in general, see Jon Elster, *Solomonic Judgments*, University of Chicago Law Review, Volume 54, 1987, pp. 1–45.

decision involving the application of the first amendment to new communications technologies, including the internet, should be narrow, because a broad decision, rendered at this time, would be so likely to go wrong. On this view, a small step is best because of the likelihood that a broad rule would be mistaken when applied to cases not before the court.

In an argument very much in this spirit, Joseph Raz has connected a kind of small step—the form usually produced by analogical reasoning—to the special problems created by one-shot interventions into complex systems.[29] In Raz' view, courts reason by analogy in order to prevent unintended side-effects from large disruptions. Similarly supportive of the small-step strategy, the German psychologist Dietrich Dorner has done some illuminating computer experiments designed to see whether people can engage in successful social engineering.[30] Participants are asked to solve problems faced by the inhabitants of some region of the world. Through the magic of the computer, many policy initiatives are available to solve the relevant problems (improved care of cattle, childhood immunization, drilling more wells). But most of the participants produce eventual calamities, because they do not see the complex, system-wide effects of particular interventions. Only the rare participant is able to see a number of steps down the road—to understand the multiple effects of one-shot interventions on the system. The successful participants are alert to this risk and take small, reversible steps, allowing planning to occur over time. Hence Dorner, along with others focussing on the problems created by interventions into systems,[31] argues in favor of small steps. Judges face similar problems, and incremental decisions are a good way of responding to the particular problem of bounded rationality created by ignorance of possible adverse effects.

From these points we can see that small steps may be better than rules or than delegation. Often an institution lacks the information to generate a clear path for the future; often no appropriate delegate has that information. If circumstances are changing rapidly, any rule or presumption might be confounded by subsequent developments. What is especially important is that movement in any particular direction should be reversible if problems arise.

The analysis is similar outside of the governmental setting. Agents might take small steps because they lack the information that would enable them to generate a rule or presumption, or because the decision they face is unique and not likely to be repeated, so that there is no reason for a rule or a presumption. Or small steps may follow from the likelihood of change over time, from the fact that a large decision might have unintended consequences, or from the wish to avoid or at least to defer the responsibility for large-scale change.

---

[29] Joseph Raz, *The Authority of Law* (1985).
[30] See Dietrich Dorner, *The Logic of Failure* (New York: Metropolitan Books, 1996).
[31] See James Scott, *Seeing Like a State* (New Haven: Yale University Press, 1998).

VII. Summary and Conclusions

A. Second-Order Strategies

The discussion is summarized in Table 3.2. Recall that the terms "low" and "high" refer to the overall costs of the decision, which are not necessarily borne by the same agent: with Low-High the costs are split between delegator and delegate; with High-Low they may split between an institution (which makes the rules, say) and an agent (who follows the rules).

B. Do People Make Second-Order Decisions?

We have not yet discussed an important underlying issue: do people, or institutions, actually make a self-conscious decision about which second-order strategy to favor, given the menu of possibilities? Sometimes this is indeed the case. A legislature may, for example, deliberate and decide to delegate rather than to attempt to generate rules; a court may choose, self-consciously, to proceed incrementally; having rejected the alternatives, a President may recommend a lottery system rather than other alternatives for admitting certain aliens to the country. Thus it is possible to think of cases in which an institution or a person expressly makes an all-things-considered decision in favor of one or another second-order strategy.

Sometimes, however, a rapid assessment of the situation takes place, rather than a full or deliberative weighing of alternative courses of action. This is often the case in private decisions, where judgments often seem immediate. Indeed, second-order decisions might be too costly if they were a product of an on-the-spot optimizing strategy; so taken, they would present many of the problems of first-order decisions.

As in the case of first-order decisions, it often makes sense to proceed with what seems best, rather than to maximize in any systematic fashion, simply because the former way of proceeding is easier (and thus may maximize once we consider decision costs of various kinds). For individuals, the salient features of the context usually suggest a particular kind of second-order strategy. Often the same is true for institutions as well.

These are intended as descriptive points about the operation of practical reason. But at the political level, and occasionally at the individual level too, it would be better to be more explicit and self-conscious about the diverse possibilities, so as to ensure that societies and institutions do not find themselves making bad second-order decisions. It is possible, for example, to find pathologically rigid rules; the Sentencing Guidelines are often criticized on this ground, and whether or not the criticism is just, pathological rigidity is a problem for societies as well as individuals. Legal formalists, like Justice Antonin Scalia, repeatedly argue for a High-Low strategy, but they do so without engaging the pragmatic issues at stake, and without showing that this strategy is preferable to the realistic alternatives.[32] Often a court or even a state would do best to

---

[32] See Antonin Scalia, *A Matter of Interpretation* (1997).

Table 3.2. Second-Order Strategies

Strategies	Examples	Potential Advantages	Potential Disadvantages	Appropriate Context
1. low-high: delegation	spouses, friends; administrative agencies	relief from direct responsibility for ultimate decisions; increased chance for good outcomes	problems relating to trust, fairness, and responsibility; possible high costs in deciding whether and to whom to delegate	availability of appropriate and trustworthy delegate; high burdens of, or perceived likelihood of error in, decision by delegator
2. low-low: picking, small steps, various heuristics	Anglo-American common law; lotteries; big personal decisions	low overall costs; reversibility; coping with change and with unintended consequences	difficulty of planning; high aggregate decision costs; multiple mistakes	equipoise/symmetry of preferences or values; aversion of drastic changes; fear of unanticipated consequences
3. high-low: rules, presumptions, routines	speed limit laws; legal formalism; criminal law; recovering addicts; rigid people	low costs of numerous decisions once in place; uniformity; facilitates planning	difficulty of generating good rules or presumptions; mistakes once in place	sheer number of anticipated decisions/decisionmakers; repetitive nature of future decisions; need for planning, confidence in ability to generate ex ante decisions
4. high-high	Hamlet; Henry James characters; dysfunctional governments	none (unless decision costs are actually pleasant to incur and decisions end up being good)	paralysis; unpopularity; individual or institutional collapse	agency or institution cannot do otherwise

proceed via small steps, in such a way as to ensure reversibility; this is an important means of avoiding the problems associated with social planning, even for those who do not believe that a general antipathy to state planning is warranted. But it is possible to find circumstances in which small steps lead to disaster, by preventing those who must deal with the law from predicting its content. People do not generally make self-conscious second-order decisions, and often this is fortunate; but the discussion here has been intended as an initial step toward making it possible to be more systematic and conscious about the relevant options.

C. Conclusion

In the course of making decisions, people are often reluctant to calculate the costs and benefits of the alternatives. Instead they resort to second-order strategies designed to reduce the burdens of first-order decisions while producing a tolerably low number of suboptimal outcomes. This is a pervasive aspect of the exercise of practical reason, and second-order decisions have large consequences for individuals, for institutions, and for societies.

Some such strategies involve high initial costs but generate a relatively simple, low-burden mechanism for deciding subsequent cases. These strategies, often taking the form of rules or presumptions, seem best when the anticipated decisions are numerous and repetitive and when advance planning is important. Other strategies involve both low initial costs and low costs at the time of making the ultimate decision. These approaches work when a degree of randomization is appealing on normative grounds (perhaps because choices are otherwise in equipoise, or because no one should or will take responsibility for deliberate decision), or when the decision is too difficult to make (because of the cognitive or emotional burdens involved in the choice) or includes too many imponderables and a risk of large unintended consequences.

Still other strategies involve low initial costs but high, exported costs at the time of decision, as when a delegation is made to another person or institution, or (in a metaphor) to one's future self. Delegations can take many different forms, with more or less control retained by the person or institution making the delegation. Strategies of delegation make sense when a delegate is available who has relevant expertise (perhaps because he is a specialist) or is otherwise trustworthy (perhaps because he does not suffer from bias or some other motivational problem), or when there are special political, strategic, or other advantages to placing the responsibility for decision on some other person or institution. Delegations can create problems of unfairness, as when delegates are burdened with tasks that they do not voluntarily assume, or would not assume under just conditions, and when the delegation is inconsistent with the social role of the delegator, such as a legislature or a court. Hence delegations can be troubling from the point of view of democracy or the separation of powers.

The final set of cases involve high costs both ex ante and at the time of decision, as in certain hopelessly indecisive fictional characters, and in highly dysfunctional governments. We have merely gestured in the direction of this strategy, which can be considered best only on the assumption that bearing high overall costs of decision is an affirmative good or even something to relish. This assumption might appear peculiar, but it undoubtedly helps explain some otherwise puzzling human behavior—behavior that often provides the motivation to consider the other, more promising second-order decisions discussed here.

4

Big Decisions
Opting, Converting, Drifting

I. Big, Small, and Medium

I want to focus on some of the limits of decision theory that are of interest to the philosophical concern with practical reasoning and rational choice. These limits should also be of interest to the social-scientists' concern with Rational Choice.

Let me start with an analogy. Classical Newtonian physics holds good and valid for middle-sized objects, but not for the phenomena of the very little, micro, sub-atomic level or the very large, macro, outer-space level: different theories, concepts and laws apply there. Similarly, I suggest that we might think of the theory of decision-making as relating to middle-sized, ordinary decisions, and to them only. There remain the two extremes, the very 'small' decisions on the one hand and the very 'big' decisions on the other. These may pose a challenge to the ordinary decision theory and may consequently require a separate treatment.

By 'small' decisions, I have in mind cases where we are strictly indifferent with regard to the alternatives before us, where our preferences over the alternatives are completely symmetrical. Every time I pick a bottle of Coke or a can of Campbell soup from the shelves of the supermarket, I have made a small decision in this sense. To the extent that we take choosing to be choosing for a reason, and choosing for a reason to presuppose preferences, it looks like we have to conclude that in such cases rational choice is precluded. As Leibniz put it in his Theodicy, 'In things which are absolutely indifferent there can be no choice...since choice must have some reason or principle.'

I have elsewhere dealt with such cases of choice without preference, referring to them as instances of picking rather than choosing.[1] My present topic however is not the picking end of the scale but its other end, that of big decisions. More precisely, I am interested in a somewhat narrower subset of decisions within the large class of what might strike us as 'big' decisions. These will be, roughly, decisions that are personal and transformative, decisions that one takes at major crossroads of one's life. I exclude from

---

[1] Edna Ullmann-Margalit and Sidney Morgenbesser, 'Picking and Choosing', chapter 1 of this volume. I should like to dedicate this essay to Sidney's memory, who passed away August 1, 2004.

this discussion the big decisions one may take in virtue of one's official position or institutional role, which primarily affect the lives of others; for example, a statesman's decision to go to war or to drop an A-bomb.

II. Big Decisions Characterized

I shall consider a decision 'big' in the sense I am here concerned to explore if it exhibits the following four characteristics:

+   it is transformative, or 'core affecting';
+   it is irrevocable;
+   it is taken in full awareness;
+   the choice not made casts a lingering shadow.

I shall refer to decisions exhibiting these characteristics as cases of *opting*. Decisions such as whether to marry, to migrate, or to leave the corporate world in order to become an artist, might be examples. Whether or not these cases do indeed qualify as cases of opting is a question I shall leave for later. First, I need to spell out the characteristic features in more detail.

The first feature of a case of opting is that it is a *big* decision in that it is likely to transform one's future self in a significant way. When facing an opting situation one stands at a critical juncture in one's life. The choice one makes alters one's life project and inner core. Now the expressions 'future self', 'life project', and 'inner core', may be helpfully suggestive but they are too broad and vague. For the notion of opting to be useful, I shall have to be more precise. So let us think of cases of opting as cases in which the choice one makes is likely to change one's beliefs and desires (or 'utilities'); that is, to change one's cognitive and evaluative systems. Inasmuch as our beliefs and desires shape the core of what we are as rational decision makers, we may say that one emerges from an opting situation a different person.

To be sure, there is a sense in which every choice changes us somewhat. The accumulation of these incremental changes makes us change, sometimes even transform, as life goes on and as we grow older. But what I am here calling attention to are the instances in which there is a point of sharp discontinuity. In these instances a person's inner core of beliefs and desires does not simply gradually evolve but undergoes, instead, an abrupt transformation.

Note that sometimes a critical juncture, a point of discontinuity and transformation may occur not as an instance of opting. I am thinking here of results of external happenings. Think of the possible transformative effect on one's life of an accident, the death of someone close, the collapse of the stock market, a draft to serve in a war, and so on. Such cases do not concern us here.

The second characteristic feature of opting situations is their irrevocability: they are points of no return. Again, in a strict, literal sense, every decision is irreversible; 'what's done cannot be undone'.[2] We can apologize for words but they cannot be literally unsaid, we can lower the arm we raised but we cannot un-raise it, a move we make we can retract but not un-make. Yet we treat a great many of our deeds, in a rather straightforward sense, as not irreversible: we compensate, return, or retreat. Various devices are available to us for restoring the situation to the way it was prior to our action or at any rate to a state of affairs sufficiently similar, close or equivalent to it. To be sure, the restoration may be costly in terms of time, money, effort or emotional outlay, but restoration it nevertheless is. So when I say that opting situations constitute points of no return I intend to mark these cases as different. When one opts, one is embarking upon a road that is one way only, leaving burning bridges behind. A reversal in the ordinary sense is impossible.

The next item on the list of characteristic features of opting situations is the element of awareness. It is constitutive of the opting situation that the person facing it is conscious of its being an opting situation. That is, not only is it, as a matter of fact, a critical juncture and a point of no return, but the person concerned also perceives it as such. We may put this more precisely in terms of two epistemic conditions: in an opting situation the person believes (a) that he or she must make a genuine choice between viable alternatives, and (b) that the decision they are called upon to make is 'big'—transformative and irrevocable. The significance of this stipulation will be seen shortly. When either of its clauses is dropped one gets instances which are no longer ones of opting but rather ones of *converting* (when (a) is dropped) or of *drifting* (when (b) is dropped). But this is already jumping ahead.

The fourth and last feature is perhaps only a derivative of the first three. Yet it deserves separate treatment. It concerns the shadow presence of the rejected option; the ghost of the Road Not Taken.

Let me explain. In an ordinary choice situation there is a set of alternatives from which the person chooses one. Upon his or her decision, the non-chosen members of this set ordinarily cease to exist as far as the decision makers are concerned. In the case of opting, however, the rejected, un-opted-for option characteristically maintains a sort of lingering presence. In other words, I suggest that what is of significance to the opting person's account of his or her own life is not only the option they have taken, but also the one they have rejected: the person one did not marry, the country one did not emigrate to, the career one did not pursue. The rejected option enters in an essential way into the person's description of his or her life. The shadow presence maintained by the rejected option may constitute a yardstick by which this person evaluates the worth, success or meaning of his or her life.

III. Big Decisions Illustrated

Having described the opting situation, we must now ask, are there instances of opting situations? I mentioned earlier decisions such as whether to marry or to migrate.

---

[2] Shakespeare, *Macbeth*, Act 5, Scene 1 (Stephen Orgel ed., New York: Penguin Books, 2000).

Think, for example, of the decision whether to have children or to quit one's job as a Director General of a high-tech company to become a Buddhist monk. Or, think of a young talented person who faces a choice between a career as a concert pianist and as a nuclear physicist.

Consider some famous cases. King Edward VIII made the agonizing decision to leave the throne 'for the sake of the woman he loved'. The early socialist Zionist pioneers in the 1920s left everything behind—home, family, religion—and came to Palestine in order to become the New Jews of their ideals. Many defected from the East-bloc countries to the West before 1989. The Biblical Ruth chose to tie her fate with that of her mother-in-law Naomi, who was returning from Moab to her native land and people in Bethlehem.

So, are these cases examples of opting? I offer them at this point as tentative illustrations of the concept. They indicate the flavor of the big decisions here under consideration—options thrust upon us in the name of love, duty or talent, of political or religious convictions, of optimistic idealism or the depth of despair.

A couple of points may be extracted from the suggested examples as they stand. First, in contrast to ordinary decision situations, opting situations are extraordinary. It is possible to go through life with only few opting occasions, even with none at all. While extraordinary, however, opting instances need not be thought of as abnormal, perverse or pathological. Anyone interested in human decision-making cannot therefore be justified in ignoring them, thinking that they lie outside the realm of 'normal' decision-making.

Second, a distinction may be called for between what can be termed opting (A, B) and opting (Yes, No). In an opting (A, B) situation one faces a decision between two new life options. In an opting (Yes, No) situation the choice is between the Yes, that is the new life option, and the No, that is the continuation of one's life in its present path (which may nevertheless not be quite what it was before, owing to the shadow presence of the Yes option).

IV. Opting vs Converting

Why were the examples offered tentatively? What stands in the way of a clear-cut determination whether a given case is a case of opting?

To approach an answer to these questions, consider two further instances. When Tolstoy made his final move to live as a peasant among his fellow Russian peasants, was he opting? When the Apostles left their families and possessions behind to join Jesus of Nazareth, were they opting? I suggest that there is a thin but significant line dividing the cases of opting as here conceived, from cases of *conversion experiences*.

The Conversion experience is familiar to us—from literature, from history, and from life.[3] Like cases of opting, converting can be about a life-transforming, core-affecting,

---

[3] Although one tends to associate conversion primarily with religious conversions, the term is by no means restricted to this phenomenon. There is, first, what Starbuck terms counter-conversion, where one

often irrevocable move. Also, instances of conversion are often dramatic. In converting, like in opting, one is aware that one is about to change one's life in a significant way. But in the conversion experiences I here call attention to it is not the case that one believes that one must make a genuine decision between two viable alternatives. From the point of view of the convert, he or she has no choice in the matter; typically, they would have a strong sense of compulsion, of there being no other way.

Another feature distinguishing converting from opting has to do with the nature of the shadow presence of the rejected option. Cases of conversion are opting (Yes, No) cases, the rejected option being the continuation on the path of one's previous life. Typically, the person who has undergone conversion rejects his or her previous life not just in a technical sense, because they now adopt a new form of life, but also normatively. Converts view their previous lives in a negative light; they evaluate them as wicked or sinful.

I have mentioned two points of difference between converting and opting: the perception of the juncture point as something other than a genuine decision situation; and the negative evaluation of one's previous life. We can readily see that both of these points are perspective oriented. They have to do with the way the people concerned see their situation. In other words, from the point of view of an outside spectator there can in fact be much similarity between cases of opting and of converting, even though from the point of view of the actors they are quite dissimilar.

This explains why I was tentative about the examples. Whether a given instance is one resulting from a big decision—'opting'—or from a conversion experience is a question that cannot be settled by a mere labeling of the act, say, as an act of defection or immigration (etc.). We need to know more. Some opting-seeming situations, including marriage, might be converting situations instead. Conversely, some converting-seeming situations might be cases of opting: 'conversion' to, and away from, communism may be cases in point (Whittaker Chambers, Arthur Koestler).[4] As for Tolstoy or the Apostles, upon a closer look they are indeed likelier to turn out converts than opters.

An evocative image for the difference between an opting situation and a conversion experience is provided by the contrast between Paul of Tarsus on the road (to Damascus) and Heracles on the crossroad (between Vice and Virtue). St Paul's powerful conversion serves as my paradigm of what I refer to as a conversion experience. It occurs when he

converts away from religion. Also, '[I]t may be from moral scrupulosity into freedom and license; or it may be produced by the irruption into the individual's life of some new stimulus or passion, such as love, ambition, cupidity, revenge or patriotic devotion.' (William James, *The Varieties of Religious Experience*, Collin: The Fontana Library, 1960 (1901–2), 181. See also James's case histories of some non-religious conversions, 183–5.) Pertinent too are conversions into, and away from, communism.

[4] Whittaker Chambers, *Witness* (Washington: Regnery Publishing, 1952); Arthur Koestler's essay in *The God That Failed* (New York: Harper, 1950), R. H. Crossman (ed.) (1951) and his three-volume autobiography, *Arrow in the Blue* (New York: MacMillan, 1952), *The Invisible Writing* (Boston: Beacon Press, 1954), and *Janus: A Summing Up* (New York: Random House, 1978).

goes to the city of Damascus to arrest Christians and bring them to punishment in Jerusalem. As he drew near to the city '... suddenly there shined round about him a light from heaven: and he fell to the earth, and heard a voice...', (*Acts* ix, 3–9). Eventually he repents of his sins, is baptized and arises to walk in the 'newness of life'. There is no decision in Paul's case: blinded by the light of the compelling new truth, he feels ordered into his transformed life. He regards his old self is an enemy of his new.

Heracles, in contrast, is described as 'debating with himself which of the two paths he should pursue, the path of virtue or of vice'. Two women personify for him the two options. Each of them tries to entice him—and the language is one of decision throughout. Vice speaks first: 'I see you, Heracles, in doubt and difficulty what path of life to choose; make me your friend and I will lead you to the pleasantest road and easiest.' Then Virtue speaks: '...I entertain good hope that if you choose the path which leads to me, you shall...' Heracles is portrayed as facing a genuine choice and he knows that it is a one way road; there will be no way back.[5]

Note however that cases of formal or technical religious conversion need not be cases of a conversion experience as delineated here. At times, they may count as quite 'normal' decisions, and occasionally as cases of big decisions of the opting variety. What I have in mind for example are the numerous instances of Jews who have converted to Christianity in order to remove an obstacle from the path of their chosen career (like Heinrich Heine or Gustav Mahler), or in order to open up doors for their children (like Abraham Mendelssohn, Felix's father). The point then is that not every case of an exchange of one religion for another is a case of a conversion experience in the sense here employed, so dramatically illustrated by St. Paul (or Ratisbonne).

Pascal's argument known as the Wager is an interesting case in point. It is an argument designed to convince non-believers to choose the Catholic faith through a deliberative-calculative process of decision-making, not by relying on being swept by a conversion experience.

V. The Rationality of Big Decisions

I have alluded to a contrast between deliberation-related opting on the one hand and a conversion experience on the other. What is behind this contrast?

In the case of opting, there is deliberation and there is an expectation that reason prevail. I shall presently examine this expectation and question it. In the case of a conversion experience, in contrast, there is no such expectation. The phenomenon of

---

[5] Xenophon, *Memorabilia* (Book II, ch. 1, 21–34). The plot is based upon a lost parable of Prodicus of Ceos (a Sophist contemporary of Socrates), *The Choice of Heracles*. In his *Memorabilia*, Xenophon has Socrates relate a paraphrase of the lost parable to Arisrtippus. (J. S. Bach bases his secular Cantata BWV 213, 'Herkules auf dem Scheidewege', on this material.)

opting is supposed to be continuous with the realm of human decision-making or practical deliberation. A conversion experience, in contrast, lies outside this realm.

In saying that opting is expected to be guided by reasons what is meant is that opters are expected to arrive at their decision in much the same way that they arrive at their ordinary, 'smaller' decisions. This in turn means that cases of opting are supposed to be open to rational-choice explanations. An ideal explanation of an action as an expression of rational choice strives to show that the action is the best way of satisfying the full set of the person's desires, given his or her set of beliefs formed on the basis of the (optimal amount of) evidence at their disposal. In addition, the further standard requirement is added that the person's sets of beliefs and of desires be internally consistent.[6]

To return to the question of the rationality of opting cases: opters are expected not only to act rationally but even superrationally, as it were. They are expected to be more rational about their opting decisions than about their ordinary decisions, simply because there is so much more at stake. This means that one would expect the opters to take extra time and care in amassing relevant information as their evidence base, to exercise extra caution in assessing the alternatives open to them—including their probabilities—and in bringing their own set of desires (valuations, inclinations, aspirations) to bear upon them, and so on. In short, one would expect an act of opting to be an exemplary candidate for the ideal rational-choice explanations just delineated.

Is this really the case? How rational are opters, and how rational ought they to be?

These are two distinct questions. The first question is empirical, the second normative. Of the first, I have little to say. There is some evidence that the attitude of people toward their big decisions is quite the opposite of the one that we might expect. That is to say, evidence seems to suggest that people are in fact more casual and cavalier in the way they handle their big decisions than in the way they handle their ordinary decisions.[7]

The normative question, how rational ought opters to be, goes to the heart of the matter. Let me begin with an (empirical) observation about how people tend to react to this question. It appears that the idea that one ought to be rational about one's big life decisions strikes some people as troublesome, even wrong. There is a view that with big decisions one ought to be guided by one's instincts, to go 'by one's gut'. The demand for cost-benefit analysis or a decisional balance sheet in the sphere of big decisions seems to some people to belittle these decisions in some sense and to detract

---

[6] I follow here the formulation of Jon Elster in 'The Nature and Scope of Rational-Choice Explanation', in *The Philosophy of Donald Davidson: Perspectives on Actions and Events*, E. Lepore and B. McLaughlin (eds.) (Oxford: Basil Blackwell, 1985).

[7] Regarding the ways people handle their big financial decisions, for example their retirement plans, see Cass R. Sunstein and Richard H. Thaler, 'Libertarian Paternalism Is not an Oxymoron'. AEI-Brookings Joint Center Working Paper No. 03–2; U. Chicago, Public Law Working Paper No. 43; U. Chicago Law & Economics, Olin Working Paper No. 185.

from their significance.[8] On this view, it is only the temperamental, intuitive leap, a 'naked act of decision' as it were, that does justice to the weight of the decision.[9]

Economists, on the other hand, care little about the phenomenology of peoples' attitudes to their decisions. Theirs is a world-view of revealed preferences, and as long as people exhibit consistency in their choices it does not much matter, from the standpoint of rationality, whether the choice was intuitive or resulted from a calculative deliberation. As we shall see, however, it is the notion of consistency that is challenged by the cases of big decisions of the opting variety.

Let us consider people who face opting situations and who want to opt rationally. We suppose that they are conscientious, fully informed and well aware of all the relevant aspects, external as well as internal, of the decision before them. We suppose that they want to choose that option which they believe more fully satisfies their comprehensive, internally consistent desires, given the consistent set of their beliefs—including of course their present beliefs about their own future states in each of the options open to them.

Think for example of a high-tech executive who, craving spirituality, considers opting for a life as a Buddhist monk. We imagine him to want the isolation, simplicity, peace of mind and closeness to nature that (he believes) characterize the life of Buddhist monks. He will seek every piece of information relevant to his decision— about the lives of Buddhist monks, about the process of becoming one, etc. He may even be able to assess his probability of success in achieving the transition and becoming the person he wants to be. As we picture him, he has, in addition to his beliefs and desires, second-order preferences as well, about the sort of person he wants to be. Being materialistic, he may prefer to have ascetic and spiritual preferences; being sex-minded, he may prefer to be a person who prefers abstention.

Now we want to consider what it means for this person to make an optimal choice, relative to his present beliefs and desires. Whose ends is he aiming to promote? Is the

---

[8] For a well-known taxonomy of decision strategies for coping under stress, time pressure, and risk see Janis, I. L. and Mann, L.: *Decision Making: A Psychological Analysis of Conflict, Choice and Commitment* (New York: Free Press, Macmillan, 1977); it includes a decisional balance sheet.

In "Feeling and Thinking" (*American Psychologist*, 1980, footnote 6), R. B. Zajonc underlines the role of affect in decision-making. He describes how, in trying to decide whether to accept a position at another university, Phoebe Ellsworth said, 'I get half way through my Irv Janis balance sheet and say: Oh, hell, it's not coming out right! Have to find a way to get some pluses over on the other side!' (I am indebted to Thomas Schelling for this quote.) A recent report of four studies on consumer choice indicates that it is not always advantageous to engage in thorough deliberation before choosing. The scientists' new advice for anyone who is struggling to make a difficult decision is, Stop thinking about it and, when the time comes to decide, go with what feels right. See: Ap Dijksterhuis, Maarten W. Bos, Loran F. Nordgren, Rick B. van Baaren, 'On Making the Right Choice: The Deliberation-Without-Attention Effect', *Science* **17** (February) Vol. 311, No. 5763, 2006 1005–7.

[9] Consider 'A Psychological Tip', a poem by Piet Hein, from *Grooks* (Cogpenhagen: Borgens Forlag, 1982), 38: 'Whenever you're called on to make up your mind/And you're hampered by not having any,/The best way to solve the dilemma, you'll find/Is simply by spinning a penny./No—not so that chance shall decide the affair/While you're passively standing there moping/But the moment the penny is up in the air,/You suddenly know what you're hoping.' (I am indebted to Thomas Schelling for this quote too.)

opter trying to promote the ends of Old Person or of New Person? The reason for casting doubt about the nature of the optimizing is that, once he opts, Old Person undergoes a personality transformation: there is no continuity in his personality identity and so there is also a problem about his being consistent in his choices.[10]

New Person is now, by hypothesis, a transformed person. Opting transforms the sets of one's core beliefs and desires. A significant personality shift takes place in our opter, a shift that alters his cognitive as well as evaluative systems. New Person's new sets of beliefs and desires may well be internally consistent but the point about the transformation is that inconsistency now exists between New Person's system of beliefs and desires, taken as a whole, and Old Person's system taken as a whole. I am not questioning his ability to actually make a choice, or his ability subsequently to assess himself as happy (or unhappy) with his choice. The question I am raising is whether it is possible to assess the rationality of his choice, given that this choice straddles two discontinuous personalities with two different rationality bases.

So: rational action is relative to the person's beliefs and desires, and the person's beliefs and desires constitute the basis against which the rationality of that person's actions is assessed. Therefore, the transformation our opter undergoes affects his or her rationality base. The opting juncture is a point of discontinuity, or break, in the opters' biography and personality and so the basis for assessing what is rational for them to do beyond this point is different from the basis for the rationality assessment of their actions prior to that point. The personality-transforming opting situation is one in which the old 'rationality base' is replaced by a new. And yet, the rationality of decision-making and of choice is predicated on the continuity of personality identity over time.[11]

Can we not describe this situation within the familiar framework of decision under uncertainty? In a sense we can, but we have to be clearer about the uncertainly that is involved here. In the opting situation it is not the future states of the world or their probabilities that one does not know but rather one's future personality. Opting is a gamble on one's future self as a transformed assessor of results and assigner of probabilities. Cases of opting involve the opting persons' explicit or implicit second-order preference for a radical change in their set of first-order preferences. These are cases, in other words, in which people have second-order preferences over their future

---

[10] I was told of a person who hesitated to have children because he did not want to become the 'boring type' that all his friends became after they had children. Finally, he did decide to have a child and, with time, he did adopt the boring characteristics of his parent friends—but he was happy! I suppose second order preferences are crucial to the way we are to make sense of this story. As Old Person, he did not approve of the personality he knew he would become if he has children: his preferences were not to have New Person's preferences. As New Person, however, not only did he acquire the predicted new set of preferences, he also seems to have approved of himself having them. How are we to assess the question whether he opted 'right'? Who is asking? Who is answering, and on whose behalf?

[11] The best known philosophical discussion of the connection between rationality and the idea of stability of personal identity over time is Derek Parfit, *Reasons and Persons* (New York: Oxford University Press, 1986), chapter XIV. However, he speaks of personal identity whereas I prefer to speak of personality identity.

selves: they want to transform themselves. Given the discontinuity in the opting person's set of preferences, can one make sense of such a decision from a rational-choice perspective? If acting rationally is optimizing, can one opt optimally?

VI. Opting Reasonably

From what I said so far, one should not conclude that when it comes to opting people are intrinsically irrational: it is not even clear what it would mean to say this. In order to be irrational about something there must also be a rational way of going about it, and the rational way of going about opting is what I am here questioning. A satisfying post-opting life is no indication of the rationality, or otherwise, of the big decision involved.

'Acting rationally' need not mean optimizing; it can also mean acing reasonably. What would it take for one to opt reasonably?

Consider a strategy people may employ in an attempt to opt reasonably: they may attempt to cut down, as it were, the opting situation into a series of ordinary 'middle-sized' decision situations. In practice, this means breaking up the big step into several steps, none of which is a dramatic leap and each of which is reversible. Small steps can be helpful. In particular, by taking small consecutive steps we can assure the continuity of our personality identity over time.

Thus, if the big decision you face is whether to marry this man or not, you may try to arrange for the two of you to live together for a while so that you can get a foretaste of your future life—and of your future self—as his wife. Or if the offer of an academic position in a country you have never been to is to you an opting situation, you may try to negotiate first for a term of teaching there, and subsequently perhaps for a year's stay in that place with your family. When the time comes for you to make your final decision, you are likely no longer to consider the last step in this series of steps as an instance of opting.[12]

That is to say, a way of resolving an opting situation is by consciously attempting to neutralize two of the characteristics that make it an instance of opting, namely, that it is a point of discontinuity in one's life, and that it involves a point of no return. These two characteristics also account for the heavy psychological burden that the opting situation imposes. Not all instances of opting may lend themselves to the application of the strategy of cutting down the opting situation to ordinary-decision size. Some cases really call for leaping across an abyss: such a jump cannot be done in small steps. But where this strategy is available I believe that it is natural, as well as reasonable, to resort to it.

---

[12] For more on the small-step strategy see Edna Ullmann-Margalit and Cass R. Sunstein, 'Second-Order Decisions', *Ethics* **110** (October 1999), 5–31. (Reprinted in: Cass R. Sunstein, *Behavioral Law and Economics*, (Cambridge: Cambridge University Press, 2000), chapter 7, 187–298.)

VII. Opting vs. Drifting

I shall now further enrich the vocabulary of big decisions by introducing the notion of *drifting*. One will be said to drift when making one's big decisions conscious of their being decisions but not of their being big. A drifting person carries on with the business of his or her life, making incremental, stepwise decisions only. It is only in retrospect that it can be seen how a particular series of such incremental steps—or in particular one step among them—had been all-important in transforming the future shape of their life and of their personality.

Consider this observation by Janis and Mann: 'Important life decisions are sometimes incremental in nature, the end product of a series of small decisions that progressively commit the person to one particular course of action. A stepwise increase in commitment can end up locking the person into a career or marriage without his ever having made a definite decision about it.'[13] Janis and Mann also report a study indicating that, 'the careers of law-breakers are often arrived at in the same stepwise, drifting fashion, without any single stage at which the offenders decide they are going to pursue a life of crime' (*Decision Making*) I think that the brief, ambiguous love affair of Fontane's Effie Briest with the Polish officer Major von Krampas is an instance of drifting, with catastrophic consequences. In contrast, Anna Karenina's liaison is surely not a case of drifting, but I leave open the question whether or not she was an opter.

It is possible that from an outside-spectator's point of view the real nature of the actor's decisions is clear. It is possible for a person to proceed as a drifter while an informed spectator would judge that the person's situation is one of opting. When this happens, I think that we can view the actor as engaged in self-deception. The actor may be ignoring aspects of his or her decision situation, which reveal it for what it is: a first commitment leading down a core-transforming, irreversible road.

By now, I have identified a number of techniques for extricating ourselves from an opting situation. One is the mechanism of resolving an opting problem by dissolving it, or by 'cutting it down' to ordinary-decision size—the small-step strategy. Another is the phenomenon of self-deception, which we may regard as a mechanism for resolving an opting problem by pretending that it was an ordinary-size decision (or a series of such). Yet another way to extricate ourselves from an opting problem is by subtly arranging it to appear to us as if it were a case of conversion. That is, we may be channeling our mental energies to make one of these alternatives appear as a compelling and inevitable *force majeur*.

I speculate that we find pure, unmitigated opting situations difficult to deal with. We find it difficult to look them straight in the eye, as it were. The speculation also is that we may in fact be badly equipped to deal with opting situations. Infrequent, exceptional and all-encompassing as they are, we can hardly draw on our own past experience or on

---

[13] Janis, I. L. and Mann, L. *Decision Making: A Psychological Analysis of Conflict, Choice and Commitment*, 1977 (see note 8 above), 35.

the experience of others in resolving them.[14] We recognize, as theorists, that big decisions test the limits of rational decision theory while we try, as practitioners, to extricate ourselves from them as best we can.

VIII.   Opting, Picking and the Absurd

I started with a distinction between the realm of decisions without preferences—picking, and the realm of 'big' decisions—opting. I want to close with a suggestion that at the deepest level of choice, picking and opting meet.

One chooses for reasons; one picks when reasons cannot prevail. This happens when the alternatives are entirely symmetrical (or incommensurate). But reasons also fail to prevail when we come to the very end of the chain of reasons, when we run out of reasons altogether. If you choose to do X for reason A and, asked to justify A, you cite B and then you give C as your reason for B and so on, you eventually reach the very bottom, the substratum of all your reasons. If reasons are forever from within a system or a framework (Wittgenstein: from within a 'language game'), the choice of the framework itself cannot be justified by appeal to reasons.

You cannot justify deduction, because there is no way to do it non-deductively. The choice to be moral cannot be justified by appeal to moral reasons. These fundamental choices, then, cannot really be choices; so are they instances of picking? These are after all the biggest, in the sense of weightiest, decisions we may ever have to make.

I believe that a similar intuition underlies Kant's position about the free yet ultimately inscrutable act of choice ('*Wilkuer*') to adhere to the maxim of the universal moral law.[15] I also believe that an intuition like this underlies the understanding of the absurd in the writings of Karl Schmidt and of the Existentialist thinkers, notably Heidegger and Sartre. At bottom, we make our most fundamental choices of the canons of morality, logic and rationality in total freedom and without appeal to reasons. They embody acts that this literature variously describes as nihilist, absurd, or leaps (of faith). The Existentialist thinkers hold that as mature adults we can step outside ourselves as it were, to find the Archimedian point from which to make the brute act of unreasoned choice of a way of life. It may be, then, that the notions of picking and opting finally meet, on the level of these profound existential decisions.

---

[14] Marrying may be an infrequent experience in the lives of each one of us but, seen globally, it is a frequent event: most people marry, at least once. Big decisions may therefore be discussed very differently—from an institutional rather than from a personal perspective. It is possible, for example, to think of incentives and institutional designs that could encourage people to make their big decisions come out in a particular way, for example to reinforce their decision to follow the path of Mother Theresa or to become a legal service lawyer instead of a corporate lawyer.

[15] See Paul Guyer, *Kant and the Experience of Freedom* (New York: Cambridge University Press, 1996 (1993)), 362–4.

5

On Not Wanting to Know

He that judges without informing himself to the utmost that he is capable, cannot acquit himself of *judging amiss.*

John Locke, *Essays Concerning Human Understanding,*
book II, chapter XXI, sec. 67.

1. Introduction

Wanting to know seems natural, and in need of no justification. Wanting not to know seems less natural and in need of some justification. But a moment's reflection suffices to make us aware that there are many types of things we may not want to know, and it seems that justifiably so. We may wish to protect ourselves from cluttering our mind and our memory, or from boredom, or from pain; we may wish to preserve our faculties of creativity and of imagination; we may wish to avoid excessive cost or unnecessary involvements; we may wish to remain impartial, or to retain an element of surprise in our lives. All of these will on occasion make us not want to know certain things.

Thus you may not want to know the number of hairs on your head, the telephone numbers of everyone in town, the exact details of the trip abroad your neighbor made or of the operation she has undergone. Perhaps you do not want to know certain things in advance, like what do all the critics think about the play you intend to see, or whether or not a surprise party for your birthday is being planned, or whether the baby you are about to have is a boy or a girl. Adopted children may wish not to know who their biological parents are. It is possible that you do not want to know precisely what your spouse is up to when you are away—and many of us may not want to know the details of how prisoners are treated in Singapore.

The phenomenon of not wanting to know, then, seems secure: it exists all right. But we may want to ask ourselves whether and to what extent it can be defended. When is not-wanting-to-know, and when is it not, inherently unreasonable or irrational? What is the relation between not-wanting-to-know and self deception? Is there an issue of morality here?

Theories of rationality conceive of rational action as the employment of appropriate means for achieving a desired end. Rational action is thus thought of as a product of two vectors. One is the vector of belief, or knowledge, or probability. The other is the vector of desires, or wants, or utility. I act rationally when I act so as to promote what I want on the basis of what I know.

Elaborate theories are constructed in order to account for these two constitutive elements, of belief on the one hand and of desire on the other. One way of looking at the present enterprise is to see what happens when we drop the assumption that these two vectors in the parallelogram of action are independent and allow them to interfere with one another. There are at least two ways in which the vectors might interact. One would be captured by the question: do we (always) know what we want? The other would be captured by the question: do we—and should we—(always) want to know? It is the second of these two questions that I focus on here.

2. The principle of total evidence

Let us consider an important component of what I have referred to as the vector of belief. It is the principle, or the requirement, of total evidence: a rational person should believe the hypothesis supported by all available relevant evidence. Addressing this issue, Rudolf Carnap distinguished the logical question of how we are to determine the degree r to which evidence E supports hypothesis H, and the practical-methodological question of what we are to do given r (however it is determined). The first is a question of theoretical reasoning, the second is a question of practical reasoning. From the fact that hypothesis H is supported by evidence E to the degree r nothing follows regarding action unless a further assumption is introduced, namely that E is the totality of evidence available to the agent. If E is indeed the totality of evidence available to the agent at time t, then, according to Carnap, the rational agent will accept the directive to believe hypothesis H at time t to the degree r and to act accordingly (e.g., to bet on H with odds not exceeding r). This Carnap calls the requirement of total evidence, tracing a distinguished historical pedigree for it, including Jac. Bernoulli (in his *Ars Conjectandi* (1713), as cited by Keynes, *A Treatise on Probability* (London: Macmillan for the Royal Economic Society, 1973 [1921], p.345–6) and Peirce.

Now when Carnap requires of his rational agents to attend to the totality of evidence available to them, he means that it is irrational for them to ignore or to disregard relevant information which they have. (Information is relevant insofar as it affects the degree r to which E supports H.) He discusses three types of cases which are meant to convince us that this is indeed so. First we are invited to consider a judge who ignores information brought before him which is relevant to the attribution of guilt to the defendant. The second case concerns a businessman who, in evaluating a proposed deal, disregards information he has about some of the risks involved. And the third is a scientist who publishes results of experiments supporting his theory but neglects to publish—or to consider—results unfavorable to it. In all three cases, according to Carnap, the procedure adopted is not rational.

However, even a cursory reflection about these supposedly paradigmatic cases brings to the fore some problems which ought to lead to further reflection. Carnap may have been insufficiently familiar with the Anglo-American adversary legal system, in which there is of course a fundamental distinction between relevant evidence and admissible evidence. A judge (or jury) often not only may but must ignore information which is brought up during the trial and which is doubtlessly relevant but which is deemed inadmissible qua evidence on social-moral grounds (evidence based on hearsay, on a wife testifying against her husband, on illegal wiretapping, etc.). A similar point may be made with regard to Carnap's third case: in science too a distinction may have to be made between relevant and admissible data. Suppose scientists are presented with results from the twins experiments conducted by Mengele, the monster doctor from Auschwitz. Should we consider them irrational—as distinct from immoral—were they to refuse to look at this information or to use it in their own research, even if it may be relevant to this research?

As for the businessman, we should note that there is much psychological literature which suggests that people as well as organizations "often expose themselves to risk because they misjudge the odds" (Kahneman and Lovallo 1993, p.24[1])—and they misjudge the odds, sometimes, because statistical knowledge "that is known to the forecaster will not necessarily be used, or even retrieved, when a forecast is made" (p.26).

This observation is discussed by Kahneman and Lovallo in connection with the distinction they make between forecasts which draw on the "inside" and those which draw on the "outside" view: an inside view anchors predictions on the specifics of the case at hand, on detailed plans, and typically on representative scenarios; the outside view ignores the details of the case at hand and is essentially statistical and comparative. For example, consider estimates of how long it would take me to finish an academic project (a paper, a book, the development of a new curriculum). My own inside view prediction is typically based on my carefully detailed work plan, and is typically overconfident: we generally tend to exaggerate our own control over events, and to underestimate the likelihood of obstacles coming our way, with the result that finishing our projects almost always takes us longer than we expected. An outside view prediction will be based on comparative statistics of how long similar projects—my own as well as other people's—took to complete.

The authors conclude that while the outside view is "much more likely to yield a realistic estimate—the inside view is overwhelmingly preferred in intuitive forecasting" (pp.25, 26). So in terms of our own concern, the point to be made is two-fold. On the descriptive level, we have the psychologists' findings that forecasters indeed ignore relevant (statistical) information available to them. On the normative level, the question may be raised whether this is always to be condemned as unreasonable. Is it not the case that the optimistic bias, which is based on ignoring unfavorable but realistic information and which leads to unrealistic bold forecasts, may yet be beneficial? Ample evidence suggests that optimism is in fact instrumental as a causal factor which contributes to successful coping with challenges. Taking the broad view, considerations of "productive enthusiasm", entrepreneurial initiative, morale, persistence in the face of difficulty etc. often speak for the benefits of unrealistic optimism (Seligman, *Learned Optimism* (New York: A.A. Knopf, 1990)).

Let us go back to Carnap's principle of total evidence and ask, what does it mean to say that evidence E is all the evidence available to agent A at time t?

Evidence 'available' to A naturally means evidence in A's possession, but it might also mean evidence accessible to A, evidence that A could acquire. Carnap concentrates on the first notion: he is concerned to establish the irrationality of ignoring information that one already has. My own focus, in contrast, is on the second notion: I am questioning the rationality (or otherwise) of acquiring information that one does not yet have. But before I move on to this second notion of available evidence, let me briefly note that even for Carnap's own purposes his notion of available evidence remains problematic. The admonition not to disregard information that is in my possession could be variously interpreted according to whether it is meant in the narrow sense of information that I am—or happen to be—aware of at t, or whether it is meant in some broader sense which might include, e.g., retrievable information that I might have, or in an even broader (and troubling) sense which includes the deductive closure of everything I know.

Consider now the idea that in order to act rationally one ought to act on the totality of evidence accessible to him or to her: "He that judges without informing himself to the utmost that he is capable, cannot acquit himself of *judging amiss*" (John Locke, *Essays Concerning Human Understanding*, book II, chapter XXI, sec. 67).

This idea too stands in need of further clarification. To get hold of all relevant information before I act makes sense, but has its price. The acquisition of further information is likely to be costly—in terms of monetary outlay, exertion, time spent, mental or emotional burden ("He that increaseth knowledge increaseth sorrow": Ecclesiastes 1, 18). So perhaps the principle of total evidence could now be recast so as to require of agents, if they are to act rationally, to act on the basis of the totality of relevant information accessible to them at a price they consider acceptable, given their goals.

But here we are in danger of rendering the whole enterprise trivial. Since there will always be some price attached to the acquisition of further information, the mere fact that on some particular occasion you do not want to know something in itself attests to the fact that you judge the price of obtaining it or of knowing it unacceptable. Hence no instance of avoiding knowledge would be considered irrational, or unreasonable.

What this suggests is that something like a cost-benefit approach may be useful here, where the value of knowledge—both intrinsic value and instrumental value—is matched against its cost. The cost divides broadly into cost of acquisition and the cost of having, and each of these can be categorized in various ways. The cost of acquiring information includes, e.g., time, money, effort, boredom, unpopularity. The cost of having information is the cost of having to come to terms with it and live with it, which may include anxiety, agitation, shame, guilt, remorse, pain, injury to self-esteem, and more. Both kinds of cost may involve strategic losses as well (a point I shall return to later).

3. The presumption in favor of additional knowledge

In light of the discussion thus far, and bearing in mind that we are focusing on practical rather than theoretical reasoning, we may at this point consider weakening the principle of total evidence, and examining a presumption instead. The presumption to be examined establishes, for purposes of rational action, a generic bias in favor of acting on the basis of more knowledge rather than on less. To defend the adoption of the presumption in favor of being maximally informed amounts to defending the belief that following it will lead, in the long run, to results which are overall better, in terms of goal fulfillment, than the results of following its antithesis (i.e. a presumption establishing a generic bias in favor of acting on the basis of less knowledge rather than on more), or indeed better than the results of a case-by-case balancing (i.e. of following no rule or presumption at all).

An important feature of a presumption as distinct from a general principle or rule is that it is rebuttable in concrete instances. In any concrete instance in which we consider applying the presumption there may be reasons, or counter-indications, which will caution us against applying it in that concrete instance. When this happens we say that the presumption is being rebutted in that particular case. A presumption is by its nature rebuttable: it has an implicit unless-and-until clause attached to it. (Thus, the presumption of legitimacy in the Anglo-American legal system establishes a generic bias in favor of treating the mother's husband as the father of her child, unless and until there are counter-indications in a specific case.) Irrespective of being rebutted, a presumption may be revised: the generic rule itself may come to be viewed as ill motivated, or as having outlived its usefulness, or as unfitting to changed circumstances, etc., and therefore may come to require revision. Revising a presumption may mean changing it, reversing it, or discarding it altogether.[2]

Can the presumption for additional knowledge be sustained? Is it reasonable to defend it as a presumptive principle of practical reasoning, or does it collapse under the weight of its counter-examples? The examples discussed so far suggest that in spite of the initial plausibility of the idea that acting on the basis of more knowledge better serves our interests in reaching our goals than acting on the basis of less, there is much that we do not want to know, and there are many situations where knowing less seems to serve our interests better than knowing more. Several categories of such cases emerged: cases involving useless or irrelevant knowledge; cases where the cost of acquisition is too high; cases where the emotional cost of having is too high; cases involving problems of impartiality; cases where knowledge incurs hedonic losses having to do e.g. with the loss of spontaneity or surprise. In addition, there are interesting cases where there are strategic problems from knowledge. Sometimes refraining from seeking knowledge may be strategically advantageous, or having more knowledge may be instrumentally dysfunctional in the sense that it may reduce the chances of success in achieving the desired goal.[3]

How are we to take all these cases where the presumption does not apply? Are we simply to view them as an accumulation of rebutting circumstances to the presumption? Or, alternatively, are we to say that the sheer volume of the types of circumstances where the presumption does not apply, as well as their sometimes systematic nature, suggest that the presumption itself needs to be reconsidered? Since the adoption of its counter-presumption (i.e. a principled bias in favor of less rather than more knowledge) is plainly irrational, perhaps the presumption ought to be revised in the sense of being localized, that is, restricted to particular contexts. Or perhaps it is to be pronounced unsustainable altogether. The latter course amounts to recommending something like a case-by-case cost-benefit approach, where the value of additional knowledge is balanced ad hoc in every particular instance against the cost—in the broadest sense—of obtaining it (where 'obtaining' is meant to cover both acquiring and having).

Now this recommendation is no light matter. There is something odd about taking the bias in favor of more knowledge as if it were just a putative technical principle of practical reasoning. It is, after all, well entrenched in our culture. Ever since the Enlightenment, knowledge in our culture has been contrasted with articulated ideologies, captured as dogmas, on the one hand, and with unfounded popular beliefs, captured as superstitions, on the other. Our culture treats knowledge—as it does freedom—not only as intrinsically valuable but as incrementally valuable, i.e. that more of it is always better than less. To be sometimes in favor of knowing less—which means to be against always knowing more—may sound like being against motherhood or friendship: it may sound like going against the grain of the culture.

In considering the question of whether the presumption for more knowledge should be sustained as a principle of practical reasoning in spite of the large number and variety of cases where it seems not to apply, or whether to abandon it altogether, one needs to look at the justification of the presumption. Broadly speaking, a presumption may be justified in instrumental terms, or it may be justified in normative terms (or, sometimes, in both kinds of terms). The first has to do with the factual question of what, in the long run, works best. The second has to do with the evaluative question, on which side we had better "err". What we have seen in the case of the presumption in favor of additional knowledge is enough, I believe, to indicate to us that an instrumental justification is shaky, at best. One would be hard pressed to show convincingly that if we adopt this presumption then, as rational actors, our interests would by and large and in the long run be better served than if we do not adopt it and proceed on a case-by-case basis instead. As for a normative justification, it seems to me that it could only be anchored in the kind of cultural considerations outlined in the previous paragraph— that is, the intrinsic as well as incremental value our culture assigns to knowledge, and the high-minded reluctance to see knowledge as just one factor among others which enter cost-benefit calculations. Yet, given that the context in which we consider this issue is far removed from the historical context of the cultural wars of the Enlightenment against the counter-Enlightenment, it seems appropriate to consider the question of the value of additional knowledge as a question which a rational actor, engaged in practical reasoning, faces on a retail and not on a wholesale basis. (Let me muse, as an aside, that our tendency to use the term 'information' rather than 'knowledge' in the context of practical reasoning and rational choice theory is not unrelated to the fact that, unlike 'knowledge', 'information' in our culture is not put on a pedestal, so to speak, and there is consequently less aversion to think of it instrumentally.)

In what follows I shall not proceed to amass direct arguments against upholding the presumption in favor of additional knowledge. I shall instead go on to explore further aspects of the phenomenon of not wanting to know, all aimed at enriching the texture of this phenomenon, and all designed to increase our skepticism about the sustainability of the presumption. In the process several more examples will be considered, and several distinctions will be introduced; the last section will take up the moral context.

4. Control of knowledge: from 3rd to 1st person

Let us consider the formula "I don't want to know x". As our first move, let us think of it as a special case of the more general formula "I don't want A to know x". This other-person formula states my wanting to prevent—or to protect—someone from knowing something; I shall be assuming here that what I do not want A to know is not some private information relating to myself. Usually when this is the case, I may be said to display paternalistic attitudes toward that person, or to engage in a manipulative power relationship with that person. If the interests I wish to promote are the other person's then it's the former, and if the interests I wish to promote are my own then it's the latter. What changes when we now switch from the third-person, general, formula to the special, first-person case where the person A is myself—when I don't want *me* to know x, so to speak?

Well, to begin with the sophist-like query may be raised, How do I know what it is that I do not want to know unless I know it already? My response to this is that while there may indeed be cases where I do not know that there is an "it" I wish I had not known until it is too late and I already know it, there are other cases where a specific question is on the table and it is the answer to this specific question ("What have you done?", "What is my test result?") that I do not want to know. And it is these cases that concern us here.

Next, the matter may be raised of the possible difference between "I do not want to know x" and "I want not to know x". While such a distinction may certainly be drawn, and in some contexts possibly even to some advantage, for present purposes I take these two formulations to be interchangeable. Both my not wanting to know and my wanting not to know imply an active attitude on my part to avoid obtaining the knowledge in question. It is not indifference to knowing which is at issue here, but aversion to knowing.

Now when the person I want not to know x is myself, can I be said to want to prevent or to protect myself from knowing x? The drift of the discussion so far is that the answer to this question is yes, I can. But when this is the case we may not wish to retain the interpretation of the formula in paternalistic or manipulative terms. To the extent that we do retain the language of paternalism or manipulation even when we talk about my not wanting me to know, I suggest that we have self-deception cases in mind.

The phenomenon of self deception, while certainly pertaining to the field I am here concerned to chart, does not exhaust it. It is even possible to maintain that cases of self deception are, strictly speaking, not cases of not-wanting-to-know. They are, typically, cases where one does know something, and at the same time is concerned to conceal this knowledge from oneself. (Or, one does know the general contours of something, and at the same time prevents oneself from being informed about its details.) This phenomenon merits, and has indeed received, special expert attention. I shall set it aside, and proceed to explore the remainder of the field.

Before moving on let us briefly consider the formula: "You don't want to know x". This is a second-person formula, where another person is advising you to shield yourself from knowing something. This formula helps underline a certain ambiguity of 'want', between a curiosity-sense of 'want' and an interest-sense of 'want'. You may not want to know x in the sense that you are indifferent to x, i.e. that you have no particular desire or curiosity to know x, as distinct from the case where you perceive it as being harmful to you, as going against your interests, to know x. Thus, I may suspect that knowing x would make you pointlessly envious or anxious or otherwise upset you, or that it would adversely interfere with your performance of the task you face, or that it may bias you one way or another where impartiality is called for. We may think of the blindfold Athena, the goddess of justice, as emblematic of this latter justification for not wanting to know.

Consider the following example. A defense attorney in a murder case may decide to avoid asking her client the direct question of whether or not he committed the crime. She will, instead, only ask him whether he wishes to plead guilty or not guilty. The attorney in such a case may say to herself "I don't want to know the answer to the question whether my client is guilty or innocent". She assesses that she will do a better and more professional job if she does not know whether or not she is defending an innocent person. Indeed, once she knows that the defendant did commit the crime, she is actually more restricted in her choice of defense strategies than she is when she does not know whether or not he committed the crime (regardless, of course, of what she happens to believe about him). Moreover, she may come to have ethical qualms about her job, which might further detract from her professional performance. So that knowing less here implies having a larger range of options to choose from— which is in normal circumstances taken to be the preferred situation for the rational decision-maker.

Thomas Schelling (in *The Strategy of Conflict* (Cambridge: Harvard University Press, 1960)) and Jon Elster (in *Ulysses and the Sirens* (New York: Cambridge University Press, 1979)), among others, have demonstrated some of the ways in which "tying our hands" in advance of action, that is to say visibly blocking off some of the courses of action open to us in a decision situation, may actually further our interests and hence be rational. The attorney example suggests something similar with regard to knowledge: that there are occasions on which intentionally arranging for ourselves to have less rather than more knowledge is strategically advantageous for us.

5.   Control of self-regarding knowledge

Next, consider the formula "I don't want to know x" when x is self-regarding knowledge.

Since the focus of the present discussion is on the question of justifying my not wanting to know, we are exempt from discussing such issues as the freedom of and equal access to information in general, or the right of the public to know. But an assertion of my right to know that which concerns me does fall within the purview of our discussion. Let me explain. I may wish to assert my right not to be denied access to knowledge that concerns me personally, to the extent that this knowledge exists and that somebody out there has access to it. To withhold from me information about myself, whether it regards my personal and family status, my health, my financial situation, my school-, army- or job records etc., is to impinge upon my autonomy. Whatever one wishes to read into the dictum that knowledge is power, it unequivocally asserts that to control knowledge is to engage power games. To withhold such knowledge from me is paternalistic at best and manipulative otherwise. (Is information about my children considered information about myself? This is a borderline case. I suppose that I have the right not to be denied access to information about my children until they reach a certain age. The other side of the same coin is that I may be denied access to certain information about myself as long as I am a child under a certain age.)

To defend one's right to knowledge concerning oneself is one thing, though, and to choose to exercise this right is quite another. The question we are now asking is whether or not one has the privilege of not wanting to know such information, and what if any are the limits of this privilege. Is not an adopted child, who may have access to information about her biological parents when she reaches the age of 18, free not to acquire that knowledge? Does a patient, who is not denied access to the results of the medical tests performed on him, have to be informed about the results? These cases point to a conflict which may exist between autonomy and welfare, with respect to obtaining knowledge. While being autonomy-increasing, knowledge about oneself may at the same time be welfare-reducing.

In many types of situations we do indeed wish to waive our right to self-regarding knowledge. In managing our lives, both externally and internally, there seems to me to be no *prima facie* reason why we should not have different tastes, which would express themselves in different preferences over our mental states in general, and over our states of knowledge in particular. People differ in the way they cope, say, with painful knowledge, and this will be reflected in their preferences over what they want or do not want to know about themselves.

The first headline on the front page of the *New York Times* on October 24, 1995 read: "If Tests Hint Alzheimer's, Should a Patient Be Told?" The story is about a gene, called apo E4, such that people with two copies of it have as high as a 90 percent chance of developing the disease by the age of 80. It is, the paper goes on to tell us, "information that nobody seems to know what to do with." The 51-year-old woman featured in the story is quoted as saying that in her family, two sisters and a brother went in for apo E tests after she learnt that she had two apo E4 genes, but four sisters refused, saying they did not want to know. She herself never hesitated about wanting to know about her apo E result; neither did her own doctor who "found the temptation to know irresistible."

This case raises fundamental practical and ethical questions for doctors and researchers whose perspective is that of the providers of information. As for the patients' perspective, which is that of the consumers of information (as it were), this case seems to me to raise no fundamental questions. It rather helps underline the point just made that, insofar as one is dealing with knowledge which pertains to one's own vital personal affairs but which one can do nothing about, people have different tastes and preferences as to whether or not they want to possess it. What one person may find "irresistibly tempted" to know, another may be to afraid to know. And just as is the case with other tastes and preferences, there isn't very much more of an illuminative, normative nature to say here.

There would be something more to say about this case had we denied the assumption that there was nothing one could do with the apo E-related knowledge. Even if it is true, and remains true, that there is no way to prevent or treat Alzheimer's disease, one may well hold that there are ways to prepare for the near-certainty of developing the disease. There are ways in which one, and one's family, may plan for the future. Once this point is acknowledged, the case under consideration can no longer be taken as a case exhibiting mere differences of taste-like preferences among people regarding their own cognitive mental states. There could then be a cogent argument for the unreasonableness of the ostrich policy of not wanting to know.

In any event, we should be clear about distinguishing cases in which I give up being informed about myself where this is merely a reflection of my personal taste, from cases in which I forego being informed about myself where this is supposed to be instrumental to promoting my ends. The latter cases, but not the former, may be evaluated as reasonable or unreasonable. Such cases may include those where I give up collecting information because it is too costly to do so, others where I want to remain impartial, and still others where having the knowledge will trouble or pain me, or strategically hurt my interests.

For example, in a case like waiving my right to read recommendation letters written on my behalf as part of my promotion procedure, my very signing of the waiver clause may causally affect the nature and quality of the procedure in a way that is ultimately more favorable to me than had I insisted on access to my file. This is a neat case where I may want to know in the curiosity sense of 'want' but not in the interest sense of 'want'. When I participate in an experiment, it may be better for me, as well as for the experimenters, if I do not know whether or not I belong to the control group. A variant on this is a case where an educational experiment is conducted on my students, and I choose not to know too many details of the experimental design so as not to be biased in my own attitudes toward the students while the experiment lasts. Or think of Rawls's veil of ignorance in the original position. One way to reconstruct this, I suppose, is to say that those entering the deliberation room are expected to ignore self-regarding knowledge that they have: they are to relinquish all knowledge about their own particular characteristics and position in society, so as eventually to come up with a more just—and presumably more rational—design for their societal institutions.

6. Hindsight

"Had I known it at the time, I would not have done what I did." This is a familiar enough phrase, with various substitutions for the "it". "Had I known the real nature of the tasks and responsibilities involved in being a chairperson of this organization (board, committee), I would never have agreed to become a candidate in the first place." "Had I known what enrolling in that particular army unit really means, I would never have signed the papers." And so on. Now it is possible that when you say "Had I known what it involved, I would never have done it" the implicature is "And I wish I had known it at the time". That is, you regret having done what you did: you acknowledge that you acted on the basis of insufficient knowledge, and as a result you judge your action to have been wrong, or suboptimal, in some sense. You reproach yourself for not having found out more, for not having been better informed.

But let us consider now the possibility that the implicature is "And boy am I glad I had not known it at the time!" That is, you acknowledge that you acted on the basis of insufficient knowledge, and, furthermore, you realize in hindsight that on the basis of fuller knowledge the course of action you chose was not the rational one to pursue and that you would therefore not have pursued it. Yet, you are happy with the result.

Of course, being a rational decision maker does not guarantee—and does not claim to guarantee—the best result on every occasion. And if you gamble against high odds without knowing them and luck out, your being happy with the result does not retrospectively make your gamble rational. But the interesting possibility to be pointed out here is the case where your not knowing contributed causally to the success of your action—whether or not it would have been the rational course of action for you to take on the basis of full knowledge. Had you known, for example, how many candidates have failed the exam you are about to take, you might either have been discouraged from even attempting it, or lost the confidence necessary for passing it. Your very ignorance of the rate of failure was thus a factor that contributed to the good result. Doubt, uncertainty or ignorance may sometimes improve performance—as may unrealistic optimism, discussed above.

7. Morality

We come, finally, to consider the aspect of morality. There are in fact two distinct kinds of cases here, which work in opposite directions. One concerns the possibility that for reasons of morality you should forego some piece of knowledge, i.e. the possibility that wanting to know is morally reprehensible. The other concerns the possibility that for reasons of morality you may not exercise your privilege not to know some piece of knowledge, i.e. the possibility that not wanting to know is morally reprehensible. The existence of both kinds of cases should further strengthen us in our conclusion that the question of obtaining additional knowledge ought to be settled on the merit of each case and not on the strength of a general rule or presumption.

With regard to the first kind of cases, recall the notion of inadmissible evidence referred to earlier. Our system of law recognizes that sometimes evidence, while clearly relevant to the question of guilt, should be disallowed. Knowledge gained by torturing a witness is a case in point. It is the procedure by which the information is obtained which is objected to here, not its content (albeit that the content of confessions obtained under physical torture is often tainted anyway). This procedure is judged to involve unacceptable social and moral cost. Note that the notion of cost here is not construed in terms of the price paid to obtain the knowledge, but rather in terms of the social consequences that the use of such knowledge might have for the future—as well as in terms of the intrinsic moral cost of the violation of a basic human right that torture necessarily involves.

Part of the rationale for not admitting this sort of evidence is the causal influence this ban is meant to have in discouraging torture in future cases. Similarly in the case of scientific research based on unethical experiments, for which Mengele's twin experiments provide an extreme example. The information such research contains may be accessible, and it may even be of scientific value. But since its very use may be construed to condone the methods by which it was obtained, it may be best, normatively as well as prudentially, to forbid its use altogether.

As for the second kind of cases, we note our familiarity with contexts where your saying "But I did not know" meets with the retort "Well, you very well ought to have known". Taken as a moral admonition, when is this retort justified?[4] Are there cases where not wanting to know is morally reprehensible? In other words, are there case where there is a moral duty to know?

The case of Nazi Germany once again provides an extreme case in point. When Germans—especially those in positions of influence—say "But I did not know what was going on", we feel that this is no defense against charges of complicity. The general point seems to be that we have a *prima facie* duty to inform ourselves about what is being done by others in our own name. Insofar as one is a citizen of a democracy, one bears some sort of responsibility not just for one's own actions, but also for the actions done on one's behalf by one's representatives. How and to what extent one can be expected to discharge this responsibility is a different issue, and a very complex one. But the point remains that at the very minimum the strategic move of shutting one's eyes, of not wanting to know, may not be a morally permissible one.[5]

A related point has to do with one's obligation to those under one's care. I may shut my eyes and be negligent with regard to my own needs; I may not want to know the medical diagnosis of my condition and what the appropriate treatment should be, and—up to a certain degree of negligence—outside interference may well violate my autonomy. But when it comes to my responsibility toward my child or my aging parent who depend on me for their care and welfare, my not wanting to know the details of their medical condition and its treatment must be morally condemned. So once again this is a type of situation where the notion of responsibility is bound up with that of knowledge in such a way that we have a *prima facie* duty to know.

A final observation, from a different angle: sometimes knowing something about somebody may put you under a special moral obligation to that person, even if this is not a person toward whom you have special obligations otherwise. The situation is perhaps analogous to the case when you happen to be passing by the beach where a drowning man calls for help: your mere presence there at that instant puts you under an obligation to do what you can to save him. Similarly, if a casual conversation with a stranger on a train turns into a confession where she starts telling you all, you may well feel that the more you know, the more freedom you are losing. You realize that you are about to lose your status of a stranger with respect to this person and that the bond that is being created between the two of you in virtue of this very conversation will make you morally obligated toward her. You may well feel, then, that as long as you don't know you don't owe. I therefore offer a distinction here, between knowing and being told. And my suggestion is that there are cases where the issue is my not wanting to be told rather than my not wanting to know. Moreover, some interesting cases involve neither my not wanting to know, nor just my not wanting to be told, but rather my not wanting to be told by x: being told by him (or her) may bind me morally against my will to a person I do not wish to be, and would not otherwise be, morally bound to. It may also establish a power relationship between us which is one I want to avoid.

Notes

1. Daniel Kahneman and Dan Lovallo, "Timid Choices and Bold Forecasts", *Management Science* Vol. 39 no.1, 1993: 17–31.
2. I have drawn here on Edna Ullmann-Margalit (1) "On Presumption", *The Journal of Philosophy LXXX*, no. 3, 1983: 143–64; (2) "Revision of Norms", *Ethics* 100, 1990: 756–67.

3. Known in game theory are cases, e.g., where a player who wants some information may nevertheless refrain from seeking it: he may not want it to be known that he wants to know—because this in itself may be compromising information about his own position.

4. In law it is often said that it is our business to know, or at any rate that ignorance of the law does not exempt from sanction. In fact, however, this situation is conceptualized within the law in terms of a fiction, or a presumption of knowledge, rather than in terms of a duty to know.

5. A delicate balance must in fact sometimes be struck here, between the duty to inform oneself on the one hand and moral urgency on the other. The duty to be well informed is sometimes used as a pretext for doing nothing, or at least for procrastination, when it is quite clear that atrocities are being committed. There are occasions in which, even if there is some unclarity about the precise details of the atrocities (and there usually is), to insist on total evidence before taking any action against them is a total abuse of the principle and must be morally objected to.

6

Holding True and Holding as True

1. Holding True

You are leafing through the pages of a scientific journal of high reputation. You come across an article by an author whom you know as a good, meticulous, and reliable natural scientist. The sentence that catches your eye is this:

"The carotenoids are isoprenoid polienes".

You do not understand the sentence. You do, however, have good circumstantial reasons to believe that it is an indicative sentence expressing a true proposition (for short: that it is a true sentence). Your situation therefore is this: you can say that you believe that the sentence "carotenoids are isoprenoid polienes" is true. At the same time, you cannot be said to believe that carotenoids are isoprenoid polienes, because you have no idea what this is all about.

This situation seems paradoxical.[1] You believe of a given sentence that it is true, because you have good external reasons to believe that it is true, but you do not believe (nor do you disbelieve, for that matter) its content—because its content is incomprehensible to you.

One way out of this problem is to distinguish between two propositional attitudes that are involved here. One is the familiar attitude of believing the proposition expressed by a sentence (in this case, believing that carotenoids are isoprenoid polienes). The other is the propositional attitude of *holding a sentence true* (in this case, holding "carotenoids are isoprenoid polienes" true). And the point of the distinction is this: when one believes that *p*, it analytically follows (*modulu* the sentence/proposition distinction) that one holds '*p*' true. The converse, however, does not hold: a person may hold something true without believing it, e.g., when one does not understand it.

There is nothing absurd about holding a sentence true without believing the proposition it expresses. Indeed we want to do more than merely point to this possibility. We want to claim that this possibility captures important phenomena. For example, the attitude towards holy scriptures, we suggest, is frequently that of holding them true. It is not unusual for people not to understand the text, or to understand it only partially or dimly. In this sense they cannot be said to believe it. At the same time they may well believe that it is true. What we have here are cases of division of epistemic labor, as it were. Part of your reason for believing that a certain given sentence, which to you is inscrutable, is true, is your belief that there are people whom you trust—scientists or priests, as the case may be—who do understand the sentence and who believe its content.

Let us explore the attitude towards sacred texts somewhat further. There is actually more than one attitude involved. That of the fundamentalist is simple. Fundamentalists believe that each and every sentence in, say, the Old and the New Testaments, is literally true. For them there is one literal—or, at any rate, straightforward—interpretation, under which each sentence is rendered meaningful and true.

Diehard fundamentalists, even if they exist, are not, by and large, typical believers. A typical believer's attitude towards sacred texts is more complex. It seems to be a mixture of straightforward belief in some of the sentences and of holding others true. More precisely, where there is no straightforward reading of a sentence in the sacred text which will enable the believer to believe it, he or she will typically hold the sentence true in the sense that they will believe that there exists an intended interpretation under which the sentence is true. (Call them phonetic believers,[2] as distinct from fanatic believers.) The interpretation, moreover, will have to be such that it will render the sentence true in a non-embarrassing way. This means, minimally, that the interpreted sentence will not overtly contradict other sentences of the same sacred text. It may also mean that the interpretation should not be too farfetched, that it should still be closer to the literal than to the altogether allegorical interpretation.[3]

There are, however, other believers, perhaps less typical, for whom the latter restriction does not apply. They will hold many sacred sentences true in the sense that they believe that there exists some interpretation under which these sentences can be seen in the best light, as revealing deep and precious truths. In order to achieve this, the interpretation may, or perhaps ought to, deviate drastically from the literal in the direction of the allegorical or even the mystical.

Regardless of the distinctions among types of believers relative to the types of restrictions they will impose on the interpretation of their sacred texts, the main point remains: the attitude of believers towards the sentences of the texts they revere is not necessarily that of belief but, rather, typically, that of holding them (or many of them) true.

2. What We Want to do

Holding true is an attitude towards the truth of a sentence related to, but still distinguishable from, belief. Another such attitude, to be introduced presently, is *holding as true*. These two notions demonstrate the richness in what is often taken as a monolithic phenomenon occupying the middle ground between mere entertaining of an idea, on the one hand, and knowledge, on the other.

In what follows, we want to uncover some of this richness, by pointing to a range of phenomena, a family of notions as it were, which is interrelated in a more complex way than can be captured by any simple hierarchy of strength.

In addition to holding true and holding as true, we shall discuss acceptance, holding as true 'come what may', and 'holding fast'. All of these notions have philosophical careers behind them. Kant, Wittgenstein, Quine, Davidson, and Harman are among those who have invoked one or another member of this family, or variants thereof. Their uses of them, however, have not been systematic and are sometimes confusing, if not confused. We shall attempt to use the holding true/holding as true distinction to set some of these confusions aright, and we shall attempt to show that these two notions have the power to organize this family of belief-related attitudes, and in part to explicate them.

A methodological aside, before we continue: the justifications for distinction may come, in general, from two opposing directions of fit. The first is the Austinian one, according to which the existence in the language of different expressions indicates that there are sufficiently different uses for them. The opposite direction starts with a conceptual distinction we are interested in, and goes on to peg the distinct concepts onto existing expressions, whether or not these expressions antecedently reflect our intended uses for them. This is often the case with turning ordinary expressions into technical or quasi-technical ones.

A useful analytical technique for pointing to a distinction—whether it is exposed or proposed—is the contrast technique, which makes use of the expression 'but not'. For example, when dealing with the distinction between "by accident" and "by mistake", Austin—the master of this technique—argued for the meaningfulness of the sentence "x killed y by accident but not by mistake".[4] With regard to the distinction between believing and holding true, we have argued above that the one-way contrastive sentence, "I hold 'p' true but it is not the case that I believe that p", is meaningful. We are not overly concerned with the question whether or not the distinction between 'holding true' and 'believing' reflects differences in the ordinary uses of these expressions. It may well turn out that no linguistic analysis of these expressions reveals just the distinction that we wish to make. More important to us is the question of the philosophical significance of the distinction.

This holds also for the further contrastive sentences which may be generated by the additional notion of holding as true. We shall have to determine just which of them are significant. It will turn out that the important ones are: "I hold 'p' as true but it is not the case that I believe that p"—*and* vice versa. There are others that relate to the notion of holding fast, and they will be examined when this notion is discussed below (Section 7).

3. Holding as True

"The client is always right", says the manager to the salespersons. Are they to attribute to her a belief in the truth of her assertion? They know, of course, just as well as she knows, that clients are often not right; that clients who return merchandise with complaints of defects often invent these defects or are themselves responsible for them. It is unreasonable for the salespeople to attribute to the manager the belief that every client is always right, or even that most clients are mostly right. Moreover, it is unreasonable for them to attribute to the manager the intention of inducing in them the belief that the client is always right. How then are we to construe the manager's assertion?

We want to suggest that the *point* of the assertion is quite clear. The manager wants her employees to behave as if the client is always right: they are not to answer clients back, not to argue, not to demand substantiation for complaints nor to prove them wrong. By telling her employees that the client is always right the manager is in effect instructing them of a house policy as to how they ought to proceed with complaining clients, regardless of what they happen to believe. We shall want to say of the manager in this case that she *holds it as true* that the client is always right, and that she requires of her salespersons to hold it as true as well.

Let us for a moment consider the salesperson as engaged in a piece of practical deliberation. One of his or her premises is the client's complaint; the conclusion is expected to state how the deliberator is to behave (proceed, respond). Now the point of the house policy is that the salesperson is to enter it as another premise that the client is right, and never mind what he or she actually believes about the truth of the complaint.

The notion of holding as true, we maintain, is a presumptive notion. We wish to draw here on the account of presumptions which was offered by Ullman-Margalit elsewhere,[5] and which takes its cue from the role of presumptions in the theory of law. The point of a presumption (that p), like the point of holding a sentence as true, is practical, not theoretical. One presumes that p in order to act on it, in a situation where the decision as to which action to take depends on whether or not p is the case. One is to enter p as a premise into one's pertinent piece of practical deliberation and to proceed as if it were true.

The case of the salesperson is thus similar in an important respect to the case of the judge who is instructed by a presumption of law that a child under the age of seven is incapable of criminal intent (or, that the father of a child born in wedlock is the mother's husband). In all these cases a person is instructed to hold something as true, i.e., to act as if that something were true. The question of whether or not the person actually believes that it is true does not arise.

Presumptions may be conclusive, or rebuttable. The legal examples just cited are examples of conclusive presumptions; the clients-are-right case may be assimilated to the class of conclusive presumptions, too. A conclusive presumption is a statement concerning matters of fact (e.g., a child under seven years of age cannot harbor a criminal intent). At the same time, however, it is endowed with a special status that places it beyond the reach of counter-evidence. In this sense it functions as a rule, or a policy.

A rebuttable presumption that p has an 'unless-or-until' clause attached to it. (Thus: "A person is innocent unless and until proven guilty".) The injunction—or decision—to proceed as if p were true is taken to obtain so long as one has no reasons to believe that not-p. Once the deliberator is in possession of (sufficient) reasons for believing that p is not the case, the presumption is rebutted and the injunction to proceed as if p is annulled. The weight of the reasons, or counter-evidence, required for rebuttal varies with the degrees of strength of the presumption, which in general depend on what is at stake.

It should be stressed that the role of presumptions is to facilitate action. We are commonly supposed to act on the basis (*inter alia*) of our beliefs, and our beliefs are supposed to be formed on the basis of evidence. What happens, however, in a situation of practical deliberation where the need for action is pressing but where there is insufficient evidence one way or the other, or where the evidence is evenly balanced? It is to avoid paralysis, or arbitrary action, in such situations that presumptions come to the aid of the deliberator. They function as means of extrication from situations of practical deliberation in which we are—or may be anticipated to be—stranded due to insufficient or balanced evidence.

Part and parcel, therefore, of the notion of presumption is the idea of burden of proof. When, in a situation of unresolved deliberation, you are armed with a (rebuttable) presumption that *p*, you have a license to act as if *p* were the case. It is up to the party who wishes to rebut the presumption to come forward with sufficient evidence that not-*p*. Unless and until this happens, you may proceed.

Returning now to the expression 'hold as true', our proposal is to equate holding '*p*' as true with having a presumption (conclusive or rebuttable, as the case may be) that *p*. It is thus possible to hold a sentence as true without believing it. *A fortiori* it will also be possible to hold a sentence as true without holding it true. (On the possibility of believing *p* without holding it as true, or even while holding its negation as true, see the example of the dean of admissions, below, in Section 4.) It is against the background of the theory of presumption that our claim about the presumptive nature of 'holding as true' gains its import and significance.

3.1. Kant's "holding for true" ("das Fürwahrhalten")

In the *Critique of Pure Reason* (the part entitled "Transcendental Doctrine of Method") Kant introduces the generic term "holding for true" ("das Fürwahrhalten"). It has, he says, three degrees: opinion, belief, and knowledge.

In order to understand this threefold division, two more dimensions of distinctions have to be considered: first, that of subjective causes vs. objective grounds, a dimension which produces a distinction between *persuasion* and *conviction;* and, second, that of practical judgments vs. theoretical judgments, a dimension which produces distinction between *pragmatical* beliefs and *doctrinal* beliefs.

Opinion has only subjective causes, and even they are insufficient. It is termed "persuasion", and dismissed as "mere illusion". Knowledge, at the other end of the spectrum, has sufficient subjective causes, which account for it being termed "conviction", as well as sufficient objective grounds, which elevates it to "certainty". That is, it has both private validity for the individual who judges, and also interpersonal validity, in the sense that it is communicable to others and that the judgments of all individuals who consider the matter agree with each other.

Belief, which occupies the middle ground, is more problematic. It is, Kant says, subjectively sufficient but objectively insufficient, and it comes into its own in the sphere of the *practical*. A belief pertains to the means for attaining a proposed end. It is interesting to note that the only detailed example Kant provides in this section concerns this notion of belief. It merits full citation:

> The physician must pursue some course in the case of a patient who is in danger, but is ignorant of the nature of the disease. He observes the symptoms, and concludes, according to the best of his judgment, that it is a case of phthisis ("die Schwindsucht"). His belief is, even in his own judgment, only contingent: another man might, perhaps, come nearer the truth. Such a belief, contingent indeed, but still forming the ground of the actual use of means for the attainment of certain ends, I term *pragmatical belief.*[6]

Bringing our terminology to bear on this example, we shall say that the physician who has formed his judgment to the best of his ability, must hold it as true and proceed to treat the patient accordingly. There is an element of urgency built into this case, as is generally typical of cases calling for the application of a presumption. The physician does not have the leisure to enter into a theoretical inquiry until he reaches the truth with certainty. The diagnosis he reaches forms the ground for his action, and the question of his epistemic attitude—to what extent he "really believes" that his diagnosis is true—is beside the point here. A Kantian belief, then, which to him is one of the three variants of "holding for true", in our terminology is a judgment one holds as true for the practical purposes of acting on it. Indeed, Kant proceeds to argue that pragmatical beliefs have degrees, "varying in proportion to the interests at stake". This echoes the notion of the strength of a presumption, which determines how much counter-evidence is required for its rebuttal.[7]

3.2. Davidson's "holding true or accepting as true"

Davidson undertakes to sketch a theory of interpretation in terms of a theory of truth. The theory of interpretation is tested, in the last analysis, by its ability to explain human behavior and actions, where the actions are described in terms free from any that belong to the theory of interpretation itself. In other words, an ideal description of the *explanandum* would be in non-intensional terms. With this as his aim, Davidson needs an intermediary level between belief and behavior.

Davidson's theorist may decide to begin by identifying the native's beliefs, or the theorist may decide that it is better to begin by identifying what the native holds true. Davidson thinks that the investigator had better begin with the minimally intensional, intermediary theoretical tool of identifying what the native holds true. However, he expresses himself in a way which lumps together the two notions of holding true and holding as true. Thus, he assigns the linkage role to what he refers to as "the attitude of *holding true* or *accepting as true*, as directed towards sentences".[8]

This is how, in a previous article, Davidson elaborates on what he takes to be the starting point for his theory of interpretation:

A good place to begin is with the attitude of holding a sentence true, of accepting it as true. This is, of course, a belief, but it is a single attitude applicable to all sentences, and so does not ask us to be able to make finely discriminated distinctions among beliefs. It is an attitude an interpreter may plausibly be taken to be able to identify before he can interpret, since he may know that a person intends to express a truth in uttering a sentence without having any idea *what* truth.[9]

Davidson seems to be groping after what we might refer to as a minimal common denominator for the range of belief-related attitudes towards the truth of sentences. His choice of terms is, from our point of view, unfortunate because it lumps together the very notions we wish to keep apart. The point here goes beyond mere semantic hygiene. Indeed, we think that for Davidson's own purposes the attitudes that he invokes of "holding a sentence true", "accepting it as true", and "believing", ought to be kept apart. That is, there are differences among them that make a difference for the theory of inter-pretation itself. For it is possible that, from a behavioristic perspective, Davidson's assumption that it is relatively easy for the investigator to identify what the native holds true does not bear out, in view of the hold-true/hold-as-true distinction. The native may, e.g., behave in such a way that leads the interpreter to take him to believe some-thing and hence to hold that something true, while the native may perhaps only hold that something as true without either believing it or holding it true.

Moreover, the exploration of the two attitudes of holding true and holding as true, as well as of the additional ones (holding true come-what-may and holding fast), does not yield the possibility of a least common denominator among them. There are, as we shall see, intricate relations among them, but no single core from which they all might be imagined to branch off.

Using our terminology, the attitude Davidson seems to need for his theory of inter-pretation is that of holding true. Given our exposition of it, it fits Davidson's idea that an interpreter may take a person to utter a truth (or, may take a sentence to assert a truth) without knowing what truth. The attitude of holding a sentence true, then, while it is not a common denominator to the other belief-related attitudes, may well be the first building block for a theory of interpretation. As for Davidson's grander aim, of linking the theory of interpretation with a general theory of human behavior and action, we suspect that this will not suffice. We suspect that, to the extent that the aim is realizable, it is the attitude of holding as true which might turn out to provide the linkage.

4. Holding as True and Acceptance

The ordinary-language differences between the uses of "believe" and "accept" are not a good enough guide for a proper distinction between these terms. Indeed, in many con-texts it seems that they are used indistinguishably. Similarly, in much of the recent philosophical literature, conditions for the rationality of believing that p and condi-tions for the rationality of accepting p have been treated indistinguishably.[10] Recall also the passage quoted earlier from Davidson, where "accepting a sentence as true" was mentioned in the same breath with "holding a sentence true" and with "a belief".

We shall take it, then, that a distinct and agreed upon role for the notion of acceptance has emerged neither from common use of ordinary language nor from the philosophical literature. Further, we want to propose that the central intuition behind the use of "accept", to the extent that it is being used distinctly, is taken care of by our notion of "holding as true". That is, one accepts a sentence when one decides to proceed or to act as if it were true, regardless of whether or not one believes that it is true.

In his important book *Change in View*, Gilbert Harman illustrates his notion of *full acceptance* with the following example:

Suppose Mark is trying to discover how to get to an address on a street called Prospect Place. Mark's "investigation" consists in asking a passerby if he knows how to get there. If the passerby is sufficiently hesitant, Mark can check the direction by asking others. (Mark may even think it prudent to ask a second person even if the first seemed quite confident.) But once Mark comes fully to accept an answer, Mark's "investigation" is over. Mark will not at that point continue to ask others how to get to Prospect Place. (Harman, *Change in View* (MIT Press, Cambridge, 1986) p. 48)

The point of Mark's "investigation" is not to enrich his body of beliefs. His concern is how to get to his destination: his is a practical, not a theoretical, quest. The problem Mark faces, therefore, is not whether to incorporate permanently the answer he receives from the passerby into his epistemic system. Rather, it is whether or not to follow the instructions he was given. For Mark to 'accept' the passerby's answer is simply to hold the information he was given as true; that is, to proceed as if the instructions are correct and to follow them, unless—or until—he has reason to doubt their truth. This takes care of the possibility Harman raises of the passerby's answer being "sufficiently hesitant". In such a case, Mark may well seek a second opinion, and then hold *it* as true and proceed to act on it. This routine is quite different from the picture conveyed by Harman. Harman's passage suggests that Mark will stand there and search his soul as to whether or not he has attained the state of fully believing the information he has received, so that he may finally declare his investigation over.

Harman introduces the notion of acceptance with the aim of distinguishing between tentative and full acceptance. His primary concern, though, is with criteria for membership in the prestigious club of our corpus of beliefs: how and when do we, or should we, adopt a new belief (and also how and when do we, or should we, discard a useless one). The example he provides, however, seems odd as an illustration for his own notion of full acceptance. At the same time, we take it to be particularly well suited to illustrate the notion of acceptance construed, as we advocate, in terms of holding as true.

Still, one may wonder whether there are any residues of the use of the notion of acceptance, which are not covered by our action-oriented, presumptive notion of holding as true, and which are worth-while preserving. In answer to this we would like to consider two contexts to which the notion of acceptance might be felt to have some sort of natural affinity. These are (i) the context of theories, and (ii) the social-ritual context.

With regard to theories, it is sometimes suggested that it is primarily a theory that one accepts, not individual, isolated sentences. Indeed, alongside such topics as explanation, observation, confirmation, etc., the topic of acceptance of scientific theories has traditionally been one of the major preoccupations of philosophers of science. It seems to us that there might be merit in reserving the notion of acceptance for the domain of theoretical inquiry in general and scientific theories in particular, and the notion of holding as true for the domain of praxis—i.e., as pertaining to sentences that might meaningfully be held as premises in someone's piece of practical deliberation. Though we see merit in this separation, and are prepared to adopt it, we shall not pursue this matter further here.

It is here that we want to consider L. Jonathan Cohen's recent version of the notion of acceptance (see fn. 10), and to compare it with our notion of holding as true. Like us, Cohen discusses acceptance of a sentence, not of a theory. Accepting that p, for him, is a mental act, and it implies "commitment to a policy of premising that p". More precisely,

to accept that p is to have or adopt a policy of deeming, positing, or postulating that p—that is, of going along with that proposition—as a premise in some or all contexts for one's own and others' proofs, argumentations, inferences, deliberations, etc.   (Cohen, 1989, p. 368)

Cohen's acceptance that p, then, like our holding p as true, consists in one's decision to use p as a premise in one's reasoning. But for him the reasoning is not necessarily, or not primarily, practical reasoning. Indeed he specifically says that what a person accepts "may...be reflected in how he or she speaks or behaves, but it need not be" (p.368) One is left with the distinct impression that for him acceptance is oriented primarily towards the speculative or theoretical. For us, as we have emphasized, the very point of introducing the notion of holding as true was to take care of situations where one's action, behavior, or response hinges on the truth of some proposition one may or may not actually believe. In that sense, the fact that what one holds as true is reflected in one's behavior is constitutive to the notion of holding as true.

This difference bears also on the durability of accepting that p as compared with holding p as true. Cohen says that acceptance involves commitment, which must be durable. (He in fact contrasts accepting that p with supposing that p, which he says is "inherently temporary".) To hold as true, in contrast, may be a transitory affair, and its presumptive nature, where not conclusive, allows for rebuttal at any stage.

As for the second context, it is sometimes suggested that, to the extent that the notion of acceptance is used in ordinary language, it has a social-ritual component that the notion of belief lacks. One way this gets spelled out is the idea that people may have to accept something, or somehow ritually to acknowledge it, in virtue of their social role (as civil servants, insurance agents, lawyers, or what have you), regardless of their actual beliefs. This may well be the case.[11] The notion of holding as true, however, is particularly well suited to capture this. Thus, the salesperson or the judge alluded to earlier may be required to accept, i.e., to hold it as true, that the client is right or that the accused is innocent because and in virtue of their roles as salespersons or judges, even if as a matter of fact they happen to believe otherwise or to have no beliefs in the matter. Likewise, the dean of admissions will be required to accept, i.e., to hold it as true, that all men and women are equal, even if he secretly harbors racist or sexist beliefs. This latter case exemplifies the possibility of holding p as true while believing not-p. Our suggestion, then, is that in some cases "acceptance that p" is to be equated with "holding p as true in virtue of one's social role".

Note that it is possible, and perhaps on many occasions natural, that one will come to believe what one has held as true by virtue of the role one has held over a long enough period of time. If you, as a social worker, are required to hold it as true that a child is generally better off with its parents than in a foster home (unless, of course, this is rebutted in some particular case), you may in time come to acquire the belief that this is so. Holding p as true may, even though it by no means must, lead to belief that p. This possibility paves the way for a certain degree of manipulability of beliefs.

5. Voluntary Attitudes

Holding p as true is a matter of decision, hence, it is voluntary. Believing that p is not. This difference is important and merits further exploration. In our body we distinguish between voluntary and involuntary muscles. If you decide to raise your hand or stick out your tongue then, under normal conditions, your hand will go up and your tongue will stick out. You cannot in the same way decide to accelerate your heart beat. Your heart beat will accelerate, e.g., if you start to run, and you may decide to do *that*. That is, while you may not directly control your heart beat, you may indirectly do so. Analogously, while our beliefs are not in general under our direct control, they may be subject to our indirect manipulation. The company one chooses to keep, the university courses one decides to take,[12] and in general the form of life one chooses may lead one to acquire certain beliefs that one may have actually set out to acquire. The distinction between the voluntary and the involuntary, then, is between that which is a direct product of decision and that which is not; the possibility that the latter is an indirect product of decision is left open.

The question of the voluntariness of belief is a long-standing philosophical issue, much discussed, *inter alia,* in the context of religious tolerance. Are heretics to be held responsible, and hence to be condemned, for their heretical beliefs—or, ought the accusation levelled against them focus on their form of life rather than on their beliefs? Our own concern in this matter is different, although it may be seen as the legitimate heir to the problem of heresy. If beliefs are involuntary, in the sense just explained, can a normative exhortation to rationality be based on them? Given that the requirement for rationality consists, in part, in the consistency of one's beliefs and in their appropriate relation to their supporting evidence, how can one be blamed for irrationality if one has no (direct) control over one's beliefs?

The alternative, we suggest, is to construe the normative requirement of rationality in terms of what one holds as true, which is subject to one's exercise of choice, rather than in terms of one's beliefs. After all, what enter as premises in our practical reasoning, and so get to be expressed in our behavior and action, are only those beliefs which we also hold as true. And this is what judgments of rationality or irrationality are ultimately concerned with. To the extent that we go along with the principle that ought implies can, we interpret the injunction 'be rational' as having to do not with our web of beliefs but, rather, with the web of that which we hold as true.

It is useful to remind ourselves, at the same time, that usually what we hold as true coincides with our beliefs. In tying rationality with what we hold as true rather than with what we (happen to) believe, we highlight two aspects of these notions. First, that which we hold as true is a product of decision and therefore is explicit. This need not be the case with beliefs. As such, what we hold as true is suitable and 'ripe' for serving as a premise in practical reasoning. And, second, as we saw, what we hold as true need not coincide with or reflect our beliefs.

Finally, what about holding true: Is it voluntary or involuntary? It seems to us that the answer to this question is mixed. Holding 'p' true, it will be recalled, involves believing of 'p' that it is true without necessarily believing that p, e.g., when not comprehending the content of 'p'. This is akin to taking something on trust, which in turn suggests a combination of involuntaristic and decisional elements. The belief that 'p' is true may up to a point 'grow in' one or 'come over' one, but only up to a certain point. To the extent that the direct and unmediated relationship with the content of 'p', which comes with full comprehension, is missing, holding 'p' true will contain an element of decision.

6. "Holding True Come What May"

In the course of his famous critique of the analytic-synthetic distinction, Quine says the following:

Any statement can be held true come what may, if we make drastic enough adjustments elsewhere in the system.[13]

How are we to construe the statement that every statement (sentence, proposition) "can be held true come what may"? And, what is Quine's notion of "holding true"?

Surely if 'holding true' is equated with 'believing', then to assert that anyone may decide to believe any statement must be wrong. All the more so regarding the idea that anyone may decide to believe any statement not just fleetingly but "come what may", and that one is able—at will—to change and adjust one's other beliefs accordingly. It is Quine himself who says elsewhere[14] that to take belief to be a matter of decision is "to stretch the term 'belief' beyond belief".

Still, it is possible to equate Quine's notion of holding true with believing and yet to interpret the quoted sentence in a way that avoids the difficulty. This interpretation shifts around the scope and the order of the quantifiers and modalities involved.

The following, we said, was plainly false:

For every person A and for every proposition *p*, it is possible for A (i) to believe that *p* is true come what may, and (ii) to introduce the necessary adjustments in A's other beliefs.

Instead, we propose this:

For every proposition *p*, it is possible that there is a person A such that (i) A believes that *p* is true come what may, and (ii) A's other beliefs are adjusted accordingly.

This interpretation gets around the problem of deciding to believe, and is compatible with Quine's program of Epistemology Naturalized. This also squares with the familiar Quinean points that beliefs don't meet the tribunal of evidence one by one, and that it is therefore possible that a person's beliefs are organized in such a way as to keep certain of them immune to revision. Moreover, different people can have different arrangements of beliefs. And it might strike me that a certain belief of mine is immune to revision even though this might seem crazy from your perspective.

However, it is not clear that this interpretation does justice to what Quine had in mind. Also, Quine can be caught using voluntaristic language regarding matters of belief at junctures too crucial for us to feel comfortable with taking this interpretation as the end of the matter. Indeed Quine often sounds as if he flatly contradicts his own avowed program. Consider:

[W]hen a set of beliefs is incompatible together, we have a choice: we can restore consistency by rejecting any one of several beliefs. And it is not always easy to decide which one had better go.[15]

Well, can we really decide which belief to give up? Is it possible to handle our beliefs by decision?

It seems to us that insofar as one's initial organization of one's beliefs is concerned, Quine may perhaps escape the charge of going against his own program. But the voluntaristic language enters as soon as he is concerned with one's *re*-organization of one's beliefs, in face of incompatibility or of recalcitrant evidence. It is with regard to passages like the one just quoted, then, that we suggest that in talking about beliefs Quine may at times have in mind the voluntaristic notion we are here referring to under the label of "holding as true". This may well apply also in the case of the passage quoted at the outset concerning "holding true come what may". That passage will thus be construed as putting forward the strong claim that anyone can decide to hold any statement as true come what may. The 'drastic adjustments' that may be required elsewhere will also affect that which one holds as true rather than one's beliefs.

For Quine an analytic sentence is a sentence which is held true "come what may": observation or experience are incapable of impinging on it. But, since in his view any sentence may be held true come what may, the proverbial privileged class (whether closed or open[16]) of analytic sentences is a myth. Put differently, but still using Quine's terminology, analytic sentences are supposed to be immune to revision. But since he claims that no sentence is immune to revision, there are no analytic sentences.

Now we have proposed to construe Quine's "holding true" in terms of our "holding as true". Furthermore, we have explicated the notion of "holding as true" in terms of a presumption. We now want to continue down the same route and suggest that "holding as true come what may" is to be taken as a conclusive presumption (in the sense explained above, Section 3). As such, it is immune to rebuttal. That is, to the extent that one is unconditionally committed to holding on to a statement and to letting it be reflected in one's behavior and action, one may as a matter of decision let no fact (or counter-evidence) touch it, however many changes one may consequently have to introduce in one's other commitments. Yet, it is still possible for one to decide to revise this commitment. We are after all talking here of what one chooses to hold on to, whether rebuttably or conclusively. In other words, our conclusive presumptions, or that which we choose to hold as true no matter what, may be irrebuttable but not irrevisable.[17]

7. "Holding Fast"

So far we have considered the belief-related notions of holding p true, holding p as true, and holding p as true come what may. We turn now to consider Wittgenstein's notion of "holding p fast".[18] I supposedly hold fast, for example, that I was born some time in the past, that I have forebears, that the earth existed long before my birth, that I have a body, and that I am never far removed from the surface of the earth. Some of these sentences, it will be recalled, were used by Moore in his defense of common sense against the skeptic. For Moore they exemplify truisms which we all know with certainty. For Wittgenstein they exemplify that which stands fast for us, and this is a very different story.

Of a sentence that I hold fast, says Wittgenstein, I cannot say that it is true (and certainly not that it is false). Also, I cannot say that I know it, nor that I believe it, nor yet that I doubt it. Let us spell this out somewhat.

For Wittgenstein, in order for a sentence to be true, it has to be grounded: "[T]he ground is not *true*, nor yet false" (Wittgenstein, 1969, sec. 205); "it is the inherited background against which I distinguish between true and false" (sec. 94). The sentences we hold fast are those that underlie our notions of truth and falsity (sec. 514).

That which I hold fast has a different status from that which I know. What I know I must have grounds for, but that which stands fast for me (or "is solid" for me) is "as sure a thing for me as any grounds I could give for it" (sees. 111, 112, 116; see also sec. 253). Also, in order for me to know something, I must be able in principle to doubt it. But there can be no doubt about that which stands fast for me: "[R]egarding it as absolutely solid is part of our *method* of doubt and enquiry" (sec. 151). "So far I have no system at all within which this doubt might exist" (sec. 247). Moreover, a propositional attitude of belief with regard to a sentence presupposes the possibility of error. But, for Wittgenstein, "when someone makes a mistake, this can be fitted into what he knows aright" (sec. 74). So, once again, it is not even clear what can count as error with respect to that which I hold fast. Indeed, the negation of the supposedly solid would not count as a mistake but, rather, as "a mental disturbance" (sees. 71, 73). It is precisely because certain sentences stand fast for me that I can be in error about others. "I should like to say: 'If I am wrong about *this*, I have no guarantee that anything I say is true'" (sec. 69).

All of this is saying what it is that we can*not* say of a sentence that we hold fast. To this we might add that a sentence held fast is also not a presupposition (sec. 153), or an axiom. Nor is it a sentence which can be distinguished in form from experience sentences (sees. 87, 98).

What, then, can be said positively about the sentences which we hold fast? To begin with, "[w]hat I hold fast is not *one* proposition but a nest of propositions" (sec. 225). What distinguishes this nest of sentences from other sentences is not any internal property they might have (e.g., logical form, simplicity, self-evidence) but, rather, their relative position with regard to the others, the special use we make of them as "a frame of reference" for the others (sec. 83). Wittgenstein tries out various analogies, images and metaphors in grappling with the need to clarify this notion. Perhaps the most helpful and suggestive one is this:

It might be imagined that some propositions, of the form of empirical propositions, were hardened and functioned as channels for such empirical propositions as were not hardened but fluid.   (sec. 96)

We have here the image of solidity. The sentences which stand fast have "hardened" while the others remain "fluid". Moreover, the hardened ones serve as conduits for the others, thereby enabling their smooth continuous flow. But crucial to this picture is the fact that the solid and the fluid can exchange roles. There is no guarantee that the sentences which are held fast will forever continue to enjoy their privileged status. The quoted passage ends with this sentence: "[It might be imagined) that this relation altered with time, in that fluid propositions hardened, and hard ones became fluid". That is, while the "solid" sentences may be immune to doubt, refutation, or rebuttal, a revision may take place which will depose them of their special status and others will come to acquire it instead. But, as long as a sentence stands fast for me, Wittgenstein says that it is "used as a foundation of research and action" (sec. 87). Again, in a language very close to that of conclusive presumptions, he says: "Doesn't this mean: I shall proceed according to this belief unconditionally, and not let anything confuse me?" (sec. 251).

The most distilled sense, perhaps, of the function and use of a sentence that I hold fast is in analogy to the function and use of an instrument. Wittgenstein compares it to a towel. "It is just like directly taking hold of something, as I take hold of my towel without having doubts" (sec. 510). What is involved here is not epistemic certainty but practical sureness. Yet it seems that Wittgenstein steers clear of voluntaristic language when he speaks of the possibility of revision. It is not as if we choose that which stands fast for us, and we do not go about changing it at will (see sec. 173). It might take "something *really unheard-of*" to happen (sec. 513), something that "threw me entirely off the rails" (sec. 517), for a revision to occur in the sentences that constitute my frame of reference.

Having said all that, we are left with the distinct impression that Wittgenstein gives us more indications as to what the held-fast sentences are not than as to what they are. Be that as it may, there is enough here to convince us that the notion of holding fast cannot be assimilated into any of the other belief-related notions we have discussed here. (This is where we might recall the 'but not' technique and the contrastive sentences it generates.) At the same time, though, it seems to share some characteristics with each of them, thereby, if you will, linking them through resemblances into a family.

The shared characteristics that have emerged are these. While holding fast, strictly speaking, is not belief *simpliciter*, the sentences which we hold fast nonetheless function as some sort of pivotal beliefs, or singularity points, which help determine the positions of all the other points in the constellation of our beliefs. That which we hold fast we also hold true in the sense that it is taken on trust. As children, Wittgenstein tells us, we have to take these sentences on trust from our elders, or there would be no learning (e.g., secs. 143, 144, 159–62). And in addition to that, the sentences we hold fast function, as we saw, in a way quite similar to that in which the sentences we hold as true function. More precisely, they play a role in our life much like the role played by our conclusive presumptions, or that which we hold true "come what may", in that they afford sureness of action.

Notes

1. This is reminiscent of Moore's paradox. Indeed, it is possible to derive a version of Moore's pardox here. The steps are the following.

   You start by asserting C (for carotenoids):

   C: "Carotenoids are Isoprenoid polienes" is true, and it is not the case that I believe that carotenoids are isoprenoid polienes.

   For the first half of C we have a well-known equivalence, an instantiation of Convention T:

   T: "Carotenoids are isoprenoid polienes" is true if carotenoids are isoprenoid polienes.

   After substitution you get Moore's paradox:

   M: Carotenoids are isoprenoid polienes and it is not the case that I believe that carotenoids are isoprenoid polienes.

2. "Phonetic Christians" is an expression we have heard from Michael Kubara.

3. Here is a case in point. In Genesis (4: 26) it is said that in the days of Enosh (Adam's and Eve's first grandson) "they began (*huḥal*) to call on the name of the Lord". Taken literally this is problematic because it conflicts with the fact that earlier in the chapter, and in reference to an earlier time, the name of the Lord is already invoked. The imaginative

solution of the Sages to this problem calls for interpreting the word *huḥal* as related to the word *ḥilul*—desecration or debasement—and not, as it is usually and naturally understood, to the word *hatḥala* which means beginning. On this interpretation, then, the sentence says that the generation of Enosh was the first to practice idolatry. (See Nehama Leibowitz: 1976, *Studies in Genesis* (3rd revised edn., Publishing Department of the Jewish Agency, Jerusalem: Alpha Press), p. 97.)

4. Austin, J. L.: 1961, 'A Plea for Excuses', in his *Philosophical Papers,* Oxford University Press, Oxford, p. 200.

5. Ullman–Margalit, Edna: 1983, 'on Presumption', *Journal of Philosophy* **LXXX**(3), 143–63. The discussion in the text necessarily touches only on a few of the points in the explication of presumption offered in this article.

6. Immanuel Kant, *Critique of Pure Reason,* A 824/B 852.

7. It is interesting to note that in this section Kant anticipates the ideas, underlying modern theories of subjective probability, that the readiness to bet may serve as a measuring instrument for degrees of belief:

   Sometimes it turns out that [someone] has a conviction which can be estimated at a value of one ducat, but not of ten. For he is only willing to venture one ducat, but when it is a question of ten he becomes aware, as he had not previously been, that it may very well be that he is in error (Kant, *Critique of Pure Reason,* A 824–25/B 852–53).

8. Davidson, Donald: 'Thought and Talk', in his *Inquiries into Truth and Interpretation* (Oxford: Clarendon Press, [1975]/1984), p. 161.

9. Davidson, Donald: 'Radical Interpretation', in his *Inquiries into Truth and Interpretation* (Oxford Clarendon Press, [1973]/1984), p. 135.

10. See Cohen, L. Jonathan: 'Belief and Acceptance', 1989, *Mind* XCVIII(391), 367–89, notes 1 and 2 for some useful references.

11. See Cohen, G. A.: 'Beliefs and Roles', in Jonathan Glover (ed.), *The Philosophy of Mind* (Oxford: Oxford University Press, [1966]/1976), pp. 53–66.

12. For a detailed story of a fundamentalist who set out to become a believer in evolution by deciding to study biology at Harvard, see Cook, J. Thomas: 'Deciding to Believe Without Self-Deception', 1987, *Journal of Philosophy* **84**, 441–6.

13. Quine, Willard van Orman, 'Two Dogmas of Empiricism', in his *From a Logical Point of View* (Cambridge Harvard University Press, [1953]/1980) , p. 43.

14. Quine, Willard Van Orman, *Quiddities* (Cambridge: Harvard University Press, 1987), p. 19.

15. Quine, Willard Van Orman and J. S. Ullian, *The Web of Belief* (New York: Random House, 1970), p. 8.

16. For the 'open list' argument and its use in defending the analytic/synthetic distinction, see Grice, H. P. and P. F. Strawson: 'In Defence of a Dogma', reprinted in (e.g.) L. W. Sumner and John Wood (eds.), *Necessary Truth* (Random House, New York [1956]/1969), esp. p. 143.

17. For more on the question to what extent the notion of conclusive presumption rescues that of analytic statements, see Ullmann-Margalit, Edna and Avishai Margalit: 'Analyticity by Way of Presumption', 1982, *Canadian Journal of Philosophy* **XII**(3), 435–52.

18. All subsequent references are to Wittgenstein, Ludwig, *On Certainty,* ed. by G. E. M. Anscombe and G. H. von Wright (Basil Blackwell, Oxford, 1969).

PART II
Social Order

7

Revision of Norms

Norm Change Versus Norm Revision

Norms, as social institutions, have careers. They emerge, endure, pass away. While they endure, they may change or be revised. Let us agree to say that a norm changes when it evolves by itself, spontaneously, over time and possibly over populations. The norm excluding husbands from the delivery room has changed so as to admit them, even to encourage their presence there. The norm for women of switching from maiden name to husband's last name upon marriage has changed in this country (not so in mine) over the past two decades. Norm revision, on the other hand, relates to situations where an existing norm is meant to be changed: where the change is instituted intentionally by some social agency.

In order for the following to go through I shall need to rely on some notion of what a norm is. I shall rely on the working definition according to which a norm is a regularity such that people generally conform with it, and, moreover, they generally approve of conformity to it and disapprove of deviance from it. This rough account is meant to encompass the wide spectrum of social norms, stretching from the diffuse, informal, non-institutional norms at one end to the institutional and legal ones at the other. (The bulk of the discussion below may in fact be weighted toward the latter.)

Given this account, it is clear that there are various ways for a norm to alter: alteration is here meant to be neutral as between change and revision. The behavior-regularity itself may alter, as may the patterns of conformity, approval, and disapproval associated with it. And in any case there is the question whether, after the alteration, we still have a norm. When we do, we may talk of the norm having been changed or revised. When we do not, we may talk of the "fall" of the norm and treat it as a case of a norm ceasing to exist. We clearly bump here into the more general question of the identity of norms and the criteria of individuation associated with them. But I shall not here be able to take up this question any further.

Let me allude briefly to two of the norm patterns discussed in *The Emergence of Norms*,[1] in order to relate them to the notions of norm change versus norm revision. Take coordination norms first. Recall that for a coordination norm to count as a coordination norm there must be at least one alternative norm (equilibrium point) which

---

[1] Edna Ullmann-Margalit, *The Emergence of Norms* (Oxford: Oxford University Press, 1977).

could have served more or less equally well as a solution to the pertinent societal coordination problem. Now the point to be made here is that, given its underlying structure—involving, as it does, systems of mutual expectations—a coordination norm is not likely to change by itself into its alternative. (And, when it does, the mechanism by which this happens calls for special explanation.) It usually takes a legislated revision to achieve that. Russell Hardin says, "Coordination rules, especially if they are not ideal, are a response to the difficulty or cost of re-coordinating on a new rule."[2] I am adding that re-coordination generally does not come about through an evolutionary process. As an example, think of the switch of driving lanes from left to right, achieved in Sweden and in many of the former British colonies and yet to be achieved, perhaps, in Great Britain itself.

With regard to PD (for Prisoner's Dilemma) norms, a norm change is entirely possible. The change involved, however, is tantamount to deterioration. Any PD norm, which represents a solution to an underlying Prisoner's-Dilemma-type problem, faces the danger of individual defection. When this happens on a massive-enough scale, the norm disintegrates. The resulting state is nonoptimal but stable: and it may, or may not, also be a norm. For example, a tax-paying society may, for a variety of reasons, evolve into a society where tax evasion is not just the regularity but is in fact the norm. Similarly, norms upholding an honor system within a given student body may deteriorate into a situation where cheating becomes the new norm. When this happens, these are cases of norm change.

Note that, in any PD-structured situation, a boot-strapping move, from the nonoptimal yet stable state to the unstable yet optimal state, is much less likely to come about spontaneously. Here a premeditated, legislated, and also enforced revision will facilitate such a move.

My concern in this article is with norm revision, not with norm change.

Presumptive Versus Conclusive Norms

I shall not here attempt to chart the terrain of norm revision in general. Instead, I propose to concentrate on certain types of revision of a certain class of norms. I shall refer to the chosen class of norms as *presumptive norms*. Let me try to delineate this class.

Suppose we begin with a general norm schema of the form "A iff *p*." That is, do *A* if *p* is the case, do not-*A* (or: refrain from doing *A*; or: do something else *B*) if *p* is not the case. For example, the organs of a deceased person are to be used for life-saving transplantation if, and only if, this accords with the wish of that person (or with the wish of their immediate family).

Not all norms lend themselves to be captured by this schema, but a good many do. This formula gives guidance for behavior in the two types of clear cases, when *p* is the case and when *p* is not the case. What, however, of the gray intermediary zone, when it

---

[2] Russell Hardin, *Morality within the Limits of Reason* (Chicago: University of Chicago Press, 1988), p. 18.

is not known whether p or not-p is the case? The question relates to the applicability of norms under uncertainty. In terms of the above example, what is to be done when an accident victim is brought to the hospital whose condition is terminal but whose heart, say, could save another life—and no indication as to his or her (or the family's) wishes concerning such transplantation is readily available?

The norm as given (i.e., "A iff p") is silent about the uncertainty zone. It provides no guidance for behavior with regard to cases falling within this zone. It throws decision making in these cases back onto some mechanism of direct deliberation on a case-by-case basis. In an important sense, then, in the presence of uncertainty such norms must be incomplete: they allow for gaps in their application.

One way of filling these gaps and rendering the norms complete is the following. The norm is supplemented by a presumptive rule according to which in cases of uncertainty as to whether or not p obtains, p (say) is determined to be the case. The presumptive rule thus in effect assimilates the gray either to the white or to the black. Gaps are construed as either affirmation (that p) or denial (that not-p), thereby assuring continuity in the application of the norm. To go back to our example, there are two possible presumptive rules concerning the organ-transplantation situation: one would determine the unknown wishes of the deceased to be permissive, the other prohibitive. The determination in either case, being presumptive, is open to rebuttal.

When a norm is thus supplemented by a presumptive rule it is useful to think of it as being recast into a new schema, which takes one or the other of the following two formulas.

1. A, unless not-p.
    That is, generally do A, but refrain from doing A when it is ascertained that p is not the case.

2. not-A, unless p.
    That is, generally refrain from doing A, but do A when it is ascertained that p is the case.

Formula 1 embodies a presumption in favor of A; formula 2, a presumption against A. The first places a burden of proof on somebody to show that in a given instance p does not obtain, in order to prevent the norm of doing A from applying in that particular instance. The second places the opposite burden—to show that p obtains, in order to prevent the application of the norm of refraining from A.

Norms which are supplemented by a presumptive rule facilitating their applicability under uncertainty will be referred to as presumptive norms. The complementary class will be referred to as conclusive norms. Conclusive norms, then, either admit of no uncertainty zone, or else they are silent about it.

In the legal theory of evidence the notion of presumption of law plays an important role. The presumption of law is propositional: it is a presumption that such-and-such is the case. For example, there is a presumption that a person who, without reasonable explanation, has not been heard from for at least seven years is dead. I have elsewhere analyzed at some length the notion of propositional presumptions and offered to import it from legal theory into the realm of practical reasoning.[3] A central thesis there was that presumptions operate as corrective devices which regulate in advance the direction of error, where errors are believed to be inevitable. A presumption, on this view, reflects a social decision as to which sort of error is least acceptable on grounds of moral values and social attitudes and goals. Thus, in connection with the presumption of innocence, Jeremy Bentham says that "in doubtful cases [the judge should] consider the error which acquits as more justifiable, or less injurious to the good of society, than the error which condemns."[4]

Going back to presumptive norms, we note that they too operate as regulative devices. The presumptive rule, which attaches itself to the norm in order to deal with uncertainty, functions as a default procedure. It gives a specific direction as to how to apply the norm in the run-of-the-mill cases of uncertainty. There is reason to change direction only when the burden of proof required for such change has been discharged by some relevant agent. And since the presumptive rule takes one of two possible alternative forms, the choice between the pair of contrary presumptions must be based, among other things, on considerations of values, goals, and attitudes.

A comment is in order about the nature of uncertainty involved. The uncertainty pertaining to presumptive norms is factual: it is uncertainty as to whether or not p obtains. This is the case, for example, when the wishes of the deceased regarding the use of their organs do not exist or are unknown. There is another sort of uncertainty, however, which is due to vagueness rather than to lack of facts. For example, consider the norms stipulating that junior faculty members will be offered tenure if and only if they have succeeded in their job, or that people will receive welfare benefits if and only if they are needy. The uncertainty involved here may relate to the questions what counts as success, or when is a person considered needy. Proper criteria need to be established so as to eliminate the vagueness involved and to allow the application of the respective norms to concrete instances. But even when the uncertainty of vagueness has been eliminated, these norms may still face factual uncertainty ("Has this person really succeeded?" "Is that person truly needy?"). It is if and when the factual uncertainty is eliminated by supplementing the norms with appropriate presumptive rules that those norms become presumptive. In the tenure case, for example, the two contrary presumptive rules are: to treat all untenured faculty as hiring mistakes unless they prove themselves worthy of holding on to their jobs, or else to treat them as fully entitled to keep their jobs unless they are shown to have failed to meet the required standards.[5]

    [3] Edna Ullmann-Margalit, "On Presumption," *Journal of Philosophy* 80 (1983): 143–63.
    [4] Jeremy Bentham, *Treatise on Judicial Evidence* (London: J. W. Paget, 1825), pp. 197–8.
    [5] For more on this, see Margaret Atherton, Sidney Morgenbesser, and Robert Schwartz, "On Tenure," *Philosophical Forum* 10 (1978–79): 341–52; Ullmann-Margalit, "On Presumption."

Patterns of Presumptive Norm Revision

1. From Conclusive to Presumptive Norms—or Vice Versa

In principle, a conclusive norm may be revised into a presumptive norm. The reasons for the revision may vary and need not detain us here. (For example, the norm may be perceived as inefficiently or unfairly crude; the direct deliberation required in the uncertainty cases, regarding which the norm is silent, may become too costly or be judged as unacceptably arbitrary; etc.) In general, the revision of a norm from conclusive to presumptive has the aura of a move toward relaxing the norm.

Consider the following conclusive norm concerning artificial insemination: a woman who applies for artificial insemination is eligible for the treatment if and only if she is married. This norm categorically excludes single (or divorced, or widowed) women and faces virtually no uncertainty zone. Consider now this revised version of the norm: a woman may be artificially inseminated if and only if she can provide for the child an environment which is economically and emotionally secure. This norm is still conclusive. However, while it does not exclude single women from the treatment, its application faces considerable uncertainty—both of vagueness (what is to count as an "emotionally secure environment"?) and factual (is this woman really capable of providing materially and emotionally for the child?).

In some instances where a revision of the original norm along such lines has been considered, the drift seems to be to make the revised norm presumptive. The favored presumption remains that of insemination within wedlock. Indeed the uncertainty-of-vagueness tends to be (partially) settled by a presumptive rule to the effect that married women can provide for their child emotionally, unless shown otherwise. What all this amounts to is that a married woman with some decent financial resources will generally be considered eligible for the treatment, while a single woman has a significant burden of proof placed upon her. But still, a revision has been effected from a conclusive to a presumptive norm.

In principle, too, a revision may be effected by turning a presumptive norm into a nonpresumptive one. The general flavor of this sort of revision, it seems, is that of a redress of some past discrimination, or preferential treatment. Consider the broad outline of the case of child custody. In Roman law, as well as in Jewish (rabbinic) and Moslem law, there is an entrenched presumption in favor of paternal custody. (The father is a "natural guardian" in Talmudic law, the mother is not.) This holds in particular with respect to boys and is subject to variation with respect to girls. At the same time, confusingly, there exists in most legal systems a so-called tender-year presumption favoring maternal custody in the case of children under the age of six. Contemporary divorce law, however, tends to make much use of the option of joint custody, and in general subjects the child custody issue to the single (conclusive) consideration of the best interest of the child, thereby freeing it from all previously entrenched presumptions.

To be sure, in their deliberations as to what constitutes the best interest of a particular child, members of the courts, or the social workers who present them with their recommendations, may be influenced, consciously or not, by, say, a presumption in favor of maternal custody. But this properly belongs in the province of prejudice, not of presumptive norms.

2. Presumption Reversal

A norm embodying a presumption against a certain practice may be revised by reversing the presumption, so that the revised norm will embody a presumption in favor of the practice. In terms of our color metaphor, this is the case where the gray zone, previously assimilated to the black, following the revision is now assimilated to the white. A paradigmatic case in point concerns the presumption of innocence in criminal law: in early times the law appears to have presumed guilt, not innocence. (Note that the imaginary "original" conclusive norm here must have been roughly of the form: punish if guilty, acquit if innocent. This norm obviously allows for a huge gray zone of factual uncertainty. Silence, or indecision, concerning this gray area is of course intolerable; hence the need for a supplementary presumptive rule—either of the two possible ones.)

Or consider the case, mentioned at the outset, of organ transplantation. A new French law stipulates that the organs of a deceased person may be used for life-saving transplantation purposes, unless specific instructions to the contrary were given by him or her prior to death (or unless the immediate family registers an objection). This law is based on what is referred to as presumed consent; it embodies a presumption in favor of the use of organs of a deceased person. This constitutes a reversal of the norm, still in force in most countries, that embodies a presumption against such use of organs unless explicit permission has been adequately provided for. Thus in England physicians are required to presume that persons not carrying donor cards object to the donation of their organs.

In the United States the presumption against use of organs unless explicitly authorized by the person concerned has not been reversed. However, a recent federal law (October 1987) devises a system designed to encourage people to become potential donors. A mechanism is in place that makes it possible for people to register their consent while filing their income-tax returns and ensures that hospitals and transplantation units are provided with updated lists of all such potential donors.

Also, consider the norms governing smoking in public places. It is still the case in many countries in the world, perhaps in most, that smoking in public places is presumed permitted unless otherwise indicated. But there are now several states in the United States, and many institutions, where the situation has been reversed, whether formally or informally. Smoking in what is considered public space is presumed forbidden, unless explicitly designated as smoking areas (or when explicit permission is given).

3. A Special Case—Affirmative Action

The concept of affirmative action has in recent years been applied to (and also tested in court in connection with) such domains as admissions procedures in universities and professional schools, training programs for industry, hiring practices, government contracting policies, and more. Supporters of the notion see it as calling for justified preferential treatment of certain groups; its opponents see it as calling for odious reverse discrimination against certain groups. Regardless of whether one is for or against it, however, and regardless of the method chosen for its application (e.g., quotas), affirmative action seems to incorporate presumption. Also, it seems to be essentially about revising past policies, practices, and norms which are judged to have been discriminatory. So that what we have here, writ large, is a sphere which involves presumptive norm revision of some sort.

To be sure, some argue that the revised, presumptive norms, adopted in the spirit of affirmative action, ought from the start to be conceived of as transitional. The argument is that in a just society there will be no reason for preferential treatment for any group—women, blacks, or ethnic minorities. In a just society norms governing procedures of hiring, admissions, etc., which embody presumptions either in favor of or against a particular gender, race, or ethnic group, cannot be defended. When all past discrimination has been put right, the pertinent norms in a just society, according to this vision, ought to be conclusive: they ought to be such that in all matters of selective competition each person will be considered and judged on his or her merit and as an individual rather than as a member of some group.

In discussing the famous case of Allan Bakke versus the Davis medical school, Ronald Dworkin questions with some skepticism the meaning of the right to be judged "as an individual" rather than as a member of some group (in this case, whites) that is being judged collectively.[6] The point he makes is that "any admissions procedure must rely on generalizations about groups that are justified only statistically." Two such generalizations at Davis, for example, concern a certain minimum gradepoint average and a certain maximum age (thirty): applicants whose averages fall below the former or whose age is above the latter are rejected out of hand—even though among them there might well be some who have personal qualities (of "dedication or sympathy") that would make them better doctors than some of the applicants within the pool. Indeed, Dworkin goes as far as saying that to the extent that one claims that the admissions procedure at Davis incorporated a presumption against whites, one would have to see it as incorporating presumptions against persons whose grade averages are below the cutoff or who are older than thirty. "If the latter presumptions do not deny the alleged right of individuals to be judged as individuals in an admissions procedure, then neither can the former."

[6] Ronald Dworkin, *A Matter of Principle* (Cambridge, Mass.: Harvard University Press, 1985), pp. 298–300.

We may still inquire into the nature of the norms governing selection procedures (in hiring, admissions, etc.) prior to the introduction of affirmative action. Are we dealing here with a revision category of type 1, that is, a switch from conclusive to presumptive norms, or with a revision category of type 2, that is, a switch involving presumption reversal?

There are certainly cases where the new, affirmative-action related norms replace older ones which explicitly excluded certain groups—women, blacks, Jews, or what have you. The interesting cases, however, are those in which the older norms did not involve explicit exclusion. The point that supporters of affirmative action emphasize is precisely this, that while the older institutional selection policies were ostensibly fair and purported to call for judging each case on its merit, the reality behind them was different. In reality they were often discriminatory because of the deep-rooted prejudices that governed their application. It is this past discrimination in application that affirmative action seeks to redress. In other words, on this view the affirmative-action-related norms exemplify presumption reversal, albeit of a peculiar kind: norms which, because of the prejudices governing their application, have come to be viewed as embodying implicit presumptions against certain (ethnic, etc.) groups are replaced—perhaps only temporarily—by norms embodying explicit presumptions in favor of those same groups.

It may be added here that the opponents of affirmative action in principle employ one of the following two strategies open to them. One is to deny the discriminatory nature of the selection policies under attack (in which case they adduce genetic or psychological evidence to account for the troublesome statistics concerning, say, the admission ratio of whites to blacks in medical schools). The other strategy is to argue that past discrimination cannot be remedied by reverse discrimination. The remedy will come, on this view, only from strict adherence to nonpresumptive (and, to use the currently fashionable expression, "colorblind") policies and norms.

Presumptive Norm Revision and Normative Reform

Let me broaden the horizon somewhat by considering two traditional attitudes toward norm revision. They may conveniently, and unsurprisingly, be referred to as the "conservative" attitude and the "enlightenment" attitude. The former incorporates an overarching presumption against norm revision, the latter—an overarching presumption in favor of norm revision.[7]

The conservative outlook rejects norms revision in the name of the self-regulating ecology of human social life and of the inherent imperfection of human knowledge. Social institutions in general, and norms governing social behavior in particular, are supposed to emerge from an evolutionary process. "Good" social norms are supposed

---

[7] For this point I am indebted to Moshe Halbertal and Avishai Margalit, *On Idolatry* (Naomi Goldblum, trans., Cambridge, MA: Harvard University Press, 1998).

to win out in an ongoing process of evolutionary competition. Existing forms and norms of social life are not to be tampered with, for fear of upsetting a precious and imperfectly understood equilibrium, conceived on an ecological model. Reason cannot comprehend the complexity of social reality and hence cannot improve on experience.

A prominent representative of this outlook is F. A. Hayek.[8] In the epilogue to his 1979 volume 3 of *Law, Legislation and Liberty*, he says that "the rules which we learn to observe are the result of cultural evolution.... We cannot redesign but only further evolve what we do not fully comprehend."[9] In "Our Moral Heritage," a lecture delivered in Washington, D.C., in 1982, Hayek says that "our morals are not the result of man's supreme intelligence discovering that they were better, but were the result of a process of cultural selection.... The social order depends on a system of views and opinions which we imbibe, inherit, and learn from a tradition that we cannot modify."[10] He is also fond of quoting the phrase that "planning is the replacement of accident by error."

It is perhaps not idle to point out that, in spite of the sweeping nature of his pronouncements, Hayek is not necessarily defending a strong thesis here. The strong thesis would claim that each and every one of our social institutions, rules, and norms is a winner in the competitive game of cultural evolution. And, further, as a survivor, it must be functional and optimal. His views reflect, I think, a weaker thesis. The weak thesis is holistic. It would claim that it is the entire fabric of our prevailing social institutions, rules, and norms which evolved from cultural selection. And so it is the system as a whole which ought to be taken as functional and optimal.[11] Therefore, much as our reason may on occasion rebel against this or that element of the system, Hayek urges us not to tamper with any.

The enlightenment attitude espouses norm revision in the name of reason and progress and, in general, in the name of the well-ordered society. The enlightenment thinkers saw tradition as saturated with superstition and prejudice. Norms emanating from the past are therefore initially suspect. It is necessary, they held, regularly to scrutinize the functions and dysfunctions of social, legal, and moral institutions; it is possible, they believed, to revise and improve upon them in the light of reason.

---

[8] I say this *pace* F. A. Hayek's own famous *Postscript* to his *Constitution of Liberty* (London: Routledge & Kegan Paul, 1960), entitled "Why I Am Not a Conservative." The question of whether Hayek should truly be considered a liberal (even a libertarian, according to some) or a conservative is a matter of some debate. It is taken up by John Grey, in "F. A. von Hayek" (in *Conservative Thinkers*, ed. Roger Scruton [London: Claridge, 1988], pp. 249–60), who decides in favor of considering him a ("modern") conservative. Be that as it may, regarding his attitude toward norm revision, Hayek certainly represents the conservative outlook.

[9] F. A. Hayek, *Law, Legislation and Liberty* (London: Routledge & Kegan Paul, 1979), vol. 3, p. 167.

[10] F. A. Hayek, *Our Moral Heritage*, Heritage Lecture 24 (Washington, D.C.: Heritage Foundation, 1983).

[11] An analogy may be drawn between this holistic thesis and the Augustinian doctrine of evil. This doctrine is one of several theodicies, which attempt to reconcile the unlimited goodness of an all-powerful God with the reality of evil. According to Augustine's doctrine, what appears to be evil when seen in isolation or in a too limited context is a necessary element in a universe which, when seen as a totality, is wholly good, "to thee there is no such thing as evil, and even in thy whole creation, taken as a whole, there is not" (*Confessions*, 7.13).

What are the pressures for norm revision? How are proposals for norm revision justified? There are in general two domains of considerations that serve to motivate or to justify norm alteration ('alteration' here, as before, is neutral between change and revision; it is also noncommittal as to whether, after the alteration, we still have a norm). The first has to do with the efficiency, or optimality, of social practices and institutions. When a social institution or norm is perceived to be less rational than some feasible alternative, pressures for alteration may be expected to develop. Where no satisfactory mechanism for spontaneous change in the desired direction can be relied upon, a revision may be proposed. Here also belong considerations that arise from increase in scientific knowledge and from technological developments. Think, for example, of the areas of organ transplantation, euthanasia, artificial insemination, genetic engineering, etc.—areas paradigmatically rife with potential for norm alteration. The second domain is that of evolving social attitudes and values. Practices and institutions may begin to be perceived as unfair, or as obsolete or out of step with emergent changes in forms of life or with changing attitudes toward such forms of life. Changing attitudes toward, say, the place of women in the work force, employment beyond the age of sixty-five, single-parent or homosexual families, etc., may well bring about norm change or motivate proposals for norm revision.

If we think of norms as established within particular game forms, we may recast the above considerations and be more concrete as to some of the possibilities that account for the pressures for norm alteration. First, with the passage of time the "players" may come to be in possession of new information that comes to light. Second, the set of strategies open to them may alter because, for example, of changing technology. And third, the preferences of the participants may alter over time (as indeed may the participants themselves). The first two possibilities correspond to the domain of rationality, the third to the domain of value.

In response to such pressures norms may die out; they may or may not alter. If the required flexibility and appropriate dynamics exist, they may change evolutionarily. But it is also possible for some agent(s) or agency that has a measure of control over the situation (the "game") to realize that such pressures have developed, that is, to notice the relevant changes in information, beliefs, strategies, technologies, or preferences and to initiate norm revision.

In conclusion, it appears that two levels have emerged on which an "interim position" on normative reform may be discerned. In considering the first, recall the distinction introduced at the outset between norm change (evolutionary, spontaneous) and norm revision (initiated). This distinction, I suggest, is less dichotomous than it may at first appear. Situations exist in which a gradual and "evolutionary" process of change in societal attitudes and values eventually gets the official cachet on the level, mostly, of institutional policy revision. Norm revision in these situations, while explicit and introduced, reflects change rather than imposes it. In this sense, then, normative reform may occupy an interim position between norm revision and norm change.

Second, the reform itself may take a moderate rather than a radical mode. On the explication I propose for this notion, moderate reform of norms takes place when it is restricted to the patterns of presumptive norm revision which affect only the uncertainty zone associated with a norm, while leaving the clear cases intact. When a revision affects the clear cases, it is, on this explication, radical—for example, life-saving transplantation of organs regardless of the wishes of the deceased, artificial insemination on demand. Note however that, as proposed, the distinction between moderate and radical reform of norms is a technical one: it is in particular not meant to prejudge their relative significance.

The "interim position" on normative reform, and in particular the concept of presumptive norm revision, may, I suggest, help explicate the notion of "piecemeal engineering" which, along with its contrasted notion of revolution, plays a central role in social change theories.

8

Invisible-Hand Explanations

1. The Setup

A long-standing tradition makes the first step towards introducing order into the plethora of the phenomena encountered by man by classifying them as either 'natural' or 'artificial'. Obvious and sensible as this classification may appear to be, it is deficient. Characterizing 'natural' phenomena as those that are wholly independent of the human sphere and 'artificial' phenomena as those that involve human agency leaves the deficiency at least partially concealed. It is brought into relief, however, once it is said that the realm of the 'natural' consists of everything that is the result neither of human action nor of human design, while the realm of the 'artificial' of everything that is the result of both: what is clearly seen to be lacking is the at least hypothetical realm of everything that is the result of human action but not of human design.

The notion that this middle realm is real rather than hypothetical is also hardly new[1], as is well attested by its articulation in the writings of the eighteenth-century Scottish school. In order to indicate its weightiness, and for suggestive purposes too, I shall refer to it as the realm of the *social*. I hasten to add, though, that this terminology should not be taken to imply that all social patterns and institutions belong here: some are, of course, the product of human execution of a human plan, and as such belong to the 'artificial' category.[2]

Those social patterns that can be viewed as results of human action but not of human design are candidates for a special kind of explanation which, following Nozick who takes up Adam Smith's cue, will be called *invisible-hand explanations*.

2. Three Paradigmatic Examples

An invisible-hand explanation, very roughly, is one that explains "what looks to be the product of someone's intentional design, as not being brought about by anyone's intentions."[3] Before attempting to fill in this rather meager formulation, let us pin down our imagination and ideas with the help of a few examples.

(i) The continuous creation of money within the banking system: No one needed to have invented the commercial banking system, nor need anyone have intended it to function so as to continuously create money. The usual story that accounts for both begins with the early goldsmiths who used to be paid a small fee for the safekeeping of people's gold and valuables. It proceeds with those intelligent goldsmiths who came to realize, first, that they don't necessarily have to give back to the customer exactly the same piece of gold that he had deposited, and, later, that since not all deposits are withdrawn together and new deposits tend to balance withdrawals, only a small percentage of the cash entrusted to them is needed in the form of vault cash. The rest of the story has to do with these shrewd bankers' investment in securities and loans of most of the money deposited with them, leading to the account of the actual creation of money through the consideration of the overall impact of this newly-developed banking system as a whole rather than of each small establishment taken in isolation.[4]

(ii) Nozick's account of the rise of the so-called ultraminimal state: This account is consciously styled as an invisible-hand explanation.[5] It begins with a Locke-like state of nature and lists the problems concerning the enforcement of individuals' rights therein. It then proceeds in successive stages through the formation of the naïve and inefficient mutual-protection associations, each member of which being liable at any time to be called upon to assist any of the other members in defending or enforcing his rights, then of the more professional private protective agencies, where there is division of labor and exchange and some people are hired to perform protective functions, and finally of the single protective agency that emerges as dominating a geographical area. The rest of the story has to do with supplying arguments as to why this dominant protective agency, which appears to fall short of being a state, actually does constitute an ('ultraminimal') state.

The invisible-hand process involved is compressed by Nozick into the following formulation:

Out of anarchy, pressed by spontaneous groupings, mutual-protection associations, division of labor, market pressures, economies of scale, and rational self-interest there arises something very much resembling a minimal state—.[6]

(iii) The development of media of exchange: In the light of Ludwig von Mises' account[7] neither a decree issued by an enlightened ruler nor explicit agreements fixing a medium of exchange need be posited. The obvious inconveniences attending the direct barter system, and the obvious value of something like gold—which, in addition to being desirable to begin with, is also scarce, divisible, non-perishable, portable, immutable, etc.—are sufficient in order to spell out the details of the invisible-hand account in question.[8]

In all of these cases the phenomenon explained is shown to be the product neither of centralized decisions nor of explicit agreements to bring it about; rather, it is presented as the end result of a certain process that aggregates the separate and 'innocent' actions of numerous and dispersed individuals into an overall pattern which is the very phenomenon we set out to account for.

But what is it that typifies that which qualifies for an invisible-hand explanation? And why does it initially look as if it is the implementation of someone's intentional design? And if it is indeed shown not to have been brought about by anyone's execution of a plan, just how *is* it claimed to be brought about?

3. Eligibility for Invisible-Hand Explanations

Suppose we encounter a crater so regular that we naturally assume it to have been carefully dug by some people according to a detailed plan. Suppose further that this crater is used as a water reservoir for which purpose, we realize, it is ideally located as well as ideally shaped. This fact of course increases our confidence in our original assumption. But now suppose some geologists chance along and convince us that this crater was actually formed as a result of volcanic action, its regular shape being satisfactorily accounted for by the application of an elaborate piece of stratigraphy to that area. Have the geologists provided us with an invisible-hand explanation of the formation of the crater?

Bearing in mind the introductory remarks of Section 1, I propose to answer this question in the negative. The geologists have replaced an explanation of the crater-as-an-artifact with an explanation of the crater-as-a-natural-phenomenon. What I want to restrict the expression 'invisible-hand explanation' to, on the other hand, are social phenomena. Moreover, in the course of explaining these social phenomena it is essential, I suggest, that not only the explanation in terms of human design, which 'naturally' suggests itself, but also the (invisible-hand) explanation that purports to replace it turn on human agency. Once again: it is with the unintended consequences of human action that we are here concerned.

At the same time, however, we would certainly want to legislate that not every unintended consequence of human action qualifies as an invisible-hand explanandum. Just think of the numerous occasions on which our children come to us in tears begging to be excused for the latest calamity they have wrought on the ground that they "didn't mean to". Quite obviously, the accidental by-products of many of our actions, even of several individuals' actions taken together, hardly constitute a promising recruiting ground for invisible-hand explanations. This holds true even if an initially plausible alternative explanation in terms of intentional design is indeed available in all these cases.

Or consider the case of someone who has a flat tyre while driving through the busy morning street. A "hidden-hand" explanation[9] of this mishap would be that someone spread broken glass there with just this purpose in mind. With some additional paraphernalia this could easily turn into a full-blown "conspiracy" explanation[10]—especially if we were to begin the story with seven punctured tyres that same morning rather than one, and if we mentioned the existence of a service station just a hundred yards down that street. But suppose it were established later that the broken glass was there completely 'by accident'—that, say, a delivery boy with a crateful of bottles had innocently tripped there earlier: would this amount to an invisible-hand explanation of the seven flat tyres (or of seven late arrivals to work that morning, for that matter)?

The answer to this question, I submit, cannot be expected to be grounded in theoretical considerations. We face, once again, a practical issue involving a decision:

given that the flat-tyres case is one in which—as required—an explanation in terms of 'human accident' replaces an explanation in terms of human intentional design, do we actually *want* it to count as having been explained invisible-handedly? My inclination is to answer this question with a No. While not attempting to defend this answer as *true*, I shall proceed to argue for it from the consideration of the explanatory import we expect invisible-hand explanations to have.

The way I see it, it is not the fact that an explanation in terms of unintended conse-quences of human action can successfully replace an initially plausible 'hidden-hand', or 'conspiracy', explanation that should be taken to bear the explanatory brunt of invisible-hand explanations. Attention should rather be directed to the fact that it is only when the social pattern or institution to be explained has a *structure* beyond a certain degree of complexity that the invisible-hand explanation of it has a point. Furthermore, I suggest that the explanatory interest of an invisible-hand explanation increases with the extent to which there is a difference in type between the overall pattern to be explained and the individual actions which are supposed to bring it about, as well as with the complexity of the intermediary process. Thus, when the aggregate result of individual actions, albeit unintended, is merely an *amplification* of these separate actions I don't quite see the point in saying that the explanation of the resultant phenomenon as the unintended (accidental) consequence of the individual actions— even when many individuals are involved—constitutes an invisible-hand explanation thereof. Think of the loud noise, in a large and crowded hall, produced unwittingly by everyone's conversing in their normal tone of voice.

To be sure, 'structure', 'difference in type', and 'degree of complexity' are hardly the most precise of expressions; nor can they be expected to be made precise in this con-text. But it seems to me that when conjoined with the paradigmatic as well as with the rejected examples presented so far these terms do indicate the direction in which the explanatory import of invisible-hand explanations lies. They also suggest, what I take to be basically true, that the explanatory import of invisible-hand explanations is a matter of degree.

To recapitulate: An invisible-hand explanation explains a well-structured social pattern or institution. It typically replaces an easily forthcoming and initially plausible explanation according to which the explanandum phenomenon is the product of intentional design with a rival account according to which it is brought about through a process involving the separate actions of many individuals who are supposed to be minding their own business unaware of and a fortiori not intending to produce the ultimate overall outcome.

It seems to me to be quite clear at this point that the onus of the explanation lies on the process, or mechanism, that aggregates the dispersed individual actions into the patterned outcome: it is the degree to which this mechanism is explicit, complex, sophisticated—and, indeed, in a sense unexpected—that determines the success and interest of the invisible-hand explanation in question.

4. Whence the Appearance of Intentional Design?

Before saying more on the invisible-hand process I would like to turn to the question of why it is that the invisible-handedly explained phenomenon 'looks like' the product of someone's intentional design. That is, why is it that an explanation in terms of the execution of a premeditated plan naturally suggests itself in the cases we are considering, and why is it that it has considerable initial plausibility? An answer to this, I surmise, will also bear on the further question of whether the availability and naturalness of such an intentional-design explanation are essential in order for the rival invisible-hand explanation to count as such, or is it merely the case that they usually happen to be concomitant features of such explanations.

By way of addressing these issues, let us put on record the observation that, when called upon to explain human actions and their results, we usually tend to do this in terms of the beliefs, intentions, and goals of a designing agent. All the more so when the phenomenon to be explained is patterned: when it exhibits structure, order, design. Now this tendency is usually successful and hence amply reinforced, since most patterned results of human action really are artifacts produced through intentional design.

Indeed, the manifestation of orderliness and apparent design in the physical universe was taken by a venerable tradition of thinkers to be the result of superhuman action, thereby suggesting—nay, proving—the existence of a superhuman, consummate designer. I am referring of course to the physicotheological tradition that stretches from Plato and Aquinas to Boyle, Ray and Newton, Locke, Clarke, Butler and Paley, and down to J. C. Maxwell. It took the powerful minds—and all the logical arsenal at their disposal—of Hume and Kant, as well as the works of Darwin and Mill, to explode the logic of this Argument from Design, even while acknowledging its deep-rooted prepossessions and its extraordinary psychological grip.

There exists, then, this bias, which we may perhaps term the 'artificer bias', that leads us to postulate a designer whenever we encounter what looks like evidence of orderliness and patterned structure—whether the model be that of the artist creating works of beauty or that of the inventor and manufacturer of elaborate machines. In addition to these, there is yet another model which may be assumed to corroborate the tendency produced by the artificer bias in the cases we are here concerned with. What I have in mind is the salient and invariable connection, within the realm of living organisms, between the manifestation of coordinated activity on the one hand and the existence of a central nervous system on the other.[11] Now, the phenomena to be invisible-handedly explained, where many individuals are involved, each doing his bit in such a way that an overall structured pattern is produced, are certainly likely to look like cases of coordinated activity. Hence the rather natural 'inference' to the existence of a central planning body that governs this dispersed activity and directs it in accordance with its intended scheme.[12]

A further consideration in this connection is that often the explanandum phenomenon performs a valuable *function*. (Thus, currency as a medium of exchange usefully alleviates the intolerable burden of finding the 'double-coincidence of wants' required for direct barter exchanges.) I shall have more to say about functions below. In the meantime I just wish to point out that when the overall pattern produced is not only well-structured but is also functional, then both the picture of the artificer manufacturing machines and the picture of a central command center controlling and coordinating dispersed activity apply. As a result the tendency to 'naturally' postulate an intentional designer in such cases is of course enhanced.[13]

The considerations dwelt upon so far show, I take it, why it is that a phenomenon eligible for an invisible-hand explanation is naturally and readily explained in terms of intentional design. Moreover, from the nature of these considerations it can be seen that the more structured the pattern to be explained is, the more it exhibits orderliness and design—and in certain cases function as well—the more likely it is that an explanation in terms of intentional design will naturally suggest itself and will look considerably plausible. At the same time, however, as has been indicated earlier, the more structured and complex the pattern, the greater the challenge it poses to whoever proposes to explain it invisible-handedly, and the more potentially successful and satisfying the explanation itself. So the naturalness and availability of the intentional-design explanation are not mere contingent concomitant features of an invisible-hand explanation worthy of the name: they are part and parcel of its very nature.

In the preceding discussion I have several times used the expression 'readily available and initially plausible' to characterize the explanation in terms of intentional design which the invisible-hand explanation purports to replace. This use was overly innocent and deserves comment. By way of unpacking it I would like to suggest that this intentional-design explanation acquires its initial plausibility precisely because it is readily available, and furthermore that it is readily available because of the saliency and grip of the two 'pictures'—the machine manufacturer model and the command-center model—discussed above. As to the *probability* of the intentional-design explanation vis-à-vis its invisible-hand rival, this is an issue I should like to come back to below, when discussing the question of the *cogency* of invisible-hand explanations.

5. The Invisible-Hand Process

Let us now pick up the thread left dangling at the end of Section 3 and focus our attention on the invisible-hand process. By 'the invisible-hand process' is meant the aggregate mechanism which takes as 'input' the dispersed actions of the participating individuals and produces as 'output' the overall social pattern. As was claimed earlier, it is this process which bears the explanatory brunt of invisible-hand explanations. When saying more on this it will be useful to keep in mind the three paradigmatic examples offered in Section 2, to which we may now add the classical account, due to Adam Smith, of the equilibrial pricing system that develops within the perfectly competitive market.[14]

As clearly emerges from these examples, the invisible-hand process is typically conveyed by means of a 'story'. Furthermore, this story usually consists of successive stages, the last of which being the pattern whose explanation is sought. As such, the full-fledged description of the invisible-hand process falls under Hempel's category of *genetic explanations* which, as he says, "present the phenomenon under study as a final stage of a developmental sequence, and accordingly account for the phenomenon by describing the successive stages of that sequence."[15]

It is my view that to look for generalizations over these stories, or to seek to unearth 'the logic' of the processes, would be a futile misplacement of the desideratum. The path that does seem to me to be worth pursuing leads in the direction of the *constraints* we assume to be—or want to see—imposed on such stories if they are to form the backbone of good invisible-hand explanations.

The first constraint I shall propose is that which makes invisible-hand explanations attractive to methodological individualists. It stipulates that the description of the initial stage from which the process is supposed to take off is to consist of nothing but the private intentions, beliefs, goals, and actions of the participating individuals, in a specified setup of circumstances. Moreover, it is laid down that these individuals do not have the overall pattern that is ultimately produced in mind, neither on the level of intentions nor even on the level of foresight or awareness.[16] The basic picture underlying invisible-hand explanations, then, is that of a bird's eye view that encompasses numerous individuals, each busily doing his or her own private narrow bit, such that an overall design, unsought as well as unforeseen by them, is seen to emerge. The point, of course, is that the emergence of the overall design is not left mysteriously unaccounted for, nor, specifically, is it attributed to accident or chance: it is the detailed stages of the invisible-hand process which are meant to supply the mechanism that aggregates the dispersed individual actions into the patterned outcome.

This leads me to the second constraint to be imposed on an invisible-hand process for it to count as adequate. Broadly speaking, it has to do with the ordinariness and normalcy of the stages of the process. By this I mean that, given the circumstances specified at the outset, the story by means of which the invisible-hand process is conveyed has got to sound like a description of the ordinary and normal course of events. It cannot hinge on the extraordinary and the freaky, or on strokes of luck or genius—even if these be logically, physically and humanly *possible*. Mere possibility is too weak a constraint on the type of stories we are after; science fiction-like stories would not yield the kind of explanatory import invisible-hand explanations are expected to afford.[17]

It would be well to comment at this point on the element of *surprise* undeniably involved in invisible-hand explanations and partly responsible for the pleasure and satisfaction derived from the best of them. What is surprising—even startling, sometimes—about invisible-hand explanations is, I suggest, their very existence: the fact, that is, that what one would have thought had to be the product of someone's intentional design can be shown to be the unsought and unintended product of dispersed individual activity. But once it is realized that it is indeed feasible to provide such an account, there should be no further surprises within the explanation itself. Indeed, among the marks of the good invisible-hand explanations are, I am arguing, the fluency and naturalness of—the very lack of surprising elements in—the description of the process involved.

6. One More Example: Schelling's Model of Segregation

Let me now consider in some detail one more example which will neatly put in relief most of the characterizing features of invisible-hand explanations discussed so far. I refer to Thomas Schelling's thought-up model of residential segregation.[18] His leading conjecture is that "... the interplay of individual choices, where unorganized segregation is concerned, is a complex system with collective results that bear no close relation to individual intent". He is concerned, then, to design abstract models which will actually show how a pattern of rather extreme segregation can be brought about not as a result of central planning or of communal agreement: rather, they will show how such patterns can be the product of the decisions and actions of individuals who, neither intending nor desiring them, only want, e.g., to reside where their own group achieves bare majority status within their immediate neighborhood.

One such model is roughly the following. We are to imagine a line (of houses in a street, chairs at a counter, or the like) along which whites and blacks are distributed, in equal number and in random order. Each of them is supposed to be satisfied in his or her location if their own color group is not in a minority in their immediate neighborhood. Those who are dissatisfied are supposed to move to the nearest point, in either direction, where the condition for satisfaction is met. Specifically, in order to see how this works, we follow Schelling in imagining a line of seventy randomly distributed individuals (thirty-five of each color) and in stipulating that an 'immediate neighborhood' consists of four neighbors (houses) to the right and four to the left. The first stage, then, can be represented by the following diagram, where the 1's stand for blacks and the 0's for whites, and with a dot marking each dissatisfied individual:

01000110100011001110110110011001100110101001110110000011100010011010110

At this point each dissatisfied individual, starting from the left, is supposed to move to the nearest point where at least half his immediate neighbors are of his own color. (Of course, some of those initially dissatisfied will become satisfied without moving, due to 'desirable' changes in their neighborhood—and vice versa.) So the second stage, which is the result of the first round of moves, is represented by the following:

000000000111101111111110000011000101011101111111110000000000000000111111

(Here there are nine dissatisfied persons, as compared with 26 in the previous stage.)

It turns out—and this is the punch—that the third stage already consists of six stable segregated clusters, with nobody dissatisfied[19]:

0000000001111111111111110000000000011111111111111100000000000000000111111

Sifting out of this model the ingredients which are of concern to us, it is evident, first, that the (segregation) pattern to be explained belongs to the social realm, and that it is well-structured. Also, there is little doubt that an explanation of it in terms of intentional design leading to coordinated action is easily forthcoming, whether it be in terms of the execution of a municipal plan, or in terms of the participants' own agreement. Moving on: the account which purports to replace the premeditated-plan one in no way has complete segregation 'in mind'. Its starting point assumptions, which set the invisible-hand mechanism in motion, have to do with the wants (bare local majority) of the individuals involved[20] and with the stipulation of their actions in pursuit of these wants. The process itself consists of well-defined, temporally ordered stages, the last of them being the explanandum phenomenon, the segregation pattern. Furthermore, the stability of this last stage (in terms of the participants' satisfaction in their location) answers the possible further question of why it is that the process actually stops there rather than go on rolling.

The way this model of Schelling's fits into—and thereby helps highlight—the account of invisible-hand explanations which I have been concerned to offer is, then, very neat. But it cannot be ignored that this neatness is bought at a certain price. The price has to do with the fact that the abstractness and quite striking oversimplification of the model rob the invisible-hand process of some of the required aura of obviousness and naturalness. And yet, it seems to me to be well worth pointing out that although somewhat unrealistic because of the oversimplification, there is nothing weird, outlandish, or abnormal in the assumptions needed in order for the mechanism to be set agoing. This indeed is what in my opinion justifies Schelling's assertion, following his acknowledgment that the model is much too abstract to be thought of as a "motion picture" of what actually takes place in reality, that "it is suggestive of some of the dynamics that could be present in individually motivated segregation."

7. Truth and Cogency of Invisible-Hand Explanations; Their Explanatory and Explicatory Import

An invisible-hand explanation, like any other explanation, is true when its premises are true; in the present case, when as a matter of historical fact the pattern explained has indeed emerged not through premeditated planning but in a way sufficiently similar to that described by the pertinent invisible-hand process. The merits of such true explanations are obvious. Independently of its truth, however, an invisible-hand explanation may be pronounced 'good' on internal standards: that is, when the degree of structure of the pattern to be explained is high, as are the degree of complexity and sophistication of the invisible-hand process and the degree of conformity of the explanation to the various constraints laid down so far. Let us agree to refer to such 'internally good' explanations as *cogent*.

Now invisible-hand explanations that are both cogent and true are too meritorious to give rise to any queries. One can only wish there were more of them. But queries do arise with regard to invisible-hand explanations that are cogent while (factually) false, as well as with regard to those cogent ones whose truth is undetermined (or maybe undeterminable): what, if any, is their worth?

Let me begin with the cogent invisible-hand explanation which is actually known—or eventually proven—to be false. Suppose, for example, that newly found archives in Venice establish it beyond doubt that, with the foundation of the Banco della Piazza di Rialto in the 16th century, Doge Nicolo da Ponte had been sufficiently shrewd and enlightened to recognize that a reserve ratio of a hundred percent was not necessary and, furthermore, that if it were to be less, then the bank could also fulfil the useful function of adding to the money supply in the state; and so he then and there thought out—and put into effect—the whole commercial banking system of Venice, reserve ratio, monetary expansion and all.

What then of our goldsmiths' story? Does the fact that the Doge beat the invisible-hand explanation to it rob the invisible-hand explanation of its explanatory import? I suggest that the answer is No, and that the argument for this answer goes beyond the mere 'feeling' we may have that the account of how something could have arisen without anyone devising it is 'interesting' or 'illuminating' in its own right.

The argument I should like to put forward is that even if the invisible-hand explanation turns out not to be the correct account of how the thing *emerged*, it may still not be devoid of validity with regard to the question of how (and why) it is *maintained*. Not every product of design, especially if we are dealing with a complex social pattern or institution, is successful and lasting. The ascertainment that there is (was) a designing agent, therefore, even when conjoined with the ability to identify him and to spell out his rationale, does not take us very far towards illuminating the nature of its success and stability. The availability, on the other hand, of a cogent invisible-hand story of how the pattern in question could have arisen—given the specific circumstances, some common-sense assumptions concerning the drives of the individuals concerned, and the normal course of events—may, I believe, contribute to our understanding of the inherently self-reinforcing nature of this pattern and hence of its being successful and lasting.

There is however another possibility. The success and durability of the intentionally designed social pattern or institution under study may in some cases be attributable to its performing a useful function. In such cases, then, the story of how it could have arisen without anyone devising it will not only not be the true account of its emergence, but it will also be of secondary importance (at best) as an account of its durability. I shall discuss this possibility below, in the broader setting of the issue of functional-evolutionary explanations.

Moving on now to cogent invisible-hand explanations whose truth is undetermined we note, first, that all that was said above concerning the explanatory import of cogent-yet-false invisible-hand explanations a fortiori holds here too. That is, even if we are unable, on the basis of available (historical) evidence, to select as true one of the two competing emergence hypotheses—the intentionally devised vs. the invisible-handedly evolved, the invisible-hand explanation will not be devoid of explanatory import as far as the continued existence of the pattern in question is concerned.

But here a further, intriguing, question may be posed. When a cogent invisible-hand explanation is given to a phenomenon heretofore 'naturally' supposed—but not proved—to have come about through intentional design, can anything at all be said about the probability that *it* is the correct account? Can the fact that an invisible-hand explanation is hit upon count as evidence in support of its own truth?

I have argued earlier (Section 4) that the more structured the phenomenon to be explained, the more easily forthcoming would an intentional-design explanation of it be, and hence the more plausible will this explanation appear. I would now like to suggest, further, that it will also be judged to be highly *probable* that some intentional-design explanation is the factually correct explanation—so long as the only alternative conceived is that the phenomenon concerned emerged through some unaccounted-for 'accident.' The reason, of course, is that the relative frequency of highly structured social patterns that come about through planning is higher than those whose origins can be attributed to mere accident. However, once an invisible-hand explanation of that same phenomenon comes upon the stage, and supposing it to be a cogent one, the comparison changes: the intentional-design account will no longer be weighted for probability against a non-account of accident, but rather against an account in terms of an explicit and detailed invisible-hand mechanism. My conjecture here is that even though its own probability cannot be determined a priori, the mere availability of a cogent invisible-hand explanation does indeed undercut the probability of the intentional-design account it purports to displace. I am, however, in possession of no further arguments capable of turning this conjecture into a proper claim. And so, unhappily, I leave the matter at that.[21]

The discussion in this section focused so far on the *explanatory* import of invisible-hand explanations. A further issue is that of their *explicatory* import. Regardless of whether or not an invisible-hand explanation is the correct account of how the pattern in question actually emerged, I contend that it is of value as an (at least partial) explication of the associated concept. By this I mean, first of all, that an account of how something could have emerged rather than the tracing down of its actual origins is generally viewed as a rational reconstruction of it, and as such it is taken to perform an explicatory task.[22]

Now with regard to our particular object of concern—cogent invisible-hand explanations—there are, I believe, two further considerations that enhance this explicatory value. First, the sense of 'could' in the expression 'how a pattern could have emerged' is here severely restricted. As was argued earlier, it is required not only that it be logically, physically and humanly possible for the pattern in question to have arisen in the specified way, but that this specified way actually conforms with what can reasonably be expected to be the normal course of events. Second, there is the element of reduction: the pattern in question is shown by the invisible-hand explanation to arise through a process involving the actions of individuals who do not have it in mind. Thus, there should in principle be no reference to the explanandum phenomenon within the spelled out explanation; the linguistic expression which stands for it need neither be used nor mentioned in the course of the explanation.

It seems to me that these two considerations taken together go a long way toward justifying our intuitive feeling that 'good' invisible-hand explanations yield substantial understanding of, and provide considerable insight into, the nature of the social patterns and institutions explained, and that as such they are of remarkable explicatory worth. There is even a sense in which the fact that a cogent invisible-hand explanation proves false is felt to be peculiarly irrelevant: the fact that someone was actually smart and quick enough to have intentionally brought about the pattern in question is felt, I think, to shed but little light on its nature—indeed is felt to be almost accidental.[23]

Since the next section will introduce a different approach to invisible-hand explanations it would be well, I think, to pause at this point and take stock. Put schematically, the distinguishing features of invisible-hand explanations that emerge from the entire discussion so far are the following.

The domain of explanation: The social domain.

The explained phenomena: Well-structured social patterns that result from human action and that look like the product of intentional design.

The nature of the explanation: A species within the genus of genetic explanations, it consists of a description of a special kind of ('invisible-hand') process, and is addressed to the question of the generation of the explained phenomenon.

The mode of explanation: Displacing the intentional-design account that 'naturally suggests itself' with an account that specifies the working of a mechanism that aggregates the dispersed actions of individuals into the overall pattern (the explanandum phenomenon), subject to the assumption that the individuals concerned neither foresee this resultant of their actions nor intend to bring it about.

Idiosyncrasies of the explanation: Its having both explanatory and explicatory import; its lending itself to be characterized as 'cogent' in addition to the usual categories of truth and falsity; its being a matter of degree (varying with the extent to which the explanandum phenomenon is structured and with the complexity of the invisible-hand process); the element of surprise attaching to it.

I prefer to regard all these as distinguishing features of invisible-hand explanations rather than as necessary and/or sufficient conditions—or as adequacy conditions, for that matter—for the following reason. I believe that the class of invisible-hand explanations is not at all sharply delineated (indeed, I take it that the picture drawn so far attests to that). The best and highest that one may aim at, therefore, is to characterize what one takes to be the *core* of this class, namely its undisputedly paradigmatic members. This is, of course, a matter of exercising judgment, and as such there is always the possibility of being persuaded this way or that. Counterexamples and problematic examples may be found and cited. They will affect the picture here drawn, however, only to the extent that they can be shown to relate to its core rather than to its fringes.[24]

8. A Different Approach: The Functional-Evolutionary Mold

There exists an altogether different approach to invisible-hand explanations, one that has to do with the nexus of functional-evolutionary explanations. In a rough and preliminary formulation, it views invisible-hand explanations as the counterpart, within the social domain, of the biological-evolutionary explanations within the domain of living organisms. In order to be able to evaluate this approach, as well as to compare it later to the one offered so far, I propose to take some space to draw the broader picture that I take to be its proper setting.

There is an abundance of recent literature on functional analysis. This is not the proper place to survey it.[25] I shall, however, venture to put forward what, on the basis of this literature, I believe to be a formulation that conveys the gist of the explanatory work a function-ascribing statement is supposed to do. It is the following:

The function of x in a system s is ϕ

means

The system s has capacity/goal ψ and the ϕing of x is an essential element in the explanation of ψ.

(The idea behind this schematic formulation is that the function of something in a system is to be construed as its contribution to the way the system operates, or to the way it attains its goal.)

There are two major areas where function-ascribing statements frequently occur: in the explanation of parts of artifacts, and in the explanation of organs of living organisms. Thus, a typical functional analysis involving artifacts will be that of the gnomon: the item, x, is the gnomon, the system, s, is the sundial, the function, ϕ, of x is the casting of a shadow on the dial beneath, and the capacity/goal, ψ, of s is to show the correct time of day. And, analogously, a typical functional analysis involving organisms will be that of the kidneys: the item, x, is the kidneys, the system, s, is the living body, the function, ϕ, of x is the elimination of wastes from the blood, and the capacity/goal, ψ, of s is its survival and well-being (or something of the sort).

It is worth noting, in passing, that while in the case of artifacts the s and the ψ—the system and its capacity/goal—vary from one analysis to the other, in the case of organisms they are virtually constant: it is usually relative to the living organism as a whole[26] and to its capacity/goal of survival that a function is attributed to some component thereof. This point will be referred to in the sequel.

Now functional analysis, however it may be construed, has as a rule been expected to be closely related to the causal story pertaining to the question of *why x is there*. A good deal of controversy and confusion, however, surround this connection.[27] As I see the matter, in the standard and archetypal cases where functional analysis is used, the interpretative formula offered above is indeed closely related to the causal-genetic story of why the functional item is 'there'. The close relation can be put thus: the functional analysis of an item yields an account of its presence through the mediation of certain specific though implicit assumptions which are—again, in the paradigmatic cases—more or less safely taken for granted.

Let me elaborate. In the case of artifacts, the mediating assumptions have to do with the intentions and beliefs (reasons, if you will) of the designer. Thus, having subjected the gnomon to functional analysis along the lines suggested above, we may arrive at its causal-genetic account by augmenting it with such assumptions as: the designer intended to produce a sundial capable of indicating the correct time of day, on the basis of his past experience and observations he believed that if the gnomon were to be installed in the particular place at the particular angle it would cast a shadow in the desired way, and, finally, that this intention and this belief led him to put it there.

In the case of the organism the mediating assumptions are drawn from the theory of evolution. The causal link here, however, is subtle and apt to be misunderstood. For one thing, the role played by natural selection is *not* analogous to that played by the designer's reasons in the artifacts case: natural selection does not 'lead' to the 'installment' of anything. The ultimate factor causally relevant to the presence of organs is that of random mutation that operates on the organism's genetic plan.[28] Thus, having subjected the kidneys to functional analysis along the lines suggested above, we may arrive at, or maybe only approximate, their causal-genetic account by augmenting it with something like the following: in vertebrates whose genetic plan specifies, due to successive mutations, a kidney-like organ, wastes are efficiently removed. Hence, by the very performance of their function, the kidneys help vertebrates incorporating them to 'succeed', i.e. to survive and be selected for, and thereby they contribute to their own *continued presence* in them.

Having said all this, I would like to emphasize that this relation between the functional analysis of an item and a causal-genetic account of its presence, although often close (in the sense just spelled out), is by no means necessary. A functional analysis of something cannot, in and of itself, be construed as an answer to the question of why this something is 'there'. In many non-standard cases the analysis of the function-ascribing statement provides no clue to, indeed has nothing whatsoever to do with, an account of "how it came to be what it is and where it is."[29]

I have in the foregoing remarks spoken of functional analysis as used in the two major domains of artifacts on the one hand and organic nature on the other. It is time now to consider how it fares in the social domain which, as indicated in the opening remarks (Section 1), can be viewed as in a sense interposed between these two.

The scheme of functional analysis presented above can in my view adequately handle cases in the social domain too.[30] Thus (to take a familiar example), it is pointed out by sociologists and anthropologists that the ostensibly superstitious and idle rain-making ceremonies of the Hopi may nevertheless be taken to fulfil an important function—to be sure, a *latent* one—that of "reinforcing the group identity by providing a periodic occasion on which the scattered members of a group assemble to engage in a common activity".[31] So here the item, x, to be functionally analysed is the rain ceremonials, the (social) system, s, is that of the Hopi, the function, ϕ, attributed to x is the enhancement of group unity and cohesion, and the capacity/goal, ψ, of s is its equilibrial survival in a state of "social health".[32]

Before going on let me allude to a point made earlier and remark that like in the case of parts of living organisms—and unlike the case of parts of artifacts—so also in the case of a social pattern or institution the system, s, and its capacity/goal, ψ, are virtually constant: it is relative to the social unit as a whole and to its capacity/goal of survival that a social institution is functionally analysed.

Now what, if any, is the relation between the functional analysis of a social pattern or institution and a causal-genetic account of its presence? It seems to me that the discussion up to now (and in particular the remark of the preceding paragraph) fairly clearly suggests that the case of functional analysis as applied to the social domain is closer in nature to the cases of its application to organisms than to artifacts. And if so, it is to be expected that the type of connection between this analysis and the causal-genetic account will be affined to that which was shown to obtain within the context of organic nature rather than to that within the context of artifacts. That is to say, the mediating assumptions required for this connection may plausibly be expected to be *evolutionary* in kind.

The intimate relationships—indeed the quite conscious cross-fertilization—between the theories of biological and social evolution hardly require documentation here;[33] besides, their elaboration right now would be beside the point. Coming to the point, my contention is the following: according to 'the other approach' to invisible-hand explanations, as I understand and interpret it, it is the functional analysis of the pertinent social institution, conjoined with the concomitant evolutionary apparatus presumed to supply the missing causal link, that constitute—together—the invisible-hand explanation of that institution.

To wit: when a social pattern or institution is to be explained within the framework of this approach, then first of all its function within the relevant social unit has to be ascertained. That is, an effort is to be made to find out its contribution (if any) to the equilibrial and frictionless survival of the society in question. Once this is successfully established, the phenomenon under study is assumed all but explained, the (implicit) filling in being that by performing its function even its faint beginnings—whatever their origins—are reinforced and selected for; consequently this institution is better capable of helping the social unit incorporating it to 'succeed', and this 'success' of the social unit, in turn, accounts for the institution's own perpetuation in it. Now this process of *selection* is supposed to be a non-man-made one: it is visualized as a large scale evolutionary mechanism that as it were scans the inventory of social patterns and institutions at any given period of time and screens through to the next those of them that are best adapted to their (respective) roles. Whence the designation of 'invisible-hand' to this mode of explanation.

Notable among the authors to whom this conception of invisible-hand explanations may be attributed is F. A. Hayek; he is also the most explicit in what he says about this matter. According to him, social institutions "did develop in a particular way because the coordination of the actions of the parts which they secured proved more effective than the alternative institutions with which they had competed and which they had displaced". And he goes on to state: "The theory of evolution of traditions and habits which made the formation of spontaneous orders possible stands therefore in a close relation to the theory of evolution of the particular kinds of spontaneous orders which we call organisms."[34]

9. The Two Molds of Invisible-Hand Explanation: A Comparison

We started out with a quest for a coherent notion of invisible-hand explanations. It now seems that we may have ended up with more than we had bargained for. For we now seem to be in the possession of two—let us call them *molds*—into which an invisible-hand explanation can apparently be cast: for convenience of reference I propose to label the first the *aggregate* mold and the second the *functional-evolutionary* mold. How are they related?—Do they converge upon, complement, or perhaps compete with each other?

I would like to begin with a delineation of the ground common to both of these two molds of explanation; this should also reveal why they both claim to the title of 'invisible-hand'. It seems to me that the motivation behind these two molds of explanation is one and the same: it is to provide mature explanations to phenomena from the realm of human action. The sense in which these explanations are supposed to be *mature* is that they are purportedly liberated from the grip of the formative—yet in certain respects primitive—picture according to which to explain is to point to a designer (conspirator), or creator. Thus, an explanation which fits either of these molds is supposed to account for a social pattern or institution as a spontaneously formed order, to account for its existence subject to the assumption of no outside intervention by any designing agency.

'To account for something's existence', however, can be construed in various ways. And, indeed, it is precisely when the question of what it is that we want explained is pushed, that the distinct contours of the two molds begin to take shape. What I shall now proceed to argue is that the basic questions to which the two molds of explanation under consideration are respectively addressed are different. Furthermore, what may be termed the *background interests* underlying these basic questions are different too. The spelling out of these differences will facilitate the assessment of the points of divergence between the two types of explanation themselves, and also between the types of social phenomena they come to explain.

The characterization of the first—the aggregate—mold of invisible-hand explanations has taken up the bulk of this study. This characterization has of course provided us with an answer to the question of what it is that we want explained within the framework of this mold: given a certain social pattern or institution, it is first and foremost asked *how did it—or how could it have—come about?* This question, however, is laden. Unpacked, it turns, as we know, into a quest for one particular mode of emergence rather than another: it is a quest for an account in terms of an invisible-hand process rather than for an account, which is assumed from the outset to be readily available, in terms of intentional design.

The basic question with which an explanation of the functional-evolutionary mold is concerned, on the other hand, is this: given that a certain social pattern or institution exists, *why is it in existence?* This question, too, has to be unfolded in accordance with the interests underlying it. It then becomes: Why is the social item under study existent rather than non-existent, or, how come it has not by now been eliminated, or, again, why does *it* exist rather than some alternative ('functionally equivalent') social arrangement. It should be noted and emphasized that an explanation of this type involves no commitment as to how the scrutinized pattern actually originated.[35] For all that it tells us the pattern in question could have come into being as a result of intentional design and careful execution, or, for that matter, it may have originated (somehow) through people's "stumbling upon establishments, which are indeed the result of human action, but not the execution of any human design."[36] An explanation that belongs within this mold decidedly leaves the matter of the origins of the explained phenomena as unaccounted for as does the notion of spontaneous and random mutation within the theory of biological evolution.

It is evident, then, that we are dealing with two quite disparate sets of questions. It follows that the molds of invisible-hand explanation corresponding to them constitute two quite disparate undertakings: the first is concerned with providing *a chronicle of* (a particular mode of) *emergence*, the second with establishing *raisons d'être*.

Further differences pertain to the social patterns or institutions eligible for explanation in either of the two molds. The explanatory onus of an invisible-hand explanation of the aggregate mold is, as was shown, on the invisible-hand process that accounts for the emergence of the item in question. The point to be stressed is that there are no prerequisites attached to the social item itself, except that it be *structured* in some interesting sense.[37] Matters are different though with an invisible-hand explanation of the functional-evolutionary mold. There it is a prerequisite that the pattern or institution to be explained have a *function*, that it perform a useful service to the social unit incorporating it. To be sure, once we allow ourselves to get immersed in the so-called functionalist school in sociology and anthropology and to adopt its viewpoint we ought presumably to grant that rather than *requiring* that the explanandum phenomenon have a function, it is indeed *presupposed* that it has one (or else it would not have arisen in the first place, or would have been eliminated in due course). But then there is of course a host of further presuppositions that this framework will commit us to: that any existing social pattern or institution, besides being 'functional', is also 'optimal' (as a 'solution') in some sense, that organic social units are self-regulating systems capable of and aiming at survival, and more. In other words, while the exposition of the aggregate mold of invisible-hand explanations constitutes a methodological undertaking dealing mainly with the formal aspects of an explanation scheme, the exposition of the functional-evolutionary mold is, in my opinion, inherently bound up with certain assumptions of substance—if not downright ideology—concerning the nature of the explained phenomena and of society in general.

Having dwelt upon the points on which the two compared types of explanation diverge, let me now, finally, indicate where they may converge—or, rather, how they may be superimposed. The point of junction is the following. Suppose a certain existent social pattern or institution is up for explanation. The attempt may first be made to subject it to the first, aggregate, mold so that—if successful—an invisible-hand account of how it (could have) emerged is obtained. It may then be pointed out that this item is functional, that it contributes to the well-being and proper working order of the society incorporating it. So, it may now be subjected to the second, functional-evolutionary, mold, yielding an invisible-hand account of its durability and prevalence (if indeed it is prevalent across societies and cultures).

Thus, suppose that the emergence of the monetary system is shown—along the lines suggested in Section 2—to be due to an invisible-hand process rather than to someone's intentional design. Suppose, further, that the (quite plausible) case is made that this 'institution' of money performs a role useful to the smooth and efficient functioning of the society in which it has emerged. At this point the evolutionary apparatus may be applied to it and as a result the continued existence of the money institution, indeed its spread, will be accounted for. That is, given that the social pattern or institution to which the first mold of invisible-hand explanations has been successfully applied is functional, the second mold may also be applied to it. This superimposition of the two explanatory molds may be expected to yield a rather satisfying answer to the question concerning the existence of this institution, since it is capable of yielding an account of its emergence and inherent stability as well as its continued existence and prevalence.

Now it is possible that many—or most, or even all—of the social patterns whose emergence is invisible-handedly explained within the framework of the first mold will be found to be 'functional' and hence amenable to the second mold as well. For myself, I prefer to withhold judgment on that; indeed, I take Schelling's model of segregation (Section 6) to serve as a warning against too easy an acceptance of a general statement on the matter. Be that as it may, however, I would like to close by emphasizing that if I am anywhere near the mark about there being a distinction between the two molds of invisible-hand explanations, it seems to me important to keep them distinct and to conceptually isolate them from each other.

Notes

1. There is a sense, of course, in which the notion of unintended consequences of human action was not only known since ancient times, but was in fact pivotal to classical tragedy. Thus, Oedipus' action, done with the intention of hitting the man in the chariot, resulted in the undesigned killing of his father. It is not, however, of such actions, which may be thought of as accidents, that the 'third realm' is supposed to consist. More on this and related issues in Section 3 below.

2. For an account of the history of writings on this 'middle realm', as well as for a vigorous statement of its importance, see F. A. Hayek, *The Constitution of Liberty* (Chicago: University of Chicago Press, 1972), Ch. 2, and F. A. Hayek, 'The Results of Human Action But Not of Human Design', in his own *Studies in Philosophy, Politics and Economics* (London: Routledge & Kegan Paul, 1967), pp. 96–105.

3. R. Nozick, *Anarchy, State, and Utopia* (New York: Basic Books, 1974), p. 19.

4. For the niceties of the full story see P. A. Samuelson, *Economics* (4th ed.) (New York: McGraw-Hill, 1958), Ch. 15.

5. Nozick, *Anarchy, State, and Utopia*, Part 1.

6. Nozick, *Anarchy, State, and Utopia*, pp. 16–17.

7. L. V. Mises, *The Theory of Money and Credit* (2nd ed.) (New Haven: Yale University Press, 1953), pp. 30–4.

8. I would like to refer the reader to a recent article by R. A. Jones, 'The Origin and Development of Media of Exchange', *Journal of Political Economy* 84 (1976), 757–75, in which he offers precise empirical models—albeit in a very specialized context and subject to rather severe restrictions on the 'trading environment'—that show how media of exchange actually emerge through the unconcerted market behavior of individuals. Noteworthy among the points made in this article are the following: (a) A stable exchange pattern is obtainable not only by full monetarization but also by 'some mixture of direct barter and use of a common good as medium of exchange'; (b) There are reasons to expect that the first commodity money to emerge in a barter economy would in fact be a very common good rather than a scarce one (like rice in Japan, beaver pelts in Canada, and more).

9. See Nozick, *Anarchy, State, and Utopia*, p. 19.

10. See K. R. Popper, *The Open Society and Its Enemies* (vol. 2) (London: Routledge & Kegan Paul, 1966), pp. 94–5.

11. See R. Cummins, 'Functional Analysis,' *Journal of Philosophy* 72 (1975), 741–65, 748.

12. It should be remarked, though, that these days any discussion of the central nervous system is likely to be itself dominated by the influence of yet another model, that of computers, electronic control, automatic command centers, and the like.

13. For Robert Boyle the model for the 'machine of the world' was the famous cathedral clock at Strasbourg, in which "the several pieces making up that curious Engine are so fram'd and adapted, and are put into such motion, as though the numerous wheels and other parts of it knew and were concerned to do its Duty". (*The Usefulness of Experimental Natural Philosophy*, 1663.) That is, not only does the existence of the clock attest to its designer, but—according to Boyle—the supreme coordination and adaptation of its parts (almost) attest to their being conscious and intentional agents.

14. The well-known Smith passage concerning the invisible hand occurs in *The Wealth of Nations* (London, 1776), I. IV.II.9. Somewhat less known is the earlier occurrence of this concept in his *Moral Sentiments* (the first edition of which was published in 1759), in a remarkable passage dealing with the distribution of means to happiness that is brought about when the landlords who, seeking to ever enhance their wealth and greatness but whose "capacity of [the] stomach bears no proportion to the immensity of [their] desires", are forced to divide with the poor what they produce above their own needs:

They [the rich] are led by an invisible hand to make nearly the same distribution of the necessaries of life, which would have been made, had the earth been divided into equal portions among all its inhabitants, and thus without intending it, without knowing it, advance the interest of the society, and afford means to the multiplication of the species. (*The Theory of Moral Sentiments*, IV.1.10. The Glasgow Edition (1976): Vol. I, pp. 184–5.)

The very first use of the expression 'invisible hand', however, appears to have been made by Smith in his *History of Astronomy* (London, 1795), III.2. But there it seems to have had theological connotations having to do with supernatural intervention. See A. L. Macfie, 'The Invisible Hand of Jupiter', *Journal of the History of Ideas* **32** (1971), 595–9. See also T. D. Campbell, *Adam Smith's Science of Morals*, George Allen and Unwin Ltd., London, 1971, esp. pp. 60–2, 71–3, 117(n). I am grateful to Allen Silver for having drawn my attention to these passages and references.

15. The Logic of Functional Analysis', in C. G. Hempel, *Aspects of Scientific Explanation* (New York: The Free Press, 1965), 447. The emphasis in Hempel's discussion, beautifully illustrated by two *historical*-genetic examples, is on the combination in these explanations of "a certain measure of nomological interconnecting with more or less large amounts of straight description" ([11], p. 449); this holds here too. As is being shown in the text, however, I take it that the invisible-hand processes are subject to more specific, as well as more severe, constraints than are the sequences in ordinary historical-genetic explanations (except possibly for the requirement of truth—see Section 7 below).

16. Nozick, *Anarchy, State, and Utopia*, p. 352, note 7) that there will be cases where some of the participating individuals foresee the ultimate outcome and intend to bring it about while others do not, and suggests therefore that the notion of invisible-hand processes might be refined to admit of degrees. Compare this to my quite different notion of invisible-hand explanations' being a matter of degree (p. 267 above).

17. Will the stipulation that the participating individuals are *rational* take care of this normalcy condition? It would seem so: the rationality of the agents' actions, relative to their beliefs and utilities as determined by the circumstances prevailing at the initial stage—as well as by the possibly changed circumstances of subsequent stages—would indeed go a long way toward insuring that the stages of the sequence not be startlingly strange or deviant. There

is, however, one level at which the requirement of rationality does fall short of the requirement of normalcy, namely the level of the beliefs and utilities themselves. That is, in addition to the requirement that the agents act rationally relative to their beliefs and utilities, we would not want to allow the invisible-hand explanation to hinge in an essential way on crazy or freakish beliefs and utilities, relative to the prevailing (and possibly changing) circumstances—unless, of course, there is *independent* anthropological evidence that such indeed were the beliefs and utilities of the people involved. It follows that the normalcy constraint, as sketchily presented in the text, may in fact be broken up into two components: the normalcy (within some vague range) of the agents' beliefs and utilities, given the circumstances, and their acting rationally, given these beliefs and utilities.

18. T. C. Schelling, 'Models of Segregation', *American Economic Review* 59 (1969), 488–93.

19. As Schelling points out, this is not the only stable 'solution' that satisfies everyone's minimum requirements. Thus, alternating 1's and 0's, or alternating pairs of 1's and 0's, will also do—as would clusters of five. But *this* is what comes out under the 'circumstances' of the particular example, i.e. with the particular random distribution of 1's and 0's we began with. (A question that seems to me worthy of consideration is this: Is there a randomly distributed series of 1's and 0's such that, were *it* to be the first stage in the process, the very same assumptions of Schelling's model would lead to its turning into a series of alternating 1's and 0's? Or is it the case that in order for this desegregated outcome to be brought about an intervening hand is inevitably called for?)

20. It is of importance to note that each participant's desire to achieve bare majority status, far from being a disguised desire for total segregation, is in fact quite compatible with the further desire to reside in a heterogeneous rather than in a completely homogeneous neighborhood. However, if indeed we attribute to our participants this further wish, then, as Schelling points out, it turns out that almost half of them remain dissatisfied on this score, since thirty out of the seventy actually end up in a neighborhood of their own color exclusively.

21. Matters are somewhat reversed with F. A. Hayek, who vehemently denounces "that factually untrue anthropomorphic interpretation of grown institutions as the product of design." 'The Results of Human Action But Not of Human Design', in F. A. Hayek, *Studies in Philosophy, Politics and Economics* (London: Routledge & Kegan Paul, 1967), p. 102. For him, it seems, every social institution is presumed to have evolved invisible-handedly, unless proven otherwise. Thus, in the context of justifying some of the criticisms levelled against Adam Smith's account of the market mechanism he emphasizes that "his [Smith's] implied assumption, however, that the extensive division of labour of a complex society from which we all profited could only have been brought about by spontaneous ordering forces and not by design was largely justified" (Hayek, 'The Results of Human Action,' p. 100). This position of Hayek's, however, should be appraised in the light of the second, functional-evolutionary, conception of invisible-hand explanations, to be introduced and discussed in Sections 8 and 9 below.

22. See R. Carnap, *Logical Foundations of Probability* (London: Routledge & Kegan Paul, 1962), pp. 576–7.

23. While mentioning this curious possibility that someone's intelligent design might come to be seen, in the light of an alternative invisible-hand account, as in a sense accidental, let me allude to Hegel's notion of the *Cunning of Reason* ('List der Vernunft'). His idea seems to

be that while the leader appears to be concerned to do 'his own thing'—to act on his own private motives—his actions, put in the wider historical perspective, are seen to fit into an overall (historical) design. Thus, the 'true' leader appears to be led by means of the 'cunning of reason' to do that which inevitably had to be done. Consider: "Thus he [Caesar] was motivated not only by his own private interest, but acted intrinsically to bring to pass that which the times required." G. W. F. Hegel, *Reason in History* (New York: The Library of Liberal Arts (Bobbs-Merrill), 1953), pp. 39–40. My interpretative reconstruction of this, suggested by the present approach to invisible-hand explanations, would be the following: A leader may (sometimes) bring about, in an initiated and premeditated way, some social pattern or institution that might otherwise have emerged—later—through an invisible-hand process. In that sense it may (perhaps) be said that, while manifesting in his deeds the cunning of reason, the leader is an 'instrument in the hands of history'. On this view see also G. W. F. Hegel, *Philosophy of Right* (T. M. Knox, trans.) (Oxford: Oxford University Press, 1967), Section 199 (p. 129), and Taylor's comment upon this section (C. Taylor, *Hegel* (Cambridge: Cambridge University Press, 1975), p. 433) in which he points out the connection between Hegel's thesis of the cunning of reason and Adam Smith's thesis of the invisible hand.

24. Having offered this interim recapitulation I would like to suggest several areas where the scope of the present analysis may possibly be broadened, thereby conferring the status of invisible-hand explanations upon cases that deviate from the core class in the systematic ways to be indicated. (a) The case can be made that an invisible-hand explanation may be offered to account not just for the *generation* but also for the *degeneration*, or disintegration, of a well-structured social pattern. A strict analogy holds between these two types of cases. (b) Given that the explanation I have been talking about consists basically of an ordered couple, the first component of which being the social pattern to be explained and the second the *expectation* that it be explained in terms of intentional design, it may plausibly be argued that the latter could be relaxed, or even ultimately abandoned. That is, it seems quite plausible to suggest that an invisible-hand explanation may be offered where there is *no* expectation at all as to what kind of explanation is called for, where one simply does not know. Moreover, if acquaintance with some (good) invisible-hand explanations that have been offered in the past and have proved successful can be assumed, one may indeed start out with the expectation that the particular social institution that is up for explanation right now would (should) be invisible-handedly explained. This shift in the expectation component, however, is thus clearly not altogether causally independent of the (known) success of some invisible-hand explanations that do belong to the core class as presented in the text. (From among the distinguishing features of invisible-hand explanations the one that will be undermined by the relaxation of the expectation condition is, obviously, the surprise factor.) (c) The requirement of methodological individualism may be relaxed to allow units larger than the single individual, such as households or firms, to be the deliberating, deciding, and ultimately acting participants.

25. Some of the central articles to have appeared recently on this subject are those of C. Boorse, 'Wright on Functions,' *Philosophical Review* 85 (1976), 70–86; R. Cummins, 'Functional Analysis,' *Journal of Philosophy* 72 (1975), 741–65; W. C. Wimsatt, 'Teleology and the Logical Structure of Function Statements,' *Studies in History and Philosophy of Science* 3 (1972), 1–80; and L. Wright, 'Functions,' *Philosophical Review* 82 (1973), 139–68. I want

to record here a special debt to Cummins's stimulating paper; some of the examples discussed in the sequel are drawn from it.

26. Possible variations here occur when the system is taken to be a whole species, or even the entire eco-system. (See Boorse, 'Wright on Functions,' and further references there.)

27. In addition to the articles referred to in note 16 above, all of which deal with this issue, one should of course mention Hempel's essay, 'The Logic of Functional Analysis', which is the *locus classicus* of all modern discussions of functional analysis (and, at least according to Cummins, also the main source of confusion regarding this question of the connection between the functional analysis of an item and a causal account of its presence).

28. Cummins, 'Functional Analysis,' "We could therefore think of natural selection as reacting on the *set* of plans generated by mutation by weeding out the bad plans; natural selection cannot alter a plan but it can trim the set."

29. The quoted phrase is A. R. Radcliffe-Brown, *Structure and Function in Primitive Society* (London: Cohen & West, 1952), p.186). For good examples of cases of functional analysis in non-standard contexts, see Boorse, 'Wright on Functions,' especially those that have to do with what he calls "accidental functions". (E.g.: the functional analysis of the bible in the soldier's breast pocket, which (happened to) function as a bullet shield, surely does not bear on its presence there.)

30. One of the main points of criticism against Boorse's article is, in my opinion, the striking absence of the social realm from it. Moreover, one of the central assumptions underlying his proposed formula of functional analysis is that the system relative to which the analysis is offered is a 'goal directed' one—and I would seriously question the applicability of this assumption (without ideological presuppositions) to the social realm.

31. R. K. Merton, *Social Theory and Social Structure* (New York: The Free Press, 1968), pp. 118–19.

32. The phrase is Radcliffe-Brown's, *Structure and Function in Primitive Society*, p. 183.

33. As is well known, it was from the rather well-entrenched views—predominantly due to the eighteenth-century Scottish school—concerning social and cultural evolution that Darwin and his contemporaries in fact derived the suggestion for their biological theories. Towards the end of the nineteenth century the biological notions were reimported into (as well as abused by) the social sciences, mainly in the form of the so-called Social Darwinism. (On this topic see, e.g., Hayek, *The Constitution of Liberty*, p. 59ff.)

34. [7], p. 101.

35. Consider, e.g., Merton's careful wording, when discussing the (latent) functions of the political machine: "*Whatever its specific historical origins*, the political machine *persists* as an apparatus for satisfying otherwise unfulfilled needs of diverse groups in the population." Merton, *Social Theory and Social Structure*, p. 127, emphasis mine.) Radcliffe-Brown, too, distinguishes between accounting for the 'history' of a social institution and accounting for its functioning (see, e.g., Radcliffe-Brown, *Structure and Function in Primitive Society*, p. 186). On the other hand I believe that for both Malinowski (e.g., B. Malinowski, 'Anthropology', in *Encyclopaedia Britannica* (1st Supp. Vol.) (London: The Encyclopaedia Britannica, Inc., 1926) p. 139) and Hayek (e.g., Hayek, 'The Results of Human Action', p. 101) the distinction is obscure, and that for both of them to explain the manner of functioning of a social institution is at the same time to answer the question of its origin or formation.

36. The phrase—it's about time that it be acknowledged—is A. Ferguson, *An Essay on the History of Civil Society* (London, 1767), p. 187. Let me mention in this connection A. A. Alchian, 'Uncertainty, Evolution, and Economic Theory,' *Journal of Political Economy* 58 (1950), 211–21, an attempt to apply evolutionary ideas to economic theory. The greater part of his argument is compressed in the following: "The economic counterparts of genetic heredity, *mutation* and natural selection are imitation, *innovation* and positive profits." (Emphasis mine.) He also points out that innovation may be achieved not only premeditatively but unpremeditatively as well—through imperfect imitation, for instance.

37. I venture, hesitantly, to suggest that whether or not the social pattern can be easily referred to by means of a conventionally codified designation ('medium of exchange', 'minimal state', 'segregation', 'free market', etc.) has something to do with its being 'structured' in the sense I am after.

9

The Invisible Hand and the Cunning of Reason

Here is a distilled list of the theses I shall discuss:

- that the idea of the invisible hand has had an impact not only on the eighteenth and the nineteenth centuries but on the twentieth century as well;
- that this idea had a curious ideological career: in previous centuries it had been used to promote ideals of secular, enlightened progress, while in our century it is used inversely, to promote conservative reverence toward traditions;
- that there are two main models for invisible-hand explanations;
- that the current, inverse, ideological use of the idea of the invisible hand by conservative circles as against liberals and social planners springs from not distinguishing between the two models;
- that Hegel's idea of the cunning of reason is historically related to the idea of the invisible hand, and that, like the latter, it is also used in contemporary political argumentation;
- that despite superficial affinity between these two ideas, they serve profoundly different doctrines.

And now to the details.

F. A. Hayek talks about the "shock caused by the discovery that [not only the *kosmos* of nature but] the moral and political *kosmos* was also the result of a process of evolution and not of design."[1] What he alludes to here is the natural human response to the phenomenon of order. Upon encountering orderliness and patterned structures, people tend naturally to interpret these as the products of someone's intentional design. If complex order is exhibited by an artifact—say, a clock—the postulated designer would be a human agent, an artist, or an engineer. If complex order is exhibited by the physical world—say, the lunar period—the postulated designer would be a superhuman agent, God. The "argument from design" (or the cosmological argument, as it is sometimes called) is indeed a most powerful argument, psychologically, for the existence of God. At the very core of religious sensibility is the conviction that the world is not just the product of divine creation, but that it is the manifestation of divine, cosmic design.

It is against this background that the idea that the *kosmos* can be seen as the result of a process of evolution rather than design is described by Hayek as "shocking." To this shock, moreover, he goes on to attribute a significant contribution in the production "of what we call the modern mind."[2] And since the nineteenth-century notion of evolution, or spontaneous order, is itself rooted in the eighteenth-century notion of the invisible hand, there is a sense in which we may take the notion of the invisible hand as expressing a major antireligious intuition. This notion was meant to replace that of the "Finger of God," or "Divine Providence." It was to play a central role in forging modern, secular sensibility.

In tracing the history of the notion of the invisible hand, it is commonly attributed to the great Scottish Enlightenment figures of David Hume, Adam Smith, and Adam Ferguson. It is Adam Smith who is credited with coining the expression "invisible hand";[3] it is Adam Ferguson who formulated the splendid, formative phrase about people's "stumbling upon establishments, which are indeed the result of human action, but not the execution of any human design";[4] and it is David Hume who is generally acknowledged to have laid the philosophical foundations for these ideas. It is intellectually pleasing, however, to go still further back and to claim, with Hayek (and others), that it was Bernard Mandeville, the Dutch-turned-English doctor, who "made Hume possible."[5] In his famous *Fable of the Bees*, subtitled *Private Vices Public Benefits*,[6] the idea is articulated that complex social order forms itself without design. Orderly social structures and institutions—law, morals, language, the market, money, and many more—spontaneously grow up without men having deliberately planned them or even anticipated them, and it is these institutions that ensure that men's divergent interests are reconciled. In discussing the growth of law, Mandeville says: "We often ascribe to the excellency of man's genius, and the depth of his penetration, what is in reality owing to the length of time, and the experience of many generations."[7]

However, even though the idea *that* order may form itself without design was expounded by Mandeville, the question *how* remained unaddressed. The initial breakthroughs in suggesting some sort of mechanisms for the workings of the invisible hand were not to be provided before the appearance upon the stage of the Scottish social and moral thinkers. Their work made it possible to delineate a mechanism that can show in specific detail how the actions of numerous individuals who pursue their own divergent interests may actually aggregate so as to bring about a well-structured yet undesigned social institution. And it is this sort of aggregative mechanism that is the heart of an invisible-hand explanation worthy of its name. Only when an invisible-hand mechanism can be pointed to, can the spell of an explanation that postulates a creator, a designer, or a conspiracy be effectively broken.

It is in this sense, and in this context, that we may allude to Wittgenstein's notion of being "in the grip of a picture": the picture is the theological picture, within which one is held in the grip of the "argument from design." The liberating role from the grip of this picture is assumed by an invisible-hand explanation that succeeds in showing, through spelling out the workings of an appropriate mechanism (or process), how the social institution in question could have come about "as a result of human action but not of human design." This liberating role firmly establishes the notion of the invisible hand as a cornerstone in the secular, rationalist worldview that we associate with the Enlightenment.

The role of the notion of the invisible hand does not end here, however. It continues to exert influence on the intellectual climate (or, on the "modern mind") down to our own time. Interestingly, though, its spheres of influence shift. The original framework in which it began playing its eighteenth-century role vis-a-vis the theological outlook was that of economic models, with Adam Smith's discussion of the working of the free market as the paradigmatic example. Later, in the nineteenth century, the locus of its influence was to be found primarily in biology, as bound with the notion of evolution and the origin of species—but also in history and historiography, as bound with Hegel's notion of the cunning of reason. In its latest, present-day manifestation, the invisible hand looms within ecology, where it relates to the equilibrium of ecosystems, and also, if we are willing to go along with Hayek, within general discussions about culture and morals.

While in the early phase of its career the invisible hand made it possible for economics, and social theory in general, to serve as a model for biology, what Hayek does in fact is the reverse. For him it is the workings of the invisible hand in biology, or in what he understands as the biological evolution of spontaneous order, which is—and which should be—the model for social structures and institutions. Now something funny happens to the notion of the invisible hand on this reverse way. When first introduced, this notion played a liberating role—in the name of light, reason, and progress—as against the religious outlook. However, within the secular outlook that came to prevail, the invisible hand is predominantly an instrument in the service of darker ideologies, conservative and counter-Enlightenment ones.

There is no other theme that Hayek, whom I shall take to be the latterday spokesman of these gloomier ideologies, emphasizes more than the need for human reason to recognize the limitations of human reason. In the more distant past, to preach for recognizing the limitations of human reason was tantamount to preaching for recognizing the supremacy of external, superhuman—that is, divine—authority. The project of the Enlightenment, which consisted in the rejection of this authority, came to be identified not only with the supremacy of human reason but with the deification of human reason. This, to Hayek, is man's ultimate, "supercilious," fatal conceit.[8]

For Hayek the recognition of the limitations of human reason, instead of leading us to accept divine authority, should rather force us to concede superiority "to a moral order to which we owe our existence . . . to a tradition which we must revere and care for . . . to a system which we must accept as given . . . to a gradually evolved set of abstract rules of which human reason can avail itself to build better than it knows . . . to structures based on more information than any human agency can use."[9] Hayek follows Hume in taking seriously the limitations of human understanding, or, more specifically, the upper bounds on the human capacity to possess, process, and compute information. He thus wages a war against the rationalist confidence in the human ability to plan and to design ("it is indeed quite difficult," he says, "to find a positivist who is not a socialist."[10]

The most we can do—the most Hayek believes we should be allowed to do—is to "humbly tinker" on a system that serves us well ("a moral order which keeps us alive") but which we can never hope to understand more than imperfectly.

The "moral order" Hayek talks about comprises in effect the entire cultural realm—the social, economic, political, and legal institutions,[11] as well as the moral tradition. For him the moral order is the product of spontaneous growth, that is, of a generations-long process of cultural evolution. As already mentioned, for Hayek the cultural evolution of traditions and habits is modeled on the biological evolution of "the particular kinds of spontaneous orders which we call organisms."[12] And, furthermore, when Hayek says of certain social institutions that they are the product of an evolutionary process, for him this seems the only adequate explication of the older, Scottish-Enlightenment idea of explaining social institutions through the workings of an invisible hand.

Now, it is one thing to say that the idea of the invisible hand paved the way for the idea of evolution, and it is quite another to conflate the two ideas. My challenge to Hayek at this point is this: while evolutionary explanations are indeed one type, or a species, of invisible-hand explanations, they are not the only species of invisible-hand explanations; they do not exhaust the genus. Moreover, while there is a strong sense in which evolutionary explanations can be said to be value laden, or, if you will, ideology laden, invisible-hand explanations as such are ideology free. This last point is of crucial significance with respect to Hayek's ideological use of the notion of the invisible hand.

Some clarification is in order.[13] I shall begin by spelling out, a bit, the nature of evolutionary explanations. First, let me recall the invisible-hand aspect of evolutionary explanations—whether biological or social. It consists, of course, in the fact that when an item, be it a social institution or an organism, is claimed to be the product of an evolutionary process, its existence is thereby taken to be explained without any reference to a designing agent. Evolutionary explanations qualify as invisible-hand explanations insofar as they are liberated from the grip of the formative—yet in a way primitive—picture according to which to account for the existence of something is to point to its creator.

The expression "to account for something's existence," however, can be taken in more than one way. And it is the basically two different ways this expression is construed that distinguish the evolutionary explanations from the other, nonevolutionary, invisible-hand explanations. One way to account for something's existence is as an answer to the question of origin: How did it come into being, how did it begin to exist? The other is as an answer to the question of endurance: Why does it persist (regardless of how it came about in the first place), why does it continue to exist? The distinction, then, is between an explanation of emergence and an explanation of endurance.

Evolutionary explanations are clearly of the second kind. Their central conceptual tool of "natural selection," and its concomitant notion of "survival of the fittest," are supposed to account for continued existence, not for origins. At this point, however, an important difference between evolutionary explanations within biology, and evolutionary explanations in the domain of society and culture, has to be noted. In the biological case some sort of an account (or, a place-holder for an account) of origins is part and parcel of the explanatory apparatus. It is, namely, spontaneous and random mutations that are supposed to account for the emergence of the items (organisms, organs) whose continued existence is evolutionarily explained. No analogue to the notion of mutation exists in the sociocultural case: an evolutionary explanation of a social institution involves no commitment, and tells no causal story, as to its historical origins.

There is yet another difference between the biological and the social evolutionary explanations, a difference that will play a significant role in what follows. It involves the notion of function. In the biological case, where the item to be explained (say an organ, like a kidney) is known to have withstood the generations-long evolutionary test, it may safely be assumed—or, at least, rebuttably presumed—that the item in question has some survival value to the organism containing it, that it fulfills a positive function contributing to its overall fitness. Matters are notably different in the social domain. When a social item is to be explained (a practice, a norm, an institution), it cannot in general be assumed that it has withstood the generations-long evolutionary test—it may be too recent for that. Nor can it in general be assumed that it fulfills a positive function that contributes to the survival and well-being of the society incorporating it—it may, for example, promote sectarian interests, or it may lack a function (in the relevant sense) altogether. The attributes of lastingness and of overall positive functionality have to be *ascertained*, case by case, rather than presupposed.

So, what an evolutionary explanation in the social domain does is the following: first of all, it ascertains that the institution in question fulfills a useful social function and identifies it (say, the continuous creation of money within the banking system); that is, it establishes its contribution to the equilibrial well-being and survival of the society incorporating it. Once this is ascertained, the explanatory schema can flow on. It assumes that by performing its useful function, even the faint beginnings of the social institution in question—whatever their origins—are with time reinforced and selected for. Consequently, this institution is seen as contributing to the evolutionary "success" of the society incorporating it, and this success, in turn, accounts for the perpetuated existence of the institution in that society. What we have here, then, is a non-man-made process of selection: a large scale evolutionary mechanism scans, as it were, the inventory of societies and of their social structures at any given period of time, and screens through to the next phase those societies whose structures and institutions serve them best. But for all that this explanation tells us, the social institution thus explained could have come about in any one of a number of ways. It could have originated, somehow, through people's "stumbling upon establishments, which are indeed the result of human action, but not the execution of any human design," in Ferguson's words. However, it could also, for that matter, have come about as a result of intentional design and careful execution by some enlightened ruler or clever committee—and yet the explanation of its continued existence would still count as an invisible-hand explanation of the evolutionary kind.

In order for an evolutionary explanation in the social domain to take off, the social institution to be explained, as we saw, has to fulfill some useful function, whether manifest or latent. Only institutions that perform a beneficial function for the society incorporating them can be candidates for an evolutionary explanation. Put somewhat differently, only institutions that promote the well-being and the survival of their society better than any alternative arrangements that happened to have been historically tried can have their continued existence explained through the evolutionary explanatory apparatus. It is through this door that conservative ideology enters the stage, by blurring the delicate distinction between *requiring* that the institution that is the explanandum phenomenon have a socially beneficial function, and *presupposing* that it has such a function.

All sociocultural evolutionary explanations align themselves with the so-called functionalist school in sociology and anthropology.[14] And within the outlook of this school it is indeed taken for granted that any social pattern, structure, or institution that has been around for some time fulfills a certain society-wide positive function—or else it would have been eliminated in due course. This outlook is further committed to more far-reaching presuppositions: that any existing social pattern, besides being "functional," is also "optimal" (as a "solution") in some sense, and that human societies are self-regulating, goal-directed, organic systems. All of these highly controversial assumptions are heavily substantive, value-laden assumptions. Somewhat crudely put, their gist is this: while it may be the case that we do not inhabit the best of all possible worlds, we do nonetheless inhabit an optimal social world that is the fittest and best adapted of all actually tried alternative worlds.

So much for evolutionary explanations *qua* invisible-hand explanations. Let me return now to the claim made earlier, that evolutionary explanations are but one kind of invisible-hand explanations, that they do not exhaust the field. Indeed, the way I see it, they are not the ones that constitute the hard core, paradigmatic cases of the invisible-hand explanations envisioned by the Scottish Enlightenment thinkers. When Adam Smith talks about an invisible hand leading to the equilibrial pricing system within a perfectly competitive market,[15] what he is referring to is an altogether different model of explanation.

The model in question envisages an invisible-hand process that is largely synchronic, not diachronic like the evolutionary selection processes. This process is an aggregate mechanism that takes as "input" the diverse and dispersed actions of numerous individuals, and produces as "output" an overall, structured, social pattern—subject to the assumption that the individuals concerned need neither foresee this pattern nor intend to bring it about. It is this process that, when spelled out, bears the brunt of the invisible-hand explanation. Such classical invisible-hand explanations, as those explaining the pricing system, or the continuous creation of money within the banking system,[16] or the development of media of exchange,[17] or the rise of the so-called ultraminimal state,[18] are all instances of the aggregate model. The aggregate model, then, supplies a chronicle of emergence and initial existence of some social pattern, while the evolutionary model is concerned with establishing reasons for the prolonged and continued existence of a social pattern.

The point to be stressed at this stage is this: for an invisible-hand explanation of the aggregate variety to go through, nothing in particular need be assumed about the social pattern that is a candidate for this sort of explanation—except, perhaps, that it be *structured* in some interesting sense. Matters, as we saw, are different in the case of an invisible-hand explanation of the evolutionary variety. There it is a prerequisite— if not, indeed, a presupposition—that the social pattern to be explained have a *function*, that it perform a useful service to the society incorporating it. This, as we saw, was where conservative ideology entered the picture in the evolutionary case. And we are now in a position to see why it is that no ideology enters the picture in the aggregate case. When the existence of a social institution is accounted for by means of an aggregative invisible-hand explanation, there is no assumption, explicit or implicit, that it is a good institution, a valuable one, one that ought to be preserved or revered.

To be sure, it is entirely possible that an institution whose emergence is accounted for in this way turns out, as a matter of empirical fact, to fulfill a function that contributes to the survival or well-being of the society incorporating it. If it does, then its endurance, or continued existence, may be subjected to the other, that is, to the evolutionary model of invisible-hand explanations. Indeed, it may even be the case that many, or most, of the social institutions whose emergence can be explained by the aggregative invisible-hand explanation, are relevantly "functional" and hence also amenable to an evolutionary invisible-hand explanation. But this is an empirical, not an analytical, connection. And as a matter of ideological hygiene, it seems to me important to keep these two models conceptually apart.

Let me return, finally, to Hayek. Put somewhat bluntly, it is my belief that for Hayek the following sweeping generalizations were true: that all the institutions constituting our social fabric can—and should—be explained invisible-handedly, that invisible-hand explanations are evolutionary explanations, and that evolutionary explanations presuppose a functionalist outlook. As I hope to have shown, none of these generalizations is strictly true. His having subscribed to them, however, made Hayek unaware that the explanations he was championing for all of our social institutions were not explanations of emergence at all. These generalizations also helped blind him to the need to subject each existing social institution to a critical examination, free of presuppositions, in order to ascertain whether it was indeed of such positive social function and of such pedigree as to make it worthy of respect and preservation. For Hayek the cited generalizations confirmed that the sociocultural sphere is "a system which we must accept as given," that it represents a "tradition which we must revere and care for,"[19] and, ultimately, that we obey reason when we submit to traditional rules that we cannot rationally justify.[20] It is in this way, then, that the notion of the invisible hand is nowadays being put to an ideological use by conservative circles; it is in this way that this notion serves as a weapon against liberals and social planners. And this way, I have argued, is faulty and misguided.[21]

*   *   *

The idea that human society produces its moral and economic institutions in an autonomous and spontaneous way had its profound impact on historical thinking as well. From Vico to Marx, the notion of the invisible hand, in one version or another, served to replace the older ideas of "the finger of God," or divine providence. The outlook according to which the meaning of history was to be extracted from some transcendent premise or promise, gradually gave way to the view that the meaning of history was immanent. A notion of particular interest in this context is Hegel's notion of the cunning of reason (*List der Vernunft*).

Hegel transformed Kant's comments on "the hidden plan of nature" into his doctrine: "This is to be called the cunning of reason, that it lets the passions do its work."[22] The higher purposes of reason—the *telos* of history—are realized, obliquely, through the exercise of the passions, self-interests, and motives of individuals. The historical agent, by acting out his own will, inadvertently acts as an instrument of reason; his "passions, ambition, jealousy, greed and the like are thus viewed as the handmaids of reason working in history."[23] The subjective freedom of the individual may appear independent of, or even in conflict with, the objective necessity of reason. But in truth, in each historical period, they coincide—their mediation being effected by the cunning of reason.

This doctrine is problematic on many counts; it is much discussed and variously interpreted by commentators. These accounts often draw attention to an affinity between the doctrine of the cunning of reason and the notion of the invisible hand. It is to this purported affinity that I should like to turn now.

The point of contact is what is sometimes referred to as the "dialectical tension" between intent and outcome. Both the doctrine of the invisible hand and the doctrine of the cunning of reason focus on the fact that the result of human action need not be the outcome of any human design. Moreover, both doctrines spring from the recognition that some unintended and unexpected consequences of human action may fulfill a purpose, may serve a valuable function, may lead to progress or to perfection. This, indeed, is why these unintended consequences appear (misleadingly) to be the result of some superb—if not superhuman—planning. And it is precisely this that the two doctrines attempt to address in terms other than superhuman planning.

This point of contact, however, while striking, does not take us very far.[24] It is important to note, by way of contrasting the two doctrines, that the notion of the cunning of reason is meant to apply to the actions of a few great men only—to the actions of the historical heroes, or the "world-historical individuals," as Hegel calls them. It is the Pericleses, Alexanders, Caesars, and Napoleons who, unbeknownst to them, are the instruments of the "deed of the world mind" that leads to the "progress of the universal spirit": it is they "whose own particular purposes comprehend the substantial content which is the will of the world-spirit." Hegel's best-known example, perhaps, is the case of Caesar, who is assassinated as soon as he has done the work of the Spirit in bringing the Republic to an end: "this," as Charles Taylor puts it, "is an example of reason using expendable instruments."[25] This feature of the doctrine of the cunning of reason stands of course in marked contrast to its parallel feature in the doctrine of the invisible hand. Namely, for an invisible-hand explanation to go through, a multitude of (nonheroic) individuals have to be postulated as privately pursuing their own particular purposes.

History, in Hegel's view, is the drama of emancipation of human consciousness, the drama of humanity's attainment of ever-growing self-understanding. The idea of history as the realization of conceptual development unfolds through the concrete actions of individuals. The world-historical individuals, as Karl Loewith puts it, "act historically by being acted upon by the power and cunning of reason, which is to Hegel a rational expression for divine providence."[26] The historical heroes contribute to this drama by their actions, while they themselves are only dimly, or "instinctively"—if at all[27]—aware of the conceptual unfolding to which they contribute. Their contribution consists not so much in a dramatic act—like a military victory—as such, nor necessarily in the founding of new orders. It consists, rather, in the undermining of existing orders, in pointing to new alternatives, in creating a critical situation, thereby preparing history for its next stage. The gap about which Hegel talks in terms of the cunning of reason is this gap between the lack of understanding on the part of the historical hero on the one hand, and his contribution to the growing self-understanding of humanity—or of the "Spirit," on the other. And when Hegel says that reason is "the sovereign of the world," and that history has a final purpose, or "ultimate design," he is not postulating agency or intentionality of some hidden mind. The design he talks about is better understood in the sense of a pattern (as in the design of an elaborate carpet) than in the sense of a plan or a plot. It is the design of the logical-ideational necessity, of the rational causality, which the historical development embodies and unfolds.

Both Hegel's cunning reason and Smith's and Ferguson's invisible hand are conceptual tools devised for the explanation of phenomena that are "the result of human action but not the execution of any human design." Interestingly, both of these tools are being put to political uses these days. While the invisible hand serves as a conservative weapon against social reform, the cunning of reason is taken to account for the spectacle of leaders who carry out a policy that is antithetical to their true desires and declared intentions.

An impressive number of big political decisions in recent times can be described as having been made by leaders who betrayed their constituencies as well as their own past. Thus we have de Gaulle who quitted Algiers, Nixon who went to China, de Klerk who terminated apartheid, Begin who withdrew from the Sinai, and more. These leaders underwent formative processes that made them come to terms with the inescapable constraints and exigencies of reality. In Hegelian terms such leaders, by acting counterintentionally, were being used by Reason as an instrument for carrying out their counterpolicy. A desire/ability dialectics is at work here, whereby the leader who wants to bring about a certain dramatic state of affairs is often politically unable to do so, while the opposing leader who intends to prevent it—and is elected to do so— will end up bringing it about, if forced to by reality. It is thus not the intentions, desires, and wishes of political leaders that count, but rather their capability and power. And the irony is that the leader who strongly and credibly opposes a certain move often has the larger maneuverability for making it, once reality brings him or her around to its imperativeness: the support of those who are anyway in favor of this move is guaranteed, while the trust of this leader's own followers—if he or she has sufficient stature— will bring many of them around as well. Indeed, in political argumentation today it is this understanding of the notion of the cunning of reason that is sometimes cynically cited by people as a justification for supporting a political candidate who in their judgement will be *capable* of carrying out the policy they favor, rather than the candidate who declares his or her intention to carry it out.

In sum, tying the various threads together, we note that the original doctrines that the notions of the cunning of reason and of the invisible hand were devised to serve differ on several fundamental counts. They differ as to the domain within which the explanation applies, as to what it is that is being explained, and as to the nature of the explanatory mechanism. In the case of Hegel the domain is spiritual history, the phenomenon to be explained is humanity's ever growing self-understanding, and the explanation consists in showing how history uses as its vehicles the results of the actions of a few heroic humans so as to unfold the execution of Reason's design. In the case of Smith and Ferguson the domain is the social order, the phenomena to be explained are social structures, practices, and institutions, and the explanation consists in showing how they come about as the result of the actions of numerous ordinary humans and of no design whatever.

Notes

1. F. A. Hayek, "Dr. Bernard Mandeville" (1978), in C. Nishiyama and K. R. Leube, eds., *The Essence of Hayek*, (Stanford: Hoover Institute Press, 1984), p. 190.
2. Hayek, "Dr. Bernard Mandeville," p. 190.
3. The well-known passage occurs in Adam Smith, *The Wealth of Nations* (London: 1776), IV.II.9. A less well known, and earlier, occurrence of the notion is in *The Theory of Moral Sentiments* (London: 1759), IV.I 10. Smith's very first use of "invisible hand" is in his *History of Astronomy* (London, 1795), III.2, but there it seems to have ironic theological connotations. Emma Rothschild, however, suggests—in "Adam Smith and the Invisible Hand" (1994)—that Smith's attitude to the invisible hand was ironic throughout.
4. Adam Ferguson, *An Essay on the History of Civil Society* (London: T. Cadell, 1767), p. 187.
5. Hayek, "Dr. Bernard Mandeville," p. 188.

6. Bernard Mandeville, *Fable of the Bees: Private Vices Public Benefits* (F. B. Kaye, ed.) (Oxford: Oxford University Press, 1924 [1714]).

7. Mandeville, *Fable of the Bees*, p. 142.

8. F. A. Hayek, "The Origins and Effects of Our Morals" (1983), in C. Nishiyama and K. R. Leube, eds., *The Essence of Hayek* (Stanford: Hoover Institute Press, 1984), p. 330.

9. Hayek, "The Origins and Effects of Our Morals," pp. 330, 326.

10. Hayek, "The Origins and Effects of Our Morals," p. 326.

11. As far as the law is concerned, Hayek's position is not entirely clear. On the one hand, he often lumps legal norms and institutions together with all other social, political, and economic norms and institutions, and makes the sweeping claim that they are all products of "spontaneous order." On the other hand, however, he acknowledges that effectively competitive markets depend on state-created legal preconditions (such as rules of property and contract law).

12. Hayek, F. A., "The Results of Human Action but Not of Human Design," in *Studies in Philosophy, Politics and Economics* (London: Routledge and Kegan Paul, 1967), p. 101.

13. In the following I draw on Edna Ullmann-Margalit, "Invisible-Hand Explanations," *Synthese* 39 (1978), pp. 263–91.

14. The prominent figures of this school are B. Malinowski and A. R. Radcliffe-Brown.

15. *The Wealth of Nations* IV.II.9. He also talks about the invisible hand leading to the optimal distribution by the rich to the poor of "the necessaries of life" (*The Theory of Moral Sentiments*, IV.1.10).

16. P. A. Samuelson, *Economics* (4th ed.) (New York: McGraw-Hill, 1958), Ch. 15.

17. R. A. Jones, "The Origin and Development of Media of Exchange," *Journal of Political Economy* 84 (1976), pp. 757–75.

18. Robert Nozick, *Anarchy, State, and Utopia* (New York: Basic Books, 1974), Part I.

19. Hayek, "The Origins and Effects of Our Morals," p. 330, n. 8.

20. Hayek, "The Origins and Effects of Our Morals," p. 325.

21. A personal note: it so happened that some years ago Friedrich A. von Hayek read my article (1978) about invisible-hand explanations. After some correspondence, he invited me to pay him a visit in Freiburg. Overwhelmed as I was by this pilgrimage, it took me a while to realize that for Hayek the mere fact that one is interested in the invisible hand meant that they are surely ideological allies of his. He seemed genuinely puzzled to find out that I was not, and I became subsequently intrigued by the question why he should have been so convinced that I must have been. The present paper represents my attempt to figure this out.

22. *Philosophie der Weltgeschichte* (1930), vol. 1, p. 83.

23. Shlomo Avineri, *Hegel's Theory of the Modern State* (Cambridge: Cambridge University Press, 1972), p. 232.

24. Consider, for example, this formulation: "In general the Cunning of Reason makes a great deal of mischief at times, and the same may be said of the Unseen Hand, another name which has been given to the summing of consequences" (Martin Hollis, *The Cunning of Reason* (Cambridge: Cambridge University Press, 1987), p. 48).

25. Charles Taylor, *Hegel* (Cambridge: Cambridge University Press, 1975), p. 99.

26. Karl Loewith, *Meaning in History* (Chicago: The University of Chicago Press, 1949), p. 56.

27. On this point, see Taylor's argument with Avineri. Taylor, *Hegel*, p. 393.

10

Solidarity in Consumption

I. Introduction

A. *Community and Consumption*

In the history of political thought, many people have objected to the pervasiveness of cash exchanges in capitalist economies.[1] The fundamental concern often involves the potential effect of money in "flattening" social experiences and eliminating important qualitative distinctions among social goods. Perhaps the concern has been vindicated in practice; but there is another side of the picture. In many ways, social norms and practices, far from having been flattened by money, have worked to "unflatten" money. As a prominent sociological study finds, "There is no single, uniform, generalized money, but multiple monies: people earmark different currencies for many or perhaps all types of social interactions . . . [P]eople will in fact will respond with anger, shock, or ridicule to the 'misuse' of monies for the wrong circumstances or social relations."[2]

One of our major goals here is to describe some related phenomena—to offer an account of important, but insufficiently noticed, features of the relationship between economic markets and social practices. Many critics of market relationships have emphasized their apparently atomistic and alienating nature, and the asocial, highly individualistic attitudes that markets seem to express and to inculcate.[3] Undoubtedly this account contains truth; but here too there is another side. Daily consumption patterns reflect a range of highly social, even communal impulses. They demonstrate that in their consumption choices, consumers relate not just to products but to other customers too. For many goods, the principal motivation for consumption is to share an experience of one sort or another, with friends, acquaintances, or complete strangers. In consuming mass-produced goods people often seek, and find, a sense of solidarity and belonging. The impulse toward shared experiences and toward multiple forms of solidarity—sometimes toward simultaneous inclusion and exclusion—persistently reasserts itself.

---

[1] See, e.g., Georg Simmel, *The Philosophy of Money* (Tom Bottomore and David Frisby trans., London: Routledge & K. Paul, 1978, [1900]).

[2] See Viviana Zelizer, *The Social Meaning of Money* (New York: Basic Books, 1994), 18–19.

[3] See Jon Elster's illuminating discussion of the themes of commodity fetishism and alienation, in *Making Sense of Marx* 100–7 (New York: Cambridge University Press, 1985).

In these respects, the decisions of ordinary consumers are anything but atomistic. They are enmeshed in efforts of sellers and buyers alike to build networks of common experiences and identifications. Advertisers of goods are well aware of this point and sometimes attempt to exploit it for economic gain.[4] But even when they do not, an emphatically social impulse plays a large role in consumption choices and in the practices that emerge from them. These phenomena help explain the undeniable pleasure that sometimes accompanies mass consumption. Consumers' enjoyment in finding solidarity thus offers another perspective on mass consumption, one very different from that offered by those who emphasize the risks of alienation and fragmentation.

B. Goods Social and Otherwise

We shall start by distinguishing among three types of goods and investigating some implications of the resulting distinctions for analyzing behavior. After refining the distinctions along several dimensions, we shall explore the potential role of law and government in creating some of the relevant goods. We paint with a broad analytical brush, in the hope of elaborating categories that may be useful for general understanding and ultimately for more detailed work, both empirical and normative.

Many goods have the value they do independently of whether other people are enjoying or consuming them. Call these *solitary goods*. The value of a cup of coffee in the morning, or of exercising on the treadmill, may be unaffected by whether others are drinking coffee of exercising (Figure 10.1). The value of other goods depends, at least in part, on whether or not other people are enjoying or consuming them too. Call these *social goods*. Social goods divide into *solidarity goods* and *exclusivity goods*. Solidarity goods have more value to the extent that other people are enjoying them; they reflect something like a communal impulse. The value of a magazine or television program focussing on a current topic (genetic engineering of food, for example) may increase significantly if many other people watch or read them (Figures 10.2, 10.3). Exclusivity goods, in contrast, diminish in value to the extent that other people are enjoying them. The value of owning an art lithograph, or of vacationing in a holiday resort, may go down, perhaps dramatically, if many others have the same lithograph or access to the same resort (Figure 10.4).

Both producers and consumers attempt to generate a wide range of solidarity goods and exclusivity goods. These are pervasive features of modern societies; market economies are pervaded by both kinds of goods.[5] Acting on their own, however, people sometimes face collective action problems in generating social goods. Rational choices by individuals can result in sub-optimal production or coordination, and here law sometimes plays a constructive role. The analysis bears on the protection of pristine

---

[4] For examples, see Malcolm Gladwell, *The Tipping Point* (Boston: Little, Brown, 2000).

[5] Compare the discussion of the search for better relative position in Robert H. Frank, *Choosing the Right Pond* (New York: Oxford University Press, 1985); the point is related mostly to our treatment of exclusivity goods, as discussed in more detail below.

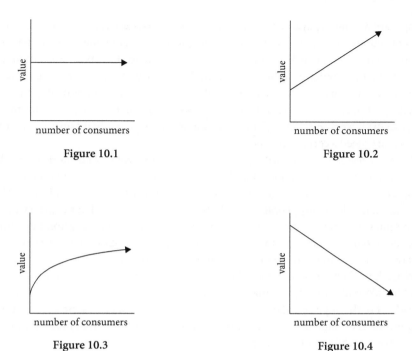

Figure 10.1

Figure 10.2

Figure 10.3

Figure 10.4

areas, on environmental and communications policy, on creation of national holidays and promotion of cultural symbols, the right of privacy, and more.

When markets fail in the production of solidarity goods, the role of government will often be to encourage people to find their way to the optimal point. Once they are there, the situation may well be self-sustaining; it is a stable equilibrium. A complication comes from the fact that some solidarity goods are bad—consider the use of unlawful drugs—and in such circumstances the role of law is to discourage their production. Our principal emphasis is on solidarity goods, as we think they received insufficient attention, especially as regards the role that their consumption plays in providing a form of social glue.

II. Goods and Persons

A. Solidarity Goods: In General

The value of many goods is a function of how many people are enjoying or consuming them. In many cases, goods become more valuable because and to the extent that they are being widely enjoyed. Consider a popular movie, the Super Bowl, a presidential debate, or a millennium celebration. These are goods that are worth less, and are possibly worthless, if many others are not enjoying or "purchasing" them too. Part of what people are willing to pay for, when they enjoy or buy the good, stems from the range of benefits coming from the fact that other people are also enjoying or buying it. Some goods would not be worth consuming, or even having for free, if others did not consume them too. Sometimes the good, taken as a solitary good, has negative value. For spouses of the sports-obsessed, the Super Bowl and the World Cup probably fall in this category. Producers of goods and services are well aware of this fact; they know that the number of viewers and users will increase, sometimes exponentially, once popularity is known to exceed a certain threshold.

What we are calling solidarity goods are those goods whose value derives, in whole or in part, from joint consumption. The very fact that many other people are enjoying them creates *positive solidarity externalities*. In such cases, part of what is good about the experience, for many people, is precisely the fact that many other people have it too. Sometimes the value of the good stems not just from *joint* consumption but actually from *simultaneous* consumption. In that case, what is good about the experience is the fact that many other people are having it at the same time.

Note that when it is said of a solidarity good that many people are enjoying it, the *it* may be taken in two ways. It may refer to the very same token of the good, e.g. the broadcast of the Super Bowl or a presidential debate. In other cases the solidarity good in question is thought of as a type, and each person enjoys a different token of this type, e.g., a drink at the end of a conference.

The value associated with a solidarity good may be intrinsic, instrumental, or both. People may find it intrinsically pleasurable to enjoy something that others are enjoying too, like a best-selling novel or songs on the car radio. Or they may think that if many people enjoy the good, this will lead to valuable social interactions, even to shared policy initiatives, business associations, or friendships.

B. Public and Private, Conformity, and Trend-Setters

To qualify as solidarity goods, it is not necessary that the relevant goods be enjoyed by people who are literally in each other's company. Some goods are *public* solidarity goods, whereas others are *private* solidarity goods. Public solidarity goods are those that people like to enjoy in the company of others. Private solidarity goods are those that people like to enjoy by themselves, but in the knowledge that others are enjoying them too. Movies in the theatre have, for many, the quality of public solidarity goods; movies rented for use on the VCR have, for many, the quality of private solidarity goods.

To enjoy solidarity goods, people need not be conformists. A conformist is someone who has a desire to narrow the distance between his or her actions and the actions of average others, or, more simply, a desire to do what others do. For a conformist, all or part of the value of action consists of its similarity to what other people are doing. Being a conformist thus presupposes a certain kind of personality. But even avowed nonconformists can enjoy many kinds of goods, say the NBA playoffs, *qua* solidarity goods.

A special case concerns trend-setting goods. If you are a trend-setter, you enjoy a good more if, as a result of your consuming it (i.e. owning, using, displaying, or subscribing to it), many others do so too. The point is especially pertinent for teen-age culture and teen-age consumer goods like fashion items, CDs, magazines, and so on. Trend-setting goods may be subsumed under solidarity goods, with a special causal twist: not only does the trend-setter enjoy the good more if many other people are consuming it too, but she enjoys it more if others consume it *because* she is consuming it. If I am known to have set the trend, part of my pleasure may have to do with fame; but even if it is not generally known that I set the trend, I may still derive pleasure from the numbers. Those who like to follow trend-setters think similarly. For them, what is important is not only the fact that many other people are consuming the good in question, but that particular, noteworthy people have started the process of widespread consumption.

When something is known to be a solidarity good, those who consume or enjoy it might well encourage others to do so as well. Such people might be trend-setters or at least trend-accelerators. Frequently their efforts are benign; sometimes they produce many individual and social gains. Consider, for example, people who are both sellers and users of desirable goods (a common selling tactic). Or consider neighborhood associations, providing voluntary agreements to enjoy certain goods together. It is easy, however, to imagine quite coercive efforts by those whose enjoyment is increased by the simultaneous activity of others. These coercive efforts may be purely private, sometimes through psychological pressure, sometimes through intimidation and even physical force. Consider efforts, within peer groups of various sorts, to require everyone to join in some activity. Prevailing social norms might develop to ensure the provision of solidarity goods; they can have coercive force. Sometimes the relevant efforts operate through the state.

Religious practices are sometimes solidarity goods, and this fact can spur both private and public action. "[M]any of the emotional and psychic rewards of religion are greater to the degree that they are socially generated and experienced. One can, of course, enjoy singing hymns alone. But that experience falls far short of singing along with hundreds of others."[6] For members of some religious organizations, the value of participation is very much a function of the number of participants, both for congregation activities and for more private and intimate experiences.[7] This point does not hold for all religions or religious organizations. But it raises many issues, taken up below, about private and public behavior designed to encourage or to force others to join in the enjoyment of what is, for many, a solidarity good.

C. Club Goods and Network Externalities: Two Contrasts

Solidarity goods have interesting relationships to club goods and network effects, both of which have received extensive recent investigation. We offer some notations here.

---

[6] Roger Finke and Rodney Stark, *The Churching of America, 1776–1990: Winners and Losers in Our Religious Economy* (New Brunswick, NJ: Rutgers University Press,1992), p. 252). Note, however, that the pleasure of singing along with hundreds of others is not restricted to religious hymns.

[7] See Laurence Iannaccone, "Sacrifice and Stigma: Reducing Free-Riding in Cults, Communes, and Other Collectives," 100 *J. Polit. Econ.* (1992) 271, 274.

1. *Club goods.* Within economics, considerable attention has been given to "club goods," created when a group of people band together and benefit from sharing a public good from which they exclude others.[8] Examples include athletic associations, exercise facilities, health maintenance organizations, and political groups with common activities. The fact that the good is shared may be attractive because per-person costs are thereby reduced, or (in a point closer to what we are emphasizing here) because people like the social interactions or feelings of membership that come from sharing. When this is the case, a club good has a central characteristic of a solidarity good—increasing benefits from increasing numbers of users. As the number of people who participate in the club increases, each person's cost may correspondingly decrease and enjoyment correspondingly increase.

But there are differences between club goods and solidarity goods as described thus far. Club goods typically suffer from crowding, which leads to a reduction in the quality or experience of the relevant services. Thus the value of a club good stops increasing, or starts to decrease, once the number of participants increases beyond a certain point (Figure 10.5). It is partly for this reason that clubs erect certain barriers to participation through, for example, membership and initiation fees, ceremonies of various sorts,[9] or selection procedures. These barriers operate to reduce the risk of congestion, and also to solve the free rider problem among insiders, by ensuring that members are actually going to contribute to the collective goals of the club.[10] For the typical solidarity good, by contrast, the value of consumption increases (perhaps up to a point) with the number of users; but there is no need to exclude or to overcome free rider problems of any sort.

For many clubs, moreover, members enjoy not only the provision of some shared service but also certain common characteristics with other members[11]; this enjoyment

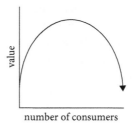

number of consumers

Figure 10.5

[8] See Richard Cornes and Todd Sandler, *The Theory of Externalities, Public Goods, and Club Goods* 347 (New York: Cambridge University Press, 1986), p. 347.

[9] Cornes and Sandler, *The Theory of Externalities.*

[10] See Iannaccone, "Sacrifice and Stigma," at 276–89, for a discussion, in this vein, of religious organizations as clubs.

[11] Cornes and Sandler, *The Theory of Externalities,* at 385.

has an exclusionary aspect. The preferred characteristics may include gender, geography, education, wealth, religion, or race. Thus clubs often form not only or not mostly to reduce the per-person costs of desirable goods but instead to form bonds of inclusion, based on the common characteristics. Here the sharing of club goods may well produce increasing benefits as the number of desired members increases (subject to the risk of crowding), but the benefits decline, for many or for all, if undesired members join. Thus many clubs depend on exclusion as well as inclusion; what members like is not only a set of common experiences, but the fact that other people, not defined in the same way, cannot enjoy those experiences. We generalize this phenomenon below; it bears on many social experiences, and is hardly limited to groups that have self-consciously created clubs.

2. *Network externalities.* With the proliferation of new communications technologies, much attention has also been paid to the existence of network effects and network externalities.[12] The standard definition of network externalities is closely related to our understanding here of solidarity goods—increases, in the value of some goods, that come from the fact that many people are using those goods. Thus "a network effect exists where purchasers find a good more valuable as additional purchasers buy the same good."[13] For example, a fax machine, or a telephone, may be worth a great deal more by virtue of the fact that other users constitute a network; the value of the good often increases continuously, and sometimes exponentially, with the number of users. Network externalities can push people firmly in the direction of certain choices, even if these choices by themselves are inferior to some alternatives. If most of your acquaintances are using a certain word-processing program, and if you want to communicate with them, it makes sense for you to use the same software, even if an alternative seems better.

The term "network effects" operates as an umbrella, capturing a number of different phenomena; but it is much narrower than the idea of solidarity goods. What we are emphasizing is not the magnified convenience and range of applications that come from numerous adoptions (as in the case of the fax machine or telephone), but the subjective benefits, hedonic and otherwise, that come from the very fact that many people are enjoying the relevant good or activity. For network goods, the paradigmatic case has to do with actual networks—goods whose purpose is to connect people to other

---

[12] See Michael Katz and Carl Shapiro, "Network Externalities, Competition, and Compatibility," 75 *Am Econ Rev* 424 (1985); Philip Dybvig and Chester Spatt, "Adoption Extenalities as Public Goods," 20 *J. Pub. Con.* 231 (1983). Mark Lemley and David McGowan, "Legal Implications of Network Economic Effects," 86 *Cal. L. Re.* 479 (1998). On the distinction between network effects and network externalities—terms often used interchangeably—see S.J. Liebowitz and Stephen Margolis, "Network Externality: An Uncommon Tragedy," 8 *J. Econ. Persp.* (1994) 133, 135 (suggesting that "network effects" apply to markets with increasing returns to scale and "network externalities" should be restricted to markets in which increasing returns create suboptimal conditions).

[13] Liebowitz and Margolis, "Network Externality," at 483.

people.[14] Because of its function, a telephone or a fax machine is obviously more valuable if many people have them. A language is a "network" in this sense. But network effects are created also by products that are not used for communication at all. Think for example of a credit card: the more popular the brand, the more businesses will accept it and even offer deals to its carriers. Conventional network effects are further created by products that are not used for communication in the strict sense, but that permit information to be exchanged more readily among people who may seek to exchange information. The value of these products, like a popular word-processing program, increases when other people are using them.

In this light, we can see that network effects turn some goods into solidarity goods of a specific kind. But the category of solidarity externalities, as we understand it here, is far larger than the category of network externalities, above all because we are emphasizing solidarity in consumption. The increase in value from a television situation comedy, stemming from the wide viewing audience for that show, is not what is meant by a network externality. As we shall see, moreover, many solidarity goods are not restricted to the causal connection that leads to the standard consequence of network effects, which is increasing returns to scale; solidarity goods come with a diverse range of value functions. But it is certainly possible to understand our analysis of solidarity goods as a large-scale expansion of the category of network effects, with the suggestion that similar effects stem from a wide range of goods and services.

D. Solitary Goods

Many goods are solitary goods. Their value is quite independent of whether other people enjoy them. For such goods, it does not matter whether many, few, or none are involved. Some people have this attitude toward sporting events and television programs; drinking a glass of orange juice in the morning, driving a Toyota Camry, or exercising on your treadmill are typical examples for many people.

The value of solitary goods, like that of solidarity goods, may be intrinsic, instrumental, or both. People may enjoy a presidential debate simply because it is fun to watch it; or they may enjoy it because they learn from the debate how to think, or not to think, about political issues. What matters is not whether the value of the good is intrinsic or instrumental, but whether value is affected by the fact that others are consuming or enjoying it.

E. Exclusivity Goods

Exclusivity goods are valued to the extent that can be enjoyed in small groups or alone. The fact that others are enjoying them makes them worth less and perhaps much less. This is true for certain status-related goods, sometimes described as positional goods,[15]

---

[14] See Katz and Shapiro, "Network Externalities," at 424; Lemley and McGowan, "Legal Implications of Network Economic Effects," at 488.

[15] The term was coined in Fred Hirsch, *Social Limits to Growth* (Cambridge, MA: Harvard University Press, 1976). See Robert Frank, *Choosing the Right Pond* (1985); Robert Frank, *Luxury Fever* (New York: Free Press, 1999), for general discussion.

and it is also true for goods that allow or create solitude—a beach house, for example, in a remote area. Often exclusive or near-exclusive enjoyment is a large part of value. In the extreme case, an exclusivity good has the value it has because only one person is able to enjoy it. (Consider: you are a Hollywood actress, and the good in question is a dress for the Oscar night. Small disasters have been known to occur when two actresses turned up with the very same dress.) Of course producers exploit this property of some goods, by emphasizing their rare or unique character; scarcity may be intentionally manufactured for this purpose, as in the case of the "rare commemorative coin," printed in limited editions.

Sole ownership, made possible by the institution of private property, does not mean that everything that is privately owned should count as an exclusivity good. While I have a right to sole ownership of my own Toyota Camry, I may be indifferent to the question how many others own a Toyota Camry as well. Indeed, my Toyota Camry may be a solidarity good for me: I may enjoy the fact that this is a popular car and that there are many others who also own a token of this type. My enjoyment of this fact, moreover, may be both intrinsic and instrumental. By contrast, a highly expensive Mercedes may, for its owners, count as an exclusivity good. If many others come to own a similar car, some people will predictably switch to a Porche.[16]

F. Demi-Solidarity Goods

There is an interesting class of goods that do not quite fit any of the three categories; call these *demi-solidarity goods*. For such goods, it is undesirable to see *either* increases in use above a certain point *or* decreases below a certain point. You might choose to attend a seminar only if it is neither very large nor very small. You may want to go to a restaurant, but you will not go either if it is very crowded or if you will be almost alone there.

Something similar is often true for decisions about clothing. Many people do not want simply to follow the crowd, but they also do not want to stand out too much. The goods should be popular, but not too popular. For demi-solidarity goods the number of users matters and may be crucial to choice. But value neither increases nor decreases continuously as a function of that number (figure 10.6).

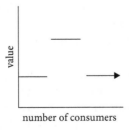

Figure 10.6

---

[16] See Frank, *Luxury Fever.*

In a related process, people may want to create organizations that represent an ideal combination of solidarity and exclusivity. Many clubs thus provide a special set of demi-solidarity goods. Such clubs are valued partly because they allow a certain group, defined in specified terms, to enjoy goods and activities in common, while at the same time excluding others, also defined in specified terms. Here the solidarity good depends on a degree of exclusivity, and vice versa. In fact group identity often depends on the right mix of solidarity and exclusivity.

III. Values and Reasons

A. *The Relational Character of Goods*

Thus far we have been writing as if goods qualify or fail to qualify as one of the various types because of what they "are." But this is an oversimplification. The nature of a good, for any particular person, depends not only on its innate qualities but also on how particular people relate to it. Here people differ from one another, often dramatically. It is not possible to "read" the nature of the good, along the dimension that we are discussing, off the good itself; it is necessary to know how people react to it, and people, groups, and even cultures typically vary along relevant dimensions.

A faculty lounge may be a solidarity good for some people, who like it best when it is crowded. But it may be a solitary good for others, who go for the coffee, and who do not care how many people are there. And it may be an exclusivity good for others, who like it best or perhaps only when it is empty. A Super Bowl may be a solidarity good for many people, who organize parties around the event, but a solitary good for others, who most like to watch it alone. A Jane Austen novel may be a solitary good for some, but for the members of a Jane Austen Society, it may be a solidarity (or a demi-solidarity) good instead. Those who market a certain good—sneakers, for example—might try to convert it into a solidarity good for many or most; they may or may not succeed.

Strictly speaking, then, the notion of a solidarity good is a relational one: a given good may be a solidarity good to me, or to you, but not a solidarity good as such. Still, in spite of possible idiosyncrasies, many goods are solidarity goods to many or to most people. These are typical cases, and we may talk of the typical cases as solidarity goods *tout court*. If a good is said to be a solidarity good, the understanding is that there exist many to whom the value of this good increases to the extent that others are consuming it too.

It is also possible to obtain some understanding of different types of people by exploring how they conceive of those goods that they most or least enjoy. Those who especially prize exclusivity goods, or who tend to think of the best goods as exclusivity goods, can often be understood as status-seekers. Or they may be loners or misanthropes. Interestingly, status seekers are social types while loners and misanthropes are asocial types, but all have in common the appreciation of exclusivity goods. Those who especially prize solidarity goods, and who tend to think of the best goods as such, obviously enjoy the comfort of belonging, in one sense or another, to a group or a crowd. Those who think of the best goods as solitary goods are to that extent independent of general opinions and social conventions. Groups and cultures as well as individuals can differ along these dimensions. These are of course brief remarks on a wider subject.

B. Varying Value Functions

There can also be complex value functions with respect to both solidarity goods and exclusivity goods. These functions include both discontinuities and sudden shifts in direction. We can imagine solidarity goods for which value steadily increases with the number of people who consume or enjoy them (figure 10.2). We can imagine goods for which value increases up to a certain number of consumers, but does not increase after that point (figure 10.3). Perhaps those who watch a presidential debate need to know that millions of people are watching, but the number of millions is not important. We can imagine an exclusivity good for which value decreases with the increase in the number of consumers, but from a certain point it stays constant (figure 10.7). Perhaps a beach is an example: once it is crowded, it does not much matter, to the privacy lover, how much more crowded it gets. As we have noted, it is possible to imagine goods whose value decreases when the number of consumers increases above a certain point, and also when the number falls below a certain point (figure 10.6). What matters with these demi-solidarity goods is that the number of participants remains between the two points. There are many possible variations here.

C. Who, Not How Many: Partnership and Fraternity Goods

Sometimes people care not only about the sheer number of consumers but also and perhaps more importantly about their *identity*. Six relevant people may be the critical ones for you; the fact that those people, in particular, are enjoying the relevant good (or not enjoying it) is what makes you especially like it. A (pro tanto) solidarity good may increase in value to you as the six relevant people simultaneously enjoy it; but others are irrelevant. Call these *partnership goods*. In the limiting case, consider a close friendship or a marriage, where the fact of joint consumption may be crucial to the underlying choice (of restaurants, or movies, or vacation resorts). In such relationships, value

number of consumers

Figure 10.7

can be greatly increased by virtue of the fact that the two people involved are enjoying the good, which has in that respect the features of a partnership good. Indeed, the fact that two particular people are enjoying it may be what gives it all or almost all of its value. If more than the two people are also enjoying it, consumption by others may be irrelevant and value may stay constant.

But what if the value decreases? What if part of what makes the partnership good valuable is that it is restricted to a number of particular people? An important feature of some goods is that value increases when a certain number of relevant people enjoy them, but consumption by others reduces value. As we have seen, this is true for some clubs; it can also be true in friendships and fraternities, and also in neighborhoods, teams, clubs, ethnic groups, and nations. People may like a good more when it is enjoyed by a large number of people thought to be relevantly like them; advertisers often try to exploit this fact and consumers may react accordingly whether or not they do. But once people in another category start enjoying the good, value decreases, sometimes dramatically.

In the case of solidarity goods, people care about the sheer number of consumers, and in the case of partnership goods people care about their particular identity. But now we recognize an additional class of goods, call them *fraternity goods*, where people care about fellow consumers falling under a certain description or belonging to a particular category (e.g. students, Catholics, athletes, gays). Fraternity goods have an excluding, discriminatory element: not only do you enjoy the party more to the extent that more Catholics come, but your enjoyment decreases if non-Catholics participate too. Here we are generalizing the idea of discriminatory clubs—groups self-consciously formed to create club goods that include the local public good of exclusion. Ordinary consumer products can have the same feature, with more informal rules of inclusion and exclusion, as, for example, when people of a certain type wear certain clothing, perhaps displaying signals that outsiders do not understand.

These points show that in some cases it is more precise to say not that goods "are" solidarity, solitary, or exclusivity goods, but that the value of a good is a function of its solidarity value, solitary value, and exclusivity value. These values can be combined in different ways, both for different people and in the social aggregate. For some people in relation to some goods, solidarity value may be real and thus positive, but it is the solitary value of the good that drives consumption. For some people and some goods, exclusivity value is crucial and makes consumption likely, while for others the exclusivity value of the good may be positive but of trivial importance. It is easy to imagine a continuum of values and many possible variations.

D. Increases and Decreases in Value

Why do some goods increase in value when others are enjoying them?

- People may be able to participate in valuable social interactions, and other activities, because of their consumption of certain goods. Part of what they get from those goods is the relevant social interactions. For example, those who watch sports event or a popular situation comedy may be able to have a range of conversations by the water-cooler at work. Those who visit national parks may be able to talk about the visit with their friends (whether this creates or reduces value for the friends is another question). People who follow a presidential campaign may be able to understand and enjoy a range of newspaper articles and television programs that would otherwise be unintelligible.

- The fact that a good is widely enjoyed may relieve people's anxiety about whether it is reasonable or legitimate to enjoy that good. People may not know whether it is appropriate or proper to enjoy a football game or a situation comedy or a cigar; the fact that other people enjoy it removes a potential sense of shame. Or people may feel proud that they are enjoying something on which others have placed a kind of stamp of approval. Here the enjoyment of others creates an informational externality (see E below).
- People care about their reputations, and if other people are doing something, it is often reasonable to infer that other people will think well of those who do the same thing, and possibly less well of those who do something different. The value of a certain activity or purchase may increase as its popularity increases, not because of the information provided by popularity, but because of the desirable reputational effects of joining the crowd (or the undesirable reputational effects of not joining the crowd). We can imagine cases in which reputational effects are the most important consideration in consumption choices. The phenomena of cascade effects and tipping points can sometimes be understood in the light of perceived reputational factors; when a critical mass is reached, a very large number of people may end up doing the same thing.[17] A closely related point is that people may engage in certain activity in order to signal their "type," and if large numbers of people will be listening, the signal might be amplified.[18]
- For some people in relation to some goods, enjoyment is heightened even if social interactions will not ensue, apparently because the social quality of the good is enjoyable for its own sake. This may seem less an explanation than a re-description; but the phenomenon is real. There is comfort in numbers. Many people would be happier to watch a sports event knowing that others are doing so, even if they do not plan to discuss it with others, and even if the fact that others are watching does not convey information about whether it is a good thing to watch. At a comedy club, holding the quality of the jokes constant, people are likely to laugh more, and thus to have a better time, when others are laughing too.

Why do some goods decrease in value when others are enjoying them? Here too there are several possibilities.

---

[17] See, eg, Mark Granovetter, "Threshold Models of Collective Behavior," 83 *Am. J. Sociology* 1420 (1978).
[18] On signalling, see Eric Posner, *Law and Social Norms* (Cambridge, MA: Harvard University Press, 2000).

- Some goods, to some people, are status goods or, somewhat more broadly, positional goods.[19] Their value comes precisely from the fact that they are not widely accessible, and people like them because ownership provides a signal about the owner's status. Ownership or enjoyment of certain goods can impose "positional externalities"[20] on those who do not have or enjoy them. Competition for status goods can create a kind of positional arms race,[21] in which one-time exclusivity goods become popular and then less exclusive, and new and more expensive exclusivity goods are sought, and they too become popular and less exclusive, and so on, to the eventual detriment of all.

- The preceding point emphasizes how the actor or owner wants to appear in the eyes of others; but sometimes more important is the person's self conception. People may value sole possession even if the good in question is not a luxury item or particularly rare. Sole possession, say of a certain fashion item or of a kilim rug from Turkey, may heighten value in the eyes of the owner not because it is a signal about monetary value, but because it says something to the owner about the sort of person that the owner is. It may enable the owner to think of herself as original, or as a person of refined taste; mass consumption of the good will make it seem vulgar.

- Sometimes people value solitude and often people hate crowds. Some exclusivity goods help to ensure solitude or relative solitude, and to prevent congestion or intrusion. This is true for a house in a secluded area, of course; but the point holds too in less dramatic and more mundane settings. People might enjoy going to a nature preserve, a museum, or a beach most when few others are there; and they might be willing to pay a premium to be able to do so.

E. Informational and Reputational Effects

We have referred to the informational and reputational effects produced by the actions and statements of other people. It will be worthwhile to say a bit more about these effects, to see how they connect to the notion of solidarity goods.

Sometimes people's behavior is greatly influenced by the information carried by the behavior of relevant others. If so many people are supporting candidate X, or concerned about global warning, or viewing a certain television show, shouldn't we assume that they're right? Whenever someone says or does something, she may well create an *informational externality*.[22] If a friend goes to a new restaurant, or invests in a new stock, or supports a particular political candidate, she provides you with a signal, carrying with it certain information, one that may turn out to be an important influence on

---

[19] See Frank, *Luxury Fever.*

[20] See Robert H. Frank, "Positional Externalities," in Richard Zackhauser ed., *Strategy and Choice* 25 (Cambridge, MA: MIT Press, 1991).

[21] See Frank, "Positional Externalities".

[22] See Andrew Caplin and John Leahy, "Miracle on Sixth Avenue: Information Externalities and Search," 108 *Econ. J.* (1998) 60.

behavior.[23] Note, however, that informational externalities may lead people to choose certain goods, without converting those goods into solidarity goods. You may go to a certain restaurant because other people do, in the sense that the actions of others suggest that the restaurant is a good one; but you might hope that on the night that you chose to go, few others will be there. In any case informational effects are a crucial part of mass consumption; producers are well aware of this fact, and they engage in pricing and other policies designed to increase the likelihood that people will learn from the apparent enthusiasm of others.[24]

From certain actions, there is also a possibility of a *reputational effect.* If people who matter to you disapprove of those who oppose affirmative action, or of those who enjoy fast-food restaurants and Star Trek, you may be unlikely to oppose affirmative action or to speak favorably of fast-food restaurants and Star Trek. You may change your views and tastes or at least keep them to yourself. Some people may watch an opera on television, or visit the Vietnam War memorial, because other people will think less of them if they do not do so. Reputational effects may thus contribute to enjoyment or consumption of solitary or solidarity goods.

Reputational effects may even convert solitary goods into solidarity goods. Your essentially solitary pleasure from watching the exhibition is enhanced when you are told that it got good reviews, and it will now have additional instrumental value for you if many people visit the exhibition, because of the social interactions that result. You may want other people to know that you saw the exhibition, because that will increase your reputation in their eyes. (This is how reputational influence differs from an informational influence: when reputation is the motivating force, you will want other people to know what you have done or refrained from doing.)

IV. The Role of Markets and States

A. *Subjective Solidarity Value, Third Party Effects, and Objective Solidarity Value*

Solidarity goods are defined as such because of the value that is created by joint or simultaneous enjoyment by many. Our emphasis here has been on the increase in subjective value that comes from a shared experience. But that increase in value can take many forms; it is not merely hedonic. To the extent that solidarity goods help unify diverse people around common symbols and experiences, they can be an ingredient in social peace. Often they provide a kind of social glue; consider national celebrations, which can help members of a heterogeneous nation create, and benefit from, a shared identity and shared experiences. In this way, solidarity goods can even help contribute to a situation in which people see the needs of others and assist in meeting them. An important

---

[23] See Robert Shiller, *Irrational Exuberance* (Princeton: Princeton University Press, 2000).
[24] Gary Becker, *Accounting for Tastes* (Cambridge, MA: Harvard University Press, 1996).

possibility, therefore, is that the existence of a range of solidarity goods that are widely consumed helps to make for desirable social cohesion. When such solidarity goods are salient and numerous, people are more likely to exhibit solidarity: they can come to see one another more distinctly and more directly as fellow citizens with common interests and experiences, rather than as depersonalized others whose experiences and internal lives seem remote and obscure.

The last point suggests an important distinction. Some goods will have desirable effects limited to those that enjoy them; consider partnership goods. Some solidarity goods will have effects on third parties, both positive and negative. Positive third party effects should be expected when, for example, people are motivated to engage in altruistic or other-regarding activities by virtue of shared experiences. Negative third party effects can be expected in the case of value functions that have a discriminatory feature, as with some fraternity goods, or that, in the extreme cases, embody or produce attitudes that lead to violence.

For those who believe that social states should be evaluated in something other than purely subjective terms, it will also be important to distinguish between subjective solidarity goods and objective solidarity goods. Suppose, for example, that we are not utilitarians, and that we believe that evaluation of social well-being does not depend solely on aggregated pains and pleasures. If so, we might think that there is objective solidarity value to programs on educational television, or to visits to pristine areas and cultural institutions, and that this objective value outruns their subjective solidarity value, especially if the latter is seen as hedonic only. If we think that the good effects of these experiences cannot be measured solely by reference to private preferences, objective solidarity value may be higher than the aggregate of subjective solidarity values. It may be lower as well; suppose that people derive subjective solidarity value from knowing that many people are enjoying a movie that is at once silly and very violent.

In thinking about a possible role for the state in such matters, there are of course questions here about the extent to which government's role is merely to satisfy existing preferences, and whether it is legitimate for government to take a stand on competing conceptions of the good.[25] Some people's enthusiasm for certain solidarity goods undoubtedly depends on a judgment that certain particular tastes and values are worth cultivating.

B. Spontaneous Generation, Cascades and Religions

It seems clear that a good society provides a wide range of solidarity goods, whether objectively or subjectively defined. A society that contains few such goods is likely to have a wide range of problems. Without the social glue that solidarity goods provide, a society might become fragmented; it might not even qualify as a society at all. Shared

---

[25] For varying views, see John Rawls, *Political Liberalism* (New York: Columbia University Press, 1993); Joseph Raz, *The Morality of Freedom* (New York: Oxford University Press, 1986); Ronald Dworkin, *A Matter of Principle* (Cambridge, MA: Harvard University Press, 1985).

experiences and memories are not merely pleasant (they may in fact be traumatic) but they can be important to social stability and a range of important social values.

Sometimes people can and will generate solidarity goods spontaneously, in the sense that government is not involved (except insofar as it creates rights of private property and freedom of contract). We have emphasized that in ordinary product markets, companies will greatly profit from selling products as solidarity goods. A sneaker company, for example, may emphasize the large number of people who are wearing its product; a television broadcaster might emphasize that its program is a kind of civic event, the kind of thing that "everyone will be talking about" on the next day. It is reasonable to speculate that a nontrivial amount of commercial success comes through this route.

But there need be no self-conscious manipulation of this kind. Acting entirely on their own, groups of consumers sometimes turn certain products into solidarity goods. Sometimes producers are quite surprised by this process.[26] Outside of the ordinary marketplace, associations and clubs form voluntarily, and one of their central functions is to generate solidarity, demi-solidarity, or fraternity goods. Indeed, associations can increase as a result of a kind of cascade, and an understanding of solidarity goods thus casts some new light on the phenomenon of social cascades.[27]

Of course cascades occur spontaneously without solidarity goods. If people are learning from the signals of others, a cascade can arise over a fully solitary good. People may like a Toyota Camry whether or not other people are driving Toyota Camrys; but they may have bought their Toyota Camrys because so many other people have done so. Especially interesting cascades occur when increasing numbers of people, with different thresholds for consuming the good, end up joining the process as the solidarity value continues to increase. Note that the value of the Camry *qua* solidarity good may be instrumental: the more popular the brand of car, the higher its value in the second-hand market, and it is also the cheaper and easier to find spare parts.

The success of new religions can be understood in these terms.[28] As we have noted, some religions construe their practices as solidarity goods. Assume, for example, that members of a church believe that an increase in membership greatly increases the value of membership. Perhaps this is so because such increases allow for more enjoyable activities, perhaps because such increases are important to the deity (and may therefore promote the wellbeing of members in this world or the next), perhaps because such increases fit with the ambition of prominent members of the church.

---

[26] See Gladwell, *The Tipping Point*.

[27] Suppose, for example, that in a society of 3000, 400 would not consume a good unless at least 100 other people are consuming it; 1000 people would not consume it unless at least 500 people are consuming it; and 1500 people would not consume it unless 1500 people are consuming it. For those eager to start a cascade, the trick is to get 100 initial consumers (perhaps people who consider this a solitary good); once they are in place, the whole society will follow.

See Sushil Biikhchandani et al., "Learning from the Behavior of Others," *J. Econ. Persp.*, Summer 1998, at 151; David Hirschleifer, "The Blind Leading the Blind," in Mariano Tommasi and Kathryn Ierulli, eds.), *The New Economics of Human Behavior* (New York: Cambridge University Press, 1995).

[28] See Finke and Stark, *The Churching of America*, pp. 237–75.

These beliefs will create a large incentive to convert more people to the faith, and thus proselytizing is a product of the solidarity value of the religious practice.[29] Along the same line and in much the same terms, it is possible to think of the political activity of an ideological political movement or party as a solidarity good.

The effort to convert people to the faith, whether religious or political, may have its flip side too. The proselytizers will want not only to increase the number of members, but also to keep them from leaving the faith. For this purpose they may resort to a variety of coercive means, for example by creating psychological pressures for continued participation or by stigmatizing deserters and outside activities. On the other hand, a risk comes with increasing numbers of members: Many might attempt to receive the benefits of membership without helping to defray the costs. When this happens, the solidarity good becomes vulnerable to the free rider problem.[30] The ultimate outcome can be coercive efforts, made privately or publicly; religious groups, or political parties, or labor unions may operate as quasi-governmental bodies, extracting taxes and otherwise imposing coercion.

C. Problems in Generating and Providing Solidarity Goods

These are tales of the spontaneous production and consumption of solidarity goods. But for such goods to be generated and provided, people must become sufficiently organized to overcome some difficulties.

1. *A solidarity game.* In some circumstances, the generation of solidarity goods can create a collective action problem, which is a particular version of a problem of coordination.[31] To see this, imagine a simple two-person society. On plausible assumptions, such a society will fail to produce a solidarity good—say, a shared viewing of a full moon—unless a collective action problem can be overcome. Assume that the benefit of individual viewing of the moon is 3; that the benefit of sleep, at the relevant time, is 4; and that the benefit of joint viewing of the moon is 5. The pay-off structure is shown in table 10.1.

Table 10.1   A Solidarity Game

	Moon watch	Sleep
Moon watch	(5,5)	(3,4)
Sleep	(4,3)	(4,4)

---

[29] See Finke and Stark, *The Churching of America*, pp. 237–75 for discussion of this process in action.
[30] See Finke and Stark, *The Churching of America*, at pp. 253–5; Iannaccone, "Sacrifice and Stigma".
[31] See, e.g., Edna Ullmann-Margalit, *The Emergence of Norms* 77–133 (Oxford: Clarendon Press, 1977); Douglas Baird, Robert Gertner, and Randal Picker, *Game Theory and the Law* (Cambridge, MA: Harvard University Press, 1994), pp. 191–5.

Note that the best cell overall is obviously the upper left. It also provides a stable equilibrium, in the sense that once both parties are there, there is no incentive to deviate; this is not a prisoner's dilemma. It may, however, be a problem for the participants to get to the right place in the first instance. Row-chooser, not knowing what column-chooser will choose, will think this: If I choose M, the worst I can get is 3 (when I'm a lone moon-watcher, while column-chooser sleeps). If I choose S, I get 4 no matter what column-chooser does. If row-chooser has no idea what column-chooser will do, and if he seeks to be on the safe side and to maximize his worst-case scenario, he will choose S. Since the situation is symmetrical, column-chooser thinks the same way. The result may well be that the two will end up at (4, 4), which is also a stable equilibrium. What they need is a method that will bring them to (5, 5) instead.[32]

Two people, or small groups, can usually solve this kind of problem on their own. A brief discussion, providing mutual assurances, should be sufficient.[33] The difficulty is more serious in larger groups, where rational and boundedly rational people may settle on inferior options simply because communication and mutual assurance can be costly and difficult. Suppose for example that many people seek a method to celebrate the memory of Martin Luther King or of Yitzhak Rabin. It is possible to make some progress simply through private efforts and educational campaigns, dedicating a certain period to their memory. Some successful efforts might eventually generate significant solidarity benefits. But it is easy to imagine circumstances in which this will not happen. Perhaps people have difficulty communicating with one another, or perhaps they lack the relevant information (involving the solidarity benefits that would follow from simultaneity).

Under certain assumptions, the best approach will be a government advertising campaign or even the declaration of a national memorial event or holiday. Note that the main function of the advertising campaign or of the declaration in such circumstances is not coercive, but rather coordinating. The goal is to signal a solution that is preferred by all. Similarly, consider a situation in which a certain television program would have a great deal of value, both distributive and collective, if and only if large numbers of people watched it. In a period of numerous entertainment options, it might be difficult to coordinate on the best outcome, in which most or all watch. Government intervention in such cases is especially attractive because once the government provides the focal point, the desirable outcome is self-enforcing and does not require further monitoring and enforcement, as opposed to, say, paying taxes or maintaining clean air. In terms of our previous example, if the government announced moon watch, and people believe that others will do what the government says (or people believe that the government accurately reveals people's preferences), then everyone will moon watch. As a real world example, consider the widespread phenomenon of "compliance

---

[32] This is a version of the so-called assurance game. See A. Sen, *Choice, Welfare and Measurement* (Oxford: Blackwell, 1982), pp. 78–9.

[33] For evidence, see Robert Ellickson, *Order Without Law* (Cambridge, MA: Harvard University Press), 1994).

without enforcement"—private compliance with laws that are enforced rarely or not at all, compliance often reflecting a solution to a problem of coordination,[34] and sometimes involving the production of solidarity goods.

2. *External benefits.* An additional problem has to do with a point mentioned above: sometimes solidarity goods produce external benefits that are not adequately captured by individual choices. Assume, for example, that the benefits of educational programming, or public affairs television, are not captured by individual viewers; much of the benefit is obtained by others, who learn from those who watch. This is a conventional third-party benefit, and such benefits can come from solidarity goods as from all other kinds. But there are also distinctive externalities associated with solidarity goods— above all, the externalities that follow from various forms of social glue.

If people are able to interact in productive and congenial ways in part because of the existence of solidarity goods, they themselves will certainly benefit; and third parties will benefit as well. The inculcation of group identity, or patriotism, and a general interest in public affairs, are cases in point. When people are generally interested in ensuring a well-functioning democracy, a range of benefits is likely to be received by the citizenry. (This is not to deny the potential bad effects of patriotism and citizen engagement.) The problem here is generating a sufficient number and density of solidarity goods of the socially desirable kind.

D. A Role for Law

If an unregulated market under-produces solidarity goods, government and law might help. Consider the following possibilities, simply for purposes of illustration:

1. *Media policy.* As several of our examples suggest, much news and entertainment programming has the quality of a solidarity good. For many people, the value of such programming dramatically increases when many people are watching. There is a no mystery why this should be so. Part of the reason is undoubtedly the social benefits that come after the show has been watched; various interactions are made possible through this route. Sometimes such programming provides desirable third party effects; sometimes it generates objective solidarity goods, together with a range of external social benefits. In these circumstances, it makes sense for government to consider policies (for example, through public subsidies) that would ensure high-quality programming, and also to provide incentives (for example, through advertising) to let people know about it and to encourage them to watch. The point bears directly on communications policy, where a democratic government, responsive to citizen aspirations, might attempt not only to allow consumers to satisfy their preferences, but to develop preferences and values of a desirable kind.[35]

---

[34] See Robert Kagan and Jerome Skolnick, "Compliance Without Enforcement," in Robert Rabin and Steven Sugarman eds., *Smoking Policy* (New York: Oxford University Press, 1994).

[35] This point raises many complexities. For discussion, see C. Edwin Baker, "Giving the Audience What It Wants," 58 *Ohio State L.J.* 311 (1997); Cass R. Sunstein, "Television and the Public Interest," 88 *Cal. L. Rev.* 499 (2000).

2. *Public celebrations and holidays.* Much of the value of public celebrations come from the fact that the celebration becomes a public event, enjoyed by large numbers of people at the same time. A national holiday is emphatically a solidarity good in both the subjective and objective sense. When the government devotes a day to celebrate national independence, or to honor the memory of a person of significance, it is not fairly subject to criticism on the ground that it is acting in an illegitimately paternalistic way. On plausible assumptions, it is ensuring a form of coordination that private persons cannot easily provide on their own. National holidays, so deemed by law and accompanied by taxpayer funds, can be justified on this ground.

A particular point here has to do with the <u>expressive</u> function of official (as opposed to purely private) action.[36] If the celebration does not have the imprimatur of the public as a whole, it is less likely to carry with it the signal that would produce the desired broad response. True, the public imprimatur may backfire when people do not trust the government, and it is also possible that some people will feel that the government has unjustifiably intruded on their freedom of action. But these adverse reactions are less likely to occur when the event in question is perceived to be a solidarity good both subjectively and objectively.

3. *Culture and the environment.* Environmental and cultural amenities often have the value they do because they have been enjoyed by many people over time, and will be enjoyed by many people in the future. When law protects a historic site, and immunizes it from development, part of the reason may be to ensure the solidarity value that comes from its continued existence. The same is true for protection of pristine areas, enjoyed by many people as such. Wildlife refuges, operating as focal points that are also solidarity goods, can be defended partly on this ground.

E. Bad Solidarity Goods

We have been speaking thus far as if solidarity goods are desirable to provide and as if society has an interest in encouraging their existence. This is not exactly false, but things are more complicated. First, the existence of a wide range of solitary and even exclusivity goods has its value too. These help insure and protect pluralism, diversity and autonomy, and they may encourage a wide range of experiments, even experiments in living. Legal rights of privacy are reasonably defended on this ground. Second, the use of public power to increase the enjoyment of solidarity goods may well represent an illegitimate interference with freedom, properly conceived. For many people, religious practices are solidarity goods, and efforts to pressure or force people to participate in the preferred religious activity might well seem attractive to powerful social groups. In cases of this sort, a rights-based constraint should prohibit any governmental effort to increase the enjoyment of what is, for many, a solidarity good. It is necessary to develop an independent account of rights to see when this sort of prohibition should apply.

---

[36] See Cass R. Sunstein, "On the Expressive Function of Law," 144 *U. Pa. L. Rev.* 2021 (1996).

Notwithstanding their status as such, many solidarity goods can cause serious problems. Consider the following possible solidarity goods: criminal conduct, including conspiracy; use of illegal drugs; use of guns; dangerous driving; smoking; discriminating on the basis of race and sex. Many people are more likely to engage in the relevant conduct, and to purchase the relevant goods, if other people are doing so, not simply because of informational and reputational effects, but also because the relevant experiences are genuine solidarity goods, providing increased enjoyment and reduced risk. There is safety in numbers. The individual interest in engaging in activity that is harmful, to self and to others, may well increase if other people are doing the same thing. If certain social bads are solidarity goods, preventive strategies immediately suggest themselves; the goal should be to reduce signals of large social involvement to the point where the numbers begin to "tip" in the opposite direction. Indeed, a whole approach to the problem of crime—the "fixing broken windows" idea—depends on the notion that crime is contagious, with epidemic-like qualities.[37]

Solidarity goods might also cause undesirable conflict. Suppose two groups compete for new members in order to enhance the solidarity value of what they provide to existing members. One way to compete for members is to make the competing group less attractive, for example by slandering it or by discriminating in one's own private business or social dealings against members of that group. Religion and ethnicity are often pretexts, or focal points, around which solidarity goods are created; they become the rallying cry when groups come into conflict. A strand of the liberal tradition is indeed suspicious of intermediary groups that come between citizen and state, and this may be part of the reason. Note, however, that the bad effects here are not strictly attributable to solidarity goods, but rather to what we have called fraternity goods, where people care about the goods' being consumed only by people belonging to a particular category.

It is important to discourage the production of solidarity goods that cause harm to others and (more controversially) to self. Interesting cases here involve a collective action problem of a distinctive kind. Suppose, for example, that people receive little solitary value from some activity X (smoking, using drugs, carrying a gun, driving dangerously). Suppose that the solidarity value is what makes them nonetheless engage in that activity. Thus far there is no problem; this is a standard case. But suppose the problem is that people wish to stop their practice.[38] They wish to be discouraged from doing what they do, through a change in the prevailing social norms. They may want, for example, a norm against using drugs, or driving dangerously, so that the social meaning of either action is not "bravery" or "rejecting oppressive convention" but

---

[37] For general discussion, see Malcolm Gladwell, *The Tipping Point* (2000).

[38] See the treatment of second-order desires in Harry Frankfurt, "Freedom of the Will and the Concept of a Preference," 68 *J. Phil.* 5 (1971).

"stupidity" or "irredeemable recklessness." The problem is that individuals cannot change that norm, and the resulting social meaning, on their own.[39] Here too government and law might help, via education, incentives, or perhaps even coercion, producing a situation in which solidarity value comes from some other source, possibly through the altered meaning of the activities in question.

V. Conclusion

We have sought to draw attention to an important characteristic of certain goods, or more precisely a characteristic of people's relations to those goods: an increase or decrease in value as a result of the number of people who are consuming or enjoying them. Some goods significantly increase in value with the increase in the number of people consuming or enjoying them, whereas other goods decrease in value for exactly the same reason. This is a central feature of human relationships, in the marketplace as everywhere else. Frequently people make consumption choices precisely in order to signal or to ensure shared experiences of one sort or another.

Contrary to a conventional concern about market relations, the communal impulse—in more or less diluted forms—continually reasserts itself in ordinary consumption choices. Advertisers and producers are well-aware of this fact and sometimes attempt to exploit it for their own benefit. But sometimes consumers, operating on their own, make unexpected choices and linkages, and solidarity goods emerge even when producers do not attempt self-consciously to promote them.[40] The increase or decrease in value might be limited to consumers or users, and indeed that is what most of our discussion has assumed. But as we have noted, solidarity goods can produce positive or negative third-party effects. Some of them count as objective solidarity goods as well or instead; environmental and communications policies can be understood in this light.

In many legal systems, the value of exclusivity goods is widely acknowledged; for example, rights of privacy tend to generate and to protect exclusivity goods. There is much less understanding of the value of solidarity goods and the occasional need for legal assistance in providing them. The bad news is that sometimes such goods, even if they have already been produced, will not become widely consumed on their own. The good news is that producers have strong incentives to overcome the resulting problems. The better news is that with relatively small encouragement, law and policy can help ensure the production of solidarity goods, and also that once produced, a large number of people will continue to consume them without much in the way of further assistance. The result will be optimal or near-optimal consumption with only a modest "push" from government and law. When this is not the case—because, for example, of

---

[39] See Lawrence Lessig, "The Regulation of Social Meaning," 61 *U. Chi. L. Rev.* 1 (1997).
[40] For examples, see Gladwell, *The Tipping Point*.

an absence of information, bounded rationality, or third party effects—a more aggressive role for law may sometimes be justified in principle.

Our main goal here, however, has not been to prescribe any particular role for law, but to provide some insights into the importance of both shared and exclusive experiences in the consumption and enjoyment of goods. A better understanding on that score casts light on a wide range of otherwise puzzling choices, both private and public, in market economies. It also helps explain the maintenance of group identifications, and the creation of new ones, in environments that might otherwise seem inhospitable to them.

11

Trust, Distrust, and In Between

The notion of trust has been the focus of intensive research in recent years. Given the negation relation between trust and distrust, a good understanding of distrust may be a useful way of shedding additional light, even if indirectly, on trust. In a similar vein, the attempts in psychoanalysis to understand the pathological mind have always been taken as contributing to a better understanding of normalcy, and a grasp of "politica negativa" as a necessary step on the way toward a more solid foundation of a positive political theory. If I want to know about the bright side of the moon, I may do well to look at its dark side, too.[1]

I approach distrust as a problem in practical reasoning, one that deals with the rules and strategies of action that we are to adopt in situations of social interaction in which the question of trust versus distrust comes up. This approach distinguishes itself from the subjective probability approach, which asks under what conditions we are to accept a hypothesis of distrust.

Normal linguistic use suggests the existence of an interim zone between clear cases of trust and clear cases of distrust. Trust and distrust, while mutually exclusive, are not mutually exhaustive. That is, I cannot both trust and distrust you, at least not with respect to one and the same matter (say, with respect to your writing a genuinely warm letter of recommendation for me), though it is entirely possible for me neither to trust nor to distrust you with respect to the same matter—or, indeed, in general. I may, in other words, be agnostic in the matter of trusting you; trust and distrust negate each other but do not complement each other.[2]

Still, if I distrust you, this surely means that I do not trust you. The converse, however, does not hold: if I do not trust you, I may actually distrust you, but this is not necessarily so. And what if I do not distrust you? Does this mean I trust you? Ordinary use would not quite accept that. This set of relationships is represented pictorially in figure 11.1. Clear cases of trust are on the right; clear cases of distrust are on the left. In between lies the spectrum of cases characterized by neither trust nor distrust. Everything to the left of the area marked as "trust" is the complement of trust, namely, "not to trust." As can be read off the diagram, the area of "not to trust" covers the area of "distrust" along with the no-man's-land of neither trust nor distrust (in the figure, "trust agnosticism"). That is, if I do not trust you, this could mean either that I distrust you—that is, that I have reasons to positively distrust you—or, more minimally, that

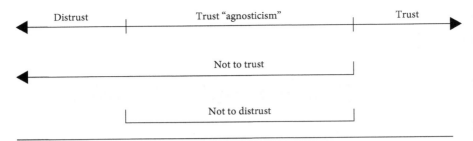

Figure 11.1

I just have no reasons to trust you (nor to distrust you either). All of this accords, I believe, with our normal and intuitive linguistic use.

Think of driving on the highway. A good driver will do well not to be too trustful of the other drivers and to resort to so-called defensive driving. At the same time, there is no reason for her to distrust all other drivers altogether. After all, she and they share an interest in not colliding and in completing their respective journeys safely. This is a common situation in which people find themselves interacting in an impersonal manner with others and in which the question of trust does come up in some "thin" sense, as relating both to the motivations and to the competence of the other(s). While there is no room for trust here, there are normally no specific reasons for distrust, either.

As can be seen from this example, the complement of "distrust" is not symmetrical to the complement of trust. Had there been symmetry, the complement of "distrust" would comprise everything to the right of the area marked as "distrust"—including, in particular, the area marked as "trust." This would mean that if I say "I do not distrust you," I could plausibly be interpreted as saying that I actually trust you. This, I believe, does not accord with accepted use.

When I say that I do not distrust my secretary, I take it that you will understand me as saying that I do not have reasons to distrust the secretary. I take it also that you will understand me, by implicature, as saying that neither do I have reasons to trust her. In other words, "not to distrust" is a narrower concept than a proper complement of "distrust" would be. "Not to distrust," then, is restricted to the middle section of the line in figure 11.1. It relates only to the no-man's-land area designated as "trust agnosticism," that is, to the area of neither trust nor distrust.

This asymmetry between the complementary notions of "not to trust" and "not to distrust" goes to the heart of the larger and much-discussed theme of asymmetries between trust and distrust. Against the backdrop of this larger theme, the bulk of the present study focuses on this middle ground, which comprises cases in which one has reasons neither to trust nor to distrust.

In the case of belief, too, there is a middle section, a no-man's-land, in which it is not the case that one believes that p nor is it the case that one believes that *not* p. However, this analogy indicates a connection between the notions of trust and belief that goes beyond the merely formal aspect. There exist, in fact, deep-level connections between the ideas of trust and belief. The Hebrew words for "trust," "belief," and "faith" all share the same three-letter root, "e-m-n." The faithful, that is, the believers, are the trust-worthy, and to believe in God is tantamount to putting one's entire trust in him. When the Lord promised Abraham a son and heir, it is said of Abraham that "he believed in the Lord"—even though he knew that his wife Sarah was barren and beyond child-bearing age. The traditional interpretation of this phrase is that Abraham trusted in the Lord. The Lord rewards him for this trust: "He counted it to him for righteousness" (Gen. 15:6; King James version).

Full Trust

The working analysis of trust presented here is an attempt to capture the conditions under which we would trust someone—or, rather, the conditions under which we would, with respect to a certain matter, trust someone in full. It relates primarily to the endpoint case, where I trust you fully about something. Note that the adjective "full" qualifies the degree of trust with respect to a given matter, not the range of matters with respect to which there is trust. When I say that he fully trusts his doctor I mean that he trusts her qua doctor to the fullest degree and without reservations. I do not mean by this that he trusts her about everything outside of their doctor-patient relationship.

I have good reason to fully trust you with respect to some matter when I believe that

1. you intend to behave or act in this matter so as to promote my interests and my general well-being;
2. you intend to promote my interests qua my interests (whether or not they coincide with your interests);
3. with respect to the matter at hand, you have the competence to behave or act so as to promote my interests.

In other words, my full trust in you requires that I attribute to you intention, right reason, and competence.

It is possible that the notion of full trust, the endpoint case, is not often applicable in practice. I start my account with it not because it is the most common case of trust but because it is a useful analytical strategy. Good grasp of the endpoint pure case gives one a handle on the range of deviations from it. The systematic possibilities of negating the notion of full trust provide us with the wide spectrum of cases that stretches from mere lack of trust to the opposing endpoint of full distrust.

Intention and Competence

Full trust, according to this analysis, is based in principle on reasons that include both intention and competence. These interact in subtle ways. They are not, in general, equal in weight: the competence component is secondary. If I have trust in your intentions—that is, if I have the required belief as regards your intentions or motives—but lack the required belief as regards your competence to act in a manner that will promote my interests, I would not say I distrust you. I may in fact still trust you. (Think of an incompetent mother: might not her children still trust her?) Not so in the converse case: if I have trust in your competence but not in your intentions, I would probably say that I distrust you. Note that when I say that I trust my surgeon, I may at times mean no more than that I think highly of his competence. That is, I assign a high probability to the surgeon's success in the operation. In such cases it will be more accurate to say that I *have confidence* in my surgeon, or that I *rely* on him, than that I trust him.[3]

In addition to the components of intention and competence, there is the additional "right-reason" component.[4] If I think someone intends to promote my interests but not for the reason that they are my interests, I do not necessarily distrust that person, though I cannot rightly say that I trust her, either. Suppose I hire a lawyer, whom I do not know personally, to represent my case strictly on the strength of what I have heard about her competence. In such a case, in which I assess that her chances of succeeding are good, I might say that I rely on her, or that I have confidence in her, or even that I have full confidence in her, but not that I fully trust her. Moreover, even if I believe that, being ambitious, she fully intends to win the case and thereby to promote my own interests, this still does not suffice to make it a case of full trust. Full trust, on the proposed analysis, requires that the lawyer's wish to promote my interests will be for the *right reason*—namely, for the reason that these are my interests, and not, say, because she wants to become rich and famous. When I fully trust my lawyer with respect to this (or any other) case, I have good reason to believe that even in the case of a conflict of interests she will take my side.

Less Than Full Trust

Still, in intermediary cases between full trust and full distrust, it may at times be in order to speak of trust. I may trust my travel agent or my teaching assistant or my representative in Congress about a given matter to some degree lower than full trust. This will be so if the conditions in the proposed analysis are relaxed in some appropriate ways. For trust that is less than full trust, we may, for example, consider dropping the condition of right reason, or the condition of competence, or both. Alternatively, we may consider weakening each or both of them rather than dropping them altogether. In the case of full trust, both of these conditions involve *good* reasons, based on full-fledged beliefs. An obvious way to weaken them, therefore, would be to turn them into conditions that involve less compelling reasons: "I have some reason to believe that—," or "I have prima facie reason to believe that—" might do.

The intention condition can be weakened in a similar manner, that is, from my having good reason for my belief in your intentions to having some reason or prima facie reason for my belief in your intentions to promote my interests.[5] This weakening notwithstanding, I am assuming that the intention component goes to the core of the notion of trust and therefore that it cannot be dropped. In one version or another, it is indispensable. This is, in principle, what distinguishes the notion of trust from the notions of reliance or confidence.

To the extent that I am in a position to assign a (sufficiently high) probability to your acting in a way that will promote my interests, I may rely on you or have confidence in you (to the appropriate degree). But it is my having reasons to believe that you *intend* to act so as to promote *my* interests that makes me trust you. This assumption becomes problematic, however, when attention is shifted from trusting an individual to trusting an institution, such as the Supreme Court or a university. The question then comes up, how are we to construe the intentions of institutions? This problem suggests that either it is possible to relax the intention condition in further ways or we must construe talk about trusting institutions in different terms.

Symmetry, Mutuality, and Familiarity

The trust relation as so far portrayed is a vector in the sense that it has direction. It is, therefore, asymmetrical: it flows from me to you. All three conditions in the proposed analysis involve my beliefs about you and not your beliefs about me. Not only does the notion of trust not emerge from the proposed analysis as a symmetrical relation, but experience shows that it is, in fact, often engendered within hierarchical relationships in which it is not—nor is it expected to be—reciprocated. Moreover, this is especially true in cases in which the hierarchical relations involve loyalty. When a secretary is known to the employer to be loyal to her, then the employer may develop trust in her secretary. Thus loyalty goes up in the hierarchy and trust goes down. This pattern characterizes such old-fashioned relations as those between kings and subjects, noblemen and vassals, and even husbands and wives in the old paradigm of marriage.

The account thus makes no assumption about mutuality. While my trustful relation toward you, as such, is asymmetrical, you may or may not trust me in return with respect to the same particular matter (or indeed with respect to additional matters). At the same time that it makes no assumption about mutuality, the trust relation emphatically does not *rule out* mutuality. Not only does it allow for mutuality, it may indeed expect it and call for it. Just consider the paradigmatic trustful relationship—a marriage of love, in which trust is assumed and expected to be symmetrical and mutual.

Note, as an aside, that the cluster of issues concerning symmetry, mutuality, and hierarchy extends in interesting ways to cases of relations of trust inside and outside of a group. Members of a family or clan may be loyal to one another and trust one another over a wide range of issues and distrust anyone from outside the family or the clan. (Consider the Mafia as an extreme case.) Moreover, a strong measure of distrust on a variety of issues on behalf of the members of some group—say, a minority—toward the members of another group—say, the majority—may create a strong bonding among the members of the first group. This bonding may even induce a relation of mutual trust among the membership of the minority group. In extreme cases, when the minority group resorts to violence against the majority, the phenomena of bonding and trust may eventually be engendered within the majority group itself.[6]

The trust relation according to the proposed analysis does, however, make an assumption about mutual familiarity and acquaintance. It assumes some preexisting relation between the parties. My fully trusting you means that I believe that you intend to act so as to promote my own well-being and, moreover, that I believe that you intend to act in that way precisely in virtue of your wanting to promote my well-being. It is not reasonable that I should form these beliefs if I do not already know you, and you me, to some extent.

Trust relations can certainly flourish when the relationships between people qualify as thick: that is, when people are connected to one another by rich networks of family, clan, neighborhood, having grown up together or gone to school together, or otherwise sharing a past.[7] But when we move on to relations of trust that involve less than full trust, thick relations are neither required nor assumed. Indeed, the force of the account is supposed to derive, in part, from its applicability to cases of casual acquaintances, that is, to cases that qualify as rather thin relations. Nonetheless, the point here is that they cannot be entirely thin: trust is, after all, a personal, not an impersonal, relation. This point again poses a problem for the institutional case. If it can be said that you trust the police, what sort of "mutual familiarity and acquaintance" between you and the police is one talking about here?

Trust Differentiated

The problem of trust is here presented within the framework of practical deliberation. When I assess my options for action, given the situation I am in, my decision as to how to act may at times depend on whether or not I have reasons to trust the person I am about to interact with. Thus framed, this is different from the theoretical problem of assigning subjective probability to the hypothesis that that person is trustworthy.

Still, the approach here offered is epistemic. The analysis of trust cites three belief conditions as reasons for my fully trusting someone. The beliefs involved are propositional: they have to do with "belief that," not with "belief in." One's faith, as expressed in one's belief in God, is related in religiously important ways to one's trust in God. But this is not the notion of trust I wish to focus on here. "Belief in" is, then, a notion from which our notion of trust has to be distanced.

Another notion from which trust has to be differentiated is confidence or reliance. The latter notions do not essentially involve the imputing of intentions; they lend themselves more readily to the subjective probability approach. I may rely on, or have confidence in, some*thing* (a bridge, for example), not only in some*one*. Trust, in contrast, relates only to people.

Finally, trust as here approached must be distanced from emotions. To be sure, when I trust you, and more so when I fully trust you, and especially when I fully trust you with respect to a wide range of issues, it is likely that there is warmth between us and that various other feelings and emotions may be involved. Trust-related emotions are worthy of analysis, but they must be kept separate from the account of trust offered here.[8]

Negating Trust

Trust and distrust, though they do not complement each other, do negate each other. How is trust negated? The proposed analysis addresses three conditions—intention, right reason, and competence—each of which begins with a belief clause. A clause that begins with "I believe that p" can be negated weakly or strongly: compare "I do not believe that p" with "I believe that *not* p." The three conditions, all beginning with "I believe that," yield various combinations of these negations. As a result there are various negations of trust, at varying degrees of strength and located at different points in the space that opens up between full trust and full distrust.

Full Distrust

When I lack the belief that you intend to act in my best interests with respect to a given matter, I do not trust you. I begin to distrust you when I am in a position to form the actual belief that you do not intend to act in my best interests in that matter. My distrust in you increases when I become suspicious of your intentions, and it increases still further when I come to form the belief that you actually intend to act *against* my interests in the matter at hand. But this is not quite the extreme case yet. My belief that you intend to act against my interests may derive simply from my perception that our interests diverge and that you take your interests to trump mine. (When the difference between our interests is large, it might not even be seen as a violation of trust that you do what serves your interests but harms mine.) More generally, my belief that you intend to act against my interests may derive from the conjunction of my belief that you are concerned with promoting your own interests and not mine and my belief that your interests diverge from mine.

A more extreme case of distrust occurs when I believe that you intend to act against my interests with respect to the given matter, fully knowing that they are my interests. The most extreme case of distrust is encountered when I believe that you intend to act, with respect to that matter, against my interests qua my interests—that is, *because* they are *my* interests.[9] The extreme opposite of full trust is arrived at when, in each of the three conditions required of full trust, the expression "to promote my interests" is replaced with "to oppose (or harm or damage) my interests." Full distrust, then, also involves an intention component, a right-reason component, and a competence component.

I have good reason to fully distrust you when I believe that you intend to behave or act so as to harm my interests, with respect to a given matter, in virtue of their being my interests and that you have the competence to thus harm my interests. As in the case of full trust, the intention component and the competence component may interact in various ways, to different effects. Suppose that I believe that you want to harm my interests because they are my interests but that I also believe that you are generally powerless or incompetent. Here I would surely distrust you a lot, but at the same time this will be of little practical consequence, and I will have little to protect myself against. Henry Fielding gives the intricate advice, "Never trust the man who hath reason to suspect that you know he hath injured you."[10] This advice serves as a reminder that human relationships that lead to trust and distrust are more complex and multidimensional than the account here offered may lead us to believe. This also helps underline that full distrust, like full trust, is a personal relationship that cannot be founded on entirely thin relations.

Self-Trust and Self-Distrust

The notion of symmetry was invoked earlier; let us here briefly consider reflexivity. Can one trust, or distrust, oneself? "If you can trust yourself when all men doubt you / But make allowance for their doubting too," says Kipling,[11] making self-trust an item on his famous list of what's required for one to be a man. Of course, the use of "trust" here is loose, such that your trusting yourself is not entirely distinguishable from your being self-confident or self-reliant. Still, the proposed analysis of trust does extend quite naturally to the idea of self-trust. It makes sense for me to believe of myself that I am motivated to promote my own interests precisely qua my own interests and also, at times, that I believe that I am competent to do so. It thus makes sense to comment on someone that she trusts herself—or, indeed, in special circumstances, that she does not.

At the same time, the proposed analysis of trust does not extend itself to the idea of self-distrust, and quite appropriately so. When John Armstrong, a U.S. army officer and the secretary of war from 1813 to 1814, says "Distrust yourself, and sleep well before you fight / 'Tis not too late to-morrow to be brave,"[12] he does not quite mean literal distrust: "do not be over-confident" is roughly what he means. The idea that I may be suspicious of my own motivations, or that I may want to hurt my interests because they are my interests, does not quite make sense—or, if it does, it belongs in the pathological department.

Samson and Delilah

Contrary to the impression that the account here offered might have created, human relationships of trust and distrust are highly complex and not always easy to disentangle. The biblical Samson did not trust his wife Delilah with the secret of his great strength. He had his reasons to doubt whether his own well-being was closest to her heart, and he had his reasons to suspect that her loyalty was rather to her kinsfolk and his bitter enemies, the Philistines. Did he actually distrust her? Delilah thought so, and she made him pay a price for his distrust. Any personal relationship that one expects to be based on trust goes sour when distrust creeps in. The disclosure of secrets is commonly taken to be a hallmark of trust, and giving secrets away as a hallmark of betrayal. Delilah kept pestering Samson to disclose to her the secret of his strength. Samson's repeated refusal to do so marred their marital relationship. "And it came to pass, when she pressed him daily with her words, and urged him, so that his soul was vexed unto death" (Judg. 16:16, King James version). Finally, perhaps to save his marriage, Samson decided to confide to his wife the secret of his strength. "If I be shaven then my strength will go from me, and I shall become weak, and be like any other man" (Judg. 16:17, King James version). The price he eventually paid for confiding his secret to his untrust- worthy wife was, of course, immense. He paid for his misplaced trust with his life.

Did Samson's distrust of Delilah change to trust when he told her his secret? Her behavior toward him up to that point certainly gave him no good reason to trust her. Could he have *decided to trust* her, even if he did not have the "right beliefs"? My account of trust precludes this possibility. But it does allow for the possibility that one who lacks the required beliefs will still proceed to act *as if* he had them. The facts (or fictional facts) remain that Samson entrusted Delilah with his secret and that she duly proceeded to betray him by making him sleep upon her knees, shaving off the seven locks of his hair, and turning him over to the Philistines. Whether by telling Delilah his secret Samson proved that his distrust in her had changed to trust or whether he was only acting as if he trusted her, thereby acting out a death wish, remains a moot inter- pretative question. But the possibility of lacking the requisite beliefs yet proceeding to act as if one had them occupies center stage in the discussion that follows.

The Presumption of Distrust

Both trust and distrust require reasons. You will trust me, to whatever degree, if you have sufficient reasons for that degree of trust; the same holds for distrust. But what if the reasons you have are not sufficient, or you have no reasons either way?

A seemingly straightforward answer in such a case would be that you should nei- ther trust nor distrust but wait until you have reasons to do one or the other. Often, however, in situations of practical deliberation, the need to act, and therefore the need to trust or distrust, is pressing, and one cannot afford to wait it out. In our social interactions, many of our decisions and actions depend to some degree on the extent to which we trust or distrust other people. If we are in a position neither to trust nor to distrust, because we lack the requisite beliefs (about the others' intentions and com- petence), we may have to resort to acting as if we had them; we may have to decide to act as though we trust or distrust.[13]

The situation, then, is this: you must act, and you must act now. How you act turns in an essential way on whether you trust or distrust me. But, so we suppose, you have no (sufficient) reasons either way. How you solve this particular problem on this particu- lar occasion may depend on what is at stake and on your personality. You may decide to play it safe and act as if you distrust me, or you may decide to take a risk on my trustworthiness and act as though you do trust me. But when you come to face this sort of situations repeatedly, and when we want to generalize from you to people in general, you may realize that what you need is a *default rule* that will tell you which way to turn in the absence of adequate reasons.

The kind of default rule we are looking for is a presumption.[14] The very possibility of a trust-distrust gap—that is, of being suspended between trust and distrust—paradigmatically suggests a role for a default rule in the form of a presumption. The presumption thus provides a link between the separate categories of belief and action: it tells you how to behave when you do not have the beliefs that would normally tell you how to behave. In this respect the situation is analogous to the case of the guilt-innocence gap in the setup of a criminal trial. Between "proven guilty" and "proven innocent" there will be cases of "proven neither guilty nor innocent." What is a judge in a criminal case to do when the time comes for a decision between conviction and acquittal but the balance of evidence leaves him or her suspended between the two? Two alternative presumptions could, in principle, provide judges with the default rule that they need: to consider the defendant guilty unless proved innocent (beyond reasonable doubt, say) or to consider the defendant innocent unless proved guilty (beyond reasonable doubt). We know which of the two our society chooses.

Regarding trust and distrust, one possible presumption would be this: In case of doubt, act as if you trust—unless or until you have (sufficient) specific reasons for distrust. Once you have such specific reasons in the concrete situation in which you find yourself, the presumption is rebutted. The alternative presumption would be this: In case of doubt, act as if you distrust—unless you have (sufficient) specific reasons for trust. This, too, is rebuttable. Of course, it is hard to know whether to act as if you trust or distrust in the abstract, without a sense of the consequences and the alternatives. Suppose I am in a situation in which I will die unless I take a risk on some stranger's trust-worthiness (with respect to a given matter): I would best act as though I trust the stranger. On the other hand, suppose that a friendly reporter, or my dinner date, asks me some personal questions whose public disclosure might be embarrassing to me. It might be best to presume distrust here, or at least to act as though I do not trust. Some rapid balancing of costs and benefits may be at work here, possibly with a bit of "maximin" thinking.

Still, in some of the literature on trust it sometimes seems to be taken for granted that "fairly generalized distrust might make sense in a way that generalized trust does not" and that, in abstraction from any specific context, suspicion and distrust are "inherently well grounded."[15] Cannot these statements be taken to constitute a sweeping recommendation for the presumption in favor of feigning distrust over the presumption of feigning trust? If so, how is this recommendation justified? After all, we all know that our world would be a much more pleasant place if it supported a general, contextless presumption in favor of trust. The issues involved need further exploration.

This exploration requires a shift of gear. The remainder of this chapter adopts a "game-theoretical," strategic approach that no longer resorts to the highly personalized notions of full trust or full distrust. General lack of beliefs that justify my trusting (or distrusting) you are assumed. Yet I take it that it is nevertheless possible for me to decide to act as if I had the requisite beliefs. This is the intended meaning of the phrase I use here, "adopting the trust (or distrust) strategy."

With these understandings, let us note that the presumption in favor of distrust is first and foremost justified on the ground that it is considered the safer of the two alternative presumptions. Consider the following rough calculation of best and worst scenarios. First, the case of trust: Acting as if you trust when trust is in fact reciprocated can lead to successful cooperation and hence to mutual benefit and potentially to significant gain. Acting as if you trust when your partner is untrustworthy and trust is not reciprocated inevitably involves disappointment. It often involves worse: being betrayed or exploited. It may lead to serious damage. Consider next the case of distrust: Acting as if you distrust when distrust is reciprocated leads to whatever gains you are able to achieve on your own. But what does acting as if you distrust, when your partner is trustworthy and does not reciprocate with distrust, lead to?

Here we may want to look at two different possibilities. One involves situations in which, when you adopt the distrust strategy, your gains are not affected by whether or not your distrust is reciprocated by your partner. Your gains remain the same regardless of whether your distrust is unilateral or reciprocated. This kind of case may in the long run breed lone distrusters who essentially expect nothing from their partners, individualists who "go it alone." They would be indifferent as to whether their partners trust them or not. The other possibility involves situations in which unilateral distrust does benefit the distrusters, at the expense of their trusting partners. In these situations the trusters are being exploited by their partners. Note that it is not two psychological types that are differentiated here but rather two different types of situations.

"Soft" Distrust

Let us refer to the two possibilities just presented as "soft" distrust and "hard" distrust, respectively. The adjective "soft" is justified by the fact that the lone distruster exhibits mere *lack of trust*. Distrust here is benign: it does not cause harm but merely protects against harm.[16] "Hard" distrust, in contrast, is exploitative of and harmful to one's partner; it involves betrayal of the partner's trust.

When payoff matrices are drawn for these two types of cases, it is easily, and unsurprisingly, revealed that cases of "hard" distrust have the structure of a prisoner's dilemma (PD) game. (For the matrices, and for further elaboration on the ideas presented in this section.[17]) In PD-structured situations, the noncooperative choice, which in the case at hand means acting as though one distrusts, dominates the cooperative choice of acting as though one trusts. Since the PD structure and its implications are well known, I focus on cases of "soft" distrust. Here too, as in the case of "hard" distrust, adopting the trust strategy can lift you high or make you fall. It can be disappointing; it is risk dominated. Adopting the distrust strategy, in contrast, is in this sort of case basically even. It leaves one on some in-between plateau that is insensitive to changes in one's environment—as well as insensitive to the disappointments one may cause to others. One neither exploits possibilities nor exposes oneself to being exploited by others.

To the extent that "playing it safe" means hedging your bets, minimizing your potential losses, being risk averse, to act as though you distrust thus seems to be the safer choice not only in the cases of hard distrust but in the case of soft distrust, as well. But suppose rather than a one-round encounter the partners are in a situation that repeats itself. If the partners start by playing it safe and adopting the distrust strategy, they will remain stuck with a suboptimal equilibrium in future repetitions of the situation.[18] If, however, they succeed in coordinating on acting as if they trust, whether through communicating with each other or somehow independently, then both will reap the fruits of their cooperation. Neither of them will be tempted to "defect" to the distrust strategy in future repetitions of the situation.

If the situation is further generalized, not just from a one-round to a repeated situation but also from two participants to a community, is the presumption of distrust justified? This may be conceptualized as a Wild West community of rugged individualists. They are honest folks who are used to relying on no one and to exploiting no one. Still, in the long run, they need be neither blind nor averse to the possibility of trustful cooperation and to its mutual benefits. In such a community the argument of "playing it safe" does not justify the adoption of the presumption in favor of distrust.

Hobbes's State of Nature

When people think of paradigmatic cases of having to choose between acting as if they trust and acting as if they distrust, it is PD-structured situations that they commonly have in mind—namely, cases of hard distrust. Many people seem to take it for granted that the distrust strategy dominates the trust strategy paradigmatically. To act as though you trust when you lack the requisite beliefs seems much worse than simply to take a chance: it seems as though it actually *means* to be a sucker, to expose yourself to exploitation.

The general outlook of hard distrust may well derive from the powerful hold that Thomas Hobbes's grim picture has over us, the picture of the state of nature as a state of suspicion of all in all and of a war of all against all. Indeed, Hobbesians often tend to interpret social interactions, whether on the micro- or macro-level, as one-round games. To the extent that these are PD-structured situations, this outlook tends to justify a general presumption in favor of feigning distrust.

But even Hobbes himself, in presenting what he calls the "precept, or general rule of Reason," distinguishes between two situations. Hobbes says that "every man ought to endeavour Peace, as farre as he has hope of obtaining it and when he cannot obtain it, that he may seek, and use, all helps, and advantages of Warre."[19] The first part of this precept contains what is for Hobbes the fundamental law of nature: to seek peace and follow it. The second part sums up what he refers to as the right of nature: to defend ourselves by any and by all means we can. There is nothing far-fetched or strained, as far as I can see, in interpreting the first part of the precept as applying to situations of soft or mild distrust and the second as applying to situations of hard or harsh distrust.

True, Hobbes did not believe that endeavoring peace in the hope of obtaining it would get one very far. A close reading of the relevant passages reveals how deeply convinced he was that we are doomed constantly to seek and use the advantages of war to defend ourselves. But the important point is that he did seem to recognize the possibility that the state of nature might be construed in terms of soft distrust as well as hard distrust.

The fact that not every situation of distrust is structured as a prisoner's dilemma is crucial here. As in those cases that fall under the category of soft distrust, mutual trust not only leads to a jointly beneficial outcome but it is a stable equilibrium, and it is accessible to the participants. This in itself suffices to cast serious doubt on the idea that the presumption in favor of distrust should be considered a universal "default" presumption.

Further Observations

To be sure, trust is fragile. As soon as breach of trust occurs, for whatever reason and by however small a number of people, a tipping-point phenomenon is likely to occur, and distrust will rapidly prevail. Like Humpty Dumpty, trust, once shattered, may be beyond repair. But to the extent that situations of soft distrust exist and are recognized as such, the precariousness—as well as the preciousness—of trust in such situations may at the same time be recognized, too. Furthermore, it is not impossible to imagine situations in which, because I decide to act as if I trust you, I eventually bring it about that you do become trustworthy and deserving of my future trust. This is what happened with Victor Hugo's priest, who chose to take the risk of acting as though he trusted Jean Valjean, thereby making him trustworthy.[20] Perhaps this is what Samson hoped against hope would happen with Delilah.

As small children we have to start out with something like an instinctive conclusive presumption in favor of sweeping trust in the adults who care for us. After all, it is hard to imagine how small children could generally get on, let alone learn a language, if they started out with an instinctive attitude of suspicion and distrust. If this is crudely true, then a case can be made that, at least developmentally, it is the trust strategy that is for many the default strategy and distrust is learned. So perhaps distrust is not a foregone social conclusion on this consideration, as well.

In thinking about the default presumption it must be noted, finally, that not only do people divide empirically into instinctive trust presumers and instinctive distrust presumers: contexts divide, too, in paradigmatic ways. We naturally catalogue situations involving economic transactions, for example, as ones in which a presumption in favor of feigning distrust is justified. Familial and communal situations, in contrast, we are often quite happy to approach with a presumption of trust. When we go abroad or are otherwise outside of our habitual contexts, we are typically in doubt. But even in such cases it is too crude to counsel in favor of acting as though we distrust. We are often able to use various social cues, sometimes quite subtle ones, to sort out different contexts and to identify those that justify taking the risk of trust. Who of us has not encountered the classical yet puzzling case on the beach, when the total strangers who happen to sit next to us ask us to "keep an eye" on their belongings until they return from their dip in the water?

It may thus be the *content* of the situation in which we find ourselves, in its wider social context, that will argue against a pessimistic and suspicious adoption of the distrust presumption. Alternatively, it may be the game-theoretical *structure* of the situation that will achieve the same purpose, once the distinction between soft and hard distrust is internalized and correctly applied. For one reason or another, it may, after all, be the case that distrust shall have no dominion.

Institutional Trust and Distrust

There is an impressive volume of social-psychological literature about trust and distrust within organizations. The bases of trust, the benefits of trust, and the barriers to trust have been studied extensively (a useful survey of this literature is given in Kramer.[21] Quite separate from this body of research that is concerned with the antecedents and consequences of trust and distrust within organizations, political theorists are also concerned with institutional trust or distrust. Their concern, however, is with the question to what extent the public displays trust or distrust toward this or that social institution, and with what implications to the polity.

It is taken to be a necessary condition of a well-functioning democracy that its citizens trust its institutions. In a sense—a somewhat ironic sense—social institutions are sometimes seen as trust mediators. On the one hand, there is the fact that in modern mass democracies, in contrast to the intimate city-states of ancient times, no level of general interpersonal familiarity and trust can be assumed. An important role of institutions, then, is to facilitate social transactions by essentially replacing the need for personal trust among citizens[22]—consider, for example, the role of legally binding contracts as a replacement for promises. On the other hand, there is the further consideration that once the institutions are in place, in order for them to fulfill their role as trust replacers, it is often supposed that citizens need to trust *them*. In terms of the example just cited, in order for contracts to work it is commonly said that people need to trust their country's legal system and its enforcement mechanisms.

A number of writers seem to diagnose a malaise in many contemporary democracies, which they believe to exhibit a general decline in institutional trust. This relates to both public and private institutions. There is substantial evidence, for example, that

institutional trust in the United States has been declining for several decades—in federal government, universities, medical institutions, and journalism as well as in several
major private companies.[23] These finding are alarming if the ability of institutions to
function properly depends in no small measure upon public trust in them.

According to another view, representative democracy and distrust go together.
"A certain amount of distrust," says Russell Hardin, "may be useful to a society or
government. Certainly, large, modern democracies work better if we can be sure that
there are professional distrusters or cynics or skeptics, people who act as watchdogs,
raise alarms, or provide contrary information."[24]

Much can be said in an attempt to explore these two views and possibly reconcile
them. How threatening—or healthy—to a democracy are various degrees of institutional distrust? Is the sort of distrust one is talking about when arguing that it is threatening quite the same as the sort of distrust one is talking about when arguing that it
is healthy? Moreover, there may be interest in following the further body of research
that tries to advance explanations, from a variety of perspectives, for the sources of
the erosion in public trust in institutions in various countries. But the question I
pursue is a different and, in a sense, a prior one. What does it mean to trust or distrust
an institution?

Institutional Trust

As it stands, the proposed account of trust and distrust will not do for the institutional
case. The analysis requires that for me to trust X, I need to entertain certain beliefs
about X's intentions and about what motivates those intentions. Since it is to persons,
not institutions, that we attribute such intentions and motivations, it would seem to be
the case that X can only be a person and not an institution. If one accepts this line of
thinking, it follows that our common, everyday talk of trust or distrust in institutions
may have to be rethought and possibly revised.

Still, in an attempt to make sense of talk about trust or distrust in institutions, several
ways may seem to be available to go around this obstacle. In principle, one may either
see one's way to attributing intentions to institutions, if not directly then somehow
indirectly, or one may see one's way to weakening the intention component or dropping
it altogether from the analysis of distrust.

One may acknowledge, for example, that even though we attribute intentions primarily to individuals, we can nevertheless attribute intentions to institutions in some
derivative or secondary sense. This line of thought puts the onus of the argument on
clarifying the derivative sense in which it may be coherent to talk about the intentions
of an institution. One way may be to argue that it is often the person who is the figure-
head of an institution that embodies for us the institution as a whole. Roderick Kramer
cites a speculation that "people may use the behavior of institutional leaders as reference points for gauging their basic beliefs... when appraising the trustworthiness of
society's institutions in general. In other words, people may draw general inferences

about institutional trust from the behavior of highly visible role models."[25] Insofar as this is so, the question of trust in the police, say, or in the Supreme Court is translated into people's beliefs about the intentions and motivations of the commissioner of police or of the chief justice.

A different route is to tinker with the intention component of the analysis of trust. Given that I trust (or distrust) you, is it really necessary that I entertain beliefs about how you intend to act and about what motivates your intentions? Is it not enough perhaps that I entertain beliefs and assess probabilities about how you are actually going to act?

I believe that this is not enough. The attribution of intentions is of the essence, so far as trust is concerned. Entertaining beliefs and probabilities about the future course of action of a person or of an institution has to do with the notions of reliance and confidence but not with trust. I believe, indeed, that as far as trust is concerned, talk of trusting an institution is misplaced. To say that we trust an institution is to be construed, rather, in terms of our reliance on an institution or of our degree of confidence in its competence and performance. This can be expressed, for example, in the probability we assign to its achieving its set goals—provided its goals accord with our interests. (I can also have confident expectations that an institution will achieve its goal and *therefore* distrust it because its goal is against my interest.)

More specifically and more crucially, talk of trusting an institution ought to be construed in terms of our degree of confidence that the institution will continue to pursue its set goals and to achieve them regardless of who staffs the institution. There is a *principle of substitutability* at work here: whenever the idea of substitutability comes up, the question to ask is what remains constant under the substitution. In the case at hand, when we express trust in an institution we express our belief that, even if the present officeholders in that institution were to be replaced with others, the performance of the institution would remain constant. In other words, so-called trust in an institution is tantamount to a belief in the *impersonality* of its performance, in addition to the belief that its goals are compatible with our interests. Given our account of trust, it is precisely this impersonality that prevents this attitude from counting as trust.

When we trust an individual, we expect his or her attitude toward us to be entirely personal. When we say we trust an institution, we expect its attitude to us to be impersonal. Can it be the same notion of trust that is invoked in both cases? I think not. Strictly speaking, in the institutional case it is a misnomer to talk of trust.

This may have to be somewhat qualified, though. Often, talk of trust is bound up with social role. I may trust my dean; you may trust the U.S. president; he may trust the federal court. What is meant here is something not entirely impersonal yet less personal than in the noninstitutional case.[26] In trusting the dean, I trust that she will not be corrupt, that she will not play favorites, that the interests of the institution will have priority at her heart, that she is competent, that she will try to do her best. These express confident expectations, not trust in the full personal sense. Nevertheless, it must be acknowledged that talk of trust here is consistent with ordinary usage and cannot easily be dispensed with.

Institutional Distrust

The case of distrust in institutions, however, is different. Here, I believe that we do attribute intentions and motivations, and not just to the figure-heads of the institution.

Consider, for example, the case of the ultraorthodox in Israel, who in recent years have expressed growing distrust in the Israeli Supreme Court. Consider also the case of the Arab Israeli minority, whose members now talk of having lost whatever trust they had in the Israeli police.[27] In expressing their distrust in the respective institutions, these people are conveying something other than a mere factual prediction to the effect that the Court or the police will act in ways that will not further their interests but will rather collide with them. Their expression of distrust has a surplus element that goes beyond expressing nonreliance or low degrees of confidence. Rather, I believe, these communities want to be understood as imputing intentions, diffusely, to those who staff the respective institutions.

What intentions can these be, given that there is no personal acquaintance and there are no personal relations between the individuals involved? At bottom, I suggest, the question of distrust in an institution boils down to one's belief in the unfairness of the institution—and to the ancillary belief that the unfairness works against one's interests. When an institution faces a crisis of trust, which is at the same time a crisis of legitimacy, this means that segments of the populace in need of recourse to the institution in question suspect it of operating in an unfair manner, a manner that goes against their interests. More specifically, in many cases this means that these members of the public tend to impute discriminatory intentions quite generally to the officeholders at all levels of hierarchy in the institution—for example, to all the judges or to all the policemen and policewomen. The discriminatory intentions may be racist, sexist, homophobic, anti-Semitic, antireligious, or what have you.

The flip side of any discriminatory intentions that make some people distrust an institution is that the very same institution may become highly trustworthy to people with other, opposing, interests. In a city where the police favor the Mafia, it may be expected that the general citizenry will distrust the police. Can we say that the members of the Mafia trust the police? Well, they sure do, in some sense. But their trust in the police is in the personal sense of trust, not in the institutional sense that is premised on impersonality and substitutability.

The mafiosi's trust in the police cannot be the trust we are after when we reflect upon the role of institutional trust in a healthy democracy. Their trust is a perversion of the trust in institutions that is claimed to be required for mass democracy to work. A necessary condition for institutional trust worthy of its name is confidence in the fairness and impartiality of the institution. (It is not a sufficient condition, though, as the element of competence is missing.) When this condition is fulfilled, there is no imputing of personal intentions to those who staff the institution; the principle of substitutability holds.

The point, then, is that in contrast to the case of institutional trust, institutional distrust does involve the imputing of intentions. It involves a shared belief among groups of citizens about the personal intentions of the officeholders of the institution. These intentions are taken to be operative while the officeholders are executing the duties of their office. The typical belief here is that these officeholders are infected with discriminatory intentions against the members of the relevant groups and that these intentions result quite generally in unfair practices. The unfair practices are believed to operate in principle against the interests of those groups of citizens.

Another possibility for institutional distrust occurs when there is widespread belief that the institution is corrupt. David Hume suggests that institutions should be designed in such a way that they would work well even if, in his well-known phrase, they were staffed by knaves.[28] Should the design fail, however, or should the level of corruption of the knaves pass a certain threshold, the institution qua institution may be perceived to be corrupt. Here, too, the attitude toward the institution turns in an essential way on people's beliefs about the personal motives of officeholders of the institution at its various hierarchical levels. Once their personal motives become suspect—as, for example, when there is a shared belief that they serve foreign interests or are open to bribes—then general distrust in the institution qua institution reigns.

There may be an interesting difference between cases in which institutional distrust is based on partiality and those in which it is based on corruption. The first tend to be cases of *group* distrust, based on membership in groups defined by race, gender, ethnic origin, sexual orientation, and so forth. The second tend to be cases of *class* distrust, in which the institution is taken to operate in such a way that the rich can get away with things that the poor cannot. The two kinds of institutional distrust may of course overlap, and there may be various intermediate cases, too.

Conclusion

The account of trust offered in this chapter is a belief-based account: roughly, I trust you when I believe that you have the right intentions toward me. Trust can be differentiated from the related but importantly different notions of reliance and confidence. The analysis also affords some insights into questions worthy of future attention, such as why trust is not, in general, a symmetrical relation and why trust can be reflexive but distrust not (that is, why it makes sense to say that I trust myself but not that I distrust myself).

The problem of trust as presented in this chapter is a problem of practical deliberation: how is one to act in a situation in which trust (or distrust) is required but the requisite beliefs are lacking? This is a problem because trust and distrust are exclusive but are not exhaustive: the absence of reasons to trust does not entail distrust, and the absence of reasons to distrust does not entail trust. Regarding those situations in which one has reasons neither for trust nor for distrust, can there be a reasoned policy in favor of acting as though one had reasons for either? The commonly held idea that the presumption in favor of acting as though you distrust is better and safer than the opposite presumption is probed. On the basis of the notion of soft distrust, this chapter argues that a pessimistic and suspicious adoption of the distrust presumption as a general rule of behavior is unfounded.

The account of trust in relation to institutions requires some modifications. Because institutions cannot have intentions in anything like the way persons have intentions, to say that we trust an institution cannot involve an ordinary ascription of intentions. What we ordinarily mean by trusting an institution should be construed not in terms of trust but rather in terms of our confident prediction that the institution will pursue its goals. Moreover, when we say that we trust an institution we expect the institution to be impersonal, whereas in trusting an individual we expect his or her attitude toward us to be entirely personal. In light of such considerations, in the institutional case it is a misnomer to talk of trust. Not so, however, in the case of distrust. Distrusting an institution is not a matter of confident predictions, and it does involve the assigning of intentions. Institutional distrust embodies one's belief that the intentions of the office-holders of the institution are discriminatory and that the institution is consequently unfair in ways that work against one's interests.

Notes

1. Avishai Margalit, "Recognition," in *Proceedings of the Aristotelian Society* Supp. Vol. 75 (2001), pp. 127–8.
2. Russell Hardin, "Distrust," *B.U. L. Rev.* 81 (2001): 496.
3. I learned about the role of competence in trust from Sidney Morgenbesser.
4. It is mostly this condition that distinguishes my account from Hardin's encapsulated-interest account of trust (elaborated in Russell Hardin, *Trust and Trustworthiness* (New York: Russell Sage Foundation, 2002). Strictly speaking, intention is subsumed under right reasons. The focus of the two conditions, however, is different.
5. The intention condition can also be strengthened. It may be the case that I believe that you intend to behave or act so as to promote my interests and my general well-being not only with respect to a particular matter but in all matters. This may be because I believe that you love me, as a parent or a spouse, or because I believe that you value me highly as a friend. We may say that in such cases my trust in you is not only *full* but also *complete*. That is, it relates both to the full degree to which I trust you with respect to any given matter and to the complete range of matters with respect to which I fully trust you: I trust you with everything and anything. Cases of full and complete trust may be rare, but they are not nonexistent. (See also note 4 for the analogous notion of *complete* distrust.)
6. See Diego Gambetta, "Mafia: The Price of Distrust," in *Trust: Making and Breaking Cooperative Relations* (Diego Gambetta ed.) (New York: Basil Blackwell, 1988); Edward Banfield, *The Moral Basis of a Backward Society* (New York: Free Press, 1958).

7. Avishai Margalit, *The Ethics of Memory* (Cambridge, MA: Harvard University Press, 2002); see also Bernard Williams, "Formal Structures and Social Reality," in Diego Gambetta ed., *Trust: Making and Breaking Cooperative Relations* (New York: Basil Blackwell, 1988).

8. Jack M. Barbalet, "Social Emotions: Confidence, Trust and Loyalty," *Int'l J. of Sociology & Social Pol'y* 16 (1996): 75–96.

9. Note that one may speak also of *complete* distrust, in analogy to complete trust (see note 3). My distrust is complete when it is not relativized to a particular matter, that is, when I distrust you with respect to everything and anything. This may be because you are my bitter enemy and I believe that you thoroughly hate me.

10. Henry Fielding, *Jonathan Wild: The Journal of a Voyage to Lisbon* (London: J. M. Dent & Sons, Ltd., 1964 [1743]), p. 94.

11. Rudyard Kipling, "If," in Daniel Karlin ed., *Rudyard Kipling* (Oxford: Oxford University Press, 1999), p. 496.

12. John Armstrong, *The Art of Preserving Health* (1804 [1744]), p. 141.

13. For a relevant discussion of an analogous distinction, between believing a proposition true and deciding to behave as if we believe it true, see Edna Ullmann-Margalit and Avishai Margalit "Holding True and Holding As True," *Synthese* 92(2) (1992): 167–87.

14. Edna Ullmann-Margalit, "On Presumption," *J. of Philosophy* 80(3) (1983): 143–63.

15. Russell Hardin, "Distrust," p. 500. While these are quotes from Hardin's article, they do not express his view.

16. See Russell Hardin, "Distrust," pp. 495–96.

17. See Edna Ullmann-Margalit, "Trust out of Distrust," *J. of Philosophy* 99(10) (2002): pp. 532–48.

18. See Russell Hardin, *Trust and Trustworthiness*, chap. 5.

19. Thomas Hobbes, *Leviathan* (C. B. Macpherson ed.) (London: Penguin 1968 [1651]), p. 190.

20. Victor Hugo, *Les Miserables* (Charles E. Wilbour trans.) (New York: The Modern Library, 1992 [1862]).

21. Roberick M. Kramer, "Trust and Distrust in Organizations: Emerging Perspectives, Enduring Questions," *Annual Rev. of Psychology* 50 (1999): 569–98.

22. See Russell Hardin, "Distrust," p. 518; also see Russell Hardin, *Trust and Trustworthiness*, chaps. 7, 8.

23. See James Coleman, *Foundations of Social Theory* (Cambridge, MA: Harvard University Press, 1990); David J. Carnevale, *Trustworthy Government; Leadership and Management Strategies for Building Turst and High Performance* (San Francisco: Jossey-Bass, 1995); Joseph S. Ney et al., *Why People Don't Trust Government* (Cambridge, MA: Harvard University Press, 1997). See also Paul Slovic, "Perceived Risk, Trust and Democracy," *Risk Analysis* 13(6) (1993): pp. 675–82, for a discussion of distrust in nationwide institutions responsible for risk management in connection with technological hazards. It would surely come as no surprise if the Enron-Anderson debacles of late were shown to have produced serious new waves of distrust in financial institutions.

24. Russell Hardin, "Distrust," p. 517. "Although often portrayed in the popular press and social science literature largely in negative terms, distrust and suspicion may constitute appropriate and even highly adaptive stances toward institutions. Vigilance and weariness about institutions, some have argued, constitute essential components of healthy and resilient organizations and societies. From this perspective, distrust and suspicion may, in a fundamental

sense, constitute potent and important forms of social capital" (Roderick Kramer, "Trust and Distrust in Organizations," p. 590). See also John Hart Ely, *Democracy and Distrust* (Cambridge, MA: Harvard University Press, 1980) and Mark E. Warren, "Democratic Theory and Trust," in Mark E. Warren ed., *Democracy and Trust* (Cambridge, UK: Cambridge University Press, 1999).

25. Roderick Kramer, "Trust and Distrust in Organizations," p. 589.

26. When I trust my lawyer qua my lawyer, this is less than full personal trust in a friend qua friend but more than just full confidence in *a* lawyer, as distinct from *my* lawyer. (Compare the lawyer example under the section "Full Trust.")

27. The acute crisis in Israel goes back to early October 2000, when the Israeli police shot to death thirteen Arab Israeli citizens during demonstrations that erupted in connection with the Palestinian uprising.

28. David Hume, "Of the Independency of Parliament," in *David Hume: Essays Moral, Political, and Literary* (Eugen F. Miller ed.) (Indianapolis: Liberty Fund, 1987).

12

The Case of the Camera in the Kitchen
Surveillance, Privacy, Sanctions, and Governance

Introduction

The incident

In the summer of 2007, a senior member of the Center for the Study of Rationality at the Hebrew University of Jerusalem arranged for the installment of a closed-circuit TV camera in the Center's kitchen. An email went to all the members, explaining that the camera was installed to solve the problem of cleanness in the kitchen.

Within minutes, a response was circulated, expressing dismay: "I find this very offensive! [–] What kind of idea is this??" This message was the first in a torrent of emails; within a week, some 120 emails were circulated, using the internal mailing list of the Center.

A week later, I, as the director of the Center, ordered the removal of the camera. I should mention that my position against the camera—as well as that of the first email writer, quoted above—was, and remained, a minority position in the Center. In what follows, I make my case against the camera. Still, I attempt to canvass the set of issues involved in an evenhanded manner.

The issues that exercised the participants in the email exchange quickly diverged and multiplied. From a mere expression of opinion for or against the camera in the kitchen, people started worrying about a wider range of concerns. Among them, the effectiveness of electronic surveillance and its morality, the difference between being watched by a person and being watched by a camera, and the methods and costs involved in confronting colleagues and in sanctioning them. Also discussed was the question of humiliation involved in cleaning after oneself as compared with cleaning after someone else, as well as the nature and status of a university research center as a community. People wondered whether, from the point of view of privacy concerns, the kitchen of such a center is closer to being a clear case of a public space (like, say, an airport) or of private space (such as one's home).

A different set of issues related to governance. What is the appropriate process that a university research center should adopt for settling such a matter; should it be a democratic vote, letting the majority opinion prevail? If so, do all Center members get to vote or should the vote be open only to those who regularly use the kitchen? Some members felt strongly that a principled moral objection to the camera, even if voiced by a small minority of Center members, ought to be accorded effective veto power overriding the majority opinion. Others felt strongly that the intense feelings of regular kitchen users whose cleanness sensibilities are offended by the occasional dirtiness of the kitchen constitute good enough reason to go along with the idea of the camera.

The incident of the kitchen camera affords us a valuable, and in some respects hilarious, opportunity to reflect upon this set of issues. It is the smallness, concreteness, and seeming triviality of the incident that helps bring this rich set of interconnected, vexing normative concerns into sharper relief. I regard the incident as a sort of peephole through which a large painted canvas reveals itself. In this essay, I try to delineate the main contours of the intricate painting that emerges, while constantly remaining aware of and referring back to the peephole itself—namely, the kitchen camera case—that gives us the particular perspective from which this exploration is undertaken.

The extensive email exchange among the members of the Center that took place during the week between the installation of the camera and its removal, serves me as an invaluable resource. I scatter quotes from it throughout the paper, under fictitious names.

Background: The Center

The Center for the Study of Rationality is an academic research center within the Hebrew University (HU) of Jerusalem. It has about 40 members (note: "members," in what follows, are professors, as distinct from "staff"), who come from more than 10 different departments of the university. The members are bound together by their interest in interactive, strategic behavior, and by loose adherence to the conceptual framework and methods of Game Theory.[1]

The Center occupies the top floor of a lovely building on campus. Its premises include office space, and public spaces such as a lecture hall, a seminar room, a common room, etc. One of the Center facilities, and a hub of activity in its own right, is a well-equipped little kitchen. Much beloved by all, it is primarily frequented for its excellent espresso machine and a more or less constant supply of cookies. The maintenance staff of the HU cleans the kitchen every morning, five days a week. Otherwise, the upkeep of a clean kitchen throughout the day is up to its users. Most users clean up after themselves, most of the time. Occasionally, however, a crisis episode occurs in the kitchen; it becomes messy and dirty, sometimes quite seriously so.

Surveillance and privacy

Cameras everywhere

> The real discussion should be about why a bunch of intelligent, well-educated, and probably well-meaning people in the center of rationality (no less!) cannot run their affairs without surveillance. I find it remarkable.
>
> (Jonathan, 5 Jul 2007, 20:46)

In recent years, people have grown increasingly accustomed to public surveillance. At airports and malls, in banks and supermarkets, in trains and subways, at the entrance to office buildings and to apartment buildings, closed-circuit television cameras are everywhere. Many of our daily steps are being watched and recorded; our private lives may be reconstructed to an unprecedented degree of accuracy and detail.

What is the appropriate reaction to the circumstance of near-ubiquitous surveillance?

Here are two contrasting possibilities. First, it seems reasonable to say that if we are becoming increasingly used to being increasingly watched by cameras, why should we care if we are being watched by one more camera? Seen in this light, a monitoring camera in a university center kitchenette seems hardly a reason to get incensed. All the more so since the camera is meant to serve the indisputable good purpose of keeping the kitchen clean, and to help eradicate asocial free riding behavior.

The second, converse, reaction asserts that, given the unfortunate circumstance of almost ubiquitous cameras, we should do everything in our individual power to draw some lines wherever possible; we should fight a rearguard battle to protect as much as we can of the shrinking private space around each of us.

Thus, while used by now to being monitored in banks, department stores, or airports, many of us find the idea of surveillance cameras in the cubicles of the toilets of these very institutions a travesty, let alone in the privacy of our own bathrooms at home. (Perhaps we recoil less, however, at the idea of cameras in the toilets of the high security wards of certain jails.) How do we feel about closed-circuit televisions in the workplace? We may not have entirely clear intuitions where to locate the workplace on the spectrum that lies between the two poles, of the public space on the one hand, and the private home on the other. Our intuitions may depend in part on the size and the type of the workplace (for example, on whether it is a public or a private outfit, or on whether or not it services members of the public).

How then do we feel about the university? A university has a variety of different kinds of "spaces." Think, for example, of classrooms, auditoria, administration buildings, cafeterias, dormitories, quads, lawns, etc. Certainly different rules apply to these different spaces. So how do we feel about a research center within the university, in particular? The relevant community here is not like a group of employees in a corporation. Neither is it like a family. It is, rather, an informal and collegiate collection of people similar, in some respects, to a social club: more a *Gesellschaft* than a *Gemeinschaft*[2] but not identical with either. The question of the appropriateness of surveillance—which is not security or crime-prevention oriented—within such a community is therefore rather troubling.

The type of space is perhaps not a good place to start; the purpose of the surveillance may be a better starting point. After all, the reason we accept the ever stepped up surveillance around us is that it is supposed to be in the service of enhancing our security. The protection of life and property is a purpose with which we do not wish to argue. Surveillance in a university setting, however, might serve quite different aims. Academic cameras installed by management may divulge faculty members who do not show up for office hours or are late for class, those who are hostile toward students or behave improperly in committee meetings, and so on. No self-respecting academic institution, as far as I am aware, will accept these "big brother" purposes as justifying surveillance.

A camera in an academic center's kitchen, however, is a different story altogether. The very first email that protested the installment of a camera in the Center kitchen as "very offensive," went on to explain: "Especially since this is meant to promote neatness, rather than to prevent theft" (Miri, 28 Jun 2007, 12:59).

The distinction between criminal and non-criminal activities seems to carry weight here. Objecting to surveillance that is meant to help catch people engaged in criminal activities, such as planting a bomb or robbing the cash register, is different from objecting to surveillance that is meant to help catch people engaged in non-criminal activities. This remains true regardless of how obnoxious these activities may be, at least in the eyes of some—whether because of their free riding nature or because of their intrinsic messiness.

Visual surveillance

Security oriented surveillance is not limited to visual monitoring. It may extend, for example, to eavesdropping and wiretapping, to mail and email scanning as well as to Internet inspection, and more. The range of the surveillance devices used in the US following the attacks on 11 September 2001 was exposed to the public at the time of the enactment of the Patriot Act, occasioning heated debates. These debates highlighted the novel types of threats to public security as well as to individual safety posed by international terrorism. At the same time, they helped articulate the sensitivities concerning the price—in terms of human and civil rights—that may have to be paid if the new challenges are to be met.[3]

Is visual monitoring worse or less bad than, say, telephone wiretapping, inasmuch as their perceived infringements on privacy and other rights are concerned? This is an interesting, and, I believe, understudied question but it need not detain us here. I shall, however, want to bring up questions that concern the comparison between several variations on the theme of visual surveillance.

> Little objection should be raised if someone were hired to sit all day long in the kitchen—for two shekels a day—in order to modify the colleagues' behavior.
>
> (Joel, 29 Jun 2007, 10:05)

How does being watched by a person, while you prepare your coffee, relevantly compare with on-screen monitoring? In fact, visual surveillance raises many questions. What is the relevant difference between the case in which the camera only transmits its pictures to computer screens in real time, and the case in which it records the images? Related to this is the question of whom to charge with the task of monitoring the screen, or with viewing the recorded tapes. How comfortable are the Center members with assigning this task to the director (or to some other members on the director's behalf) as compared, say, with charging the administrative staff with this responsibility? And how comfortable will he (or she or they) be with this task?

One interesting suggestion in this context that came up in the exchange was to connect the computers of all of the members of the Center to the closed-circuit television camera in the kitchen. The thinking behind this suggestion is that in this way the surveillance will be carried out by all (or by some or none) of the members themselves, but not by any "central" authority, nor by the administrative staff.

If filmed, you may have further questions. You do not quite know what the camera caught, or how it will be interpreted or by whom. You also do not know whether there will be "secondary use" of these images without your consent,[4] or when, by whom, or for what purpose. Finally, what is the line separating surveillance from voyeurism, anyway?

"Reasonable expectations of privacy"

> Altogether, I don't understand how the matter of privacy applies to a common kitchen. What would one want to do there "privately?"
>
> (Isaac, 4 Jul 2007, 00:19)

An academic kitchenette is not a private space in the sense in which one's own kitchen in one's own home is. US law has a doctrine about "reasonable expectations of privacy," according to which unless there exists a "reasonable" expectation that what one does or says in a certain place will not be seen or heard by someone else, a surveillance operation by law enforcement authorities in that venue does not require a warrant or some other court order. Importantly, neither the simple desire for privacy in a particular place, nor the fact that one took some steps to obtain it, entitles one reasonably to expect it. The question turns on how one establishes whether, in a given instance, one's expectation of privacy is "reasonable."

One criterion laid down for establishing reasonable expectations of privacy is "the degree of privacy afforded by certain buildings or places." (The other three criteria have to do with general legal principles, with the question of whether there exists a vantage point from which anyone, not just a police officer, can see or hear what was going on, and with the sophistication, and invasiveness of the surveillance technology employed.) Thus, while reasonable at a public phone booth, the expectation of privacy is not reasonable on a public highway. Nor, it would seem, would the expectation of privacy be reasonable in an academic kitchenette.[5,6]

However, a lawful search and seizure operation by local police conducted even without a warrant for purposes of law enforcement is a far cry from surveillance activity conducted in the kitchenette of an academic center for the disciplinary purpose of catching the messy users. The latter purpose is unrelated to unlawful behavior, let alone to terrorist activities. Even if, according to traditional legal concepts, expectations of privacy are not reasonable in the Rationality Center's kitchen, and hence strictly speaking no violation of privacy can occur when a closed-circuit television monitors the kitchen, one may still reasonably object to the surveillance on broader privacy related grounds.

One such objection will be based on the chilling and inhibiting effects of the camera; "chilling effects" is a legal term used mostly in the US to describe a situation where conduct in general, and speech in particular, is self-suppressed for fear of being penalised. (A standard example is the threat of a costly and lengthy lawsuit, which might prompt self-censorship, and have a chilling effect on free speech.)

Surveillance of any sort can create chilling effects on people's conduct, inhibiting them from acting spontaneously and unselfconsciously. Surveillance cameras are interventionist measures: their introduction affects people's behavior, and not always in foreseen and intended ways. Such effects are acknowledged as harmful in the political context, where free speech and other rights essential for democracy might be chilled. The harmful effects will surely be at least as obvious and immediate in an academic context, where spontaneity, jest, mutual trust, and the free flow of ideas are all-important—and in the normally friendly, informal environment of an academic kitchen, all the more so.

The grounds for another objection to the camera in the kitchen will be a recent theory, labeled "contextual integrity," according to which it is possible for violation of privacy to occur in a CCTV-monitored kitchen, depending on certain specific contextual features of the case. This approach tries to explain why the commonly accepted theoretical approaches to privacy, developed over the years to meet traditional privacy challenges, do not yield satisfactory conclusions where public surveillance is involved; public surveillance seems to fall entirely outside the range of application of the traditional approach to privacy protection that has dominated public discussion in recent decades.[7]

Introduced by Nissenbaum[8] and further developed by her and others,[9] the theory is designed to articulate a framework for addressing the problem of public surveillance, aiming at a theoretical account of a right to privacy as it applies to information about people. It offers a model of informational privacy in terms of contextual integrity, defined as compatibility with two types of overarching norms—regarding information appropriateness, and informational flow, or distribution. The theory posits that whether or not a particular action violates the norms is a function of several specific contextual variables. When the machinery of this theory is applied in detail to the Rationality Center kitchen, it appears to yield the conclusion that the installment of a closed-circuit television camera does constitute a violation of relevant norms; whether or not this constitutes a violation of privacy depends, in the last analysis, on one's chosen definition of privacy.

"Nothing to hide"

> I see no reason for people to object to the camera in the kitchen, UNLESS THEY HAVE SOMETHING TO HIDE. And if they have something to hide, it should not be done in the common area.
>
> (Alex, 4 Jul 2007, 12:42)

> The idea that the people who object to the camera have something to hide is so preposterous that it could only cross the mind of one who thinks everything in life is a simple strategic game.
>
> (Miri, 4 Jul 2007, 18:06)

As it turns out, the argument that a person who has nothing to hide should have no problem with surveillance comes up frequently in discussions of privacy issues. It is one of the primary arguments made when balancing privacy against security. "In its most compelling form, it is an argument that the privacy interest is generally minimal to trivial, thus making the balance against security concerns a foreordained victory for security."[10]

In truth not only privacy in the kitchen, but also cleanness in the kitchen, are rather trivial concerns, at least in comparison with the "Global War on Terror." Still, in non-security contexts, people come up with a number of instinctive retorts in response to the seemingly compelling "If you've got nothing to hide, you've got nothing to worry about" argument. Among the typical examples: "This is not about something I want to hide: this is about it being none of your business," or "If you had nothing to hide you would not have curtains."[11]

Of relevance to these concerns is the following question, published in the weekly column "Readers Ask" of the Israeli daily *Maariv*:

I am a student in the school's photography department. For an assigned project, one of my fellow students proposed to photograph people in an elevator, without their knowledge. I believe this would constitute a gross violation of their privacy, even though no intimate scenes are anticipated. My friend claims that as the photos are intended for an academic project only, and will not be displayed anywhere else in the world, no harm is involved. Who is right?[12]

The columnist's answer was given the large-print title BEWARE, A PHOTOGRAPH HAS A LIFE OF ITS OWN. It said, in part,

From the moment a photo was taken it has a life of its own. It cannot be confined to an academic project. It cannot be assigned just one interpretation... Do not be mislead into thinking that the seemingly innocent photo of people in an elevator cannot start wandering into all sorts of areas and uses, some of which might involve the infringement of the privacy of the photographed persons, of their rights, of their good name, or more. Hence, refrain from carrying out this project.[13]

I note that a key element in this contemplated camera-in-the-elevator project involves photographing people without their knowledge. This element does not apply in the camera-in-the-kitchen case that concerns us here. Other aspects of these two cases, however, as highlighted by the columnist's reply, are comparable. Most likely, no reasonable expectations of privacy (in the sense explained above) pertain to either the case of the elevator or to the case of the kitchen.

Concealment pertains not only to criminal acts. People are much preoccupied with concealing wrinkles on their faces or their loss of hair. Elton John had a perfectly just complaint against the paparazzi who showed him to the world without his wig. People's attitude to their private parts, intimate relationships, serious illnesses, or the details of their bank accounts makes them want to shield all these from anyone's uninvited gaze.

"Something to hide" is obviously taken by most people as a much broader category than wrongful doing or something of which to be ashamed;[14] and what people want to protect as "personal" goes beyond what is strictly defined as "private." The concept of intimacy indeed presupposes concealment; where everything is known and revealed to all, intimacy is precluded.

"We don't want to expose ourselves completely to strangers even if we don't fear their disapproval, hostility or disgust," says Thomas Nagel, in his insightful chapter on the larger topic of what he takes to be the importance of concealment as a condition of civilization. "The boundary between what we reveal and what we do not, and some control over that boundary, is among the most important attributes of our humanity."[15]

"The 'nothing to hide' argument…forces the debate to focus on its narrow understanding of privacy."[16] There is more to privacy than wanting to hide.

Being watched

> Cameras are feared more than people because people are there and you adjust
> your behavior.
>
> (Rachel, 30 Jun 2007, 08:12)

What difference does it make whether we are being watched by a person or by a camera?

One difference concerns symmetry. When a person watches you, you can watch him or her back. When you know that you are being watched but cannot watch back, an asymmetrical relationship is initiated, leading to an asymmetrical power structure with the potential to engender feelings of humiliation.

The one-sided mirror—say between an employer's room and the employees'—provides an example. Or think of that quintessential scene from war movies, where the sergeant major inspects the new recruit, moving his eyes over the rooky from top to bottom, and back and forth, while the new recruit has to fix his gaze straight ahead.[17] The asymmetry of gaze strongly attests to the asymmetry of power. Movies by directors like Kieslowski or Egoyan come to mind too for exploring with detail and fascination the theme of voyeurism, or the uninvited asymmetrical gaze, and its ramifications.

When you are in the public space, say when you walk about in the mall or the municipal park, you know that every step you make may be watched by someone. There is no problem here. There is a problem, however, when one particular person is or may be watching your every step. This can be sinister; you are being followed, stalked, or worse.[18]

The problem with surveillance, then, is not the fact that everything you do may be watched by someone—but rather the subtly different fact that there may be someone who is watching everything you do. This, to me, is the heart of the matter, one of the main insights I have come away with from researching this issue: that so much hangs on this switch in the order of the quantifiers.[19] The corollary problem with video monitoring is that it is basically a setup that in principle makes it possible that there should be someone who is, or may be, watching you all the time.

In addition, it is often the case that the video monitoring is equipped with a recording device as well, without warning anyone about it. Also, once captured on tape, you may be watched over and over again. All of these elements are serious aggravating circumstances that go beyond the mere asymmetry of the gaze.

The panopticon and beyond

Much attention was given in recent years to Bentham's quaint notion of the panopticon—a type of prison building whose design allows a God-like overseer to observe all prisoners without being seen by them. Foucault, famously, used the idea of the Panopticon as a formative metaphor of the project of modernism, highlighting the total loss of individual privacy—equated with the total loss of protection from centralized systems of unwanted gaze. Indeed Foucault took the idea of the panopticon an important step further by talking about the drive to self-monitoring through the belief that one is under constant scrutiny.[20]

The subtitle of Bentham's treatise *Panopticon or the Inspection House* comprises a list of establishments other than prisons, "in which Persons of any Description are to be kept under Inspection."[21] Among them hospitals, madhouses, schools, and various work places. As the proverbial locus of privacy, the home of course provides the starkest contrast to the panopticon, and to the other "inspection houses": home is meant to provide protection from any, and all, unwanted gaze. Where on this spectrum should we locate an academic research center within a university? Do we want to see it as a "workhouse" in Bentham's sense, thus closer to the penitentiary end of the spectrum, or rather as closer to the home end?

I take this occasion to note that the interface between my discussion of general issues raised by the kitchen camera case on the one hand, and their relevance to the specific case of the kitchen camera on the other, is delicate, indeed sometimes tenuous. Of course, the kitchen in the Rationality Center would not have become a panopticon had the camera remained, so it may strike one as an overexaggeration to bring up the notion of the panopticon in this context. A similar feeling of disconnect may occur with regard to the discussion (above) of the chilling effects of the camera, or to the problem of shaming sanctions discussed below, and possibly to further issues as well. I therefore reiterate the peephole simile mentioned at the outset, and point out that, rather than arguing for direct relevance, I take the incident of the kitchen camera as an opportunity to reflect upon a wide set of normative issues, and suggest some normative conclusions.

Here is a different tale about a camera in another academic kitchen. It might throw a different—and helpful—light on our case.

> If I remember correctly, the first web-cam was used exactly to monitor a shared coffee room in a university. It involved computer science students who didn't want to walk to a different floor to get coffee if the pot was empty. So they set up a camera via the Web, to be able to see whether the coffee pot was full. This didn't cause any discussion of privacy.   (Ofer, 4 Jul 2007, 18:48)

The email message concludes: "It seems to me that the problem with the camera is not really the issue of privacy but rather of being 'checked up on'."

This is a correct insight. It seems as if the fact that one's image and activities are pro-jected onto a screen is not, in and of itself, what one objects to in general; it also seems as if the violation of one's privacy is not what one objects to in particular. What people find objectionable in the case of the Rationality Center kitchen camera is "being checked up on." People object, first, to the disciplinary purpose behind the installment of the camera. Secondly, people seem to be sensitive to the grotesque disproportionality of the surveillance device, relative to the purpose behind its installment.

Regulation and governance

Disciplining behavior

> Confronting people who were spilling coffee and sugar or not cleaning their cups based on video records is not going to be a lovely scene.   (David, 29 Jun 2007, 09:25)

Suppose the closed-circuit television is connected to the computer screens of all mem-bers of the Center, so that anyone can watch what goes on in the kitchen in real time. No "central agency" is charged with the disciplinary action; rather, the charge is equally distributed among all Center members.

This idea of peer discipline may appear attractive but its effectiveness is dubious. When it is everyone's responsibility to catch transgressors, it ends up being the respon-sibility of no one. Depending on who happens to be watching their screens at the relevant time, catching the culprits becomes a matter of happenstance.

If people do not make it their habit to connect to the closed-circuit television, the solution offered by it is ineffective. It they do, and they happen to see a colleague mess-ing up the sink, or leaving the milk outside the fridge and the foam pipe unwiped, what exactly are they supposed to do? Whatever they do, they might find themselves dealing with phenomena such as recrimination, badmouthing, rumor spreading, whistle blowing, or shaming.

All of these constitute part of the price that the Center community might have to pay for the methods it chooses to use for catching the culprits, and for punishing them. The adverse effects on the working atmosphere within the Center, and the possible damage to the values essential to the fabric of the Center community, need to be balanced vis-à-vis the value to the Center community of a clean kitchen.

Suppose, next, that a taped record is kept of all images transmitted from the camera to the monitors. Surely, the potential effectiveness of the camera for disciplinary purposes in this case increases significantly. Not only is it possible to discover who was remiss, but it is also possible to confront the wrongdoers with "proof" of their misdeeds.

However, the very existence of the taped record cannot be taken lightly. Some rules and regulations have to be decided upon ahead of time, regarding questions such as who can see the tapes, how to prevent their misuse or abuse in general—and access to them by non-approved parties in particular, how long they are to be kept, and more. Moreover, some second-order questions need to be addressed: what are the correct procedures to settle the procedural questions just posed (e.g., who decides who can see the tapes, etc.). I am not suggesting that these issues are insurmountable; but I am saying that they are delicate matters, to be addressed with tact, and with due transparency.

Let us now consider the act of confronting the transgressors with on-camera proof of their misdeeds, reminding ourselves that the transgression in question is not a criminal offense or felony. Nor is it even a disciplinary offense in the usual sense (like cheating in an exam, or plagiarism) but rather misdeeds of a different, "softer" nature.

The idea of using surveillance cameras (or polygraphs, for that matter) within the family is, to most people, unthinkable. When you find a dirty sink, or unwiped coffee stains on the floor at home, you may tell your children off, even punish them. But already when it comes to your spouse, the question of confronting him or her is not an altogether simple matter. Family politics and issues involving baggage from the past are often complicating factors.[22]

When the culprits are one's colleagues, the issues are comparably complex, perhaps even more so. In analogy to the case of the family, it may be better, and wiser, to hold back. Moreover, it may be wrong to see the act of confronting a transgressor with proof of his or her misdeeds as a triumphal act, parallel to the clinching climax of a criminal court case: we must see it, rather, in the different light of an act of shaming.

Shaming and shame sanctions

We also need a mechanism to deal with those who are "caught". I suggest that the first step will be a discreet conversation with [the Director] or somebody.

(Rachel, 30 Jun 2007, 14:25)

To treat a person who forgot to return the milk to the refrigerator as someone who is "caught" and who will, "as a first step," be summoned to a "discreet" conversation the Director, is mind boggling.

(David, 30 Jun 2007, 21:59)

Shame is a private emotion. I am ashamed when I realize that what I said or did diminishes me in my own eyes; when I privately experience embarrassment and loss of self-respect.[23] Shaming is a social act; one person putting another person to shame. It can also be public, when the act of shaming occurs in the presence of an audience, or of witnesses. Shame induced by a second party intrinsically involves elements of derision and contempt, and hence loss of dignity and humiliation.[24]

In the Jewish sources, "whitening" someone's face in public, namely shaming them, is likened to spilling that person's blood. The commandment not to shame is comparable in its importance to "Thou shall not kill."

The theme of shame sanctions has gained growing presence in the legal literature since the mid-1990s.[25] Shame sanctions have a strong element of spectacle for the spectators, and shame for the offender. Their effects on the public can be politically dangerous; their effects on the offender violate human dignity.

Public punishments (whipping, flogging, dunking, branding) used to be an integral part of the old punishment traditions but have largely faded away. The current US practice "takes milder forms, such as requiring offenders to wear shirts describing their crimes, publishing the names of prostitutes' johns, or making offenders sit outside public courthouses wearing placards" (e.g. "I am a Drunk Driver").[26]

Caught by a closed-circuit television camera, offenders are exposed red-handed, or actually dirty-handed. The exposure here is quite literal: one is seen misbehaving; perhaps one's misconduct is even broadcast on tape in the presence of others. The very exposure is meant to be, and to do, the condemnation.

Informal shaming sanctions may comprise scolding and rebuking, and also ridicule, contempt, avoidance, shunning, and more. Of their several idiosyncratic features, one is that people's reaction to them is extreme: either one finds them easy to ignore, or one finds them particularly harsh, and "cripplingly diminishing of self-esteem."[27] The effectiveness of such sanctions on people of the first sort is nil; with respect to the second sort, the effect is likely to be overkill, and hard to predict (Whitman 1998).[28]

Also, shaming sanctions seem particularly vulnerable to the phenomenon of diminishing effects. So, while the administering of a shaming sanction for the first time may have overkill effect, with consequences that are difficult to control and predict, its repeated use may prove ineffectual.[29]

Stigmatization imposes costs on the enforcers too. In order for it to work, stigma relies on the active cooperation of individuals who must incur costs in privately sanctioning the offenders; the effectiveness of private sanctions is based on the willingness of individuals to incur such costs. "Other things being equal, the larger the costs private enforcers incur in the imposition of private sanctions, the less the willingness of private enforcers to stigmatize, and consequently, the less effective stigma becomes."[30] Assessing the costs borne by private enforcers is crucial therefore for predicting the effectiveness of the proposed scheme of stigmatization.

An academic center like the Rationality Center, as a community, must face the consequences for its morale and esprit de corps once it becomes a surveillance community. It must face the possibility that some of its members will become peeved, even humiliated, by the effects of shaming.[31] It must also be concerned with the question of whom to charge with delivering the rebuke, whether this charge is fair, and what its costs might be. (And, how about the idea of a camera recording the sanctioning proceedings too, in the spirit of "guarding the guardians?")

Deterrence and its limits

> Game theory teaches us that one can modify people's behavior with the right incentives.
>
> (Alex, 6 Jul 2007, 10:51)

> We put the camera, and if that does not work, then I suggest a high voltage fence as the next step...
>
> (Andre, 3 Jul 2007, 10:23)

The camera as such does not clean the kitchen. But can it guarantee a clean kitchen? Evidently some in the Center not only hoped that it will, but were convinced that it will. Why?

One line of thinking is, surely, that the camera deters potential transgressors from transgressing. The complementary line of thinking is, presumably, that if transgression does occur, then the camera enables catching of the culprits. Once the culprits are caught and punished—and the news goes around—deterrence kicks in again and transgression stops.

Deterrence can work—up to a point. It is clear that sustained cleanness in the kitchen cannot rely on the camera's deterrence effect alone. Incidentally, for partial deterrence the camera may not in fact be necessary. As one contributor to the email exchange pointed out, "in some experiments by behavioral economists, merely having a poster of a face with big eyes on the wall markedly improved compliance."[32]

So much for deterrence. Let us now probe the complementary argument, about catching the culprits. What is the causal chain that supposedly connects the catching of the culprits with a forever clean kitchen? With what degree of confidence can we expect people's behavior to improve as result of disciplining measures?

Changing people's behavior is a notoriously complex business. Much of social science—and most of education—is about this. Psychologists and priests, criminologists and political activist, sales persons, and advertising agencies—all of these and many others attempt to affect and change people's behavior. The methods they come up with range widely over persuasion, propaganda, brainwashing, coercion, conditioning, manipulation, formal and informal sanctions, incentives and disincentives, carrots and sticks. In an open society, the choice may be somewhat restricted.

Confronting a person with evidence of his wrongdoing, and punishing him for messing up the kitchen may have the desired effect of "teaching him a lesson." But then, it may not. Or it may have the desired effect for a while and then wear off. When his colleagues hear about this, some may indeed improve their behavior in the kitchen. But then, some may not.

Why do some people react one way, and others the other? Under what conditions is one reaction likelier than the other one, and by how much? This is the stuff of complex social science. The puzzling point to me was realizing that for several of the participants in the exchange, the full success of the surveillance device was a sure thing. In their minds, the installment of a camera amounted—as a matter of necessary truth and logical certainty—to the achievement of 100 percent cleanness in the kitchen. Consider: "The dichotomy is not a false dichotomy; it's a real, practical one. If we want to keep the kitchen open—AND I DO—we either have the camera, or the administrative staff keeps cleaning it" (Isaac, 5 Jul 2007, 17:46).[33]

In fact, the unbearable lightness of accepting this means–end connection was characteristic of the proponents of the camera, who saw the chain as an ultimate winning argument. Strikingly, this was not the case for the camera opponents, who had qualms with the normative aspects of the means–end chain. Here is a particularly telling comment, revealing how people's views regarding the anticipated efficacy of the camera device intertwine with people's views about its normative acceptability: "I suspect that the people who think this measure [i.e., the camera] is repugnant also don't think it will work, and the people who think it WILL work, don't find it repugnant" (Miri, 30 Jun 2007, 17:17).

One factor the proponents of the camera did not consider, but we surely must, is that the presence of the camera may start altogether unanticipated chain reactions, bringing about unintended consequences. For example, people may wish to avoid any encounters with the camera, and hence leave their dirty coffee cups all over the place rather than return them to the kitchen—thus raising the general messiness level at the Center, not reducing it.

The point is that people do not always respond in the way that somebody intended them to respond. Their reaction to the camera may diverge from the causal chain meant to improve their cleanness behavior in the kitchen. The design of human response to a novel technical device has its limits; sometimes it even backfires.

An attempt by a respected Los Angeles medical doctor to improve his colleagues' cleanness related behavior was reported not long ago by Stephen J. Dubner and Steven D. Levitt (of *Freakonomics* fame). Many medical studies have shown, they say, that hospital doctors wash or disinfect their hands "in fewer than half the instances they should."[34]

The story highlights how hard it is to change people's entrenched habits, and how much effort can be required to solve the seemingly simple problem of changing people's hand washing behavior.

In contrast to the hospital case, cleanness in the Center kitchen serves no distinct instrumental purpose. Nobody is going to die because of a substandard level of cleanness in the kitchen. (Besides, the following morning the cleaner arrives.) In the hospital, a policy of zero tolerance toward transgressors is instrumentally justified; not so in the case of an academic kitchen. Bluntly put, I believe that zero tolerance toward cleanness offenders is intolerable within the context of an academic community. True, habitual free riders and offenders should not be tolerated, but occasional lapses and instances of absentmindedness should. A machinery of spying, catching, confronting, shaming, and sanctioning—all in the name of reaching 100 percent cleanness in the kitchen—is in my view unacceptable.

Decision-making

> Let me suggest to conclude this lengthy and sometime heated debate by casting a vote (electronically) among the Center's members.
>
> (Benny, 5 Jul 2007, 12:22)

Who should have made the decision about the kitchen camera, and how?

The way it actually happened was that a senior Center member, who had entered the kitchen and found it in a particularly disgusting mess, felt that he had finally "had it."[35] Set on an energetic problem solving course, he went ahead and installed the camera, technically aided by two administrative staff persons. The office then immediately sent an email saying, "For your information we have installed a closed-circuit camera in the Center's kitchen. Please do your part to keep the kitchen tidy. Thank you for your cooperation."

In real time, Center members were not aware of what had actually taken place. Indeed, they probably imagined it quite differently. An early contribution to the email exchange expressed the following opinion: "We have a highly effective administration/ staff team... If they have decided to put a camera in the kitchen, I am sure it was done after serious internal deliberation, and therefore we should all (and I do) support it" (Eli, 1 Jul 2007, 14:16). Several members expressed instant support for this position. Another put it thus: "I trust the management. If they felt that the situation calls for such an arrangement, which is not trivial, I trust them that the problem is real. The fact of the matter is that most places do not reach such a solution" (Rachel, 5 Jul 2007, 15:13).

It appears, then, that at least for some members it was perfectly acceptable that the management of the Center (director, executive committee, or senior staff) should be making such a decision. Other members wondered whether the Center has any authority to install a camera in the first place, and whether the university administration should not have been consulted about the matter.[36] A democratic alternative to both the executive and the administration options is that the Center-wide community should decide the matter. Namely, first, the members should have reached a general agreement among themselves that the cleanness of the Center kitchen is indeed a problem they, as a collective, want solved; second, they should have agreed upon a mechanism for arriving at a solution; and only thereafter should they have gone ahead and implemented the agreed upon solution. "Agreed upon" might involve any number of techniques: majority vote, forming a kitchen committee to present options that would be voted on later, desig-nating a special "kitchen czar" invested with full authority to solve the problem as he or she sees fit, assigning the responsibility to the Center director, etc.

Presented with a similar problem, different communities, and different workplaces would find either the executive option or the democratic option (in one of its versions) more suitable. The question of which option fits an academic community such as the Rationality Center is, in my view, nontrivial. Basing himself on proper governance principles and theories, at least one Center member was very clear that the answer to this question must be the executive:

A sub-unit of an organization is not a democracy, and its director need not abide by a majority rule...The only duty of a director is to run his or her unit well, sometimes against the wishes of the majority...The Center is not a pirate ship owned by its members...The university governance [has] clear and continuous chains of command....Since you [namely me, EUM] were nominated by the Hebrew University administration to direct the Center, you are, indeed, authorized to decide on the camera issue, unless overruled by someone higher up the HU administrative hierarchy.   (Joel, 6 Jul 2007, 00:42; 13:00)[37]

Others felt that the democratic option was more suitable for the Center. But here, too, there was no agreement as to whether all should be assigned equal weights. "Those who hold offices in [the building] should be assigned more votes than those who do not; four-to-one, say? Let's debate now this ratio, take the vote, and finalize" (Joel, 5 Jul 2007, 18:28). Another member suggested a secret ballot, "to compensate for the status quo effect: the camera has been installed (and therefore this is the status quo now)" (Yoav, 5 Jul 2007, 14:42). Reacting to these messages, one member quipped: "I enthusiastically abstain" (Emanuel, 5 Jul 2007, 15:39).

If the executive option prevails, then the director (or a body on the director's behalf) decides one way or the other, and this settles the matter. But let us suppose democracy is opted for, and a general discussion takes place among Center members about the pros and cons of the camera in the kitchen.

Clearly, if the outcome of the discussion is that aversion to electronic self-surveillance is overwhelmingly stronger than the desire to catch those who violate the cleanness norm, then the camera solution will be rejected. Judging from the contributions to the email exchange, however, I am not clear that this would have been the probable result in the case of the Rationality Center, had such a general discussion taken place. What happens, however, in the opposite case, namely if there is a majority in favor of the camera, but no unanimity? In particular, what happens if the minority who object to the camera feel very strongly about the issue, basing their objection on deeply held convictions and principles? Should the majority simply overrule this minority? Is this case to be decided by the counting of votes, or is this a case in which veto power might be granted to the opposition, no matter how small?

I find this question troubling. It is troubling to me partly because I suspect that, had my own opinion been pro-camera, I might probably not have seen the point of even raising this question in the first place, and partly because I do not have a proper grip on the arguments that might justify vetoing rather than voting. As citizens, most of us take it for granted that the polity is to go by majority rule even about issues which, to some segments of the citizenry, pertain to defining core convictions (for example, abortion in the US, or sovereignty over Jerusalem in Israel). However, regarding smaller communities, semi-formal, and voluntary associations, this might be less clear-cut.

How do we think in this connection about a small, semi-formal, and voluntary academic community, organized as a university research center? In all likelihood, layers of common background beliefs and shared worldviews bind such a community together, transcending differences along political or religious dimensions. Also, in all likelihood such a community is only rarely called upon to take a decision that touches upon the deepest convictions of its members. So on the rare occasion that a community like this must make such a decision, is it to be taken for granted that majority rule prevails? Is the ardent and deeply felt desire, on the part of the majority of members of an academic community, to be able to make their coffee in a clean kitchen comparable to the deeply held desire on the part of the minority, to avoid turning the community into a surveillance community? I leave this question hanging in the air, because I do not know how to ground it.[38]

Epilogue

I don't think that Rabelais or Swift or Waugh could have invented something as hilarious as the discussion that took place here. Keep the good work, folks.

(Jonathan, 1 Jul 2007, 10:00)

What are my lessons from this incident?

One lesson has to do with the notion of solution. As noted by one email, "A dirty kitchen is disgusting. A camera-surveyed kitchen is repugnant. On balance, I am not sure the solution is better than the problem" (Miri, 3 Jul 2007, 16:03). Reflecting on the matter, I realize that a lot hangs on what one means by a solution here. Is it appropriate to strive for a solution that guarantees 100 percent cleanness, such that no dirty episode occurs in the Center kitchen, ever?

If we focus on the notion of the "problem" rather than on the "solution," perhaps we shall come to realize that this may be one of those cases (familiar to clinical therapists), in which a solution—or a resolution—is achieved largely by learning to accommodate to, and to live with, the problem. Namely, perhaps the solution here lies with teaching ourselves to live with somewhat lower standards of cleanness than what some of us expect at home, and with wiping up after others, occasionally. In any case, we can comfort ourselves with the thought that by the next morning the place will be clean again.

A second lesson derives from a striking observation about the email exchange. It is that most Center members made up their minds about the issue instinctively and instantaneously; their instincts were made up before their minds were. This contrasts with the attitude of many people to moral dilemmas, where they find themselves agonizing long and hard about what their opinion should be.

The corollary observation is that most of the participants in the exchange felt that the natural light of obviousness is on their side; they seemed not to recognize the potential validity, or even legitimacy, of the opposite attitude. People on each side of the argument tended to see the alternative to their own view as ridiculous, disingenuous, and even perverse.

So I gained the insight that cases of public surveillance are troublesome because they seem to "drive opponents into seemingly irreconcilable stances."[39] The new methods of gathering information drive some people into indignation, while others remain unconvinced and even puzzled by what they consider a mere dislike of new technologies and practices. It seems that traditional theoretical frameworks fail to handle these conflicting attitudes and stances.

Having said that, I should mention incipient work proposing novel uses of a variety of new technologies—including, but not limited to, surveillance—to help constrain and regulate antisocial behavior. As an example, consider the program launched in Cincinnati, whereby spectators can report hooligan behavior of football fans in the local Bengals stadium by calling a certain hotline telephone number. The behavior of the suspect fans is then monitored with the help of the stadium's CCTV cameras, making it possible for security officials to remove, and even arrest, the misbehaving individuals. "Given the problems associated with soccer hooliganism around the globe, the innovation deserves serious attention."[40]

The idea here is to combine the mechanism of individual reporting with the use of surveillance cameras, to achieve control of undesirable behavior. As such, it fits in with the budding body of literature concerned with exploring innovative ideas for the use of information aggregation technologies for the purpose of deterring, detecting, and, where needed, punishing people's misconduct. A good example of this is the proposal by Strahilevitz to put to use "How's My Driving"-style programs in a variety of social contexts.[41] Among them, in addition to the area of traffic regulation, he mentions the behavior of soldiers, police officers, hotel guests, sports spectators, and participants in virtual worlds.

In all of these, the suggestion is that the applications of reputation tracking systems will help "transform loose-knit environments, where reputation often fails to constrain antisocial behavior, into close-knit environments, where reputation constrains misbehavior more effectively."[42] Intriguingly, however, I note that the kitchen camera case demonstrates that close-knit environments do not guarantee the success of constraining misbehavior: indeed, it shows that precisely because a close-knit environment is involved, in which the reputation of participants counts, the problems of shaming sanctions become worrisome.

Innovative and fascinating, this new set of ideas merely begins to scratch the surface of the host of issues that come together to form a heterogeneous field of study that concerns itself with what might be termed "regulation through observation."[43] At issue is the intricate, and as-yet intractable, interface between a number of disparate concerns—with surveillance, control, privacy, shaming, and social norms. In a way, the camera in the kitchen incident serves as a paradigmatic case study—a microcosm of sorts—of this study area. Its triviality notwithstanding, this case attests to the fact that regulation by observation touches some basic chord in the minds of people. This chord, moreover, seems connected to a variety of key sensibilities that are involved in determining people's essential life choices and core convictions about broad social issues.

Postscript

In the months following the Kitchen Camera incident, I had occasions to tell various people the story of the "Curious Incident of the Camera in the Kitchen." The idea of an academic community acting as its own "big brother" in the name of kitchen cleanliness variously regales, and appalls, the listeners. In addition, I am invariably asked how clean the kitchen now is. The answer is that, well, overall it has been kept "reasonably clean, thank you very much."

This is of course partly attributable to the effect of the email exchange itself, which helped heighten people's awareness of their personal responsibilities in the kitchen. Also, a number of additional measures were taken. For example, the doorstopper was removed, so that the kitchen door now slams shut, and can only be opened with a key, thus reducing the chance that unauthorized persons will use the kitchen, and, again, serving as a reminder.

Finally, in a brilliant move, one Center member put up a big sign next to the electric fan on the kitchen wall (where the camera was), proclaiming "CLOSED-CIRCUIT fan IN OPERATION." In doing so, he succeeded in artfully reminding people of the note about the camera that was there before, and thus, vicariously, in gently nudging them to clean up. He thereby also succeeded in producing some good-natured smiles—which may well be the appropriate response to the Curious Incident of the Camera in the Kitchen anyway.

Notes

1. For more about the Center, see: http://www.ratio.huji.c.il.
2. F. Tönnies, *Tönnies: Community and Civil Society (Cambridge Texts in the History of Political Thought)* (Jose Harris ed.) (Cambridge, UK: Cambridge University Press, 2001 [1887]).
3. For more H. Nissenbaum, "Privacy and Contextual Integrity," *Wash. L. Rev.* 79 (2004): 113.
4. "Secondary use" refers to the use of data obtained for one purpose for a different and unrelated purpose without the person's consent.
5. This doctrine was developed in connection with the Fourth Amendment's protections (enacted in 1791) against "unreasonable searches and seizures." For more see W. R. LaFave, *Search and Seizure: A Treatise on the Fourth Amendment* (3rd ed.) (St. Paul: West Publishing Co., 1996); Nissenbaum, "Privacy and Contextual Integrity," pp. 112, 117–18); *Katz v. United States*, 389 U.S. 347, 360–1 (1967), and also http://www.notbored.org/privacy.html (New York Surveillance Camera Players).
6. How about the privacy of a suicide attempt in public? In a landmark 2003 decision, the European Court of Human Rights has ruled that a British man's right to respect for his

private life was violated when closed-circuit television footage of him attempting suicide was released to the media. The court awarded him damages of £7,800. R. Bingham, "Liberty Wins Key CCTV Privacy Case," posted on January 28, 2003 at http://www.liberty-human-rights.org.uk/about/index.shtml (the website of Liberty and the Civil Liberties Trust: 21 Tabard St, London, SE1 4LA).

7. See, e.g., R. Gavison, "Privacy and the Limits of Law," *Yale L.J.* 89 (1980): 421–71.

8. Nissenbaum, "Privacy and Contextual Integrity."

9. See, e.g., "The Logic of Privacy, *The Economist* (Jan. 4, 2007).

10. D. J. Solove, " 'I've Got Nothing to Hide,' and Other Misunderstandings of Privacy," *San Diego L. Rev.* 44 (2007): 2.

11. Some guide books to Amsterdam, in their section about the famous Red Light District, talk of Calvinist open-curtain culture to show the world that nothing untoward is happening behind their front doors; the architecture of many Dutch houses indeed allows for an uninterrupted view from front to back.

12. A. Baruch, "Beware, a Photograph Has a Life of its Own," *Maariv Weekend* (Aug. 24, 2007): 103 (in Hebrew; author's translation).

13. A. Baruch, "Beware, a Photograph Has a Life of its Own."

14. For an opposite view, consider Posner's, according to which privacy consists of a person's right to conceal discreditable facts about oneself. R. A. Posner *Economic Analysis of the Law* (7th ed.) (New York: Aspen Publishers, 2007 [1973]).

15. T. Nagel, *Concealment and Exposure* (New York: Oxford University Press, 2002), p. 4.

16. D. J. Solove, " 'I've Got Nothing to Hide,' and Other Misunderstandings of Privacy," p. 23.

17. A. Margalit, "Privacy in a Decent Society," *Social Research* 68 (2001): 255–69.

18. Consider the lyrics of the well-known song of the "Police": "Every breath you take/Every move you make/Every bond you break/Every step you take/I'll be watching you." Sting, "Every Breath You Take," *The Police*, A&M label, UK (1983). The beauty of the song notwithstanding, the situation it describes is uncomfortably close to stalking.

19. The benign case is "For every step *s* that you make, there is, or there may be, person P, such that P is watching *s*." The sinister case, in contrast, is "There is, or there may be, person P such that, for every step *s* that you make, P is watching *s*."

20. D. Wood, "Foucault and Panopticism Revisited," *Surveillance and Society* 1(3) (2003): 234–39.

21. J. Bentham, "Preface to Panopticon or the Inspection House," in *The Panopticon Writings* (Mirin Bozovic ed.) (London: Verso, 1995 [1787]), pp. 29–95.

22. E. Ullmann-Margalit, "Family Fairness," *Social Research* 73 (2006): 575–96.

23. B. Williams, *Shame and Necessity* (Berkeley: University of California Press, 1993), p. 89.

24. M. Nussbaum, *Hiding from Humanity: Disgust, Shame and the Law* (Princeton: Princeton University Press, 2004); A. Margalit, *The Decent Society* (Cambridge, MA: Harvard University Press, 1996).

25. D. Kahan, "What Do Alternative Sanctions Mean?, *U. Chicago L Rev.* 63 (1996): 591–653; T. Massaro, "The Meanings of Shame: Implications for Legal Reform," *Psychology, Public Pol'y & L.* 3 (1997): 645–704; E. A. Posner, *Law and Social Norms* (Cambridge, MA: Harvard University Press, 2000).

26. J. Q. Whitman, "What Is Wrong with Inflicting Shame Sanctions?," *Yale L.J.* 107 (1998): 1056.

27. B. Braudway, "Scarlet Letter Punishment for Juveniles: Rehabilitation through Humiliation?," *Campbell L. Rev.* 27 (2004): 80.

28. D. M. Kahan and E. A. Posner, "Shaming White-Collar Criminals: A Proposal for Reform of the Federal Sentencing Guidelines," *J. L. & Econ.* ` 42 (1999): 386, also make the point that the stigmatizing effects may often be too large or too small, and thus they do not render themselves easily to achieving the desired results.

29. A. Harel and A. Klement, "The Economics of Stigma: Why More Detection of Crime May Result in Less Stigmatization," *J. Legal Studies* 36 (2007): 355–78.

30. A. Harel and A. Klement, "The Economics of Stigma," p. 358.

31. There is, however, a different approach, according to which not all shaming is bad. This approach (J. Braithwaite," Shame and Criminal Justice," *Canadian J. Crim.* 42 (2000): 3; E. Ahmed et al., *Shame Management through Reintegration* (Melbourne: Cambridge University Press, 2001)) contrasts stigmatization, conceived as disrespectful shaming, with reintegrative shaming, where society's disapproval of the offender is communicated within a framework of respect for the offender. Shaming done within a cultural context of respect for the offender can, according to this approach, be both an efficient and a just form of social control, provided the social conditions for such shaming are successfully identified and implemented.

32. M. Bateson et al., "Cues of Being Watched Enhance Cooperation in a Real-World Setting," *Biology Letters* 2 (2006): 412–14, report an elegant study that backs up this statement, with regard to norms of generosity.

33. Note, too, that the causal (not logical) means-end connection here is not free of potential obstacles and glitches of a technical nature. We might think, for example, of the possibility that the view of the camera is blocked, supposing two or more people are in the kitchen at the same time, or that someone obstructs the view on purpose. Again, the quality of the tape might be bad, or nobody is monitoring the closed-circuit television when a transgression occurs (assuming no recording takes place), and so on.

34. S. J. Dubner and S. D. Levitt, "Selling Soap," *N.Y. Times Mag.* (Sept. 24, 2006).

35. "I have had it with people leaving the milk out of the fridge, using half a liter of milk to make foam for one cup, and then leaving the rest to spoil and stink there, spilling coffee and sugar everywhere and not cleaning, not washing their cups, throwing garbage on the floor,... and the list just goes on and on" (Alex, 28 Jun 2007, 23:06).

36. In the wake of the kitchen camera incidence, a Center member sent a letter to the president, and to the legal adviser of the HU, asking them what the HU policy is regarding the installation of CCTV by individual units of the university, if indeed such a policy exists. Ten days later a memorandum was circulated by the Secretary to the Administration, addressed to all schools, departments, and units, announcing that it is strictly forbidden to install cameras within the premises of the university, and that any request to do so requires appropriate coordination and special permission.

37. Intriguingly, the person who wrote this had suggested, in an earlier message, to take a vote. He prefaced the quoted passages with the comment/apology: "Indeed, my previous call for a vote was a mistake, inconsistent with what I have been teaching in the last few years." For more on the pirate ship analogy, see L. A. Casey, "Pirate Constitutionalism: An Essay in Self-Government," *J. L. & Politics* 8 (1992): 477–537.

38. Consider a different case where the question of majority rule may be troubling: a group of people is traveling in a car. Some find the air in the car stifling and want the window open

for fresh air, the others get chilled when the window is open and want it kept closed. What is to be done?

39. Nissenbaum, "Privacy and Contextual Integrity," p. 101.
40. Reported by Brunsman (cited in L. J. Strahilevitz, "'How's My Driving' for Everyone (and Everything?)," *N.Y.U. L. Rev.* 81 (2006): 1763).
41. L. J. Strahilevitz, "'How's My Driving' for Everyone (and Everything?)."
42. L. J. Strahilevitz, "'How's My Driving' for Everyone (and Everything?)," p. 1699.
43. I am indebted to Cass R. Sunstein for this label. It echoes, of course, Foucault's "Surveiller et punir."

13

Considerateness

A stranger entering the store ahead of you may hold the door open so it does not slam in your face, or your daughter may tidy up the kitchen when she realizes that you are very tired: both act out of considerateness. In acting considerately one takes others into consideration. The considerate act aims at contributing to the wellbeing of somebody else at a low cost to oneself.

Focusing on the extreme poles of the spectrum of human relationships, I argue that considerateness is the foundation upon which our relationships are to be organized in both the thin, anonymous context of the public space and the thick, intimate context of the family.

The first part of the paper, sections I–III, explores the idea that considerateness is the minimum that we owe to one another in the public space. By acting considerately toward strangers we show respect to that which we share as people, namely, to our common humanity. The second part, sections IV–VIII, explores the idea that the family is constituted on a foundation of considerateness. Referring to the particular distribution of domestic burdens and benefits adopted by each family as its "family deal," I argue that the considerate family deal embodies a distinct, family-oriented notion of fairness.

The third part, sections IX–XV, takes up the notion of family fairness, contrasting it with justice. In particular I take issue with Susan Okin's notion of the just family. Driving a wedge between justice and fairness, I propose an idea of family fairness that is partial and sympathetic rather than impartial and empathic, particular and internal rather than generalizable, and based on ongoing comparisons of preferences among family members. I conclude by characterizing the good family as the not-unjust family that is considerate and fair.

I. The Considerate Act

In acting considerately one shows thoughtfulness for others. As a variety of dictionary entries for 'consideration' tell us, the considerate act takes others into account: it takes sympathetic notice of others, displaying regard for the circumstances, feelings, and comfort of others.[1] To help explore the sense in which we sometimes act while *taking others into consideration*, let us consider a few examples:

- You enter the lavatory in an airplane. On the mirror above the sink a little note says: "Out of consideration for the next passenger, please use your paper towel to wipe the wash basin clean."
- I am talking on a public payphone. It is intermission time at the theater, and I notice that someone is standing outside the booth, waiting her turn. I cut my conversation short.
- As you walk toward your parked car, you notice a desperate driver in search of a spot in the full parking lot. You motion to the driver to follow you, and you accelerate your pace.
- I am entering the department store. I push the heavy glass door, glance over my shoulder and hold the door open for the next person.
- You sit next to me at a meeting. You are momentarily called out of the room and I cover your cup with the saucer, to keep the coffee warm.
- Given how late you returned from your trip last night, I let you sleep a little extra this morning and I take over some of your morning chores.

These cases provide us with an initial stock of examples of considerate behavior. Looking for what they have in common we see that in acting considerately one takes others into consideration; more specifically, one takes into account the wellbeing of other people. Here is a preliminary way of describing the phenomenon:

A considerate act is designed to decrease someone else's discomfort at near-zero cost to oneself.

Let me elaborate on this formula by taking apart its constituent elements, in light of the examples above.

1. *"Decrease the Discomfort."* When I act out of consideration toward you, I have your wellbeing in mind. My considerate act is typically intended to decrease your discomfort, alleviate your inconvenience, or minimize an injury to your welfare. Occasionally it is intended to prevent these altogether and sometimes indeed to contribute to your comfort or in general to increase your wellbeing.

Whether looked at in the positive or in the negative, the benefit to you is small: you are spared a longer wait, or the need to push the door, or the unpleasantness of an

---

[1] The thesaurus lists the following different roots for 'consideration': 1. *thinking* (as in argument, belief, contemplation, and more); 2. *importance* (as in esteem, regard); 3. *accounting* (as in taking into account); 4. *considerateness* (as in care, concern, attention/attentiveness, and more).

Here is a useful way of linking these four, seemingly disjoint, meanings in a chain of near-identities or causal/psychological connections: to think of X => to have regard for, and respect X => to take X into consideration => to care for X's wellbeing. Interestingly, the Hebrew three-consonant root *kh-sh-v* serves all four meanings (*lakhshov, lehakhshiv, lekhashev/kheshbon, lehitkhashev*).

unclean sink. 'Small' is a relative and context-dependent term. Still, whatever one's yardstick, considerate acts involve benefits that are at the low end of the scale. Note however that their being small does not mean that they are trivial or negligible. At a low cost to myself my considerate act allows me to confer on you a benefit that, while small, is meaningful to you. Moreover, I judge the benefit, small as it may be, to be worth to you more than its cost to me. This presupposes that I can compare my cost with your benefit. Such comparisons, while quite often and naturally made, raise non-trivial issues to which I shall come back later.

A considerate act thus has leverage-power to transmute a low-cost gesture of mine into a small yet meaningful benefit to you. "For others expect of us only the deeds we can render without inconvenience to ourselves, nor do we expect more of them; but it often happens that deeds that cost others little profit us very much" (Montaigne).[2] Gestures involving larger benefits to you usually correspond to higher costs to me; in general, these are no longer acts of consideration but rather cases of altruism and sacrifice.

In choosing one's action or the manner of its execution, the considerate person takes into consideration the presence, needs, or interests of others. This "taking into consideration" has both a physical and a mental component. In being considerate, you acknowledge the impact on others of your bodily being as well as your potential impact on the others' feelings. You want to minimize any unfavorable consequences that your bodily presence might have upon those around you. You might, for example, lower yourself a bit in your seat at the theater in consideration of those in the rows behind you, or stand on the right when stepping onto the escalator conveying people up toward the subway exit in consideration of anyone behind you who might be in a hurry, or eliminate your traces from the bathroom before you vacate it.

We often speak of being considerate toward other people's feelings. One wants to spare the other's feelings and to avoid hurting them unnecessarily, for example in telling a joke or breaking bad news. These cases are primarily about omissions: they concern what you avoid doing or what you refrain from saying, taking into account people's sensitivities. Here, as in the standard cases of considerateness, the cost to you of putting extra checks on your words or deeds is usually low. In any case, what matters is that you judge it lower—sometimes significantly lower—than the chagrin spared from the other. In omission as well as commission, the considerate person endeavors primarily to reduce to the minimum the adverse effects that his or her deeds and words might have on others.

2. "*Someone else.*" Who is the "someone else" who benefits from one's considerate acts? I intend to focus on two contrasting categories of people toward whom we may direct our considerate acts. One is total strangers, and the other is our immediate family. Friends, colleagues, acquaintances, and many others are to be found between

---

[2] Michel de Montaigne, *Essays*, trans. M. A. Screech (London: Penguin, 1991), pp. 176–7.

these two extremes and may, of course, be on the receiving end of our considerateness as well. With regard to people located somewhere on the imaginary continuum that stretches between the utter strangers and the closest relatives, I assume that our considerateness toward them will best be understood in terms of some mix between the two ends of the continuum. (Consider the case of my covering someone's coffee cup, cited among the examples above. I may do this to a stranger or to an acquaintance, and the analysis will somewhat vary accordingly.)

In the anonymous context of the public space, I act considerately toward people I do not know: indefinite people, anyone and no-one-in-particular, *Jedermann*. In this case, if you benefit from my considerateness, it is not because of the particular person you are but because you happen to be in my orbit, whoever you might be. I am considerate toward a concrete yet anonymous person; a man (or a woman) without qualities, as it were. He or she has needs and wants that, insofar as they pertain to my considerateness, are situational and not person-specific. In holding the entrance door from slamming in your face as you enter the store behind me, I am being considerate toward you as the person-who-enters-behind-me, not you as the highly individual person that you are. Your need or wish I am responding to is that the heavy glass entrance door should not slam in your face: it is a need or wish that anyone in that situation would have. I need to know nothing about you beyond this situational description; even eye contact between us is not required.

The beneficiary of my considerateness, then, is you as an accidental representative of humanity: it could have been anyone. In acting considerately, I do not expect gratitude.

You may say "thank you"—but then, you may not. Beyond the impersonal, fleeting moment of contact between us, my considerate act does not establish nor does it invite a more lasting relationship, let alone a relationship between gift giver and gift receiver.

We think of considerateness very differently in the context of the family. Here the beneficiaries of one's considerateness are one's nearest and dearest: parents, spouse, siblings, and children. Far from generic human beings, they are the highly specific people one knows most intimately. The family is the context of the thickest of human ties in contrast to the public space, where what ties people together is nothing but their shared humanity—the thinnest of ties. Even though considerateness plays out differently among strangers and among close relatives, I believe that many of our acts of considerateness we typically direct toward these two very different categories of people.

My goal here is to explore the idea that considerateness is the foundation upon which our relationships are to be organized both in the thin, anonymous context of the public space, and in the thick, intimate context of the family. The considerate public space and the considerate family provide us with the minimal pre-moral normative bedrock for the civilized society. The terms 'just society' and 'decent society' have become terms of art with rather strict and technical definitions.[3] I think of the civilized society, with considerateness at its core, as the common denominator underlying both. I start with considerateness among strangers; I will take up the case of the family in section IV.

3. *"Near-Zero Cost."* A considerate act benefits someone else at near-zero cost to oneself. How small is 'near zero'? The examples give some indication in what sense my considerate acts cost me little; still, this question cannot be given a precise answer.

The cost may be some slight discomfort to my self. If we had a system of interpersonally calibrated units of comfort and discomfort I would say that the degree to which I inconvenience myself by my considerate act is smaller, and often much smaller, than the degree to which I expect to be contributing to your overall wellbeing. We can often come up with such a rough judgment even without well-calibrated units of wellbeing. As I said before, while the small reduction of your discomfort due to my considerate act is not trivial, I think it is mostly the case that I judge the cost to me of such acts as trivial. The low cost is measured not only by its small size, however. Think of the cost as if it were a vector, so that it has direction as well. Considerate acts as a rule do not require me to change the course on which I am already set; typically, by acting considerately I do not go out of my way. While favorably affecting the beneficiary's wellbeing, my considerate act often involves only a minimal disruption of the course I was pursuing anyway. It requires only slight changes in the pace, timing, or flow of what I am already doing.

When the cost to me is significant, and the benefit to you is positive and large, we do not say that I am being considerate to you. Rather, perhaps, that I am being altruistic toward you. When the cost is somewhere in the middle range we may say that I am being generous toward you or that I am doing you a favor. If my cost is so high that it goes beyond any reasonable scale, we tend to think of this as a case of sacrifice. I shall deal with some examples below.

Performed at near-zero cost to my self, my considerate act should not be considered, in and of itself, as self-effacing. In being considerate toward you, I am not being over-deferential toward you. The signal I am emitting is not that I hold you in higher regard than I hold myself: it is that I do not hold you in lower. Since the 'you' in the case of considerateness in the public space is impersonal, the message I am conveying is one of humanity-wide respect and solidarity.

II. Taking Others into Consideration

If you complain that I have not been considerate to you, what is the nature of your complaint? What charge can you press against me for inconsiderate behavior?

---

[3] John Rawls, *A Theory of Justice* (Cambridge: Harvard University Press, 1971); Avishai Margalit, *The Decent Society* (Cambridge: Harvard University Press, 1996).

In being inconsiderate toward you, I am not infringing on any of your rights. You do not have the right to my parking spot before I have vacated it or the right to have the entrance door held for you. You may have expectations regarding these matters, but not rights. I may inconvenience, irritate, or aggravate you in my acting inconsiderately but I do not wrong you in the sense of depriving you of anything that is rightfully yours. Still, is there a sense in which there is a normative expectation of me to be considerate and in which it is something that I owe you?

There is wide understanding that in a decent society we owe one another a host of negations or abstentions, such as not to subject one another to cruelty, torture, or humiliation. There is also wide understanding that in a liberal society we owe it to one another not to violate each other's liberties. In a society ruled by law, the law backs up most of these expectations. Our expectations from one another, however, often reach further than what the law protects. We may expect non-rudeness and civility. These expectations are normative in nature; we hold up certain norms of behavior. The law does not back these expectations, however, and it does not punish their breach. The degree to which their breach is punishable by informal sanctions varies greatly from one social group or society to another.

To act considerately is to take into consideration others when one acts. 'Considerately' is an adverb; it tells us something about the way the action is done and it qualifies the action in a certain respect. To the extent that we take considerateness as a duty or a norm, its injunction to take others into account is general and vague. It does not specify how one is to go about satisfying it or what it is about the others that one is to take into account: their interests, needs, or wishes—or possibly something else altogether? In acting considerately toward people I know well, I may have an idea of what it means to take them into account. I may know not only their needs and wishes but also their vulnerabilities, so I have a pretty good sense how I may avoid inconveniencing them or hurting their feelings beyond necessity. But what of the case involving people I do not know? When I act with consideration toward strangers all I can take into account about them is what they have in common with all other human beings: that they have, in Shylock's words, "hands, organs, dimensions, senses, affections, passions"—that they bleed when pricked and laugh when tickled and die when poisoned.

In other words, their shared humanity is what people take into consideration when they act considerately toward one another in the anonymous public space. And in being taken into consideration, common humanity is thereby respected. Considerateness thus encapsulates the minimal unit of one's positive acknowledgement of the other qua fellow human being, with a body and a mind. It encapsulates the minimum that we owe to one another in a positive rather than negative way, giving content to the indistinct notion that our shared humanity is worthy of respect.[4] The considerateness we owe

---

[4] In his book entitled *What We Owe to Each Other* (Cambridge: Harvard University Press, 1998), T. M. Scanlon offers a fully fledged (contractarian) moral theory. My use of the expression is more literal: I explore considerateness as the minimum that we owe to each other irrespective of the particular moral theory we espouse.

one another falls short of kindness: kindness lies beyond the scope of what we might truly owe to one another in virtue of the barest minimum that we all share, which is our common membership in the human race.

Seen in this light, my considerate act toward you seems implicitly to be stating something like the following. I recognize that you are "in the orbit" of my action. I recognize that, to some extent, my person might inconvenience you as a person. I recognize that you and I temporarily share the same space (physical or mental) and that this very fact might have nuisance implications for you. In acting considerately toward you I mean to convey to you this complex of recognitions and at the same time to minimize the inconvenience I may engender in you. Implicit in this is my recognizing you as a fellow human being and my respect for you as such.

Another aspect of the message conveyed by acts of considerateness toward strangers involves reciprocity. In being considerate toward the anonymous other, I broadcast my expectation—both factual and normative—to be met with considerateness in return. This expectation need not mean that my considerateness toward you is conditional upon my belief that you will reciprocate in the short run. Rather, it is to be construed in the spirit of Ecclesiastes, "Cast your bread upon the water, for in the fullness of time you shall find it." My act of considerateness thus expresses a hope that the world I live in is or will be inhabited by considerate people; at the same time my act does its share toward ushering such a world in.[5]

Returning to the question posed at the beginning of this section, we can now appreciate the nature of the complaint against inconsiderate behavior. While not wronging me in the sense of infringing on my rights, it is entirely appropriate for me to feel affronted, to take offense. Your inconsiderate act toward me is a disrespectful act; it is an insult to the genus 'human being'. In contrast to being on the receiving end of impoliteness, inconsiderateness is a slight to a fundamental aspect of being a human being.

III. Considerateness Differentiated

To get a better grasp of considerateness is to get a better grasp of what it is not. It must be differentiated from notions that are its closest neighbors in our conceptual scheme, as well as from those notions that clearly contrast with it. Altruism, sacrifice, supererogation, gift giving, kindness, politeness, chivalry—all of these, and possibly more, come to mind as belonging to the first group; selfishness, rudeness, disrespectfulness, and 'tit for tat' are included in the second. The disparity between acting selfishly and

---

[5] The question may still be raised whether considerateness does not pay in the long run and within the larger picture—and whether this might not be the motivation for considerateness. See Elster's discussion of Becker's example of an altruistic husband and a selfish wife: he likes reading in bed, but her sleep is disturbed. She may nevertheless let him read if she benefits from his reading in that "at the higher utility level...he will more than compensate her for her loss of sleep." Her behavior, Elster points out, is the same as that of a considerate wife, but the underlying motivation differs; see Jon Elster, "Altruistic Behavior and Altruistic Motivations," in S. C. Kolm and J. Mercier-Ythier, eds., *Handbook of the Economics of Giving, Altruism, and Reciprocity* (Amsterdam: North-Holland, 2006).

acting considerately is perhaps the most obvious and the most telling. A considerate act, which takes into account other people, stands in stark contrast to a selfish act, which is self centered and oblivious to the existence and concerns of others. So too with rudeness and the other notions that contrast with considerateness; there seems to be little need to dwell on those. But to demarcate considerateness from its neighboring concepts is a less obvious task. Doing so thus holds the promise of casting considerateness in sharper relief.

1. *Supererogation.* I said earlier that the considerate act toward strangers involves low, or near-zero, cost to the actor. When the cost to the actor is higher and the benefit to the recipient is correspondingly larger, we no longer think of the act as one of considerateness but we think, rather, in terms of the actor doing the recipient a favor. We speak, in an increasing scale, of the act as being one of generosity, altruism, or sacrifice. The distinctions here are matters of degree but, imprecise as these degrees may be, they eventually amount to important distinctions in kind. In being considerate, one is not engaged in supererogatory acts; considerateness is distinct from generosity, kindness, altruism, or sacrifice.

Donating a kidney to a relative, risking one's life trying to save someone from drowning, or giving up one's annual vacation in order to do refugee relief work—these acts go way beyond acts of considerateness. They require one to go a very long way out of the way to perform them and they typically imply a major disruption in the routine of one's life. Acts of considerateness, in contrast, involve no disruption, or perhaps only a minimal one, in the course one was pursuing anyway. The examples just given are of course rather extreme cases of supererogation. Other cases of supererogation in the strict sense of the term, namely, going beyond the call of duty, need not be so dramatic. They may involve simple, everyday examples of kindness and generosity such as cooking a meal for a sick friend, standing in for a colleague who must leave work early, giving alms to a street beggar, or donation to a charity.

The Good Samaritan, we are told (Luke 10, 30–35), sees a wounded man lying by the side of the Jericho road and stops to help him. He sees that the wounded man is a stranger but he also sees him as a human being who needs help. The story contrasts the Samaritan with the Priest and the Levite who happened to be going down the same road earlier and when they saw the man "passed by on the other side." Their moral failure, the story implies, is compound. The Priest and the Levite failed, first, in that they avoided seeing the wounded man qua fellow human being. But they also avoided seeing him qua co-religionist of theirs—a fact that is supposed to impose special obligations on them toward his wellbeing. The Good Samaritan went far beyond considerateness; his was a supererogatory act. He went much out of his way to help: "He bandaged his wounds, pouring on oil and wine." Then he took the wounded man to an inn and even paid the innkeeper two silver coins for continuing to take care of the patient.

Still, in being considerate toward people, you are doing something for them. Are you not doing them a favor? Are you not being kind toward them? Well, I suppose in some sense you are. As evidence, we may cite the simple fact that often people respond with a "thank you" when they are on the receiving end of a considerate act. However, this evidence does not go very far. Kind and generous people will be considerate people as well, but the opposite does not in general hold; to act considerately one does not have to have a kind or generous disposition. Invoking a somewhat artificial distinction here, we may observe that through the kind act one typically intends to contribute in a positive way to the wellbeing of the other. By the considerate act, in contrast, especially toward a stranger, one typically intends to reduce the discomfort one may be causing the other in virtue of one's mere presence.

2. *Politeness.* Might not being considerate be tantamount to being polite to one another? Up to a point it is possible, I think, to see politeness as overlapping with consideration, but the overlap can only be partial. Much of politeness has to do with decorum and etiquette (think of table manners, for example). These involve highly conventional and rule-governed behavior, concerned to a considerable degree with demarcation of social hierarchies as well as with preventing social embarrassments. It would seem that this rule-following aspect of politeness has little to do with considerateness. A gentleman stands up when a lady enters the room or walks between the lady and the traffic because he knows that this is the polite way to behave, not out of considerateness. Except that this last example actually suggests that at least initially some rules of politeness may have evolved out of considerateness: the gentleman of some long-past century considerately wished to protect the lady's dress from the mud slung by the passing carriages in the narrow alleyways—and, with time, this became the rule. Examples like these abound; after all, connections between etiquette and ethics are not altogether accidental.[6]

Still, those aspects of politeness that might more clearly overlap with considerateness must surely be found among the more spontaneous, less non-rule governed expressions of politeness. Also, one may expect to find an overlap where acts of politeness are not culture specific but are rather directly oriented toward people as people, regardless of culture or social rank. When one gives up his or her place in the queue for a frail elderly person to go first it is hard to determine—and somewhat pointless to try—whether this act is done out of natural politeness or out of considerateness. The line is fine here and not too much should be made to hang on it.

Suppose you belong to a culture or society in which not letting pregnant women or elderly people sit in the bus counts as flouting a norm of politeness. Still, by standing up and giving them your seat you are showing consideration. You are making a gesture

---

[6] For a wealth of examples and information on the history of politeness and etiquette consult Norbert Elias, *The Court Society,* trans. Edmund Jephcott (Oxford: Blackwell, 1983), and Elias, *The Civilizing Process: Sociogenetic and Psychogenetic Investigations* (Oxford: Basil Blackwell, 2000, first published in German in 1939). The following quote is from the latter book: "Politeness, *courtoisie,* required that one blow one's nose with the left hand if one took meat with the right. But this precept was in fact restricted to the table. It arose solely out of consideration for others."

that shows your recognition, or awareness, of their existence and of their particular physical condition. At the same time you are giving up a certain amount—small, to be sure—of your own comfort in order to decrease their discomfort by an amount that you judge to be more significant. And you make the gesture without much going out of your way.

Many years ago I used to take bus rides in England. I was surprised on more than one occasion to realize that unless I let a pregnant woman sit, no one did. Puzzled by this, I asked around for explanation. The answers I got suggested that the norm of respecting other people's privacy, and more generally of minding one's own business, was stronger than the ordinary norms of politeness. Getting up to let a pregnant woman sit implies that one had observed her and noticed her condition and this is taken as a violation of the code of strict non-interference in other people's life and affairs.

I do not know for sure if this explanation reports a true empirical generalization. But if it is true, I find the value system that it reflects puzzling. Gazes and stares, to be sure, are often unwanted and may at times be experienced as intrusive; spying clearly constitutes an invasion of privacy.[7] But does noticing a woman's pregnancy fall in these categories? Looking ordinarily implies seeing, and seeing ordinarily implies the drawing of some immediate inferences. This is normal and expected in the course of normal, everyday life. So to behave as if you did not see would seem more like avoiding the other than like respecting the other's privacy.

Of course, if you know the person you are avoiding you may have a variety of reasons to want to avoid eye contact with her. But if she is a stranger, then in avoiding her you are treating her as if she were thin air: you are not avoiding *her* for the particular person that she is, but avoiding her qua fellow human being. Considerateness requires one not to be oblivious to people in one's environs: to look, and to see. And, upon seeing a pregnant woman in the full bus the considerate person is expected to recognize her condition and to help her to a seat. She may decline the offer, for whatever reason. Even if she does, this is not inconsistent with her recognizing the act of considerateness for what it is.

The notion of tact offers a further interesting comparison. In "Tact: Sense, Sensitivity, and Virtue," David Heyd analyzes tact as a virtue of sensitivity, lying between moral virtues and the virtues of politeness.[8] Unlike either morality or politeness, tact is not rule governed. It is a skill, says Heyd, expressed in the right measure of sensitivity exercised in particular states of affairs and toward a particular individual toward whom the

---

[7] The idea of Bentham's *panopticon* comes to mind in this connection: the all-seeing viewer induces in the observed person (the prison inmate) a state of "permanent visibility" that assures the ultimate imbalance of power between observer and observed. See also Michel Foucault, *Discipline and Punish: The Birth of the Prison* (1975), trans. A. Sheridan, 2nd ed. (New York: Vintage Books, 1995), esp. pp. 195–228. The idea of the *panopticon* is in vogue in the current literature about the "war on terror" and the privacy-curtailing legislation it has given rise to.

[8] David Heyd, "Tact: Sense, Sensitivity, and Virtue," *Inquiry* 38 (1995): 217–31.

agent is sensitive and sympathetic. The position of tact between ethics and etiquette, or between the obligatory and the merely conventional, "opens the door to characterize it as supererogatory." Considerateness, in contrast, underlies both morality and politeness. It is a non-supererogatory norm enjoining one to recognize that one's presence and actions have consequences for others.

IV. The Considerate Family

The first part of this paper dealt with considerateness in the context of thin relations between strangers in the public space. The considerate person was presented as one who is not oblivious to the existence of relevant others in one's orbit of action and who takes them into consideration in the way one acts. Specifically, the considerate person designs his or her action so as to minimize the discomfort—or sometime to increase the comfort—of relevant others. Considerateness was described as the least that we owe to one another in virtue of our sharing public space as fellow human beings.

In the context of family relationships, the thickest of all human relationships, considerateness plays out very differently. The relevant others we take into consideration when we act considerately are our family members: not anonymous fellow human beings but the people we know most intimately. I shall now have to spell out more fully what it means and what it takes for family members to be considerate toward each other.

A word is in order first about the family as a social institution. It is often said that the family is a special social institution; that in some respects it is a social institution like any other, and in other respects it is different and special. As an "association of individuals"[9] the family typically consists of a small group of people, yet it is often referred to by theorists as a "major" or "fundamental" social institution.[10] Scholars ask whether the family is an inevitable social institution, and also to what extent the family can be seen as a natural institution, as distinct from a conventional one. Even if it can be argued that for any of us to belong to a family is natural, this is not quite the same as to argue that the family we belong to is natural.

The traditional, male-headed, monogamous, heterosexual family that for centuries was considered, at least in the West, unchallengeable as well as natural can no longer be taken for granted. Variations on the traditional theme of the family abound, as do questions concerning the definitional core of what the family is and what it is that remains constant under the plurality of current domestic arrangements. "Despite its importance," says the entry on "Family, Anthropology of" in the *International Encyclopedia of the*

---

[9] Rawls, *A Theory of Justice*, p. 467.

[10] "By major institutions I understand the political constitution and the principal economic and social arrangements. Thus the legal protection of freedom…, competitive markets, private property…, and the monogamous family are examples of major social institutions" (Rawls, *A Theory of Justice*, p. 7). Rawls also lists the family as one among several "fundamental institutions" in *Political Liberalism* (New York: Columbia UP, 1993), p. 258.

Social & Behavioral Sciences, "the word 'family' has no clearly defined meaning.... Three elements are *interrelated* in complex ways in the various uses of the word family: marriage, relatedness, or kinship and domestic or household organization. Each usage of the term carries different combinations of these elements."[11] I shall assume that for present purposes we can make do with a broad characterization of the family as a small and intimate grouping of people that share domestic organization; and that it is the locus of individualized care in which a parental link of some sort typically exists.[12]

Considerateness within the family is supposed to be reflected in the first instance in the set of arrangements regarding the way the family members share or divide the burdens and responsibilities they face. I refer to these arrangements as the 'family deal' and I shall say more about it presently. The prime motive in arriving at a family deal is not "what's in it for me" or "how can I get away with less." Rather, it is the thoughtful regard for one's family members. It is one's parent, sibling, spouse, or child as concrete people, in their full particularity, that one is supposed to be taking into consideration when one is acting in the family context. About strangers one knows nothing, except that they are fellow human beings with bodies and minds. In taking strangers into consideration, therefore, one cannot be supposed to consider anything in particular about them, only what they have in common with everyone else. But of family members one has intimate knowledge. One knows their needs, tastes, wishes, and quirks, all of which have to be considered when one acts while taking one's family members into consideration.

The family enterprise in the case of the good family is never a zero-sum game. One person's loss cannot be another's gain. Even though the interests of the family members need not be harmonious and cannot in general be assumed to coincide perfectly (contrary to what some thinkers maintain),[13] their enterprise is nevertheless inherently a cooperative one. Moreover, it is characterized by an ongoing desire on the part of the family members to act in such ways that will alleviate pressures from the other members of the family and will in general ease and benefit their lives. By 'ongoing desire' I do not mean a burning all-consuming desire that is top priority for each member of the family at all times. I am thinking rather in terms of a steady "backburner" wish that is somewhere on the priority list of the family members and informs their activity, behavior, and decisions on an ongoing basis.

---

[11] J. S. La Fontaine, "Family, Anthropology of," in Neil J. Smelser and Paul B. Baltes, eds.-in-chief, *International Encyclopedia of the Social & Behavioral Sciences* (Amsterdam: Elsevier, 2001), p. 5307.

[12] See Veronique Munoz-Darde, "Rawls, Justice in the Family and Justice of the Family," *Philosophical Quarterly* 48 (1998): 335–52, at p. 350.

[13] Jean-Jacques Rousseau, *Discourse on Political Economy*, trans. from Rousseau's *Oevres Complètes* (Paris: Pleiade, 1959–1969), 3:241–2; David Hume, *Enquiry Concerning the Principles of Morals*, ed. L. A. Selby-Bigge from the 1777 edition (Oxford: Oxford University Press, 1975), p. 185, and also *A Treatise of Human Nature*, ed. L. A. Selby-Bigge (Oxford: Oxford University Press, 1978), pp. 493–6; Michael Sandel, *Liberalism and the Limits of Justice* (Cambridge: Cambridge University Press, 1982), pp. 30–5; and see the discussion of this issue in Susan Moller Okin, *Justice, Gender, and the Family* (New York: Basic Books, 1989), pp. 26–33. See also the discussion below, in section XI.

As an aside, I note that the English language is missing a verb. The meaning of the German verb *vergönnen* is 'not to grudge', for which there is no equivalent word in English.[14] But in fact this verb denotes more than just not-begrudging or wishing someone else well. It conveys the sense of delighting in the success of someone else, of taking active pleasure in the wellbeing and good fortune of the other. When I am *vergönn*ing to you, my wellbeing increases when yours does. Good teachers or mentors may be *vergönn*ing to their pupils and close friends may be *vergönn*ing to each other. But the clear cases of *vergönn*ing are surely to be found in family relationships, most paradigmatically in the attitude of parents to their children. The desire of parents to see their offspring thrive and the positive, heartwarming pleasure they take in their child's success is what the notion of *vergönn*ing is essentially about. This often applies in the case of siblings as well.

V. The Family Deal

A family is established, typically, when two people decide to share their lives. They start a joint household; with time children are added. There are many variations on this conventional theme. Current trends tend toward ever greater diversity of family structures that are increasingly acceptable socially as well as recognized by the law. Families are formed by couples of opposite or of the same sex and sometimes by a single person of either sex. Families break, unite, and start again in a variety of configurations. Children are had in the natural or in high-tech kinds of ways; no fixed assumptions hold about the biological relation of a child to the one or two heads of the family who raise it or to the other children in the family. Membership in the family unit is constantly negotiable and in flux. This must all be borne in mind even when, for the sake of non-cumbersome presentation, the discussion that follows seems to focus on the conventional family.

Even under the most romantic circumstances the sharing of a household involves ongoing series of decisions to be made, domestic labor to perform, and in general a multitude of chores, tasks, and duties. Upon establishing a family, the "founding" members arrive at a certain initial understanding how they are going to share or divide all of these. The initial understanding reached by the couple is usually only partially explicit; it is often the product of subtle and largely tacit negotiations. It would be wrong to think of this understanding as a contract. 'Covenant', 'treaty', and the like will also not quite capture the nature of the process that is going on or of its product. It is not easy to pin this notion down with an appropriate term and yet I believe that there is something important here that needs to be captured. I shall refer to it as the *family deal*.

---

[14] My native tongue of Hebrew also lacks this verb but it has imported the word from the German via its Yiddish form. And so in current spoken Hebrew there is much usage of the verb *le-fargen*, from which a noun is also formed, *firgun* (to rhyme with the Hebrew word *Irgun* that will be familiar to some readers from an altogether different context).

The array of divisions of tasks and responsibilities that the parties arrive at reflect the delicate, initial balance of power between them that they bring into their union, as well as their mutual caring and intimate knowledge of each other. It reflects their preferences and aversions, their different competences and skills, their relative strengths, weaknesses, and vulnerabilities, as well as their fantasies, whims, and special needs. Who shops and who cooks, who cleans and who launders, who takes care of the bills and who deals with the social calendar, who makes the decisions about work or leisure or about how the family budget is to be allocated, and (typically at a somewhat later stage) who does what with regard to the burdens of child care—these are some of the most mundane and familiar examples. They belong perhaps to the repertoire of the traditional urban middle-class family, but they can easily be generalized to (or replaced by) examples pertaining to different sets of circumstances as well as to non-traditional kinds of family.

The initial family deal reached by the founding couple is in constant flux. With time it gets modified and extended in response to changes in circumstances. It stands in need of adapting to the unfolding life cycles of the members of the family. This is true in particular when a child is added to the family and at each new stage in the children's lives. But it is also true when someone falls ill, goes away or starts new work, when an elderly relative moves in or when the family moves out. Family arrangements regarding the allocation and distribution of burdens and benefits are continuously renegotiated and redefined.

The parties who reach the family deal and who keep renegotiating and redefining it partake of this process as highly concrete individuals who are known to themselves and to each other in the most distinctive and intimate details. Contrary to what economists and welfare theorists might tell us, couples and siblings know each other's preferences very well. Moreover, they have a pretty accurate sense of the intensities of these preferences too. They know to whom that extra hour of sleep is worth more and who minds less doing the dishes. And so, in the process of establishing and revising the family deal, the parties are typically engaged in fully fledged interpersonal comparisons of utilities.

VI. "Little Women": The March Family

A chord will no doubt be struck in some readers' minds to be reminded of the way the March family is portrayed in the opening pages of Louisa May Alcott's *Little Women*. In particular, let us recall the role considerateness plays in the lives of members of this family:

The clock struck six and, having swept up the hearth, Beth put a pair of slippers down to warm. Somehow the sight of the old shoes had a good effect upon the girls, for Mother was coming, and everyone brightened to welcome her... Jo forgot how tired she was as she sat up to hold the slippers nearer to the blaze.

"They are quite worn out. Marmee must have a new pair."

"I thought I'd get her some with my dollar," said Beth.

"No, I shall!" cried Amy.

"I'm the oldest," began Meg, but Jo cut in with a decided—

"I'm the man of the family now Papa is away, and I shall provide the slippers, for he told me to take special care of Mother while he was gone." "I'll tell you what we'll do," said Beth, "let's each get her something for Christmas, and not get anything for ourselves."

"That's like you, dear! What will we get?" exclaimed Jo.

A little later the "tall, motherly, noble-looking" Mrs. March arrives home. Casting her "can-I-help-you" look about her and making a series of maternal inquires,

Mrs. March got her wet things off, her warm slippers on, and sitting down in the easy chair, drew Amy to her lap, preparing to enjoy the happiest hour of her busy day. The girls flew about, trying to make things comfortable, each in her own way. Meg arranged the tea table, Jo brought wood and set chairs, dropping, overturning, and clattering everything she touched, Beth trotted to and fro between parlor and kitchen, quiet and busy, while Amy gave directions to everyone, as she sat with her hands folded.[15]

The loving and affectionate March family is a highly idealized case of the "good" family in the sense I here seek to explore—sweetened to a point just short of parody, perhaps. Still, there is something to gain from examining the quoted passages with the notions of considerateness and the "family deal" in mind.

The girls brighten to welcome their mother, engaging in a cheerful sisterly conversation peppered with endearments. For the mother, homecoming is the happiest hour of the day. We note the gesture of warming Mothers' slippers before she arrives, and the girls' efforts "to make things comfortable, each in her own way" in what amounts to a cooperative family enterprise, tacitly undertaken. We note also the competition between the sisters, who will use her only dollar to buy Mrs. March new slippers, the idea being that the one who gets to make this sacrifice is the winner. In addition, we learn from this passage that adjustments needed to be made in the life of the family when Father left home to fight in the war. Tomboy Jo sees herself now as the "man of the family" and it appears that she was in fact singled out by Father, who conferred on her the extra responsibility of taking special care of Mother when he is away.

Let us look a little closer at the way the girls "make things comfortable, each in her own way." Looking at what each of them is described as doing, it is quite evident that the way they go about the various chores does not exactly amount to an equitable distribution of labor among them, objectively speaking. Nor is it intended to be. What we have here is a description of a natural, familial division of labor, not an artificially imposed one. It is meant to convey to the reader a preliminary sketch of the different

---

[15] Louisa May Alcott, *Little Women*, 1868 (New York: Alfred A. Knopf, 1988), pp. 6–9.

personalities, abilities, and characters of the four sisters as these are reflected in the way the girls self-select and divide the various domestic tasks between them. What matters, for our present concerns, is that each of them does what she is inclined to do and possibly does best. The sisters naturally complement each other in what they do. The resulting arrangement—we must assume—is on the whole acceptable to them as fine and fair; presumably it also works in the sense that it gets things done.

Toward the end of the book Amy says to her mother, "I never ought to [despond], while I have you to cheer me up, Marmee, and Laurie to take more than half of every burden" (p. 475). Wanting to take "more than half of every burden" just about sums up the essence of domestic, familial considerateness at its most idealized. One of the OED dictionary entries for 'consideration' is, we recall, "Regard for the circumstances, feelings, comfort, etc., of another"; a more apt example may be hard to come by.

VII. A Second Tier of Considerateness: Gestures

Considerateness as characterized in the first part of the paper had a caveat concerning cost. The considerate act is not only supposed to contribute to someone else's wellbeing but to do this at near-zero cost to the actor. Acting considerately toward strangers, it was pointed out, typically involves no going out of one's way but rather incorporating regard for relevant others while proceeding in one's own business. In the case of the family this caveat does not necessarily apply. Considerateness in the family often involves going out of your way toward your spouse, child, sibling, or parent at a more-than-trivial cost to yourself. This brings me to discuss a second point of entry for considerateness in family affairs. I want to claim that considerateness plays a two-tier role in the life of the good family: first, when the family deal is set up or revised and, second, when the deal is honored in instances of its considerate breach.

Let me explain. I am distinguishing here between two types of things that can happen to an existing set of arrangements. One may, on the one hand, adapt, adjust, or revise them in light of changing circumstances, or one may deviate from them, or go beyond them without actually challenging them, on the other. The family deal, as I see it, is a configuration of tasks, responsibilities, benefits, and privileges that is not only revisable but also invites friendly deviations from it. And it is considerateness that plays a key role in both revision and deviation. That is, in the good family considerateness largely determines the configuration of the family deal in each of its evolving phases, and it also often motivates breaching the family deal in any of these phases. Since I have spoken about the role of considerateness in setting up and revising the family deal, I need to say more about the role of considerateness when the deal is flouted.

I am of course not talking about "bad" deviations from the deal but about "good" ones; it is after all the exemplary family I am concerned to explore. Bad deviations are exploitative while good deviations are considerate; the former go against the family deal and the latter go beyond it. For example, Ann may go beyond whatever it is that her family deal calls on her to do and surprise her father by picking him up from the airport on his return from a particularly grueling trip. Or Ben may decide to get up early tomorrow morning to make breakfast for his sister who is taking an important exam and had too little sleep lately preparing for it.

The way consideration plays a role in going beyond the family deal is typically through considerate *gestures*, small or large.[16] Gestures usually involve some sacrifice—buying a gift, making a special trip, getting up early, giving up a coveted concert ticket, standing in for someone, or taking up their turn in performing some household chore, and the like. As considerate gestures, they are also characterized by their motives, namely, other-regarding motives such as the desire to please others, to decrease their pressure or increase their comfort, and in general to contribute to their wellbeing and flourishing. Considerate gestures are not supposed to be made on a tit-for-tat basis or to be subjected to bookkeeping. Still, the possibility is not excluded of a tacit understanding to the effect that, under opportune circumstances, gestures of considerateness will be reciprocated in kind. This is true in the family, as well as in other social institutions.[17]

A gesture is an expressive action. It is an action intended for effect, for a demonstration of feeling or attitude. An act is perceived as a gesture, typically, when there is a surprise element to it: when it stands out in that it was not quite to be expected in the normal run of things. So when we are given a neutral description of an action—for example, 'he held the door open for her' or 'she drove him home'—we cannot tell that it is a gesture. We need to know more about context, intention, and expectations to determine whether or not it is a gesture.

People in love often make gestures toward their beloved. The gestures of people in love tend to be big, oversized, at times "crazy." He might serenade outside her window, she might send him a bouquet of a hundred roses. When we focus on loving relationships in normal, ongoing family life, however, we realize that what the family members feel for each other often also gets expressed through gestures, though they tend not to be oversized. Considerate gestures within the family, as distinct from lovers' gestures, will typically occur by way of going beyond the current family deal. *Tier I considerateness* is incorporated into the deal that forms the background against which the gesture is made; *tier II considerateness* is the gesture that honors the deal in its considerate breach.

---

[16] My view of gestures in this context is meant to contrast with a received view according to which there is room for "free donated labor" and "voluntary work" within the family, above and beyond the rights-based organization of domestic labor. See, for example, Munoz-Darde, note 12 above, p. 349.

[17] The expectation of eventual reciprocation can go to extremes and get sinister and manipulative, as in the case of the Potlatch. This ceremonial feast of the American Indians of the northwest coast is marked by the host's gestures of giving lavish gifts to demonstrate wealth and generosity, with the expectation of gifts in return. See also Colin Turnbull, *The Mountain People* (New York: Simon & Schuster, 1972), for an account of gift and sacrifices among the Ik (esp. at p. 146).

VIII. Going Wrong

How might things in the family go wrong? The question surely strikes us as odd. We are more likely to want to ask instead, can things in the family ever go right? Or, perhaps, why is it so difficult for things in the family to go right?

The account I gave of the considerate family was meant as a conceptual and normative analysis, not a descriptive one. I set out to explore the ideal-type of the family, the institution of the family at its best—not the average or median family. But we may nevertheless wish to judge empirical families in light of this account and to assess the distance of the typical from the prototypical. Two points, pointing in opposite directions, need to be made. First, the considerate family is not an empirical impossibility: considerate families, or near-considerate families, can and do exist. Second, considerate families are likely to be rare: to achieve the standard of the considerate family requires a highly delicate balancing act; many things can go wrong, in many different ways.

Rawls makes the point that family members on occasion exhibit such higher moral virtues and sentiments as benevolence, mercy, and self-sacrifice in relation to one another. But he also points out that only saints and heroes, not ordinary people, can consistently adhere to such standards of morality.[18] I agree, yet I emphasize that the considerate family is not predicated on saints and heroes or on supererogation generally. The reason why it is rare must be located elsewhere.

To be considerate toward our family members is to be disposed to take their well-being into consideration in our choices and actions. It is not difficult to make considerate gestures toward someone we love. Difficulties begin with securing the coordinated and sustained considerateness of every member of the family, upon which the considerate family deal depends. Ordinary family life takes place in circumstances of close physical proximity. Family members share space that is often tight, and facilities that are often scant; they share bedrooms, bathrooms, living rooms, and kitchens. When we consider the normal friction of human relationships under such conditions and the objectively taxing nature of many of the domestic burdens involved we realize what a feat it is for a family deal to be a considerate one. This is true regardless of social class and socio-economic status. But of course the lower the circumstances of the family are, the more difficult it becomes to be considerate.

One member of the family who does not quite cooperate may destroy the whole delicate balance. Dealing with recalcitrance is particularly vexing in the family situation. Sanctions of various sorts are likely to misfire in the sense that, even if they achieve their purpose in the short run, they may lead to an overall loss of good will, and lack of good will on the part of all involved, as already indicated, is detrimental to the project of the considerate family deal. While we are in principle supposed to love all members

---

[18] Rawls, *A Theory of Justice*, pp. 191, 479; also Okin, *Justice, Gender, and the Family*, note 13 above, pp. 28–9. Rawls's use of the expression 'saints and heroes' is meant to evoke John Urmson, "Saints and Heroes," in A. Melden, ed., *Essays in Moral Philosophy* (Seattle: University of Washington Press, 1958).

of our family, we do not in fact always do, and anyway not equally so. Familial love, quite apart from its complex relation to romantic love,[19] is volatile and ambiguous. Moreover, in too many people's minds familial love is compatible with bad and even monstrous behavior, such as exploitation or abuse (and worse).

It is not uncommon for family members to think, or say, that they love each other. But this is not quite enough for the family to be good. If our standard for the good family is that it is a considerate family then we must accept that good families are not likely to be prevalent. This standard requires, as we saw, that family members should genuinely want "to take more than half of every burden" and that they should be able to stick by this for the long haul; it requires, moreover, that they should want and be able to go even beyond this with considerate gestures every once in a while. While not supererogatory, this standard is quite demanding. It is certainly more demanding than in the anonymous public space context, where the typical cost for one's considerate act is near zero.

Familial love helps a great deal; where there is love considerateness may come naturally and costs are liable to be easily met, even dismissed as irrelevant. Still, familial love is not a sure guarantee that the considerateness standard will be met. On the other hand, it is not a necessary condition either. People may find it in them to behave considerately toward their family members, even consistently so, in the absence of love, or after it has faded away.

IX. Family Fairness

In forging the family deal considerations of fairness apply. They apply as well in the subsequent process of continually readjusting the deal in response to changing circumstances. Members of the good or exemplary family will want to be fair to each other and will attempt to ensure that their family deal, as it evolves and changes, is guided by considerations of fairness.[20] However, family members' notion of family fairness is likely to reflect an understanding of fairness that is different from the way fairness is understood in the context of other social institutions. In particular, 'fair' within the family tends not to be equated with 'equal'.[21]

---

[19] Harry G. Frankfurt, *The Importance of What We Care About: Philosophical Essays* (Cambridge: Cambridge University Press, 1988).

[20] I am here taking issue with Sandel, for whom the appeal to fairness in the "more or less ideal family situation…is preempted by a spirit of generosity in which I am rarely inclined to claim my fair share"; see Sandel, *Liberalism and the Limits of Justice*, note 13 above, p. 33.

[21] Consider: "Many of the individuals who might recognize the inequalities within their [domestic] relationships also consider their circumstances fair.… Family members are trading in different currencies"; see Christopher Carrington, *No Place Like Home: Relationships and Family Life among Lesbians and Gay Men* (Chicago: University of Chicago Press, 1999), p. 21. This is an observation based on Carrington's ethnographic study of "family life" among fifty-two (lesbian and gay) families. The broader point he makes is that the blurring of the two quite distinct categories of fairness and equality is necessary for many in order "to maintaining the myth of egalitarianism" (p. 177).

A basic intuition about justice is the idea that similar cases ought to be treated similarly. What is to count as similar and when do differences make a difference that would justify departure from similar treatment—these are questions of both principle and interpretation, on which different theories of justice differ. Now the flip side of this "justice coin" states that dissimilar cases allow for, or indeed require, dissimilar treatment. I take this as the clue for the notion of fairness in the family. Treating similarly-placed family members similarly is a hollow precept: each member of the family is uniquely placed. The considerate family deal embodies the idea of treating the dissimilarly situated members of the family dissimilarly, yet fairly.

To appraise the fairness of my family deal I must take into account my spouse or partner in his or her fullest particularity. Furthermore, I must engage in a comparison of our preferences and of their intensities: the economists' myth notwithstanding, in the context of the family we do this all the time. If my family consists of more than myself and my partner I must take into account all the members of my family in their fullest particularity too, and engage in similar inter-personal comparisons among all of us. 'Fullest particularity', as already indicated earlier, comprises more than needs and desires. It must comprise all aspects of the personality, such as each family member's competences, talents, and strengths as well as their problems, special needs, weaknesses, and vulnerabilities; even their idiosyncrasies and fantasies. Moreover, fullest particularity includes family members' positional and comparative attributes, in addition to the ordinary non-comparative ones; 'old', 'younger than', or 'neediest' illustrate the point.

Reaching beyond synchronic time slices, the comparisons of preferences have a diachronic dimension as well. Families are communities of memory. Family history matters; past deprivations, sacrifices, privileges, or bonuses count. For my family deal to be fair, the distributive package that constitutes it must also be path dependent. Family fairness takes the long view. It has to take into account how each of us got to be where we are and it has to have corrective, compensatory, and rewarding aspects. Furthermore, in appraising the fairness of my family deal I must be conscious that the future weighs too, not only the past. The plans, projects, and fantasies of my family members must often be accommodated by the family deal whose fairness I am trying to appraise. My teenage daughter's hope to go to college, for example, and the various ramifications of this hope, might have to be factored in.

I have used first-person language in the previous paragraph advisedly. I think that while we have a license to try to appraise the fairness (or otherwise) of our own family deal, we do not have a license to appraise that of another family. To be sure, we may sometimes form opinions, even strong ones, about other families. We may think that a family we know has managed to work out a wonderfully fair deal, or we may assess another family's deal as rotten unfair. But then we are advised always to be careful to add to this opinion a caveat like "but of course what do I know, I am not a member of that family" or "still, this is only how it looks from the outside."

Such caveats suggest that we intuitively sense two important points. First, that we take the category of fairness to apply, in some broad sense, to family deals; second, that the appraisal of the fairness of a family deal is essentially an internal affair. It has a perspective dependent aspect and can therefore only be undertaken from within one's own family. In other words, a counterfactual seems to be implicit here: if we knew everything that is to know about the other family and its members, we would be in a position to pass judgment about the fairness of its deal. At the same time, however, we recognize that we cannot ever know everything there is to know about another family.

Having said that, I note that even to appraise the fairness of one's own family deal is a tricky matter. One complication here concerns children. Until a certain age children are not capable of making fairness evaluations and it is the parents who make them on the children's behalf. (A twist on this point is that at the same time that parents may wish to ensure the fairness of the deal they are giving their children, they have to be also fully aware that one of the things young children need most is to be treated *partially*.)[22]

From a certain age children think they can make fairness claims and indeed they make them, even with vengeance. But it is not at all clear that they are competent to make them, much less to assess them. As for grown-up children (which is, after all, what we all are), we often wonder whether they can ever really be fair in their appraisal of the fairness of their parents in general and of the deal their parents dealt them in particular.[23]

Generally speaking, there are no set criteria for the fairness appraisal of one's family deal, and it is not clear that there is a "right answer" whether or not one's family deal is fair. There is no algorithm to calculate the fair deal or a systematic way for working out how it is to be achieved, beyond assuring that it passes the not-unjust test. Yet it does seem to be the case that family members are capable of weighing whether the current family arrangements in their own family are fair toward them. I ponder this matter vis-à-vis the other members of my family and also as compared to alternative family arrangements my family might have adopted. In addition it seems to be the case that it is possible for me to ponder whether current arrangements are fair not just toward me but, say, toward my son—again, vis-à-vis the other members of the family. Some notion of everyone getting their weighted due seems to be operative here.

---

[22] Aware of this point, I encountered a problem when my twin daughters were little and would ask me which of them I loved more. My strategy was to tell T "I love you most" and then tell R "and I love you even more" and then repeat to T "I love you still more" and so on and on, tirelessly. My sense was that the "proper" answer, namely, "I love you both exactly the same," is not what little children want or need to hear. It is partiality children need, not logic or consistency.

[23] Recall Philip Larkin's immortal lines: "They fuck you up your mom and dad / They may not mean to, but they do; / They give you all the faults they had, / And add some new ones just for you." But note that this is from the point of view of the children, not the parents. (At the end of the poem he gives his advice, whether sad or tongue in cheek, "Get out as quickly as you can, / And don't have any kids yourself.")

Moreover I can be quite clear about the various considerations that do and should enter this appraisal. I can also well envision a family dinner-table conversation about this issue. In light of what gets aired in such a conversation, it might result in a decision to change some of our current arrangements so as to improve on their overall fairness. But I cannot envision such a dinner-table conversation taking place behind a veil of ignorance, masking from view the family members' particularities. The notion of fairness that drives the process of forging the family deal is heavily weighted by the particularities of the participants and the idiosyncrasies of the family circumstances. Consequently, useful generalizable principles can hardly be expected to emerge from this process; nor can the specific deal itself be expected to be usefully generalizable to other families.

Two newspaper reports in late 2004 highlighted families with autistic children and their "fight for the ordinary."[24] The reports make the point that "it is a relentless, labor-intensive and harrowing task, overwhelmingly performed by mothers." This is a task that "tests the strength of marriages, the resilience of siblings and the endurance of the women themselves." The first story goes on to describe what this means in the case of the Krieger family, affording us a glimpse into their family deal: "For Ms. Krieger it has meant accepting that her husband's patience with Gina is more limited than her own; being careful not to overburden or ignore her 6-year-old daughter, Nicole; and arranging occasional telecommuting so she can continue working." In the second story we are told that "Derek can certainly be annoying, but [his brother] Mark is used to it and sees the silver lining. 'He brings us together more, because we're in it as a family', Mark said. Still, he is hyper-vigilant, more an auxiliary parent than a brother to Derek no matter how many times his parents tell him that it is not his job."

Is it fair that Mr. Krieger gets away with having less patience than his wife? Is it fair that Ms. Krieger should be the one who makes career changes so that she can work from home?[25] Is it fair that 15-years old Mark takes upon himself to be an auxiliary parent to his younger brother Derek? These are vexing questions. The overall picture that emerges, however, is of two families who are by and large admirably successful in their struggle to work out a family deal that adjusts to the trying circumstance of autism in the family, and remain functional. Here is how the story about Derek ends, providing a touching instance of a son's considerateness toward his mother: "One blustery evening, for instance, his mother was enjoying a cup of tea when, upstairs, Derek's steady gait turned to jump-up-and-down pounding and his high-pitched singsong to a shriek. That usually means his brother is happy, Mark said, but you can never be too careful. 'I'm going up to check on him', he said."

---

[24] Jane Gross, "For Families of Autistic, the Fight for Ordinary," *New York Times*, October 22, 2004, and "For Siblings of the Autistic, a Burdened Youth," *New York Times*, December 10, 2004.

[25] Given gender stereotypes, the case would have served as a more poignant example had the Kriegers' roles been reversed—as relates both to their different patience levels and to their jobs.

X. Partiality

Family fairness, as presented and discussed above, is not impartial. On the contrary, it relies in an essential way on the family members' intimate acquaintance with the full particularity of each other. It is also predicated on comparisons of preferences among the members of the family and even on comparisons of their intensities. We saw moreover that the fair family deal has to be sensitive to the past and to the future, and that in any case its appraisal is highly perspective dependent and hence internal.

The capacity for empathy, which is the ability to see things from the perspective of others, is sometimes mentioned as essential for the sense of justice.[26] I suggest that sympathy, the capacity for fellow-feelings,[27] is essential for the sense of family fairness. It is the power not only to see things from the perspective of others but to be favorable to their perspective. What the blindfolded goddess Athena is prevented from seeing might, for the purpose of doing justice, be irrelevant. But for the purpose of appraising family fairness, what she does not see may be highly relevant.

Is Rawls's notion of the veil of ignorance applicable to the family deal? Could family members have "hypothetically agreed to their structure and rules from a position in which they did not know which place in the structure they were to occupy"? (Okin, p. 94). Rawls developed his idea of the original position as a device of representing impartial concern in the attempt to arrive at social institutions that are just. With regard to the family, Rawls's view has been the focus of much criticism, most especially his definition of the contracting parties behind the veil of ignorance as "heads of family" or "heads of households." (Rawls subsequently modified this position somewhat.)

In Rawls's general scheme of things the deliberating parties behind the veil of ignorance are supposed to be mutually disinterested individuals, devoid of any "ties of sentiment."[28] They do not know who they are. They are all assumed to think identically, none of them being in a position to tailor principles to their own personal advantage. The "direction of fit" in this scheme goes from the principles arrived at by these abstracted, disembodied, veiled agents to the flesh-and-blood people who will then apply the principles to their real-life situations. That is to say, the real and particular people must abide by the principles they arrive at when behind the veil of ignorance, and in this sense they must fit themselves to these principles. If they fail to do so then the failure of fit is with them, not with the principles.[29]

---

[26] See for example Okin, note 13 above, p. 21.

[27] Adam Smith, *The Theory of the Moral Sentiments*, 1759, part I, section I, chapter II ("Of the Pleasure of Mutual Sympathy").

[28] For the purpose of his "just savings principle" and the cause of intergenerational justice, however, Rawls does allow for ties of sentiment between generations. Each head of family in Rawls's original position is supposed to care about the wellbeing of some persons in the next generation (Rawls, pp. 128, 146, 292; Okin, p. 92). Commentators continue to debate, however, whether care about descendants contradicts the idea of the original position as a device of representing impartial concern.

[29] This remains essentially true even after we take into account Rawls's notion of "reflective equilibrium." The method of reflective equilibrium determines a set of principles rooted in the human sense of justice. It is a coherentist method for the epistemic justification of moral beliefs that allows for some give-and-take—but

Matters are different when we come to apply these ideas to the case of the family. The participants forging the family deal—the founding couple, initially—bring themselves to the task in their full particularity. After all, when deciding to marry, it is a highly particular person—warts and all—that one marries, not an imaginary person who would score highest on a "partner's description" devised ahead of time. People who decide to share their lives do so not as mutually disinterested bargainers but, to the contrary, as mutually interested parties who intend to work out their domestic arrangements in a way that reflects the strongest "ties of sentiment" between them. They are to be thought of as being in a position to tailor the package of domestic burdens and benefits to their mutual advantage and sometimes even to each other's advantage rather than to their own personal advantage.

Moreover, as already pointed out, interpersonal comparisons of preferences are a matter of routine in family life. "You mind this more, so let me do it" is a common feature of sound domestic arrangements. The "direction of fit" in the case of the family is thus the reverse of what it is in the case of other social institutions, flowing from the particular members of the family to the principles and arrangements. We, as the highly concrete individuals that we are, arrive at the set of domestic arrangements that fit us best and that give each of us our weighted due in the broad sense here expounded. Should there be failure of fit, it is typically the arrangements we have arrived at that are at fault and in need of being re-thought.

XI. Justice and the Family

According to Rawls an institution is just if its rules and workings could in principle be established by its members agreeing to them from behind a veil of ignorance. For Susan Okin this applies to the family as well. What she calls a "better-than-just" family is one that, in addition to being just, is regulated by intimacy and love. Okin holds that the institution of the family must be built on a foundation of justice before it can be adorned (as it were) by "the best of human motivations and the noblest of virtues" (p. 32): justice first, noble virtues—optionally—later.

The position I am putting forward here is that the institution of the family should be built upon a foundation of considerateness, which embodies a distinct notion of fairness referred to as family fairness. But where does this leave the question of justice in the family?[30] Can the family be just? Should it be just?

---

this remains on the level of the principles and beliefs. The give-and-take does not affect the direction of fit that eventually flows from the set of principles, properly adjusted and stabilized, to their application to concrete cases.

[30] A distinction is sometimes invoked between the question of justice *in* the family and the question of the justice *of* the family (see Munoz-Darde, note 12 above). The first concerns, primarily, the division of labor within the family; the second asks whether the very existence of the institution of the family is not an impediment to social justice, for example because of the way it can be a barrier to equality of opportunity. I am here concerned with the first question only.

Rawls's view is that justice is the "primary virtue" of all social institutions. If so then the family cannot be thought of as falling outside the bounds of justice.[31] Rawls does not explicitly address the question of justice in the family as such, however. For various purposes he needs the family to be thought of as a just institution and so he posits it as just: "I do assume that in some form the family is just."[32] At the same time however Rawls upholds the separation of the public from the domestic sphere. He sees questions concerning the division of domestic labor as private family matters which are governed by natural sympathy rather than by principles of justice.[33]

Susan Okin has written a powerful book, *Justice, Gender, and the Family*, to champion the cause of applying the standards of justice to the family. She criticizes classical liberal thinkers who take the family to be a male-headed natural unit and consider internal relations among family members as falling outside the bounds of justice.[34] Okin argues, on the descriptive side, that "typical current practices of family life...are not just" and, on the normative side, that "until there is justice within the family, women will not be able to gain equality in politics, at work, or in any other sphere" (p. 4). For Okin the family is not merely one among many institutions that have to be just in order for society to be just. Her position, rather, is that the just family is the very basis for a just society; the family, she says, is "a school of justice."

To defend her claim that the family ought to be based on justice Okin must go beyond the attempt to extend Rawls's theory of justice to the domestic sphere. In fact, it is not even clear that the project of extending Rawls's ideas to the family unit is entirely coherent and free of internal contradiction. In a fairly straightforward sense, the just family is an essential building block in Rawls's edifice. Yet, as indicated, he relegates the family to the private sphere, and he maintains that behind the veil of ignorance men make their deliberations and choices qua heads of families and not strictly qua individuals. These considerations stand in the way of seeing the family simply as one more social institution to which Rawls's principles can and perhaps should apply.

Rawls's position on the family as a just institution, then, is not free of ambiguities. Entirely unambiguous about the question of justice in the family are two different clusters of doctrines that must be briefly considered in the context. Both of them stand in clear opposition to the notion that the relationships among the members of the family ought to be regulated by justice. Each of these doctrines holds that it is inappropriate to apply the category of justice to the family, but for different reasons. Michael Sandel is considered by Okin the most prominent contemporary proponent

---

[31] "In Rawlsian terms, the only thing that can be demanded is...that the family should fit together with other main institutions so that the principles of justice operate" (Munoz-Darde, p. 347).

[32] Rawls, *Political Liberalism*, note 10 above, p. xxix; see Okin, p. 27 and chapter 5.

[33] For more, see Will Kymlicka, "Rethinking the Family," *Philosophy and Public Affairs* 20 (1991): 77–97, at p. 79.

[34] See Kymlicka, p. 78.

of one of these doctrines and Allan Bloom, who is following in the footsteps of Rousseau, of the other.[35]

The first doctrine sees the family as an intimate group characterized by harmony of interests. As such the family is taken to be above justice; it is an institution that is expected to be "more than" just or "better than" just. Justice on this view is considered inappropriate to the family in that it belittles the family or misses its point, as it were. While justice is a virtue, it is taken by this doctrine to detract from the nobility of family relationship. The second doctrine considers justice inappropriate to the family because it sees the institution of the family as inherently and naturally unjust. Given the hierarchical structure of the family and the gender differences between its members, the family on this view can not and should not be thought of as an arena for just divisions of burdens and benefits. Justice on this view is a virtue alien to the family, even harmful to it.

The second, old fashioned approach is more extreme in its outright rejection of the notion that family relationships be based on principles of justice. It rejects equality for women as contrary to nature and embraces the notion that nature determines a gender-dependent, hierarchical structure for the family that is necessarily unjust. The first, sentimental approach, in contrast, does not altogether reject the notion of the just family but rather sees justice as irrelevant for the ideal family. Maintaining that the interests of each member of the family are entirely convergent with those of the family's patriarch, this position sees the insistence on justice in the family as pointless. On this view, in Okin's words, "An intimate group, held together by love and identity of interests, the family is characterized by nobler virtues" (p. 26).[36]

Okin's vigorous rebuttal of both these doctrines is animated by her thesis that underlying the social inequalities that exist between the sexes in our society is the unequal distribution of labor in the family. I believe that it is possible to agree with Okin on this general thesis and yet not to accept her view that the institution of the family is on a continuum with all other social institutions and that as such it must, like them, be built on a foundation of justice.

XII. The Good Family

My own unease with the idea that the family is to be constituted on principles of justice is by no means an endorsement of the idea that the family should be allowed to be unjust. To the contrary, the argument I offer is that a precondition for the good family

[35] Sandel, *Liberalism and the Limits of Justice*, note 13 above; Allan Bloom, *The Closing of the American Mind: How Higher Education Has Failed Democracy and Impoverished the Souls of Today's Students* (New York: Simon & Schuster, 1987).

[36] See also Susan Moller Okin, *Women in Western Political Thought* (Princeton: Princeton University Press, 1979), p. 202, and Kymlicka, note 33 above, p. 78.

is that it is not unjust. In other words, the elimination of injustice is in my view a threshold condition for the good family. Putting it this way, in terms of a double negative, indicates that I do not see 'just' and 'unjust' as complementary adjectives. To characterize an institution as not unjust does not amount to characterizing it as just. An institution might be in an interim zone as it were, where it will be considered not-unjust and yet it will not quite qualify as just either, in light of some positive strictures of justice.[37]

Aiming to explore the idea of a family that "works" and is functional (as distinct from dysfunctional), I refer to it as a "good" family. The thrust of my discussion of the good family is normative. Yet I choose not to talk about the *ideal* family in order to avoid the impression that the good family is unattainable. An ideal alludes to the notion of a regulative idea, a high-above star that shows you the way by shining bright at the end of the path but remains distant and unattainable the closer you think you have approached it. The considerate family is a good family. This is a reachable ideal; it is a normative notion that is also descriptive. From experience as well as from literature, we all know good, considerate families; the lucky ones among us recognize in this notion their own family.

Tolstoy famously said that happy families are all alike. A happy family may perhaps be easy to recognize even if it is not so easy to pin down conceptually, and anyway it may be that only the good family, in the sense here expounded, can be happy. All good families are also alike, in some important respects. It is these respects that I focus on: my account of considerateness attempts to explore what they have in common and what makes them good. Tolstoy may have meant to imply that the happy family is intrinsically uninteresting and only the unhappy ones—each unhappy in its own way—are of interest. With regard to the good family, however, I want to make the opposite case. I believe that breaking the code of the good family, examining what it is that makes it work and function, is a worthwhile undertaking.

Once a prototype, in any domain, is better understood, the countless ways of deviating from it can also be better understood; indeed in some instances a metrics can be devised to measure the distance of the deviants from the prototype. Regarding the family it may remain true, perhaps even be reaffirmed, that each dysfunctional family is dysfunctional in its own way. But then these less fortunate cases will stand a greater chance of being better analyzed and understood.

A family whose domestic arrangements are unjust cannot be considered good. The absence of injustice is a threshold condition for the goodness of the family. Purged of injustice, the good family is one whose family deal is considerate. The not-unjust, considerate family is fair, in the distinct family-oriented sense of fairness discussed earlier.

---

[37] Consider the analogy to trust and distrust: my not distrusting you does not amount to my trusting you; see Edna Ullmann-Margalit, "Trust, Distrust and In-Between," in Russell Hardin, ed., *Distrust* (New York: Russell Sage Foundation, 2004), pp. 60–82, at 60–1.

XIII. "Not Unjust"

I need to say more about the elimination of injustice in the context of the family. Injustice is here meant to refer to clear cases of injustice as judged by prevailing standards of justice. These include as an important special case any practice or arrangement that is legally unjust. "Legal constraints that apply to all individuals and associations should also apply to the family" (Munoz-Darde, p. 349). We would nowadays consider it unjust for a wife not to be allowed to inherit her husband, or for a daughter not to be allowed to inherit her parents if she has brothers.[38] The eighteenth-century doctrine of "coverture," according to which the married woman's property as well as her body, her children, and her legal rights belong to her husband, would be considered unjust by the standards of the twenty-first century.

Blatant inequality, gender-based or otherwise, in the access to family resources such as property, money, or leisure, would likewise be judged unjust. Male tyranny within the family over his womenfolk's bodies and lives, systematic exploitation, discrimination, coercion, and physical abuse all count as clear cases of injustice by our current societal standards.[39] Also unjust are domestic arrangements that are based on the systematic sacrifice of one particular, usually female, family member[40] (the wife/mother, an eldest daughter, or as folklore would have it, a "spinster aunt"). To be sure, sacrifice gestures do and perhaps should occur in the course of normal life of the normal family.[41] But the reliance on systematic self-renunciation, especially if it is habitually expected of the same person, is no different from exploitation.

I believe that to eliminate unjust family arrangements, as appraised in light of prevailing standards of justice, is a move in the right direction. Still, this leaves room for a margin of troublesome borderline cases. If in a poor family the man is out of the home, breadwinning all day long, and the woman is charged with all of the responsibilities of home and children, the division of labor in this family may strike us as unfortunate but it can hardly be pronounced unjust. If the man in this family does not bring home his

---

[38] This is the biblical law (see Numbers 27:8). The Mishna goes further and rules that even if a father wills his property to his daughter his will is null and void. To circumvent this injustice a writ of gift was invented; three cases of such gifts were found among the Judean Desert papyri.

[39] As evidence of changing societal norms regarding justice in family matters, consider the recent twist in the struggle against family injustice offered by the British movement "Fathers 4 Justice." "The divorced and separated fathers who belong to Fathers 4 Justice say they hope to accomplish one thing: ensuring they get a fair shake at equal custody of their children... there are many fathers —and the number is growing— who want to see more of their children and are unsatisfied with their custody arrangements... They say judges have been slow to recognize the changing roles of fatherhood, including the fact that 50 percent of the British work force is made up of women. Fathers argue that the system is biased against them... What is really needed, they emphasize, is for the court to presume a 50-50 custody arrangement from the start, and then work from there"; see Lizette Alvarez, "Disobedient British Fathers Act to Reclaim Children," *The New York Times*, Nov. 11 2004.

[40] "The supererogation that is expected in families often occurs at women's expense" (Okin, *Justice, Gender, and the Family*, p. 31, and further references there).

[41] On the idea that family members commonly exhibit such higher moral virtues as heroism and self-sacrifice in relation to one another, see Rawls, *A Theory of Justice*, pp. 129–30, 438–9.

daily wages but drinks them away in the local pub every evening, this will strike us as unjust.[42]

But consider now an ultra-Orthodox Jewish family, for example in the Me'a She'arim quarter in Jerusalem. The man is out all day studying, while the woman stays home to take care of their many children, having to make do with the small state allowance that her husband receives for devoting his life to study. Voluntarily entered into by both husband and wife, the domestic arrangements of this family are quite typical of a sizeable community. A man's lifetime devotion to the study of Holy Scripture is, for the members of this community, the highest value; the wife enjoys reflected glory to the extent that her husband excels in his studies. How are we to appraise the division of labor in the families belonging to this community? It may be tempting to hurl accusations of "false consciousness" at the women in this community, inasmuch as they express contentment with their lives. I suspect that Okin would assail these families' division of labor as outright unjust. But I find this case troublesome. While hardly to be seen as just, I would hesitate to qualify the domestic arrangements of these ultra-Orthodox families as unjust either.

XIV. Equal Sharing of Domestic Labor?

Injustice makes for the badness of the family, as it makes for the badness of any other social institution. The elimination of injustice is a necessary condition for the working of the good family. As was pointed out already, to eliminate injustice is not quite the same as to instate justice. But what does 'just' mean in the context of the family anyway?

For Okin the answer is unambiguous. Her ultimate, long-term goal is a "just, gender-free family" that is part of a just, gender-free society. In the just family there will be "equal sharing by men and women of paid and unpaid work, or productive and reproductive labor" (p. 171). In particular, it is the equal sharing of domestic labor that is in Okin's view the condition for justice in the family.[43] I find this view wanting and too restricted in several respects. In general, the condition of equal sharing of domestic labor is in my view neither a necessary nor a sufficient one for the good family.

Let me note, first, that labor cannot be the sole concern here; there is more to justice in the family than equal distribution of labor alone. Family life involves an intricate package of domestic burdens and responsibilities, as well as benefits and privileges, the distribution of all of which is relevant to the issue of justice. Let us notice, also, that

---

[42] See, e.g., Frank McCourt's harrowing autobiographical account, *Angela's Ashes* (New York: Scribner, 1996).

[43] Since same-sex families carry an obvious potential to corroborate or undo this hypothesis, many scholars have recently been developing this research agenda. "These scholars offer the lesbi-gay family as a model for the future," notes Carrington. His research, however, "seriously challenges the effort to place the lesbi-gay family in the vanguard of social change, a model of equality for others to emulate. Such assertions are based on the ideology of egalitarianism, not on its actual existence" (Carrington, note 21 above, p. 218).

from much of Okin's writings one might form the impression that the family unit consists of a couple or even, more accurately, of a man-and-woman couple.[44] Since her primary concern is justice between the sexes, her interest in the family is primarily as a major locus of sexual inequality. But the wider-ranging questions regarding the working of the good or functional family do not interest her beyond making the point that men and women should be equally responsible for domestic life and that all assumptions about male and female roles within the family should be abolished.

Okin's cause is equality for women and her book is a crusade for the recognition of women's unpaid domestic labor and against women's domestic exploitation. Let us imagine, however, that domestic labor has indeed been sufficiently recognized by society for its worth and let us suppose further that, given this recognition, a particular woman opts of her own free will to take upon herself the domestic labor of home and children. Of course, as in the case of the ultra-Orthodox family discussed above, the question of how free is free choice in such instances is hard to settle and the lurking danger of false consciousness, here too, is a complicating factor. Still, given these caveats, would it be possible for Okin to sanction this woman's choice? If, as I suspect, it would not, I find it troubling.

When Okin's discussion goes beyond the couple unit and includes children as part of the family, she tends to see the children merely as contributing additional domestic labor to be shared by both their parents. This may be understandable given Okin's perspective of concern with justice for women and sexual equality. But if the focus is the functioning of the good family then we must be thinking in more general and in more dynamic terms. For example, we must be thinking that in families with children the children may be expected, from a certain age, to share some of the burden of domestic labor. Indeed children have to be thought of as continually growing up and as being gradually initiated by their parents into the family's ever-evolving array of domestic burdens, responsibilities, benefits, and privileges.

We must also be taking into account that questions concerning the distribution of resources and responsibilities apply horizontally, among siblings, as well as vertically between the generations. Sometimes the vertical axis eventually changes direction and the children may have to assume responsibilities toward their parents. In addition we must allow for the open-endedness of membership in the family. People are added to the family, as when a new child is born or a grandparent moves in, and people leave the family, as when somebody goes away or dies.

I take all of these considerations to show that Okin's position is too restricted. But quite apart from these considerations, I question the idea that "equal sharing of domestic labor" is, in and of itself, adequate for capturing the working of the good family. At any rate not when equality is "measured with a plumb line" (Carrington, p. 206). The idea that the couple can be imagined to go through some procedure in which they list

---

[44] "Okin seems to equate a 'gender-free' society with a society of heterosexual couples who (inter alia) share domestic labor. She often treats 'adult members of the family,' 'parents,' 'both parents,' 'couple,' and 'mother and father' as synonyms" (Kymlicka, note 33 above, p. 84).

all the domestic tasks and chores and then divide them more or less mathematically down the middle, possibly even drawing lots as to which half should fall to each, is a recipe for frustration and failure. In the workplace it is possible to compile lists of tasks and job descriptions and then to hire suitable people to perform them and to fire them if they fail. But the family is a radically different sort of institution. Family is for life,[45] and "home is the place where, when you have to go there, they have to take you in."[46] The family is expected to cater for its members throughout their full life cycles and continually to accommodate their personalities and problems, strengths and weaknesses, whims and vulnerabilities, foibles and fortunes.

Of course, if the notion of justice in the family is stretched to apply to any not-unjust distribution of domestic labor that "works," in the sense that the members of the family accept it and feel comfortable with it, then by stipulation the good family will be just. But this stipulation comes at a price: the notion of justice as it applies to the institution of the family will be very different from the notion of justice as it applies to all other social institutions. This implies accepting that the family is an exceptional sort of institution, or taking family justice as an exceptional sort of justice, or both.

I suspect that most liberal theorists and some feminist ones will reject both options. They will want to see the family as continuous with all other social institutions and to see the notion of justice applying to it as to all other social institutions.[47] The position I present here in effect embraces both options and sees them as intrinsically connected. I embrace the notion that the family is an exceptional sort of institution, and I maintain that the set of domestic arrangements—the family deal—is assessed not for justice but rather for fairness, in the sense here expounded.[48]

XV. Conclusion

The family, I argued, is constituted on a different foundation than other social institutions. Family fairness, not justice, underlies the working of the good family, via the notion of the considerate family deal.

---

[45] Even if marriage can no longer be assumed to be for life, as it was in previous times (see Okin, p. 32).

[46] Robert Frost, "The Death of the Hired Man." The fuller quote is interesting in the present context; it is a dialogue between two voices:

- "Home is the place where, when you have to go there, / They have to take you in."
- "I should have called it / Something you somehow haven't to deserve."

[47] For Okin the family remains "a peculiarly *preliberal* anomaly in modern society" which would improve if it were to conform to contractual liberal principles (p. 122). Kymlicka believes that if one pushes this position to its logical conclusion one ends up with Hobbesian and Orwellian views that no liberal is willing to endorse (pp. 91–2). Munoz-Darde says that "the only thing that feminists should ask from Rawls is that he should *refrain* from saying too much about the family, and that he should treat it exactly as any other association" (p. 348).

[48] Discussing long-term same-sex families, Carrington observes that "Interestingly, these … families conceive of their circumstances as *equal*, although I suspect they really mean *fair*. They consider things fair in light of a whole series of spoken and unspoken matters ranging from the number of hours someone works for wages to the pleasures one garners from domesticity" (p. 187).

Social institutions other than the family are assessed for their justice. Within the Rawlsian framework, the assessment is made in reference to a set of principles and practices impartially adopted by the members of the institution with "eyes wide shut"—namely, in an imagined original position, behind a veil of ignorance. Within the family, in contrast, the array of not-unjust and continually re-adjusted domestic arrangements is being assessed for its family fairness. This assessment, as I have shown, is in principle internal, in the sense that it can be made only by the members of the family themselves. The fair family deal is adopted considerately and partially, with "eyes wide open"—namely, with the family members sympathetically taking into account the full particularity of each, and in light of fine-grained comparisons of preferences between them. I conclude that it is the not-unjust, considerate, and fair family that is good.

Epilogue: Final Ends and Meaningful Lives

1

Given that some outcomes are of greater value to us than others, it is undesirable to behave at random.

(Frankfurt, sec. 3)

A life constituted entirely by activity of that sort [i.e. random, pointless, non-purposeful activity] would be, in an important sense, a meaningless life.

(Frankfurt, sec. 3)

People who successfully identify their interests and values, and who spend their lives in pursuit of their interests in accordance with their values, are likely, Professor Frankfurt tells us, to lead a meaningful life. Let us accept that, for the time being. There are people who successfully identify their interests, and who systematically go against them. Such people are self-destructive, to be sure. But their aim, of consistently behaving so as to violate their interests and frustrate their desires, may nevertheless be correctly described as a final end, however perverse. And their lives, spent in pursuit of this end, may accordingly be seen as meaningful.

But let us now imagine a person who has a life program of total indifference and arbitrariness. This person may be motivated by some notion of an *Übermensch*, or of an "extraordinary man," or possibly by some version of the Eastern systems of thought Frankfurt mentions (n. 8), which advocate an "extinguished self." Such a person will desire neither to further his or her interests nor to systematically violate them but to pursue, instead, a life-plan of utter pointlessness. It will be a consistent life-plan of behaving inconsistently with respect to one's interests.

Is this impossible? I do not see, within the framework of Frankfurt's discussion, why this should be impossible, nor indeed, why a life spent acting out this program should not count as a meaningful life. Moreover, in order to act out such a program it may well be desirable to behave at random. Random behavior may actually be the only possible way to pursue the final end of total indifference and arbitrariness.

2

Aiming is important because it makes a difference to us what we hit.

(Sec. 3)

This statement has a pleasant air of unassailability to it: it sounds like a slogan. It is related by Frankfurt to the previous point, about the undesirability of behaving at random, but I will use it to highlight a different point.

There may be cases where the "targets" represent states of affairs that are incommensurate to us. When this is the case I may want to say that although it does make a difference to us what we hit, it may nevertheless not be true that it is important, or even desirable, for us to aim. Two final ends may involve, to use Frankfurt's own terminology, two very different "networks of feeling, emotion, thought, and action" (sec. 5); say, a life as a performing musician and a life as a creative mathematician. Consequently a person may be unable to compare them on a single scale of value or desirability, and come up with a verdict as to which one is "better." Even though it obviously makes an immense difference whether one ends up a musician or a mathematician, it is not clear that "aiming," in the sense of a reasoned choice, is that which is called for: *force majeure*, drifting, an arbitary incident, or random selection may be the alternatives.

Incommensurate states of affairs may roughly be equally good (as in the above example), or equally bad or even horrible. An extreme case like that of Sophie's choice, where the Nazis made her choose which of her children will escape with her and which will stay behind and be killed, underscores the point that random selection rather than a reasoned choice may be the only way that will enable a person to live with the consequences of his or her action. It may be better to shoot at random, if shoot one must, than to take responsibility for having aimed.[1]

3

Living without goals or purpose is living with nothing to do.

(Sec. 3)

I suppose that this is in general true, with one possible exception.

Living as an end in itself, living for the sake of continuing to live, may call for a great deal to do. I am sometimes struck with this thought when watching the elderly or the disabled. Where every bodily movement and every act is an effort, merely going on with the business of living fills the day.

---

[1] For an instructive discussion of incommensurability that bears on these points see Joseph Raz, *The Morality of Freedom* (Oxford: Clarendon, 1986), chap. 13.

Does living for the sake of living count as purposeful activity? If it does, then surely the ascription of purposeful activity will have to apply not just to human beings but also to all animals who busy themselves with survival. If it does not, then it is not true to say that living without purpose is living with nothing to do.

4

A person's life is meaningful only if he spends it, to some considerable extent, in activity that is devoted to things that he cares about.

(Sec. 4)

Working to reach desirable ends is essential to meaningful life; a person's life is meaningful, indeed, only to the extent that it is devoted to pursuing goals that are important to him.

(Sec. 9)

Take a devout, activist communist, or take a person who was trained to be a Jesuit priest. These two exemplify well, I think, Frankfurt's point about the meaningful life. They spend their entire lives in pursuit of their chosen goals; their lives consists of activities devoted to things they are committed to and care about. They have final ends toward the attainment of which they have much instrumentally valuable work to do. They are indeed likely to perceive their lives as meaningful, regardless, as Frankfurt rightly points out, of how much they actually accomplish. And so are we, as spectators, likely to judge their lives to be meaningful.

Suppose, however, that they now undergo a transformation, or, if you will, a conversion. As a result, our committed communist becomes a disillusioned ex-Marxist (say, à la Koestler), and our Jesuit priest becomes a lapsed Catholic. They now see the world, and their own lives, very differently. There will be a sharp discontinuity between their previous final ends and their present ones. They will come to care about different things. Moreover, it is possible that from their present perspective, now that they have come to "see the light" (or to see a different light), the things they cared about before seem to them not to be worth caring about. So even though their lives up to the conversion consisted of purposeful activities and hence count, on Frankfurt's account, as meaningful lives, these activities may now be perceived by them to have been mistaken, misguided, even pointless.

What effect does this have on the question of the meaningfulness of their lives? Are the lives of these transformed persons more meaningful, equally as meaningful, or less meaningful—whether to themselves or to us—than their lives had they continued them in their previous courses without any transformation?

I am aware that the question is not yet focused enough. But even if we had world enough and time to go through the necessary stages of clarifying the issues involved, distinguishing classes of cases, etc., I still believe that the conceptual framework provided for us by Frankfurt would not enable us to address this question. Frankfurt's concept of the meaningful life mirrors in an important respect a familiar concept of happiness. Happiness, on this view, is additive. The total amount of happiness is an aggregation of the happy (or pleasurable) moments of a person's life, minus the aggregate unhappy (or painful) moments. No point in time, whether early or late in life, is supposed to be privileged with respect to this calculation. Similarly, for Frankfurt meaningfulness has to do with the amount, or perhaps with the percentage, of activities in one's life devoted to things one cares about. I think this insight is essentially correct and valuable. But I also think that with the meaningfulness of life a mere additive function of locally meaningful moments will not do. The situation here may more instructively be compared to a plot of a story. A plot is not a mere collection of events; it has direction. Early events are perceived and judged differently in the light of later ones. It is the narrative as a whole which is capable of endowing the constituent events with meaning or depriving them of it. I think that this notion of perspective in which one sees one's life, past as well as future, is indispensable for the notion of the meaningfulness of life. This is true, I believe, for people whose lives are more or less continuous, and it is even truer in the case of people whose lives exhibit points of conversion-like discontinuity.

This, at any rate, seems to be the case with regard to the internal, subjective point of view of the person whose life is being considered. If, however, one wishes to argue that from the external, objective point of view of the spectator the meaningfulness of life is nevertheless an additive function of the meaningful moments spent on activities the actor cares about *at the time*—and I do not know whether Frankfurt wishes to take this line—one still has much ground to cover.

5

The goals that it would be most desirable to achieve are not necessarily those that it would be best to seek.

(Sec. 5)

Frankfurt justifies this statement by arguing that "the pursuit is also desirable as an end in itself" (sec. 9). That is, the very seeking of a goal may have value in virtue of the meaningful activities it entails. And so the pursuit of one goal may imbue the life devoted to it with more meaning than the pursuit of another, even though the latter may—as such—be judged to be more valuable than the former. This sounds, I suspect, somewhat like saying that in sports to participate sometimes counts more than to win.

Be that as it may, there are two comments that I wish to make here.

First, take a woman whose final end is to look forever young. This final end requires—to use Frankfurt's words—"invigoratingly complicated and wholehearted attention." It requires a strict regime of diets, exercises, creams, face-lifting operations, beauty masks and beauty baths and beauty sleep, regular visits to the hairdresser's as well as to various other salons, and much else besides. All of this will surely fill this woman's life with purposefulness. But I wonder whether Frankfurt would wish to claim that "in this respect" (sec. 5) her life would be more meaningful than the life of a person who adopts a final end of great value but such that the activity required in order to attain it is significantly more meager. At the minimum I suggest that this "respect" in virtue of which one life may be judged more meaningful than another stands in need of further refinement.

Second, the quoted statement can, I believe, be justified on grounds different from those offered by Frankfurt. I wish to invoke here the notion, introduced by economists, of the *second best*. The idea is this: when one's ideal cannot be attained, it is sometimes irrational to continue to pursue it with the intention of coming as close to it as possible. Instead, the rational thing to do would be to identify another ideal, one's second-best ideal, and pursue *it*.

For example, let us take the case of shooting. If you know that your chosen target is at a distance which is outside the reach of your weapon, it makes no sense to shoot toward it regardless. You would do better to aim at your second-best target, which is within your reach, and shoot at that. Another example comes from 1 Corinthians 7: 8–9: if your supreme moral ideal is celibacy, but you know you cannot trust yourself to achieve it, attempting to pursue it would result in occasional episodes of fornication, which you consider sinful. It might be better—more moral, perhaps—to forsake this ideal and opt for the second best one, namely, faithful marriage.[2]

6

The importance of anything depends upon considerations outside itself.

(Sec. 8)

The exception to this principle, says Frankfurt, is one's importance to oneself:

The importance of a person to himself is clearly intrinsic, in that it depends exclusively upon his own characteristics.

(Sec. 8)

The distinction Frankfurt is presenting here is a distinction between extrinsic and intrinsic importance. I myself am important to myself—if indeed I am important to myself—solely because of my own characteristics; hence it is intrinsic. Everything else which is important to me is important because of things *other* than its inherent characteristics; hence it is extrinsic.

Approaching the matter from the extrinsic-intrinsic perspective, however, blurs the real distinction. The real, and important, distinction here is, I submit, between what one might term attitudinal importance and relational importance. Thus, things may be important or unimportant to me because of my attitude (feelings, intention) toward them. But my own importance to myself is not because of my characteristics but precisely because I am I. That is, this importance is in virtue of my standing in a certain

---

[2] See Avishai Margalit, "Ideals and Second Best," in Seymour Fox (ed.), *Philosophy for Education* (Jerusalem: The Van Leer Jerusalem Foundation, 1983).

relation to myself, namely, the relation of identity. Similarly, and more broadly, my mother or my child are important to me *qua* my mother and my child—quite apart from my attitude toward them and quite apart from any characteristic they might have. Of course, we may be ambivalent toward our children or parents, just as we may be ambivalent toward ourselves and our own self-importance. But this ambivalence does not count against the relational importance in question. On the contrary, the possibility of such ambivalence would serve as a cornerstone in any attempt to flesh out the notion of self-importance that is here evoked by Frankfurt.

It is of course obvious that the distinction between attitudinal and relational import-ance bears crucially upon the notion of the meaningful life discussed here. How are we to strike a balance between that which is attitudinally important to us and that which is relationally important to us—first and foremost ourselves? How are we to judge the meaningfulness of a life devoted to oneself, whether to self-realization, to self-aggrand-izement, to self-probing, or whatever, as compared with a life devoted to final ends which are attitudinally important to the person? I would like in this context to quote a passage from Colin McGinn's review of Ray Monk's recent biography of Wittgenstein:

[Wittgenstein] approached his own soul like a kind of moral engineer: there was a fault in the design and it had to be dismantled, tinkered with, reconstructed, possibly scrapped altogether. Gazing inward, poking around inside, was the way to rid the spiritual machine of its imperfec-tions. The obvious flaw in this approach to himself was that it inevitably ran the very risk it was supposed to eliminate — the narcissistic absorption in his own being that stood between himself and the outer world. Another method—if method there must be—would be to try to turn a bored eye and ear away from one's own soul and towards the lives and feelings of others, hoping that one's own moral improvement will occur while one was, as it were, otherwise engaged.[3]

7

Assigning weights to the various considerations that are pertinent to a decision concerning how to live is the same as deciding how to live.

(Sec. 10)

This underlies a certain paradox that Frankfurt discusses in the last two sections of his paper. He refers to the question of *how to live* as "systematically inchoate" ("until it has been answered, it is impossible to understand fully what it asks.") He avoids going all out and calling it a paradox, but he does talk of circularity.

I agree that the question of how to live, or the alternative questions that are offered by Frankfurt, like how to choose one's final ends, what are we to care about, and what is to be important to us, smack of paradox. But I do not think that these are ever the questions that we ask. Instead, I offer to replace the above quote with the following amended statement:

---

[3] Colin McGinn in the *London Review of Books*, Nov. 22, 1990 (on Ray Monk, *The Duty of Genius* [New York: Free Press, 1990]).

> Assigning weights to the various considerations that are pertinent to an *assessment* as to *how one has lived* is the *basis for* deciding how *to go on living*.

It is of course a myth that we ever stand at the very starting point of life, at "point zero" as it were, and decide how to live. And yet we do, occasionally, make crucial decisions about how to live. The way we go about it is in two stages. First we look back and take stock. Then, in the light of this, we make forward-looking decisions about how to proceed. The first stage involves an assessment of one's past. It does not however consist of a passive enumeration of the past events in one's life. It is rather an active and creative task of constructing one's past, of interpreting it, of using the "raw material" of the succession of events to put it in the form of a narrative. Frankfurt says that a person "must define the respective roles that *are to be played* in his life by feelings, by desires, by morality, by various personal commitments and ideals" (sec. 10; my emphasis). I submit that one cannot do this: how can one define the role that is to be played in one's life by personal commitment to one's children before one has any? But what *is* possible is for one to discern the respective roles that *have been played* in one's life by feelings, personal commitments, etc. And, further, one may like what one discerns, or one may dislike it. And this assessment will form the basis for one's decisions concerning how one is to live from now on. This two-tier process, I think, is not in general contaminated by a paradox.[4]

There still remains the problem that Frankfurt addresses in the last section of his paper. Taking stock is possible only at points along the course of one's life, not at its starting point. How are we to construe what happens at the starting point?

Frankfurt says that one is never in a position in which one is unguided by any "volitional predisposition," and that "the pan-rationalist demand for selfless objectivity is in this context not a reasonable one." I agree. But I disagree with what he takes to follow from this. For him the conclusion is that there must be things that we *cannot help* considering important, and that we are "antecedently in the grip of some such necessity" (sec. 11). I would like to suggest, however, that the order of the modalities is wrong here (i.e., that the necessity should be construed as *de dicto*, not *de re*). The reformulation of the above statement, thus, would be: It is necessary that we should be antecedently gripped by something-or-other. Further, I suggest that this something-or-other that antecedently grips us does not have to be considered as something about which we *cannot help* caring, but rather as something which we *happen* to care about, or which we *find* ourselves caring about.

Finally, "it is not implausible to suggest that we are 'born into' preferences, or conditioned in various ways to having them."[5] This is intimately connected with the Existentialist notion of the *absurd*, and with the notion of the free moral *project* that man "launches out of his own nothingness."

---

[4] But see my "Opting: The Case of 'Big' Decisons," in the 1985 *Yearbook of the Wissenschaftskolleg zu Berlin.*

[5] Chapter 1 of this book.

Bibliography

Ahmed, E., N. Harris, J. Braithwaite, and V. Braithwaite. *Shame Management through Reintegration.* Melbourne, Cambridge University Press, 2001.

Alchian, A. A. "Uncertainty, Evolution, and Economic Theory." *Journal of Political Economy* 58 (1950): 211–21.

Alcott, Louisa May. *Little Women.* 1868. New York: Alfred A. Knopf, 1988. 6–9.

Alighieri, Dante. *The Paradise.* Edited with translation and notes by Arthur John Butler. London: Macmillan, 1885. 38.

Alvarez, Lizette. "Disobedient British Fathers Act to Reclaim Children." *New York Times,* Nov. 11 2004.

Armstrong, John. *The Art of Preserving Health.* 1744. "Prefixed," a critical essay on the poem, by John Aikin. Philadelphia: Printed for Benjamin Johnson, 1804.

Atherton, Margaret, Sidney Morgenbesser, and Robert Schwartz. "On Tenure." *Philosophical Forum* 10, no. 2–4 (Winter-Summer 1978–79): 341–52.

Augustine. *Confessions.* [Translated by William Watts. Cambridge: Harvard University Press Year: 1961. Esp. 7.I3.

Austin, J. L. "A Plea for Excuses." In *Philosophical Papers.* Oxford: Oxford University Press, 1961. 20.

Avineri, Shlomo. *Hegel's Theory of the Modern State.* Cambridge: Cambridge University Press, 1972.

Ayres, Ian, and Robert Gertner. "Filling Gaps in Incomplete Contracts." *Yale Law Journal* 99 (1989): 87.

Baird, Douglas, Robert Gertner, and Randal Picker. *Game Theory and the Law.* Cambridge: Harvard University Press, 1994. 191–5.

Baker, C. Edwin. "Giving the Audience What It Wants." *Ohio State Law Journal* 58 (1997): 311.

Banfield, Edward. *The Moral Basis of a Backward Society.* New York: Free Press, 1958.

Barbalet, Jack M. "Social Emotions: Confidence, Trust and Loyalty." *International Journal of Sociology and Social Policy* 16 (1996): 75–96.

Bardach, Eugene, and Robert Kagan. *Going by the Book: The Problem of Regulatory Unreasonableness.* Philadelphia: Temple University Press, 1982.

Barrett, William. *Irrational Man.* New York: Doubleday Anchor, 1962. 247.

Baruch, A. "Beware, a Photograph Has a Life of its Own." *Maariv Weekend.* Translated by Edna Ullmann-Margalit. August 24, 2007. 103.

Bateson, M., D. Nettle, and G. Roberts. "Cues of Being Watched Enhance Cooperation in a Real-World Setting." *Biology Letters* 2 (2006): 412–14.

Becker, Gary. *Accounting for Tastes.* Cambridge: Harvard University Press, 1996.

Benn, S. I., and R. S. Peters. *Social Principles and the Democratic State.* London: Allen & Unwin, 1959. 111.

Benn, S. I., and R. S. Peters. *The Principles of Political Thought.* Glencoe, IL: The Free Press, 1965. 127–8.

Bentham, J. "Preface to Panopticon or the Inspection House." 1787. In *The Panopticon Writings*, edited by Mirin Bozovic. London: Verso, 1995. 29–95.

Bentham, Jeremy. *Treatise on Judicial Evidence*. London: J. W. Paget, 1825. 197–8.

Bernoulli, Jacob. *Ars Conjectandi*. 1713. Brussels: Culture et civilization, 1968.

Biikhchandani, Sushil, et al. "Learning from the Behavior of Others." *Journal of Economic Perspectives* (Summer 1998): Vol. 12(3), 151.

Bingham, R. "Liberty Wins Key CCTV Privacy Case." *Liberty and Civil Liberties Trust* (blog), January 28, 2003. http://www.liberty-human-rights.org.uk/about/index.shtml.

Bloom, Allan. *The Closing of the American Mind: How Higher Education Has Failed Democracy and Impoverished the Souls of Today's Students*. New York: Simon & Schuster, 1987.

Boorse, C. "Wright on Functions." *Philosophical Review* 85 (1976): 70–86.

Boyle, Robert. *Some Conditions Touching the Usefulness of Experimental Natural Philosophy*. London: Oxford Hall, 1663.

Braithwaite, J. "Shame and Criminal Justice." *Canadian Journal of Criminology* 42, no. 3 (2000).

Braudway, B. "Scarlet Letter Punishment for Juveniles: Rehabilitation through Humiliation?" *Campbell Law Review* 27 (2004): 63–90.

Campbell, T. D. *Adam Smith's Science of Morals*. London: George Allen and Unwin, 1971. Esp. 60–2, 71–3, 117(n).

Caplin, Andrew, and John Leahy. "Miracle on Sixth Avenue: Information Externalities and Search." *Economic Journal* 108 (1998): 60.

Carnap, R. *Logical Foundations of Probability*. 1950. London: Routledge and Kegan Paul, 1962.

Carnevale, David J. *Trustworthy Government: Leadership and Management Strategies for Building Trust and High Performance*. San Francisco: Jossey-Bass, 1995.

Carrington, Christopher. *No Place Like Home: Relationships and Family Life among Lesbians and Gay Men*. Chicago: University of Chicago Press, 1999. 21, 206.

Casey, L. A. "Pirate Constitutionalism: An Essay in Self-Government." *Journal of Law and Politics* 8 (1992): 477–537.

Chambers, Whittaker. *Witness*. [City]: Regnery Publishing, 1952.

Cohen, G. A. "Beliefs and Roles." 1966. In *The Philosophy of Mind*, edited by Jonathan Glover. Oxford: Oxford University Press, 1976. 53–66.

Cohen, L. Johnathan. "Belief and Acceptance." *Mind* 98 (1989): 367–91.

Coleman, James. *Foundations of Social Theory*. Cambridge, MA: Harvard University Press, 1990.

Collingwood, R. G. *The Idea of Nature*. Oxford: Clarendon Press, 1945. 41.

Conlisk, John. "Why Bonded Rationality?" *Journal of Economic Literature* 34 (1996): 669.

Cook, J. Thomas. "Deciding to Believe Without Self-Deception." *Journal of Philosophy* 84 (1987): 441–6.

Cornes, Richard, and Todd Sandler. *The Theory of Externalities, Public Goods, and Club Goods*. New York: Cambridge University Press, 1986. 347–8, 385.

Cummins, R. "Functional Analysis." *Journal of Philosophy* 72 (1975): 741–65.

Davidson, Donald. "Thought and Talk." In *Inquiries into Truth and Interpretation*. 1975. Oxford: Clarendon Press, 1984. 161.

Davidson, Donald. "Radical Interpretation." In *Inquiries into Truth and Interpretation*. Oxford: Clarendon Press, 1984. 135.

Dijksterhuis, Ap, Maarten W. Bos, Loran F. Nordgren, Rick B. van Baaren. "On Making the Right Choice: The Deliberation-Without-Attention Effect." *Science* 17, Vol. 311, No. 5763. (February 2006): 1005–7.

Dorner, Dietrich. *The Logic of Failure*. New York: Basic Books, 1996.

Dubner, S. J., and S. D. Levitt. "Selling Soap." *The New York Times Magazine*, Sept. 24, 2006.

Durham v. United States, 214 F. 2d 862 741–49 (D.C. Cir. 1954).

Dworkin, Gerald. "Is More Choice Better Than Less." In *The Theory and Practice of Autonomy*. New York: Cambridge University Press, 1991.

Dworkin, Ronald. *Taking Rights Seriously*. Cambridge, MA: Harvard University Press, 1975.

Dworkin, Ronald. *A Matter of Principle*. Cambridge, MA: Harvard University Press, 1985. 298–300.

Dybvig, Philip, and Chester Spatt. "Adoption Externalities as Public Goods." *Journal of Public Economics* 20 (1983): 231.

Elias, Norbert. *The Court Society*. Translated by Edmund Jephcott. Oxford: Blackwell, 1983.

Elias, Norbert. *The Civilizing Process: Sociogenetic and Psychogenetic Investigations*. Oxford: Basil Blackwell, 2000, first published in German in 1939.

Ellickson, Robert. *Order Without Law* Cambridge: Harvard University Press, 1994.

Elster, Jon. "The Nature and Scope of Rational-Choice Explanation." In *The Philosophy of Donald Davidson: Perspectives on Actions and Events*. Edited by E. Lepore and B. McLaughlin. Oxford: Basil Blackwell, 1985.

Elster, Jon. *Ulysses and the Sirens*. New York: Cambridge University Press, 1979.

Elster, Jon. *Making Sense of Marx*. New York: Cambridge University Press, 1985. 100–7.

Elster, Jon. "Solomonic Judgments: Against the Best Interests of the Child." *University of Chicago Law Review* 54(1) (Winter 1987). 36–122.

Elster, Jon. "Altruistic Behavior and Altruistic Motivations." In *Handbook of the Economics of Giving, Altruism, and Reciprocity*. Edited by S. C. Kolm and J. Mercier-Ythier. Amsterdam: North-Holland, 2006.

Ely, John Hart. *Democracy and Distrust*. Cambridge, MA: Harvard University Press, 1980.

Encyclopedia Britannica, [15th ed.]. "Neuroses." Chicago: Encyclopedia Britannica, 1980.

Feinberg, Joel. *Social Philosophy*. Englewood Cliffs, NJ: Prentice-Hall, 1965. 100–2.

Ferguson, Adam. *An Essay on the History of Civil Society*. London: 1767.

Fielding, Henry. *Jonathan Wild: The Journal of a Voyage to Lisbon*. 1743. Introduction by A. R. Humphreys. London: J. M. Dent & Sons, 1964.

Finke, Roger, and Rodney Stark. *The Churching of America, 1776–1990: Winners and Losers in Our Religious Economy*. New Brunswick: Rutgers University Press, 1992. 237–75.

Foucault, Michel. *Discipline and Punish: The Birth of the Prison*. Translated by A. Sheridan. 2nd ed. New York: Vintage Books, 1995. Esp. 195–228.

Frank, Robert H. *Choosing the Right Pond* New York: Oxford University Press, 1985.

Frank, Robert H. "Positional Externalities." In *Strategy and Choice*, edited by Richard Zeckhauser. Cambridge: MIT Press, 1991. 25.

Frank, Robert H. *Luxury Fever*. New York: Free Press, 1999.

Frankfurt, Harry. "Freedom of the Will and the Concept of a Preference." *Journal of Philosophy* 68 (1971): 5.

Frankfurt, Harry G. *The Importance of What We Care About: Philosophical Essays*. Cambridge: Cambridge University Press, 1988.

Gambetta, Diego. "Mafia: The Price of Distrust." In *Trust: Making and Breaking Cooperative Relations*. Edited by Diego Gambetta. New York: Basil Blackwell, 1988.

Gavison, R. "Privacy and the Limits of Law." *Yale Law Journal* 89 (1980): 421–71.

Gladwell, Malcolm. *The Tipping Point*. Boston: Little Brown, 2000.

Goodman, Nelson. *Language of Art*. London: Oxford University Press, 1969. 99–109.

Granovetter, Mark. "Threshold Models of Collective Behavior." *American Journal of Sociology* 83 (1978): 1420.

Grey, John. "F. A. von Hayek." In *Conservative Thinkers*, edited by Roger Scruton. London: Claridge, 1988. 249–60.

Grice, H. P. William James Lectures. 2nd lecture. Harvard, 1968.

Grice, H. P., and P. F. Strawson. "In Defense of a Dogma." 1956. In *Necessary Truths*, edited by L. W. Sumner and John Wood. New York: Random House, 1969. Esp. 143.

Gross, Jane. "For Families of the Autistic, the Fight for Ordinary." *New York Times*, October 22, 2004.

Gross, Jane. "For Siblings of the Autistic, a Burdened Youth." *New York Times*, December 10, 2004.

Guyer, Paul. *Kant and the Experience of Freedom*. New York: Cambridge University Press, 1996. 362–4.

Halbertal, Moshe and Margalit, Avishai. *On Idolatry*. Cambridge: Harvard University Press, 1992.

Hardin, Russell. *Morality within the Limits of Reason*. Chicago: University of Chicago Press, 1988.

Hardin, Russell. "Distrust." *Boston University Law Review* 81, no. 3 (June 2001): 495–522.

Hardin, Russell. *Trust and Trustworthiness*. New York: Russell Sage Foundation, 2002.

Harel, A, and A. Klement. "The Economics of Stigma: Why More Detection of Crime May Result in Less Stigmatization." *Journal of Legal Studies* 36 (2007): 355–78.

Hart, H. L. A. *The Concept of Law*. 2nd ed. New York: Oxford University Press, 1996. 127–30.

Hayek, F. A. "Why I Am Not a Conservative." In *Constitution of Liberty*. London: Routledge & Kegan Paul, 1960.

Hayek, F. A. *The Constitution of Liberty*. Chicago, 1960. Gateway Ed. Chicago: University of Chicago Press, 1972.

Hayek, F. A. "The Results of Human Action but Not of Human Design." In *Studies in Philosophy, Politics and Economics*. London: Routledge & Kegan Paul, 1967.

Hayek, F. A. *Law, Legislation and Liberty*. London: Routledge & Kegan Paul, 1979. 3:167.

Hayek, F. A. "Our Moral Heritage." Heritage Lecture 24. Washington, DC: Heritage Foundation, 1983.

Hayek, F. A. "Dr. Bernard Mandeville" (1978). In *The Essence of Hayek*, edited by C. Nishiyama and K. R. Leube. Stanford: Hoover Institute Press, 1984.

Hayek, F. A. "The Origins and Effects of Our Morals." In *The Essence of Hayek*, edited by C. Nishiyama and K. R. Leube. Stanford: Hoover Institute Press, 1984.

Hegel, G. W. F. *Philosophie der Weltgeschichte*. Edited by Georg Lasson. Leipzig: Felix Meiner, 1930.

Hegel, G. W. F. *Reason in History*. The Library of Liberal Arts. Indianapolis: Bobbs-Merrill, 1953.

Hegel, G. W. F. *Philosophy of Right*. 1952. Translated with notes by T. M. Knox. Oxford: Oxford University Press, 1967.

Hein, Piet. "A Psychological Tip." In *Grooks*. Copenhagen: Borgens Forlag, 1982.

Hempel, C. G. "Aspects of Scientific Explanation." In C. G. Hempel, *Aspects of Scientific Explanation*. The Free Press, New York, 1965.

Hempel, C. G. "The Logic of Functional Analysis." In *Aspects of Scientific Explanation*. The Free Press, New York, 1965.

Heyd, David. "Tact: Sense, Sensitivity, and Virtue." *Inquiry* 38 (1995): 217–31.

Hirsch, Fred. *Social Limits to Growth*. Cambridge: Harvard University Press, 1976.

Hirschleifer, David. "The Blind Leading the Blind." In *The New Economics of Human Behavior*. New York: Cambridge University Press, 1995.

Hobbes, Thomas. *Leviathan*. 1651. Edited by C. B. Macpherson. London: Penguin, 1968.

Hollis, Martin. *The Cunning of Reason*. Cambridge: Cambridge University Press, 1987.

Holmes, Stephen. *Passions and Constraint*. Chicago: University of Chicago Press, 1995.

Howard, Phillip. *The Death of Common Sense*. New York: Random House, 1994.

Hugo, Victor. *Les Miserables*. 1862. Translated by Charles E. Wilbour. New York: The Modern Library, 1992.

Hume, David. *Enquiry Concerning the Principles of Morals*. Edited by L. A. Selby-Bigge. Oxford: Oxford University Press, 1975. 185.

Hume, David. *A Treatise of Human Nature*. Edited by L. A. Selby-Bigge. Oxford: Oxford University Press, 1978. 493–6.

Hume, David. "Of the Independency of Parliament." 1748. In *David Hume: Essays Moral, Political, and Literary*, edited by Eugene F. Miller. Indianapolis, IN: Liberty Fund, 1987.

Hunter, Kathryn. *Doctors' Stories*. Princeton: Princeton University Press, 1993.

Iannaccone, Laurence. "Sacrifice and Stigma: Reducing Free-Riding in Cults, Communes, and Other Collectives." *Journal of Political Economy* 100 (1992): 271, 274, 276–89.

James, William. *The Varieties of Religious Experience*. 1901–02. Collin: The Fontana Library, 1960. 181–5.

Janis, I. L. and Mann, L. *Decision Making: A Psychological Analysis of Conflict, Choice and Commitment*. New York: Free Press, MacMillan, 1977. 165.

Jones, R. A. "The Origin and Development of Media of Exchange." *Journal of Political Economy* 84 (1976): 757–75.

Kagan, Robert and Jerome Skolnick. "Compliance Without Enforcement." In *Smoking Policy*, edited by Steven Sugarman and Robert L. Rabin. New York: Oxford University Press, 1994.

Kahan, D. "What Do Alternative Sanctions Mean?" *Chicago Law Review* 63 (1996): 591–653.

Kahan, D. M., and E. A. Posner. "Shaming White-Collar Criminals: A Proposal for Reform of the Federal Sentencing Guidelines." *Journal of Law and Economics* 42 (1999): 365–91.

Kahneman, Daniel, and Don Lovallo. "Timid Choices and Bold Forecasts: A Cognitive Perspective on Risk Taking." *Management Science* 39 (1993): 17–31.

Kant, Immanuel. "Transcendental Doctrine of Method." In *Critique of Pure Reason*, A 824/B London: Macmillan, 1973, 852.

Kaplow, Louis. "Rules and Standards: An Economic Analysis." *Duke Law Journal* 42 (1992): 557.

Katz v. United States, 389 U.S. 347, 360–1 (1967).

Katz, Michael, and Carl Shapiro. "Network Externalities, Competition, and Compatibility." *American Economic Review* 75 (1985): 424.

Katzner, Louis I. "Presumptions of Reason and Presumptions of Justice." *The Journal of Philosophy* 70 (Feb. 22, 1973): 89–100.

Keynes, John Maynard. *A Treatise on Probability*. 1921. London: Macmillan, 1973. 345–6.

Kipling, Rudyard. "If." 1910. In *Rudyard Kipling*, edited and with an introduction by Daniel Karlin. Oxford: Oxford University Press, 1999.

Koestler, Arthur. "A Faith is Not Acquired by Reasoning." In *The God That Failed*, edited by R. H. Crossman. London: Hamilton, 1951.

Koestler, Arthur. *Arrow in the Blue*. New York: Macmillan, 1952.

Koestler, Arthur. *The Invisible Writing*. Boston: Beacon Press, 1954.

Koestler, Arthur. *Janus: A Summing Up*. New York: Random House, 1978.

Kolata, Gina. "If Tests Hint Alzheimer's, Should a Patient be Told?" *New York Times*, October 24, 1995.

Kramer, Roderick M. "Trust and Distrust in Organizations: Emerging Perspectives, Enduring Questions." *Annual Review of Psychology* 50 (1999): 569–98.

Kymlicka, Will. "Rethinking the Family." *Philosophy and Public Affairs* 20 (1991): 77–97. Esp. 79.

LaFave, W. R. *Search and Seizure: A Treatise on the Fourth Amendment*. 3rd ed. St. Paul, MN: West Publishing, 1996.

La Fontaine, J. S. "Family, Anthropology of." In *International Encyclopedia of the Social & Behavioral Sciences*, edited by Neil J. Smelser and Paul B. Baltes. Amsterdam: Elsevier, 2001. 5307.

Lamb, James W. "Knowledge and Justified Presumption." *The Journal of Philosophy* 69, no. 5 (Mar. 9, 1972): 123–7.

Leibniz, Gottfried Wilhelm. *New Essays Concerning Human Understanding*. Translated by Alfred Gideon Langley. New York: Macmillan, 1896.

Leibniz, Gottfried Wilhelm. *Theodicy*. Translated by E. M. Huggard. London: Routledge & Kegan Paul, 1951. 148–9.

Leibowitz, Nehama. *Studies in Genesis,* 3rd revised edn, Publishing Department of the Jewish Agency. Jerusalem: Alpha Press, 1976. p. 97.

Lemley, Mark, and David McGowan. "Legal Implications of Network Economic Effects." *California Law Review* 86 (1998): 479, 483, 488.

Lessig, Lawrence. "The Regulation of Social Meaning." *University of Chicago Law Review* 61 (1997): 1.

Levi, Edward. *An Introduction to Legal Reasoning* Chicago: University of Chicago Press, 1948.

Liebowitz, S. J., and Stephen Margolis. "Network Externality: An Uncommon Tragedy." *Journal of Economic Perspectives* 8 (1994): 133, 135.

Llewelyn, J. E. "Presuppositions, Assumptions and Presumptions." *Theoria*, 28 (1962): 158–72.

Locke, John. *An Essay Concerning Human Understanding*. 1689. Esp. Book 2, Chapter 21, sec. New York: Oxford University Press, 2008. 67.

Loewith, Karl. *Meaning in History*. Chicago: The University of Chicago Press, 1949.

Lyons, David. *Forms and Limits of Utilitarianism*. New York: Oxford, 1965. 124.

Macfie, A. L. "The Invisible Hand of Jupiter." *Journal of the History of Ideas* 32 (1971): 595–9.

Malinowski, B. "Anthropology." In *Encyclopaedia Britannica*, 1st Supplementary Volume. London: The Encyclopaedia Britannica, 1926.

Mandeville, Bernard. *Fable of the Bees: Private Vices Public Benefits*. 1714. Edited by F. B. Kaye. Oxford: Oxford University Press, 1924.

Margalit, Avishai. "Ideals and Second Best." In *Philosophy for Education*, edited by Seymour Fox. Jerusalem: The Van Leer Jerusalem Foundation, 1983.

Margalit, Avishai. *The Decent Society*. Cambridge, MA: Harvard University Press, 1996.

Margalit, Avishai. "Privacy in a Decent Society." *Social Research* 68 (2001): 255–69.

Margalit, Avishai. "Recognition." *Aristotelian Society Suppl.* 75 (2001): 127–39.

Margalit, Avishai. *The Ethics of Memory*. Cambridge, MA: Harvard University Press, 2002.

Mashaw, Jerry, *Greed, Chaos, and Governance*. New Haven: Yale University Press, 1997.

Massaro, T. "The Meanings of Shame: Implications for Legal Reform." *Psychology, Public Policy and Law* 3 (1997): 645–704.

McCourt, Frank. *Angela's Ashes*. New York: Scribner, 1996.

McGinn, Colin. "Ray Monk, The Duty of Genius." *London Review of Books*, Nov. 22, 1990.

Merton, R. K. *Social Theory and Social Structure*. Enlarged edition. New York: The Free Press, 1968.

Mises, L. V. *The Theory of Money and Credit*. 2nd ed. New Haven: Yale University Press, 1953.

Montaigne, Michel de. *Essays*. Translated by John Florio. 3 vols. London: J. M. Dent & Sons, 1965. 2: 333.

Montaigne, Michel de. *Essays*. Translated by M. A. Screech. London: Penguin, 1991. 176–7.

Morgan, Edmund M. "Some Observations concerning Presumptions," *Harvard Law Review* 64 (1931): 906–34.

Morgan, Edmund M. "Instructing the Jury upon Presumptions and Burden of Proof." *Harvard Law Review* 67 (1933): 59–83.

Munoz-Darde, Veronique. "Rawls, Justice in the Family and Justice of the Family." *Philosophical Quarterly* 48 (1998): 335–52. Esp. 350.

Nagel, T. *Concealment and Exposure*. Oxford, NY: Oxford University Press, 2002.

New York Surveillance Camera Players. http://www.notbored.org/privacy.html.

Ney, Joseph S., Philip D. Zelikov, and David C. King. *Why People Don't Trust Government*. Cambridge, MA: Harvard University Press, 1997.

Nissenbaum, H. "Privacy and Contextual Integrity." *Washington Law Review* 79 (2004), 101–39.

Nozick, Robert. *Anarchy, State, and Utopia*. Blackwell, Oxford. New York: Basic Books, 1974.

Nussbaum, M. *Hiding from Humanity: Disgust, Shame and the Law*. Princeton, NJ: Princeton University Press, 2004.

Okin, Susan Moller. *Women in Western Political Thought*. Princeton: Princeton University Press, 1979. 202.

Okin, Susan Moller. *Justice, Gender, and the Family*. New York: Basic Books, 1989. 26–33.

Olafson, F. A. "J. P. Sartre." In *Encyclopedia of Philosophy*. Edited by Paul Edwards. 8 vols. New York: Macmillan, 1967. 7: 292.

Parfit, Derek. *Reasons and Persons*. Oxford: Oxford University Press, 1986. Esp. chapter 14.

Parkinson, G. H. R. *Logic and Reality in Leibniz's Metaphysics*. Oxford: Clarendon Press, 1965. 100.

Popper, K. R. *The Open Society and Its Enemies*. Vol. 2. 1945. London: Routledge and Kegan Paul, 1966.

Posner, E. A. *Law and Social Norms*. Cambridge, MA: Harvard University Press, 2000.

Posner, R. A. *Economic Analysis of the Law*. 1973. 7th ed. New York: Aspen Publishers, 2007.

Prior, A. N. "Can Religion Be Discussed?" In *New Essays in Philosophical Theology*, edited by A. G. N. Flew and Alasdair MacIntyre. London: SCM Press, 1955. 7–9.

Quine, Willard van Orman. *Word and Object*. Cambridge, MA: The MIT Press, 1960. 59.

Quine, Willard van Orman. "Two Dogmas of Empiricism." 1953. In Willard van Orman, *From a Logical Point of View*, Cambridge, MA: Harvard University Press, 1980. 43.

Quine, Willard van Orman. *Quiddities*, Cambridge: Harvard University Press, 1987. 19.

Quine, Willard van Orman and J. S. Ullian. *The Web of Belief*. New York: Random House, 1970. 8.

Radcliffe-Brown, A. R. *Structure and Function in Primitive Society*. London: Cohen & West, 1952.

Rawls, John. *A Theory of Justice*. Cambridge, MA: Harvard University Press, 1971. Esp. 129–30, 191, 438–9, 479.

Rawls, John. *Political Liberalism*. New York: Columbia University Press, 1993. 258.

Raz, Joseph. "Reasons for Action, Decisions and Norms." In *Practical Reasoning*, edited by Joseph Raz. New York: Oxford, 1978. 128–43.

Raz, Joseph. *The Authority of Law*. New York: Oxford University Press, 1985.

Raz, Joseph. *The Morality of Freedom*. Oxford: Clarendon, 1986. 23–31.

Raz, Joseph. *Practical Reason and Norms*. 2nd ed. New York: Oxford University Press, 1990. 37–45.

Reid, Thomas. *The Works of Thomas Reid, D. D.* Preface, notes and supplementary dissertations by Sir William Hamilton, Bart. 4th ed. Edinburgh: MacLachlan & Steward, 1854. 238.

Rescher, Nicholas. "Choice without Preference." *Kant Studien* 51 (1959–60): 143.

Rescher, Nicholas. *Methodological Pragmatism*. New York: NYU Press, 1977.

Robert Frost. "The Death of the Hired Man." In Robert Frost: Collected Poems, Prose, and Plays. New York: Library of America, 1995.

Rothschild, Emma. "Adam Smith and the Invisible Hand," *The American Economic Review* Vol. 84(2) (May 1994): 319–22.

Rousseau, Jean-Jacques. "Discourse on Political Economy." In *Oevres Complètes*. Paris: Pleiade, 1959–1969. 3:241–2.

Samuelson, P. A. *Economics*. 4th ed. New York: McGraw-Hill, 1958.

Sandel, Michael. *Liberalism and the Limits of Justice*. Cambridge: Cambridge University Press, 1982. 30–5.

Scalia, Antonin. *A Matter of Interpretation*. Princeton: Princeton University Press, 1997.

Scanlon, T. M. *What We Owe to Each Other*. Cambridge, MA: Harvard University Press, 1998.

Schauer, Frederick. *Playing By The Rules*. New York: Oxford University Press, 1993.

Schelling, T. C. "Models of Segregation." *American Economic Review* 59 (1969): 488–93.

Schelling, Thomas. "Self-Command in Practice, in Policy, and in a Theory of Rational Choice." *American Economic Review* 74, no. 1 (1984): 1.

Schelling, Thomas. *The Strategy of Conflict*. Cambridge: Harvard University Press, 1960.

Schoenbrod, David. *Power Without Responsibility*. New Haven: Yale University Press, 1993.

Scott, James. *Seeing Like A State*. New Haven: Yale University Press, 1998.

Seligman, Martin. *Learned Optimism*. New York: Vintage Books, 1991.

Sen, Amartya. "Choice." In *Choice, Welfare and Management*. Cambridge: Harvard University Press, 1982. 78–9.

Shakespeare, William. *Macbeth*, Act 5, Scene 1.

Shiller, Robert. *Irrational Exuberance*. Princeton: Princeton University Press, 2000.

Simmel, Georg. *The Philosophy of Money*. 1900. Translated by Tom Bottomore and David Frisby. New York: Routledge, 1978.

Slovic, Paul. "Perceived Risk, Trust and Democracy." *Risk Analysis* 13(6) (1993): 675–82.

Smith, Adam. *The Theory of Moral Sentiments*. 1759. The Glasgow Edition. Vol. I. London, 1976. Esp. art 1, section 1, chapter 2 ("Of the Pleasure of Mutual Sympathy"). 184–5.

Smith, Adam. *The Wealth of Nations*. London: 1776. Esp. IV.II.9.

Solove, D. J. "'I've Got Nothing to Hide,' and Other Misunderstandings of Privacy." *San Diego Law Review* 44 (2007): 1–23.

Stockton, Frank R. *The Lady, or the Tiger? and Other Stories*. New York: Scribner's, 1884.

Strahilevitz, L. J. "'How's My Driving' for Everyone (and Everything?)." *New York University Law Review* 81 (2006): 1699–765.

Sullivan, K. "Foreword: The Justices of Rules and Standards." *Harvard Law Review* 105 (1993): 22.

Sunstein, Cass R. "On the Expressive Function of Law." *University of Pennsylvania Law Review* 144 (1996): 2021.

Sunstein, Cass R. "Television and the Public Interest." *California Law Review* 88 (2000): 499.

Sunstein, Cass R. and Richard H. Thaler. "Libertarian Paternalism Is not an Oxymoron." *University of Chicago Law Review* 70, no. 4 (2003).

Taylor, Charles. *Hegel*. Cambridge: Cambridge University Press, 1975.

Taylor, Charles. *Hegel and Modern Society*. Cambridge: Cambridge University Press, 1979.

Thayer, James Bradley. *A Preliminary Treatise on Evidence at Common Law*. Boston, 1898.

The Economist. "The Logic of Privacy." January 4, 2007.

The Police. *Every Breath You Take*. A&M. 1983.

Tönnies, F. *Tönnies: Community and Civil Society*. 1887. In *Cambridge Texts in the History of Political Thought*, edited by Jose Harris. Cambridge: Cambridge University Press, 2001.

Turnbull, Colin. *The Mountain People*. New York: Simon & Schuster, 1972.

Ullmann-Margalit, Edna. *The Emergence of Norms*. Oxford: Oxford University Press, 1977. 77–133.

Ullmann-Margalit, Edna. "Invisible-Hand Explanations." *Synthese* 39 (1978): 263–91.

Ullmann-Margalit, Edna. "On Presumption." *Journal of Philosophy* 80, no. 3 (1983): 143–63.

Ullmann-Margalit, Edna. "Opting: The Case of 'Big' Decisions." In *The Yearbook of the Wissenschaftskolleg zu Berlin*, Berlin: Wissenschaftskolleg zu Berlin 1985.

Ullmann-Margalit, Edna. "Revision of Norms." *Ethics* 100 (1990): 756–67.

Ullmann-Margalit, Edna. "Not Wanting to Know." In *Reasoning Practically*. Oxford: Oxford University Press 1998.

Ullmann-Margalit, Edna. "Trust out of Distrust." *Journal of Philosophy* 99(10) (2002): 532–48.

Ullmann-Margalit, Edna. "Trust, Distrust and In-Between." In *Distrust*, edited by Russell Hardin. New York: Russell Sage Foundation, 2004. 60–82, at 60–1.

Ullmann-Margalit, Edna. "Family Fairness." *Social Research* 73 (2006): 575–96.

Ullmann-Margalit, Edna, and Avishai Margalit. "Analyticity by Way of Presumption." *Canadian Journal of Philosophy* 12, no. 3 (1982): 435–52.

Ullmann-Margalit, Edna, and Avishai Margalit. "Holding True and Holding As True." *Synthese* 92, no. 2 (1992): 167–87.

Ullmann-Margalit, Edna, and Sidney Morgenbesser, "Picking and Choosing," *Social Research* 44, no. 4 (Winter 1977): 757–83 n. 27.

Ullmann-Margalit, Edna, and Cass R. Sunstein. "Second-Order Decisions." *Ethics* 110 (October 1999), 5–31. Reprinted in Cass R. Sunstein, *Behavioral Law and Economics*. Chapter 7. Cambridge: Cambridge University Press, 2000. 187–298.

Underwood, Barbara D. "The Thumb on the Scales of Justice: Burdens of Persuasion in Criminal Cases." *Yale Law Journal* 86 7(1977): 1299–348.

Urmson, John. "Saints and Heroes." In *Essays in Moral Philosophy*, edited by A. Melden. Seattle: University of Washington Press, 1958.

Warren, Mark E. "Democratic Theory and Trust." In *Democracy and Trust*, edited by Mark E. Warren. Cambridge: Cambridge University Press, 1999.

Weick, Karl. "Small Wins." *American Psychology* 39 (1984): 40, 48.

Whitman, J. Q. "What is Wrong with Inflicting Shame Sanctions?" *Yale Law Journal* 107 (1998): 1055–92.

Williams, B. *Shame and Necessity*. Berkeley: University of California Press, 1993.

Williams, Bernard. "Formal Structures and Social Reality." In *Trust: Making and Breaking Cooperative Relations*, edited by Diego Gambetta. New York: Basil Blackwell, 1988.

Wimsatt, W. C. "Teleology and the Logical Structure of Function Statements." *Studies in History and Philosophy of Science* 3 (1972): 1–80.

Wittgenstein, Ludwig. *On Certainty*. Edited by G. E. M. Anscombe and G. H. von Wright. Oxford: Basil Blackwell, 1969.

Wood, D. "Foucault and Panopticism Revisited." *Surveillance and Society* 1(3) (2003): 234–9.

Wright, L. "Functions." *Philosophical Review* 82 (1973): 139–68.

Xenophon. *Memorabilia*. Cambridge: Harvard University Press, 1980. Esp. Book II, Ch. 1, 21–34.

Zajonc, R. B. "Feeling and Thinking." *American Psychologist* (1980): Vol. 35 No. 2.

Zelizer, Viviana. *The Social Meaning of Money* New York: Basic Books, 1994. 18–19.

General Index

Index of Persons

Printed in the USA/Agawam, MA
May 19, 2020

755273.055